CROOM HELM
London & Sydney

3354

© 1985 Richard J.A. Talbert and contributors
Croom Helm Ltd, Provident House, Burrell Row,
Beckenham, Kent BR3 1AT
Croom Helm Australia Pty Ltd, First Floor,
139 King Street, Sydney, NSW 2001, Australia

British Library Cataloguing in Publication Data

Atlas of classical history.
  1. History, Ancient — Maps
  I. Talbert, Richard J.A.
  911'.3   G3201.S2

  ISBN 0-7099-2421-6
  ISBN 0-7099-2448-8 Pbk

Printed and bound in Great Britain

CONTENTS

PREFACE

In all likelihood this book has its origin in a chance encounter between Richard Stoneman, the humanities editor of Croom Helm Ltd, and myself at the classical societies' Oxford Triennial Conference in summer 1981. The subject of our conversation on that occasion eludes me. At any rate it was an unexpected pleasure to be approached by Richard in the autumn with a tentative proposal for the compilation of an atlas of classical history. We soon found that we were in close agreement on what was needed: a volume in which lucid maps offered the high school student and the undergraduate a reasonably comprehensive, up-to-date and scholarly coverage of classical history down to the time of Constantine, accompanied by modest elucidation of the material and by some suggestions for further reading. Explanation and discussion were felt to be especially important, so long as they did not outweigh the maps.

A concern to keep production costs under control has restrained us from including everything that we might have wished. The same concern has affected the size and number of pages in the atlas, while colour printing has proved out of the question. Use of some standard bases has helped to limit expenditure on cartography. Equally, without the help of expert colleagues the desired coverage of classical history would have been impossible to achieve. The warmest gratitude is therefore due to those throughout the British Isles who agreed with alacrity to contribute to the atlas and have done such excellent work. It has been deliberate editorial policy to be ready with guidance when required, but otherwise—in view of the contributors' specialist knowledge—to leave them a fairly free hand in the presentation of their material. Inevitably, however, restraint did have to be exercised when texts submitted overran their allotted space.

In particular no standard convention for the spelling of names has been imposed. Since a convention which meets with general satisfaction has yet to be devised, in a work of this character an editor who sought to impose one of his own making would only face exceptions, pleas, arguments, delay, as well as increasing the possibility of mistakes and diverting attention from more important issues. Whatever an editor does, he has no hope of pleasing everybody where this perennial controversy is concerned. As it is, notably outlandish or unusual spelling of names has been discouraged, Latin forms have been recommended where serious doubt has arisen, and an effort has been made to keep each individual contributor's usage consistent (since sometimes it was not!). Nonetheless, throughout the atlas as a whole inconsistency does still remain. While any distress caused to purists who read through from cover to cover is regretted, arguably the degree of inconsistency present should hardly cause undue difficulties of comprehension anywhere, and should prove of little account to those who refer just to two or three maps at a time.

No matter how carefully plans are laid in advance, in a complex project of this type the need for certain changes and improvements will only emerge as work proceeds. Such developments are the principal cause of failure to publish the atlas during 1984, as had originally been intended. However the remarkable fact that this target will be missed by so very few months is due above all to the efforts of Jayne Lewin and Richard Stoneman.

Taking over from A. Bereznay at an early stage, Jayne has executed the cartographic work for nearly the entire volume with artistry, speed, efficiency and good humour: her responsiveness to contributors' diverse requirements has been especially appreciated. Richard, as well as initiating the project and contributing to it, has offered all possible encouragement and support throughout. Not least my own debt to him is enormous: no editor could have been served better.

In Belfast, too, my colleagues (especially Raymond Davis) have given unfailing support and have patiently sought to answer my astonishing range of queries. Janis Boyd's secretarial work has been superb. I continue to appreciate the high quality of the University Library's holdings, and the assistance of University funds towards travel and research. In addition thanks are due to N.G.L. Hammond, W.V. Harris, R. Hope Simpson, A. Powell and M.L. Pringle. But above all this atlas has been a collaborative effort. If it succeeds in its principal aim of stimulating the readers for whom it is designed, then there will be cause for joint satisfaction on the part of all those who have worked hard to achieve it.

Richard Talbert

Queen's University
Belfast
1984

CONTRIBUTORS

M. Alden, Queen's University, Belfast.
A.E. Astin, Queen's University, Belfast.
M. Ballance, Eton College.
R.P. Davis, Queen's University, Belfast.
J.F. Drinkwater, University of Sheffield.
J.D. Falconer, Winchester College.
M.G. Fulford, University of Reading.
J.F. Gardner, University of Reading.
R.H. Jordan, Methodist College, Belfast.
M.J. McGann, Queen's University, Belfast.
E.J. Owens, University College of Swansea.
T.W. Potter, The British Museum.
A.G. Poulter, The University, Nottingham.
N. Purcell, St. John's College, Oxford.
P.J. Rhodes, University of Durham.
J.B. Salmon, University of Lancaster.
C.E. Schultze, Queen's University, Belfast.
A.R.R. Sheppard, London.
E.M. Smallwood, Queen's University, Belfast.
R. Stoneman, Beckenham.
R.J.A. Talbert, Queen's University, Belfast.
C.J. Tuplin, University of Liverpool.
B.H. Warmington, University of Bristol.
J.P. Wild, University of Manchester.
R.J.A. Wilson, University of Dublin.

EQUIVALENT MEASUREMENTS

1 hectare = 10,000 sq metres = 2.47 acres

1 Roman foot = 0.295 metres
1 Roman mile = 5,000 Roman feet = 1475 metres

1 metre = 1.09 yards
1000 metres = 1 kilometre = 0.62 miles
10 km = 6.21 miles
50 km = 31.07 miles
100 km = 62.14 miles

THE MEDITERRANEAN WORLD: PHYSICAL

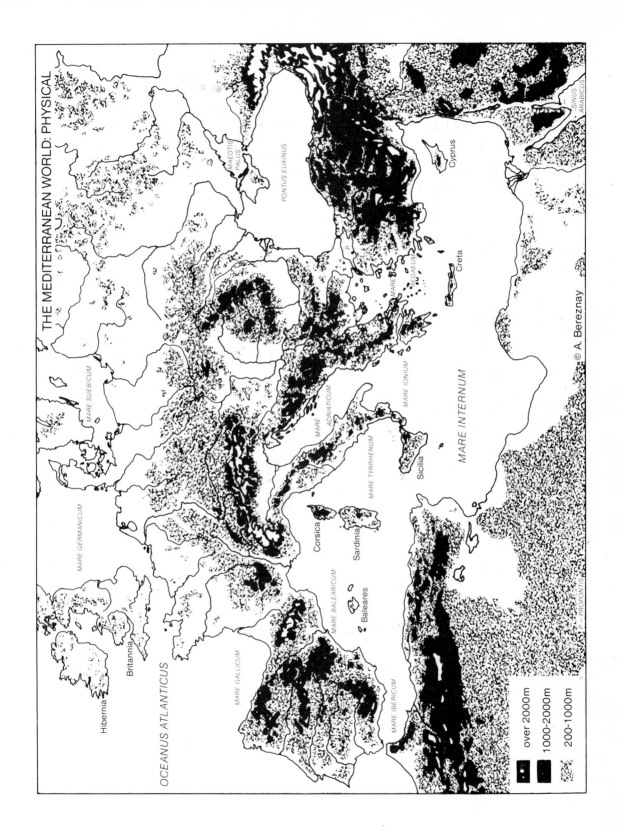

© A. Bereznay

Hibernia

Britannia

OCEANUS ATLANTICUS

MARE GERMANICUM

MARE SUEBICUM

MAEOTIS PALUS

PONTUS EUXINUS

Cyprus

Creta

SINUS ARABICUS

MARE AEGAEUM

MARE ADRIATICUM

MARE IONIUM

MARE INTERNUM

Sicilia

MARE TYRRHENUM

Corsica

Sardinia

MARE BALEARICUM

Baleares

MARE GALLICUM

MARE IBERICUM

PROPONTIS

- over 2000m
- 1000-2000m
- 200-1000m

1

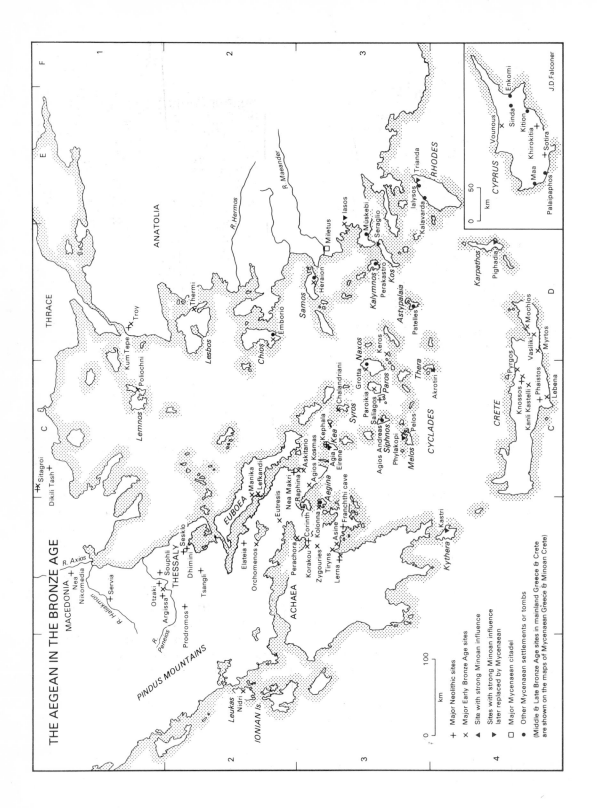

THE AEGEAN IN THE BRONZE AGE

MACEDONIA

THRACE

ANATOLIA

THESSALY

PINDUS MOUNTAINS

ACHAEA

IONIAN Is.

EUBOEA

CYCLADES

CRETE

RHODES

CYPRUS

J.D.Falconer

R. Axios
R. Haliakmon
R. Peneios
R. Axios
R. Hermos
R. Maeander

Sitagroi
Dikili Tash
Servia
Nikomedia
Nea
Souphli
Otzaki
Argissa
Prodromos
Sesklo
Dhimini
Tsangli
Orchomenos
Elateia
Perachora
Korakou
Corinth
Zygouries
Tiryns
Mycenae
Lerna
Asine
Nidri
Leukas
Kythera
Kastri
Franchthi cave
Eutresis
Nea Makri
Raphina
Agios Kosmas
Askitario
Kolonna
Aegina
Eirene
Agia
Kephala
Kea
Agios Andreas
Saliagos
Paroikia
Paros
Siphnos
Phylakopi
Melos
Pelos
Chalandriani
Syros
Grotta
Naxos
Keros
Thera
Akrotiri
Manika
Lefkandi
Kum Tepe
Troy
Poliochni
Lemnos
Lesbos
Thermi
Chios
Emborio
Samos
Heraion
Miletus
Iasos
Müskebi
Seraglio
Perakastro
Kalymnos
Kos
Astypalaia
Patelles
Kalavarda
Ialysos
Trianda
Karpathos
Pighadia
Knossos
Kanli Kastelli
Phaistos
Lebena
Vasiliki
Myrtos
Mochlos
Pyrgos
Vounous
Enkomi
Sinda
Kition
Maa
Khirokitia
Sotira
Palaipaphos

km
0   100

km
0   50

Legend

+   Major Neolithic sites

✕   Major Early Bronze Age sites

▲   Site with strong Minoan influence

▼   Sites with strong Minoan influence later replaced by Mycenaean

☐   Major Mycenaean citadel

●   Other Mycenaean settlements or tombs

(Middle & Late Bronze Age sites in mainland Greece & Crete
are shown on the maps of Mycenaean Greece & Minoan Crete)

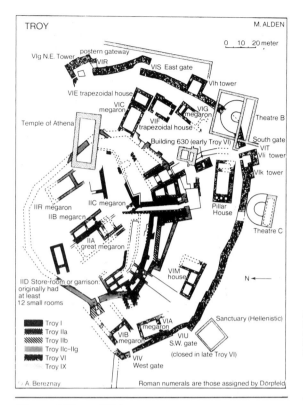

TROY   M. ALDEN

0 10 20 meter

VIg N.E. Tower — postern gateway
VIR
VIE trapezoidal house
VIC megaron
VIG megaron
VIF trapezoidal house
Temple of Athena
Building 630 (early Troy VI)
VIS East gate
VIh tower
South gate
VIT
VIi tower
VIk tower
Theatre B
IIR megaron
IIC megaron
Pillar House
IIB megarcn
Theatre C
IIA great megaron
VIM house
N ←
IID Store-room or garrison: originally had at least 12 small rooms
Sanctuary (Hellenistic)
VIA megaron
VIB megaron
VIU S.W. gate (closed in late Troy VI)
VIV West gate

▰ Troy I
▨ Troy IIa
▧ Troy IIb
▤ Troy IIc–IIg
▰ Troy VI
   Troy IX

A. Bereznay   Roman numerals are those assigned by Dörpfeld

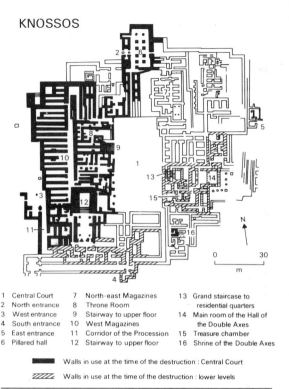

KNOSSOS

N

0   30
m

1 Central Court
2 North entrance
3 West entrance
4 South entrance
5 East entrance
6 Pillared hall
7 North-east Magazines
8 Throne Room
9 Stairway to upper floor
10 West Magazines
11 Corridor of the Procession
12 Stairway to upper floor
13 Grand staircase to residential quarters
14 Main room of the Hall of the Double Axes
15 Treasure chamber
16 Shrine of the Double Axes

▬ Walls in use at the time of the destruction : Central Court

▨ Walls in use at the time of the destruction : lower levels

Troy (Hissarlik)

Before excavation the city of Troy (later Ilion) was a tell more than 31 metres high. Excavations by Schliemann (1870–90), Dörpfeld (1893–4), and the University of Cincinnati (1932–8) revealed 46 separate strata, making up nine major layers (I–IX), each with a number of subdivisions. Occupation dates at least from the beginning of the Early Bronze Age, and the wealthy city of Troy II (Treasure of Priam) has fortifications comparable in grandeur with those of the approximately contemporary sites of Thermi on Lesbos and Poliochni on Lemnos. Troy VI, in which the horse first appears here, is the settlement which spans the Middle Bronze Age and earlier part of the Late Bronze Age: it seems to have been destroyed by an earthquake around 1300 BC. Mycenaean IIIB pottery in Troy VIIa, destroyed by fire *c.* 1260, has led to its identification with Homer's Troy, the destruction of which was traditionally placed in 1184 by Eratosthenes on genealogical grounds. The city continued through various vicissitudes to be inhabited until *c.* AD 500.

Knossos

The Cretan city of Knossos and its king, Minos, appear several times in the Homeric poems; Knossians led by Idomeneus take part in the expedition against Troy. In 1878 the site was investigated by Minos Kalokairinos, who found a tall earthenware storage jar (*pithos*), now in the British Museum. Full-scale excavations were begun by Arthur Evans in 1900. The earliest levels were found to be preceramic Neolithic. Despite destructions occupation continued through all phases of the Bronze Age. Evans named the phases of the Cretan Bronze Age 'Minoan' after King Minos. The Middle Minoan palace at Knossos, destroyed *c.* 1700, was replaced by the magnificent one shown here. It was built around a central court, with state rooms, storage magazines, and several storeys of luxurious residential apartments. It suffered destruction *c.* 1450. Afterwards it alone among the Cretan palaces was re-occupied, albeit on a reduced scale; the new inhabitants were probably Mycenaeans. The final destruction was by fire, *c.* 1375–50.

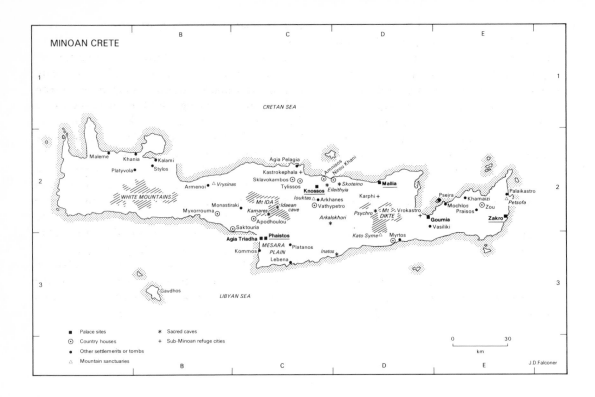

The Aegean in the Bronze Age, Minoan Crete, Mycenaean Greece

Pages 2, 4 and 6 show the most important sites at which excavations have revealed settlements or tombs in the period from 6500 to 1200 BC. *The Aegean in the Bronze Age* gives Neolithic and Early Bronze Age sites for the whole area, as well as later Bronze Age sites for the islands, Asia Minor and Cyprus. Later sites in Crete and mainland Greece are shown on the other two maps.

The most heavily settled areas in the Neolithic period (*c.* 6500–2900) seem to have been the fertile plains in north east Greece, but in the Early Bronze Age there was a change in the settlement pattern corresponding with a move from an economy based on cereals to a mixed economy of olives, vines and cereals. Settlements were made in the more rocky terrain of the islands, Crete and the Peloponnese, and a particularly prosperous and artistic culture flourished in the Cyclades. While in Crete the Early Bronze Age settlements seem to

have led without a break to the founding of the first great palaces in the twentieth century BC, on the mainland the end of the Early Bronze Age was marked by the violent destruction of sites and the arrival of a new people from Anatolia. These were probably the ancestors of the Greeks. In the next period (the Middle Bronze Age, *c.* 2000–1550) Crete replaced the Cyclades as the most prosperous civilisation in the western Aegean, while Asia Minor and the eastern Aegean were dominated by the city of Troy VI, also settled about 2000 BC by newcomers from Anatolia.

After the first Cretan palaces had been destroyed *c.* 1700, probably by earthquakes, they were rebuilt on an even grander scale. By the beginning of the Late Bronze Age (*c.* 1550) Crete was extending her influence widely across the Aegean, so that several of the island sites became culturally and perhaps also politically dependent on Crete. One of these, the town of Akrotiri on the volcanic island of Thera, was destroyed *c.* 1500 by an eruption which was followed shortly afterwards by the great explosion of the whole island. The precise sequence of events on Thera and their relation to the burning and abandonment of all the major Cretan sites except Knossos *c.* 1450 has been much debated, but however these sites were destroyed, their destruction marked the end of the Cretan dominance in the Aegean.

For the next 200 years (*c.* 1400–1200) the Mycenaean Greeks replaced the Minoans as masters of the Aegean. That their prosperity had been growing since *c.* 1600 is shown by the rich burials in the two Shaft Grave circles at Mycenae, and later by the construction of the monumental *tholos* tombs. After the Thera eruption the Mycenaeans moved into Knossos, and by 1400 seem to have had control of the whole of Crete,

until the palace was finally destroyed a few years later.

In the fourteenth and thirteenth centuries there was relative peace in the eastern Mediterranean, and the Mycenaeans traded widely in the Aegean and beyond, replacing the Minoans in the island sites and establishing a major settlement at Miletus. On the Greek mainland palaces were built and some sites were heavily fortified. In the second half of the thirteenth century, probably as a result of internal wars, many of the Mycenaean sites were destroyed, the palace civilisation came to an end, and much of the population fled to Achaia and the Ionian islands in the west, and to Euboia, the Cyclades and Cyprus in the east. However, Mycenaean society continued in Greece for a further hundred years until early in the eleventh century, by which time all the major sites except Athens had been abandoned.

Mycenae

The citadel occupies a low hill, with Mounts Profitis Elias and Szara to the north and east. Sherds suggest that habitation dates from the Neolithic period, but the site seems to have risen to importance during the Middle Bronze Age, when the wealthy Grave Circles A (found by Schliemann in 1876) and B were established; they form part of an extensive Middle and Late Bronze Age cemetery on the north west slopes. The Late Bronze Age city consisted of a palace on the hill, with houses, workshops and storerooms below. At first only the summit was fortified, though by the late thirteenth century a large area was enclosed, including the Cult Centre and Grave Circle A. Even with its massive walls and underground spring the city declined during the twelfth century, and was eventually burnt. However the area continued to be inhabited and in the Archaic period had a temple of Athene. Mycenae was sacked by the Argives in 468, but re-occupied in the Hellenistic period.

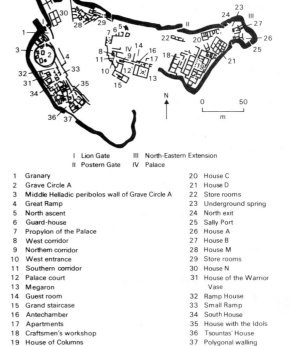

MYCENAE

| | I Lion Gate | III North-Eastern Extension |
| | II Postern Gate | IV Palace |

1	Granary	20	House C
2	Grave Circle A	21	House D
3	Middle Helladic peribolos wall of Grave Circle A	22	Store rooms
4	Great Ramp	23	Underground spring
5	North ascent	24	North exit
6	Guard-house	25	Sally Port
7	Propylon of the Palace	26	House A
8	West corridor	27	House B
9	Northern corridor	28	House M
10	West entrance	29	Store rooms
11	Southern corridor	30	House N
12	Palace court	31	House of the Warrior Vase
13	Megaron		
14	Guest room	32	Ramp House
15	Grand staircase	33	Small Ramp
16	Antechamber	34	South House
17	Apartments	35	House with the Idols
18	Craftsmen's workshop	36	Tsountas' House
19	House of Columns	37	Polygonal walling

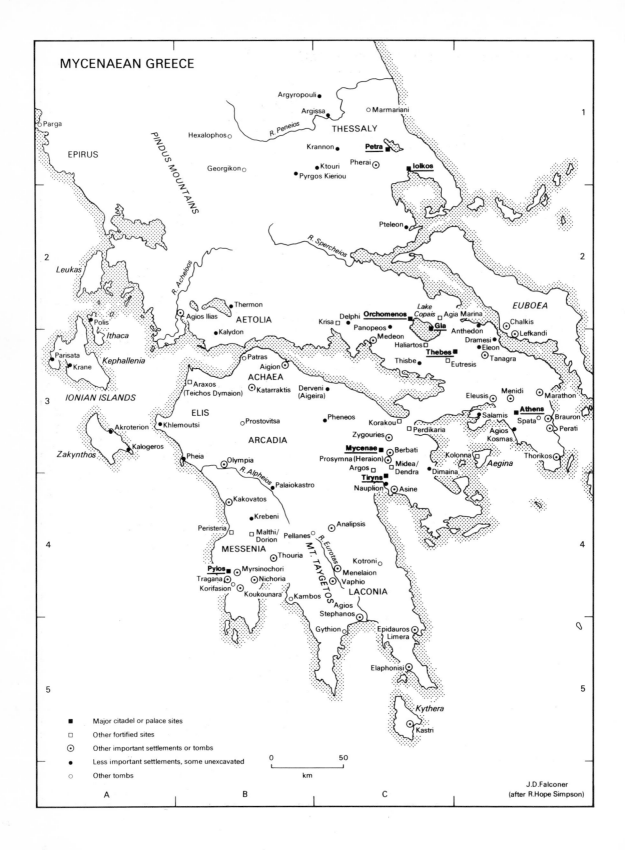

MYCENAEAN GREECE

Parga

EPIRUS

PINDUS MOUNTAINS

Argyropouli
Argissa
Marmariani
THESSALY
Hexalophos
R. Peneios
Krannon
Petra
Georgikon
Ktouri
Pherai
Pyrgos Kieriou
Iolkos

Pteleon

R. Spercheios

Leukas

Thermon
Agios Ilias
AETOLIA
Polis
Kalydon
Ithaca
Krisa
Delphi
Orchomenos
Lake Copais
Agia Marina
EUBOEA
Panopeos
Gla
Anthedon
Chalkis
Parisata
Medeon
Lefkandi
Krane
Kephallenia
Haliartos
Dramesi
Eleon
Patras
Thisbe
Thebes
Tanagra
Aigion
Eutresis

IONIAN ISLANDS
Araxos
(Teichos Dymaion)
ACHAEA
Derveni
(Aigeira)
Eleusis
Menidi
Marathon
Katarraktis
Athens
Akroterion
Khlemoutsi
Pheneos
Korakou
Salamis
Spata
Brauron
Zakynthos
ELIS
Prostovitsa
Perdikaria
Agios
Kosmas
Perati
Kalogeros
Zygouries
Pheia
Olympia
ARCADIA
Mycenae
Berbati
Kolonna
Thorikos
R. Alpheios
Prosymna (Heraion)
Midea/
Dendra
Aegina
Palaiokastro
Argos
Dimaina
Kakovatos
Tiryns
Nauplion
Asine
Krebeni
Peristeria
Analipsis
Malthi/
Dorion
Pellanes
MESSENIA
R. Eurotas
Kotroni
MT. TAYGETOS
Thouria
Menelaion
Pylos
Myrsinochori
Vaphio
Tragana
Nichoria
LACONIA
Korifasion
Koukounara
Kambos
Agios
Stephanos
Gythion
Epidauros
Limera

Elaphonisi

Kythera
Kastri

■ Major citadel or palace sites
□ Other fortified sites
⊙ Other important settlements or tombs
● Less important settlements, some unexcavated
○ Other tombs

0   50
km

J.D.Falconer
(after R.Hope Simpson)

A   B   C

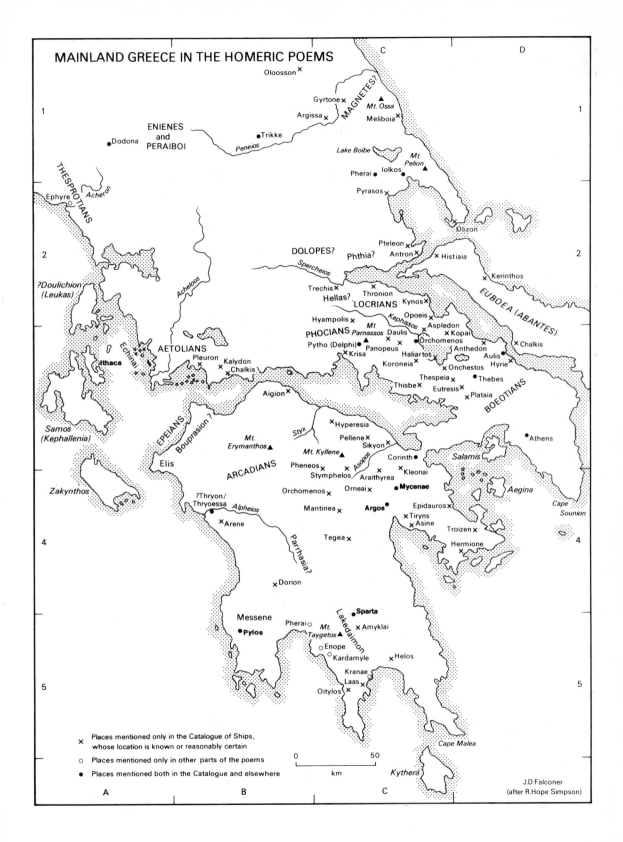

MAINLAND GREECE IN THE HOMERIC POEMS

Oloosson ×

Gyrtone ×

MAGNETES?

Argissa × Mt. Ossa ▲

Meliboia ×

ENIENES
and
PERAIBOI

• Dodona

• Trikke

Peneios

Lake Boibe Mt. Pelion ▲

THESPROTIANS

Pherai • Iolkos •

Acheron

Pyrasos ×

Ephyre ×

Olizon ×

Pteleon ×

DOLOPES? Phthia? Antron × Histiaia ×

?Doulichion
(Leukas)

Spercheios

Trechis × Thronion Kynos × Kerinthos ×

Hellas? LOCRIANS

Hyampolis × Opoeis ×

Acheloos

Kephissos Aspledon ×

PHOCIANS Mt Parnassos Daulis × Kopai ×

Pytho (Delphi) • Panopeus × Orchomenos × Anthedon × Chalkis ×

AETOLIANS Pleuron × Krisa × Haliartos × Aulis ×

Echinai Ithaca Kalydon × Koroneia × Onchestos × Hyrie ×

Chalkis × Thespeia × Thebes •

Thisbe × Eutresis × Plataia × BOEOTIANS

Aigion ×

Samos
(Kephallenia)

Hyperesia ×

Styx Pellene × Athens •

EPEIANS Mt. Erymanthos ▲ Sikyon × Salamis

Bouprasion? Mt. Kyllene ▲ Asopos Corinth •

Elis Pheneos × Araithyrea × Aegina

ARCADIANS Stymphelos × Kleonai ×

Zakynthos Orchomenos × Orneai × Mycenae • Cape Sounion

?Thryon/ Mantinea × Argos • Epidauros ×

Thryoessa Alpheios Tiryns ×

× Arene Tegea × Asine × Troizen ×

Parrhasia? Hermione ×

× Dorion

Sparta •

Messene Pherai ○ Amyklai ×

• Pylos Mt. Taygetos ▲

Lakedaimon

○ Enope

○ Kardamyle Helos ×

Kranae ×

Laas ×

Oitylos ×

Cape Malea

× Places mentioned only in the Catalogue of Ships,
  whose location is known or reasonably certain

○ Places mentioned only in other parts of the poems

• Places mentioned both in the Catalogue and elsewhere

0   50
km

Kythera

J.D.Falconer
(after R.Hope Simpson)

Mainland Greece in the Homeric Poems and The Homeric World

Mainland Greece in the Homeric Poems and *The Homeric World* are intended as a guide to readers of the *Iliad* and *Odyssey*, and show the known or probable location of the main places referred to by Homer. Like other aspects of the poems, Homer's geography is a mixture of memories from the Mycenaean world, contemporary knowledge of the eighth or early seventh century BC, and fairy tale. The most detailed geographical information is given by the Catalogue of Ships in *Iliad*, Book 2, which names 152 towns or districts in Greece and the islands, and 19 in Thrace, the Troad and Asia Minor. The position of many of these was unknown even to the Greeks of historical times, and it is likely that at least the Greek section of the Catalogue was a survival from the Mycenaean Age reflecting the settlement pattern of that period rather than of Homer's own time. Further evidence for this is provided by places in the Catalogue which archaeology has shown to have been unoccupied after the Mycenaean period (e.g. Eutresis, Krisa, Dorion and Pylos), and by the grouping of the towns into kingdoms which are quite unlike anything known in historical Greece. Although the Catalogue cannot originally have been composed to form part of the *Iliad* as we know it, the rest of the *Iliad* is broadly consistent with it in its picture of a Greece dominated by the important Mycenaean centres of Mycenae and Pylos.

The Trojan section of the Catalogue is far less informative than the Greek. Although the Troad itself is described in some detail, the territories of the Trojan allies cannot be located with any certainty. The Trojan Catalogue appears to describe Asia Minor before the Ionian migrations of around 1000 BC, with no reference to any of the later Greek cities on the coast, apart from Miletus which is specifically said to be occupied by 'barbarian-speaking Carians'. But whether this means that the Catalogue was composed in the Mycenaean period, or merely represents later ideas of what Asia Minor was like at the time of the Trojan War, is still disputed. On the geography of the Troad, the rest of the *Iliad* adds details that are sometimes surprisingly accurate—for example, the fact that Poseidon could see Troy from the peak of Samothrace—and this feature has led to the suggestion that Homer may have had personal knowledge of the area.

It has also been claimed that the *Odyssey*'s description of Ithaca and the islands round it was based on first-hand knowledge, but this has been questioned on the grounds that the account of the relative position of the islands is inaccurate. While the identification of Ithaca with modern Ithaki is now generally accepted, there is probably as much fiction as fact in the topographical details of caves, springs and bays on the island.

The main action of the *Iliad* and *Odyssey* takes place in a world enclosed by Ithaca in the west, Troy in the east and Crete in the south. However, the boundaries of the Homeric world are extended by references to more distant peoples and places, Egypt and Libya in the south, Sidon and the Phoenicians in the east, as well as to a number of more or less mythical tribes, the Ethiopians and Pygmies in the south, the Taphians in the west and the Cimmerians in the north. Finally there are the wanderings of Odysseus, from the time when he was blown off course round Cape Malea. The origins of these stories lie in folk tales without any specific geographical location, but attempts were made quite early on by the Greeks themselves to fit them into the geography of the Mediterranean, so that the Phaeacians were placed on Corfu, Circe at Cape Circeo near Naples, Scylla and Charybdis in the Straits of Messina and the Cyclopes on Mount Etna. This location of Odysseus' wanderings in the west probably reflects the opening up of Sicily and south Italy to Greek trade and colonisation in the seventh century.

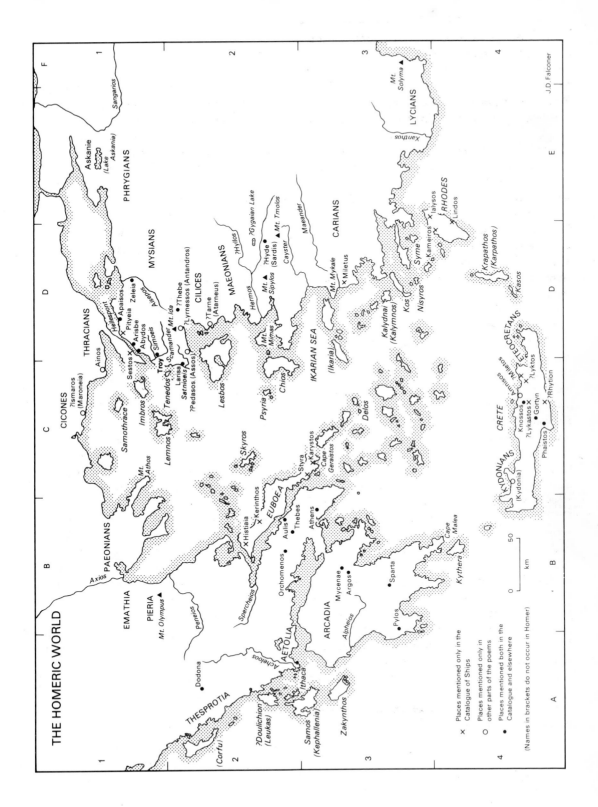

THE HOMERIC WORLD

Places mentioned only in the Catalogue of Ships — ✕

Places mentioned only in other parts of the poems — ○

Places mentioned both in the Catalogue and elsewhere — ●

(Names in brackets do not occur in Homer)

J.D. Falconer

9

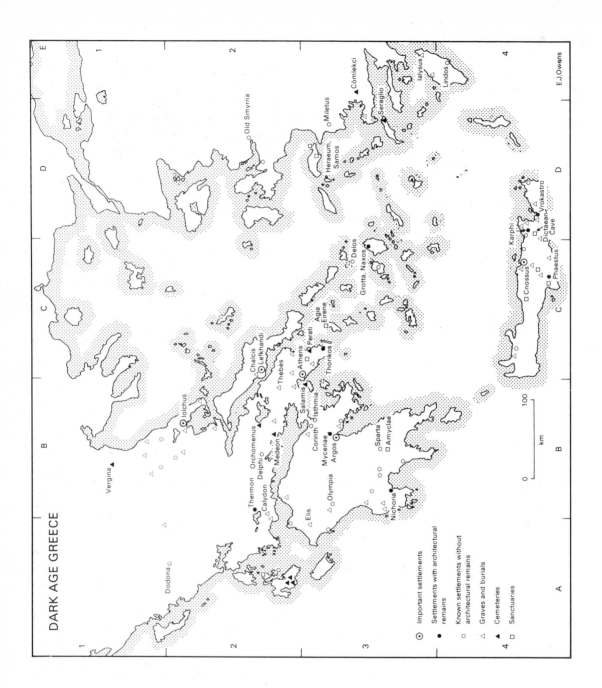

DARK AGE GREECE

E.J.Owens

Important settings

Settlements with architectural remains

Known settlements without architectural remains

Graves and burials

Cemeteries

Sanctuaries

Dodona

Vergina

Thermon
Calydon
Delphi
Orchomenus
Medeon
Elis
Olympia
Nichoria

Iolchus

Chalcis
Lefkhandi
Thebes

Corinth
Isthmia
Salamis
Mycenae
Argos
Sparta
Amyclae

Athens
Perati
Agia
Eirene
Thorikos

Old Smyrna

Heraeum.
Samos
Miletus

Grotta, Naxos
Delos

Cömlekci

Seraglio

Ialysus
Lindos

Cnossus
Karphi
Vrokastro
Dictaean
Cave
Phaestus

km
0   100

10

Dark Age Greece

After the collapse of Mycenaean civilisation during the course of the twelfth century BC Greek history enters an era of darkness, which was not totally dispelled until the middle of the eighth century. This period is 'dark' both because information is lacking, and because such information as exists indicates an extreme cultural recession, characterised by depopulation, isolation and poverty. The substantial reduction in the number and size of occupied sites is proof of widespread depopulation: indeed some areas of the Aegean have so far produced no evidence of habitation during this period. Depopulation was accompanied by regional fragmentation and isolation, as communications ceased not only within the Aegean but also with areas beyond. A significant feature of the Dark Age is the scarcity of architectural remains at most sites. This reflects the uncertainty of the times and, together with the poor quality of the other material remains, indicates the low quality of life. Except on Crete, where Bronze Age building traditions continued, graves alone supply the bulk of the evidence throughout these centuries. Technical and artistic skills, such as bronze working, writing and figured art, were also lost for a time.

The Dark Age, however, is not a period of total demoralisation. Life continued in certain areas, albeit at a much reduced level. In particular, Attica, the Argolid, parts of Thessaly and Crete managed to survive the worst difficulties of the age, and it was in these areas that the foundations of the eventual recovery of Greece were laid. New metal working technology was developed, and old skills rediscovered. Iron appears in several areas, and the cupellation of silver was undertaken at Argos and Thorikos by 900. Bronze working reappears at Lefkandi. Athens leads the rest of Greece with the development of the proto-Geometric style of pottery, from which evolved the full Geometric style from c. 900 onwards. Lefkandi has arguably become one of the most important sites for the elucidation of the Dark Age: here the excavation of several rich burials must modify our view of total poverty, at least from the later tenth century onwards. With the appearance of open air sanctuaries there is also the first indication of a change in places of worship. Before 1000 BC, too, the first tentative steps were taken to colonise the Aegean with the implantation of settlements along the west coast of Asia Minor.

This evidence must not be over-emphasised. Most parts of Greece remained depressed throughout the ninth century, and full recovery did not begin until the eighth century. But then remarkable changes and advances can be noted. A substantial increase in population is evident, both from the increased number of sites and the increased size of many settlements. As communications were opened up, areas of Greece for which evidence of settlement had been lacking, were again occupied. The west coast of Asia Minor and the Aegean islands were fully colonised. Contact with the Near East, which brought fresh impetus to many aspects of life and artistic development, was intensively renewed. The colonisation of the western Mediterranean was also begun.

Graves and cemeteries continue to supply the bulk of the evidence for the eighth century, but there is important information regarding architecture from such sites as Emborio, Old Smyrna and Zagora on Andros. Their substantial remains also confirm a more settled and prosperous existence. However the defensive nature of many sites, often in inaccessible or hidden locations, and the construction of fortification walls at Old Smyrna and Zagora suggest that life was still by no means secure.

Many new sanctuaries appear during this period, and it is clear that some were gaining a reputation beyond their immediate area. About half contain remains of temples. The dedication of votive offerings at Bronze Age sites is indicative of an interest in the heroic past. With the introduction of writing from the Near East, Greece can be said to have finally put aside the Dark Age and to be emerging into the full light of history.

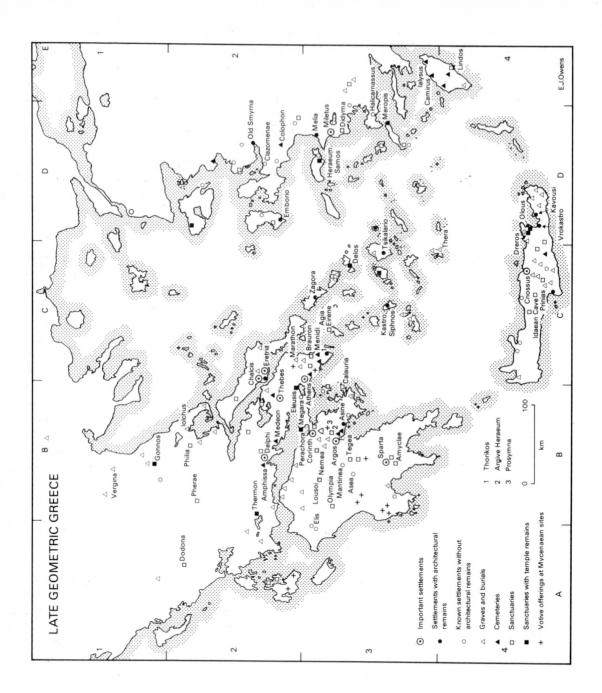

LATE GEOMETRIC GREECE

Important settlements ⊙
Settlements with architectural remains ●
Known settlements without architectural remains ○
Graves and burials △
Cemeteries ▲
Sanctuaries □
Sanctuaries with temple remains ■
Votive offerings at Mycenaean sites +

1 Thorikos
2 Argive Heraeum
3 Prosymna

0   km   100

E.J.Owens

Vergina
Dodona
Pherae
Gonnos
Philia
Thermon
Amphissa
Delphi
Medeon
Elis
Olympia
Lousoi
Nemea
Mantinea
Asea
Tegea
Argos
Asine
Sparta
Amyclae
Calauria
Corinth
Perachora
Megara
Eleusis
Athens
Eirene
Agia
Menidi
Brauron
Marathon
Thebes
Chalcis
Eretria
Zagora
Delos
Tsikalario
Kastro
Siphnos
Thera
Emborio
Old Smyrna
Clazomenae
Colophon
Melia
Miletus
Didyma
Heraeum
Samos
Halicarnassus
Meropis
Camirus
Ialysus
Lindos
Cnossus
Idaean Cave
Prinias
Dreros
Olous
Kavousi
Vrokastro
Iolchus

12

Greek Colonisation (Eighth to Sixth Centuries BC)

By *c.* 800 Greek traders had begun to venture beyond the Aegean with such confidence and regularity that Euboeans from Chalcis and Eretria had set up a 'trading station' (*emporion*) at Al Mina (the place called Posideion by Herodotus?) on the R. Orontes delta, excavated in the 1930s. Arguably these traders sought iron and copper above all. A comparable 'trading station' which Euboeans founded before 750 at Pithecusae in the gulf of Naples was succeeded during the latter part of the eighth century by their establishment of 'ports of call' at Zancle and Rhegium, and of settlements in fertile areas at Cumae, Leontini and Catane. Though Greeks were not blind to trading opportunities and other attractions, it was principally the prospect of good land free for occupation which prompted others to follow the Euboean example, in an effort to gain relief from the generally acute problems of increased population and unequal division of land holdings throughout Greece. Further sites on the eastern seaboard of Sicily were quickly settled, and in the seventh century these acted as the springboard for foundations on the north and south coasts of the island. In south Italy development of the same type occurred simultaneously, with settlers from Achaea taking the lead.

In a northerly direction it was again Euboeans who led the way with the establishment of settlements in Chalcidice during the late eighth century. In the seventh century other Greeks settled further along the northern shore of the Aegean, either side of the Hellespont, and around the Propontis. Despite its harsher climate the Black Sea was even penetrated by a few settlers at this date, but the main wave of foundations here did not come until the sixth century, mainly at the instigation of Miletus.

Elsewhere Greeks principally from Asia Minor were permitted to establish a 'trading station' and settlement at Naucratis, 50 miles up the Canopic branch of the Nile Delta, in the late seventh century. Cyrene near the North African coast was founded from Thera *c.* 630; later, early in the sixth century, Phocaea in Asia Minor planted settlements as far distant as southern France, Spain and Corsica. These areas, together with western Sicily, were also being settled by Phoenicians and Carthaginians. Though their motives seem to have been broadly similar to those of Greeks, hostile relations were the exception, usually the result of provocation.

The modern translation 'colony' for the Greek *apoikia* misleads if it is taken to imply any degree of long-term dependence upon, or control by, the founders from mainland Greece. Rather, from the outset the settlements were intended to be independent, self-supporting communities, whose links with their founders would in normal circumstances be no more than those of culture, religion and sentiment. Each foundation would indeed enjoy the formal sponsorship of a community, which was thus recognised as the *metropolis* or 'mother city'. This community would appoint a leader (*oikistes*), furnish ships or other help, and gather colonists, who did not necessarily have to be its own citizens. However, its positive role would often lapse at this point, even though links of the type just mentioned would always remain strong. In special circumstances, where the social or agrarian problems of a community were particularly bad, the colonists might not even be volunteers—as, for example, in the cases of the Spartan foundation of Tarentum or the Theran foundation of Cyrene.

This last instance stands out as one of the best documented colonial ventures, thanks to the survival of an inscription embodying at least the gist of an archaic record to supplement Herodotus' narrative. Among ancient authors he and Thucydides furnish the most useful information about colonisation; later writers, like Strabo, have much less of solid value to offer. Excavation and the analysis of material remains (especially pottery) have therefore played a key role in illuminating further the character and development of colonisation, even if there is a limit to what may be securely deduced from such evidence. It is frustrating that so little written material survives to deepen our insight into the major topic of the relations between colonies and the local, normally less civilised, peoples of the areas settled.

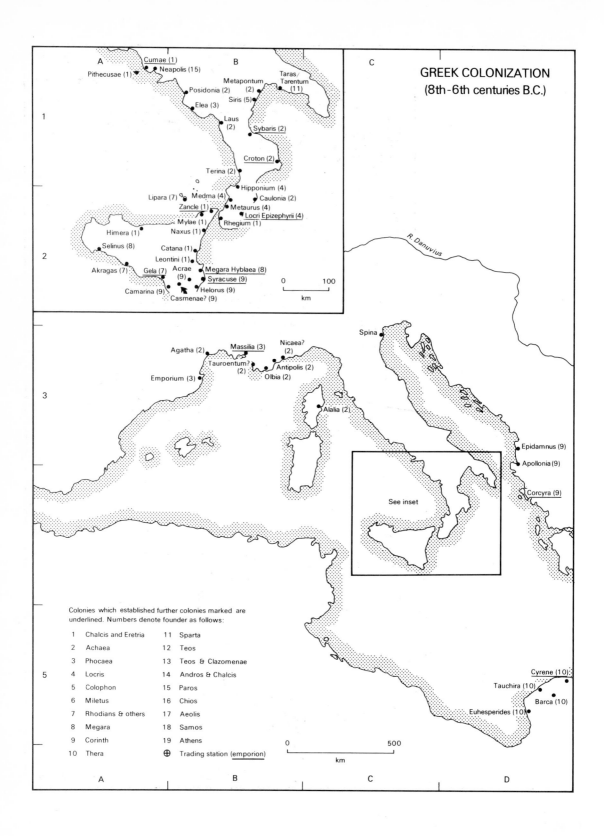

GREEK COLONIZATION
(8th-6th centuries B.C.)

Cumae (1)
Neapolis (15)
Pithecusae (1)
Metapontum (2)
Taras Tarentum (11)
Posidonia (2)
Siris (5)
Elea (3)
Laus (2)
Sybaris (2)
Croton (2)
Terina (2)
Hipponium (4)
Lipara (7)
Medma (4)
Caulonia (2)
Zancle (1)
Metaurus (4)
Locri Epizephyrii (4)
Mylae (1)
Rhegium (1)
Himera (1)
Naxus (1)
Selinus (8)
Catana (1)
Leontini (1)
Akragas (7)
Gela (7)
Acrae (9)
Megara Hyblaea (8)
Camarina (9)
Syracuse (9)
Helorus (9)
Casmenae? (9)

0   100
km

Spina

R. Danuvius

Agatha (2)
Massilia (3)
Nicaea? (2)
Tauroentum? (2)
Antipolis (2)
Emporium (3)
Olbia (2)

Alalia (2)

Epidamnus (9)
Apollonia (9)
Corcyra (9)

See inset

Colonies which established further colonies marked are
underlined. Numbers denote founder as follows:

1	Chalcis and Eretria	11	Sparta
2	Achaea	12	Teos
3	Phocaea	13	Teos & Clazomenae
4	Locris	14	Andros & Chalcis
5	Colophon	15	Paros
6	Miletus	16	Chios
7	Rhodians & others	17	Aeolis
8	Megara	18	Samos
9	Corinth	19	Athens
10	Thera	⊕	Trading station (emporion)

Cyrene (10)
Tauchira (10)
Barca (10)
Euhesperides (10)

0   500
km

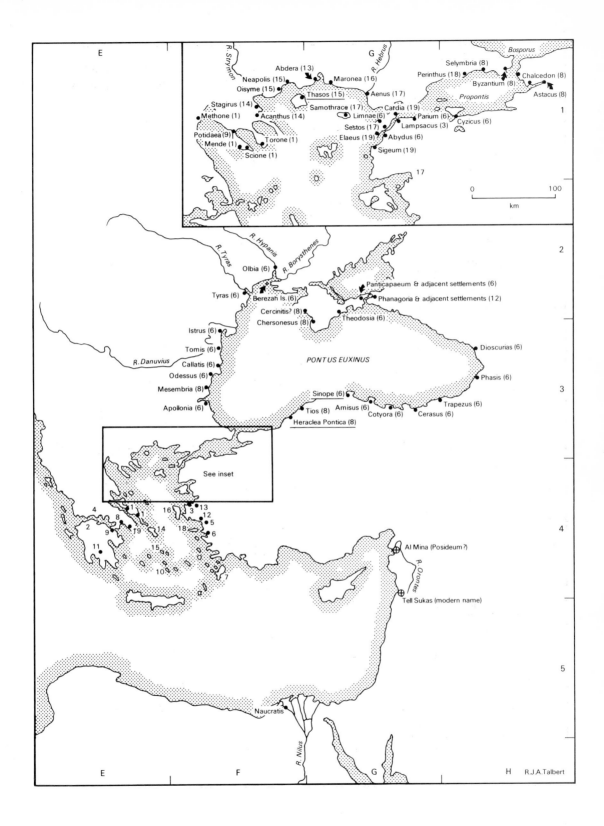

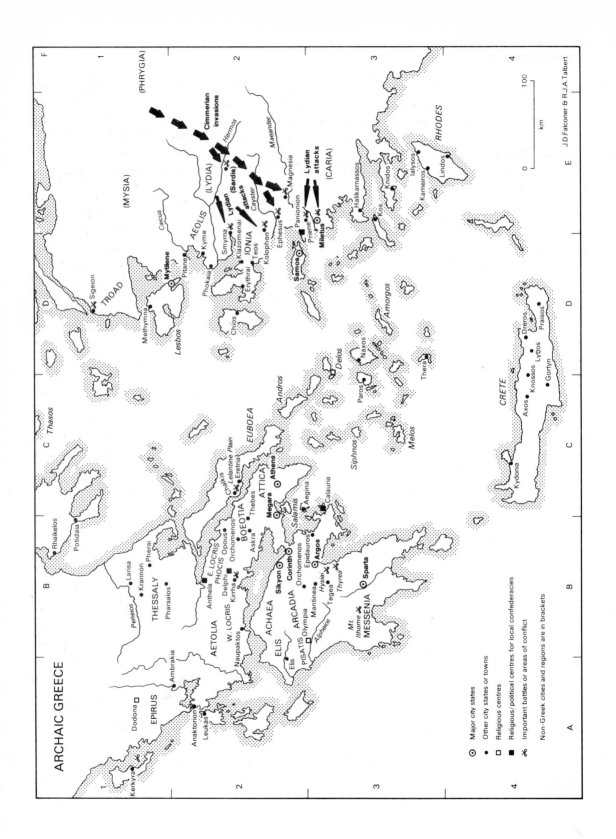

ARCHAIC GREECE

Major city states ⊙
Other city states or towns ●
Religious centres ☐
Religious/ political centres for local confederacies ■
Important battles or areas of conflict ✗
Non-Greek cities and regions are in brackets

J.D.Falconer & R.J.A.Talbert

0   100 km

(PHRYGIA)

Cimmerian invasions

(MYSIA)

(LYDIA)

Hermes

Maeander

Lydian (Sardis)

Lydian attacks

(CARIA)

RHODES

Halikarmassos
Knidos
Kos
Ialysos
Kameiros
Lindos

AEOLIS
Caicus
Kyme
Pitane
Smyrna
Phokaia
Klazomenai
Teos
Erythrai
Kolophon
Ephesus
Magnesia
Panionion
Priene
Miletus

IONIA
Lydian attacks
Cayster

Mytilene
Methymna
Lesbos
Chios

Sigeion
TROAD

Samos

Delos

Andros
Amorgos

Naxos
Paros

Siphnos
Melos
Thera

CRETE
Kydonia
Axos
Knossos
Lyttos
Gortyn
Dreros
Praisos

Thasos

Rhaikelos
Potidaia

THESSALY
Larisa
Krannon
Pherai
Pharsalos
Peneios

EPIRUS
Dodona
Anaktorion
Leukas
Ambrakia
Kerkyra

AETOLIA
W. LOCRIS
Naupaktos
Antheia
E. LOCRIS
Opous
PHOCIS
Delphi
Kirrha
Orchomenos
Askra
BOEOTIA
Thebes
Chalkis
Eretria
Lelantine Plain
EUBOEA

ACHAEA
Elis
ELIS
PISATIS
Olympia
Alpheios
ARCADIA
Orchomenos
Mantinea
Tegea
Sikyon
Corinth
Argos
Epidauros
Aegina
Salamis
Calauria
Hysiai
Thyrea
Mt. Ithome
MESSENIA
Sparta

Megara
Athens
ATTICA

A   B   C   D   E   F

Archaic Greece

The seventh and sixth centuries constitute an exciting formative period of the utmost importance in Greece. For the first time Greek history is now illuminated significantly by written records as well as by archaeology. Though its origins lie obscurely in the preceding Dark Age, unquestionably the emergence of the *polis* as the predominant political and social unit in Greece was a crucial step forward. Autonomous communities of this type—centred on a defensible town in control of its surrounding territory—became a distinctive feature of Greek civilisation throughout the Mediterranean and beyond.

However this is not to overlook wide variations in the speed and character of change. In many areas of Greece, especially the north and west, there was at best only a slow shift away from tribal organisation. Elsewhere Crete (see further pp. 155–6) and Sparta are distinguished by their idiosyncratic development. The latter, having at last achieved success in a struggle to conquer fertile Messenia shortly before 700, was then faced with bitter hostility not only from Messenians permanently subjected as helots, but also from jealous neighbouring states, Argos especially. A great battle at Hysiai in 669 resulted in a narrow Argive victory. During the late seventh century the strain which Sparta faced in containing a prolonged Messenian rebellion led to a permanent transformation in the character of the state: most strikingly the Spartiates, or citizen males, became an exclusive military caste. Only during the sixth century was Sparta able to extend her influence further in the Peloponnese. Checked by an initial failure to annex Tegea, she proceeded instead to forge alliances, a policy which led to the formation of the Peloponnesian League under her leadership. By the late sixth century Sparta was the strongest of the mainland states.

As seen above (pp. 13–15), the Archaic period was one of widespread expansion and of increasing prosperity through trade and settlement. Communities either side of the Aegean—like Chalkis, Eretria, Miletus and Samos—were especially well placed to benefit, as was Crete to the south. On the Greek mainland this growth caused constant rivalry between ambitious neighbours such as Athens, Megara and Corinth. The latter built up a formidable fleet and consolidated her influence in north west Greece. She was also one of the first states where the impact of new wealth weakened the exclusive hold of a traditional landed aristocracy upon government. As a consequence of such strife (*stasis*), Corinth was seized around 655 by a single ruler or 'tyrant'—not necessarily a pejorative term. Elsewhere too (as at Argos, Sikyon and Samos in particular) powerful tyrants established themselves for one or two generations before giving way to oligarchy or democracy. At Athens—not yet among the leading states—a political and economic crisis was alleviated in 594 by a mediator, Solon. But faction fighting persisted, so that eventually from 545, at his third attempt, Peisistratus set himself up as tyrant: he proved a wise ruler who, followed by his sons, did much to unify and stabilise Attica over 35 years, as well as to strengthen the economy. Athenian interest in Sigeion and the Thracian Chersonese, on the trade route to the Black Sea, dates from the sixth century.

On the eastern seaboard of the Aegean, the Greek cities first withstood Cimmerian incursions, and then from the 670s more persistent onslaughts by the Mermnad rulers of Lydia, a power which came to stimulate its Greek neighbours as well as to antagonise and dominate them. Coinage, for example, was a Lydian invention imitated by Greeks from about 600. The most successful military resistance was that of Miletus, arguably the greatest Greek city of the day, celebrated for its encouragement of culture and scientific enquiry as well as of colonial ventures northwards. Yet Lydia, and with it the Greek cities beyond, fell to Persia in the mid-sixth century. Thereafter Persian encroachment westwards was to make a lasting impact upon Greek history.

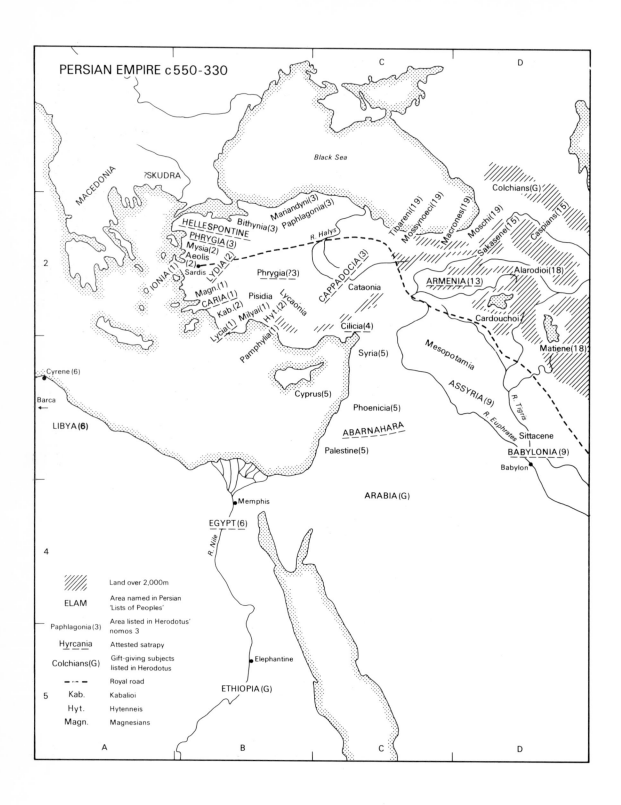

PERSIAN EMPIRE c550-330

Black Sea

MACEDONIA

?SKUDRA

Mariandynii(3)
Bithynia(3) Paphlagonia(3)
HELLESPONTINE
PHRYGIA(3)
Mysia(2)
Aeolis
(2)
O IONIA(1) Sardis LYDIA(2)
Magn.(1)
CARIA(1)
Kab.(2)
Lycia(1) Milyai(1) Hyt.(1)
Pamphylia(1)

R. Halys

Phrygia(?3)

Pisidia
Lycaonia
CAPPADOCIA(3)
Cataonia

Cilicia(4)

Syria(5)

Cyprus(5)

Tibareni(19) Mossynoeci(19)
Macrones(19)
Moschi(19)
Sakasene(15)
Caspians(15)

Colchians(G)

ARMENIA(13)

Alarodioi(18)

Cardouchoi

Matiene(18)

Mesopotamia

ASSYRIA(9)

R. Tigris

R. Euphrates Sittacene

BABYLONIA(9)

Babylon

Cyrene (6)

Barca

LIBYA(6)

Phoenicia(5)

ABARNAHARA

Palestine(5)

ARABIA(G)

Memphis

EGYPT(6)

R. Nile

Elephantine

ETHIOPIA(G)

	Land over 2,000m
ELAM	Area named in Persian 'Lists of Peoples'
Paphlagonia (3)	Area listed in Herodotus' nomos 3
Hyrcania	Attested satrapy
Colchians(G)	Gift-giving subjects listed in Herodotus
– · – · –	Royal road
Kab.	Kabalioi
Hyt.	Hytenneis
Magn.	Magnesians

18

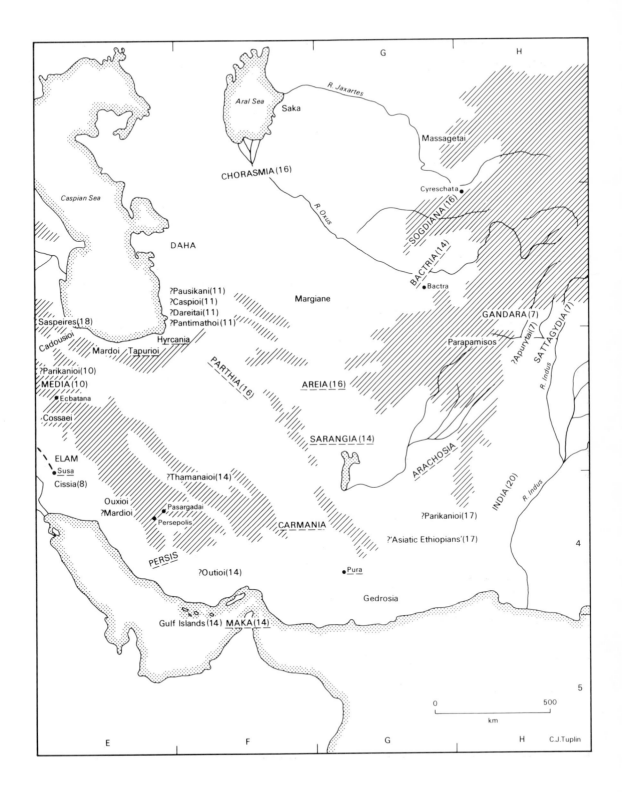

G · · · · · · · · · · · H

R. Jaxartes

Aral Sea　Saka

Massagetai

CHORASMIA(16)

Cyreschata ●

Caspian Sea

DAHA

R. Oxus

SOGDIANA(16)

BACTRIA(14)

Margiane

Bactra ●

?Pausikani(11)
?Caspioi(11)
?Dareitai(11)
?Pantimathoi(11)

GANDARA(7)

Saspeires(18)

Hyrcania

Parapamisos

?Apurytai(7)

SATTAGYDIA(7)

R. Indus

Cadousioi

Mardoi　Tapurioi

?Parikanioi(10)

PARTHIA(16)

AREIA(16)

MEDIA(10)

Ecbatana ●

Cossaei

SARANGIA(14)

ARACHOSIA

ELAM

Susa ●

Cissia(8)

INDIA(20)

R. Indus

?Thamanaioi(14)

Ouxioi
?Mardioi

Pasargadai ■

Persepolis ◆

CARMANIA

?Parikanioi(17)

?'Asiatic Ethiopians'(17)

4

PERSIS

?Outioi(14)

Pura ●

Gedrosia

Gulf Islands(14) MAKA(14)

5

0 · · · · · · · · 500

km

E · · · · · · · F · · · · · · · G · · · · · · · H　C.J.Tuplin

19

Persian Empire c. 550–330

The empire was largely created by the absorption in turn of four previous Near Eastern great powers. First, c. 550, the Median empire, stretching from the R. Halys to an uncertain eastern frontier. By 522/21 Persian rule ran as far as Sogdiana and eastwards across the Hindukush, but some of this area may have been acquired separately by Cyrus, who died trying to advance beyond the R. Jaxartes. Second, c. 540, the Lydian empire, extending west of the R. Halys to the sea. Third, from 539, the Neo-Babylonian empire, consisting of Mesopotamia, Susiane and Abarnahara ('Beyond the River', i.e. Syria/Palestine). Fourth, from 525, Egypt, extending south along the R. Nile to Elephantine/Syene. In addition, Cyprus came as either a precursor or a consequence of the conquest of Egypt; Cambyses had Arab help in 525 and Darius claimed 'Arabia' as subject in 522/21; Cilicia voluntarily submitted to Cyrus, retaining a native dynasty almost continuously until the fourth century. Herodotus and Persian 'Lists of Peoples' show significant additions by Darius: c. 518, India (West Indus valley); some east Aegean islands—Samos, Lesbos, Chios among them—and c. 513 Greek cities on the north Aegean coast; c. 513/12, Thracians south, and possibly north, of Mount Rhodope; c. 512 or 492, Macedonia; c. 513, Libya. The Persian lists alone add Ethiopia, Caria (not a new conquest) and, untruthfully, 'Scythians beyond the Sea'. Two new names appear in Xerxes' reign, Akaufaka (unlocated) and Daha. However his Greek failure ended expansion and brought permanent loss of European subjects, though, exceptionally, Persian occupation of Doriscus persisted for decades.

At best the empire now stretched from west Anatolia, the Levant and Egypt to Bactria/Sogdiana and India. Chorasmia was certainly lost by the 330s, though some Indians did fight at Gaugamela in 331, coming perhaps from areas where Alexander later encountered native rulers still calling themselves hyparchs or even satraps. Even so, the empire never truly included *all* areas lying within the geographical limits outlined. Mysia, Pisidia and the Cardouchi, for example,

appear autonomous c. 400, and this may be the norm at all periods. Throughout the empire's history rebellion was a chronic problem—both nationalist secession, and satrapal attempts to seize the throne or to establish independent principalities. In 522 Darius' usurpation occasioned rapidly suppressed disturbances in Elam, Babylonia, Assyria, Armenia, Egypt, Media, Parthia-Hyrcania, Sagartia, Sattagydia, Scythia, as well as in Persia itself. Lydia had revolted immediately after Cyrus' conquest, the Asiatic Greeks and Caria in 499–4, parts of Cyprus in 498–7 and possibly 478, Egypt in 486–5, Babylon in the late 480s. Certain unsatisfactory satraps had to be forcibly removed—like Oroetes at Sardis (c. 520), and Aryandes in Egypt (after 513).

After 480/79 the Asiatic Greeks rebelled again and were only regained securely by the King's Peace of 387/86. Egypt was persistently troublesome with two major rebellions: the first in the late 460s was not suppressed until c. 455, with instability in the Nile Delta lasting even longer; the second, c. 404, brought independence until 343. There soon followed a third Egyptian rebellion between 338 and 336. Various parts of Phoenicia, Cilicia and Cyprus saw disturbances in the 380s, late 360s and early 340s. There were rebellions by satraps in Abarnahara (440s, Megabyxos; c. 416, Artyphius), Lydia (c. 416, Pissouthnes; 401, Cyrus; late 360s, Autophradates), Hellespontine Phrygia (360s, Ariobarzanes; 350s, Artabazus), Caria (360s, Mausolus), Cappadocia (late 370s and 360s, Datames), and Armenia (late 360s, Orontes). Further east the evidence is less good, but shows a Median rebellion c. 408, a period of Cadusian secession from 405 to the 350s, and rebel satraps in Bactria (late 460s), Hyrcania (425/24, Ochus, alias Darius II), and possibly eastern Iran (under Darius II, Teritouchmes).

The political geography of the empire is a contentious topic. The present map seeks at least to take account of four types of enumeration of its constituent parts, though location is often conjectural and in some cases has not been attempted:

(a) the subject peoples in various, mostly Darian, royal texts (*not* satrapy lists);

(b) the 20 *nomoi* or satrapies in Herodotus 3.89 ff.;

(c) the nations found in Persian armies, especially those of Xerxes and of Darius in 331; in the former instance, the account of Herodotus 7.61 ff. is nearly identical with (b) above;

(d) the nations represented, either singly or in conjunction with others, in attested satrapal titles; this is a fluid list, especially in better documented areas, compiled almost entirely from *Greek* sources.

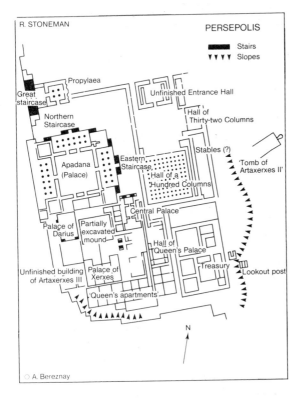

Persepolis

The ceremonial capital of the Persian Empire lies in south west Iran, on the north side of the plain of Marvdasht. Though the site may have been used by Cambyses II, it was Darius the Great (522–485) who was responsible for the foundation of the present complex. Most of the building was accomplished in the reign of Xerxes, in the thirteen years following 485. Buildings of this period include the Gateway of All Lands, the Hall of a Hundred Columns, and the Northern Staircase. Persepolis was the gathering place for the annual presentation of tribute to the Great King. This scene is represented in the magnificent reliefs of the Northern Staircase. The palace was destroyed by fire by Alexander the Great—by accident or design—in 330. Many of the stone slabs exhibit the marks of cracking by fire. Further columns have collapsed with the passing centuries. A few miles to the west are the tombs of the Achaemenid kings at Naqsh-e-Rustam, and further north Pasargadae and the tomb of Cyrus.

MARATHON, 490 B.C.

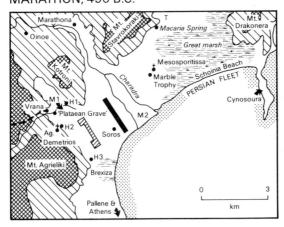

Marathon, 490 BC

The presumable position of the Athenian camp by the western foothills (at a Herakleion, not securely identified), and the certain position of the *Soros* (Athenian mass-grave), guarantee the main battle's location west of the R. Charadra; and if the remains of the later trophy were not significantly moved when reused in the Middle Ages, they may confirm the slaughter of fleeing Persians by the Great Marsh, shown in the Stoa Poecile painting. (The supposed 'Plataean Grave' near Vrana, and all dependent suppositions about the battle, should be rejected.) Much about the campaign is disputed. Did the Athenians move their camp during the days before the battle? What eventually precipitated the engagement? Likewise with regard to the battle itself, were the lines parallel with, or at right angles to, the shore? In this connection Herodotus' reference to the Persian centre pushing towards the *mesogaia* is unhelpful. Why did the Persian cavalry make no significant contribution?

Persian Wars

The 'Persian Wars'—*ta Mēdika*, 'Median things'—conventionally describes the two occasions on which Persian armies had to be driven out of the heart of mainland Greece.

(1) In 490 Datis led across the Aegean a seaborne expedition against Eretria and Athens, the two mainland states which briefly participated in the 'Ionian revolt' of Persia's Greek subjects in western Asia Minor (499/4). Persian aspirations on the mainland extended beyond Eretria and Athens. An earlier, unsuccessful punitive expedition against them had been instructed to conquer whatever it could, and Darius sought formal submission from other Greek cities in 491/90. But there was no general movement by the Greeks to resist Datis. Only Athens helped Eretria, and only Plataea helped Athens. The Spartans did march north, but arrived too late. When Eretria fell through treachery after a brief siege, the population was deported to Cissia. However a different fate was presumably intended for Athens, since the exiled tyrant Hippias, who accompanied Datis, was hardly going to be restored to a deserted, smoking ruin. In the event the Athenians chose not to await a siege, but confronted the Persians where they landed in Attica, at Marathon (see p. 21). Despite their defeat here the Persians did then sail on to Athens, but proved unwilling to risk an opposed landing, and so returned to Asia Minor.

(2) Xerxes' expedition (480/79) was much larger in scale, and was confronted by a more concerted resistance from the Hellenic League. The Serpent Column erected at Delphi as a thank-offering after Plataea listed 31 participants in the war, though it omits states which medized after initial resistance and some others. Xerxes planned a steady advance into the Greek peninsula from the north by army and fleet acting in conjunction. The overriding concern of the Spartan leaders of the League—protection of the Peloponnese—was not shared by Athens, whose fleet was vital to the Greek cause. There were therefore persistent and deep-rooted differences over strategy among the Greeks. But they did agree upon successive attempts to halt Xerxes at Tempe (abandoned as unsuitable before his arrival there), Thermopylae/Artemisium (p. 24), and Salamis/Corinthian Isthmus. Both the latter were co-ordinated land/sea positions designed to keep the enemy army and fleet out of mutual contact; in the event the Persian army never actually reached the Isthmus. After the defeat at Salamis in September 480, Xerxes, together with his fleet and part of the army, retired to Asia Minor. The remainder, under Mardonius, wintered in Thessaly and Macedonia.

Neither side hurried into action the following year. In particular the Hellenic League, dominated by Sparta, showed little enthusiasm for searching out the Persians in northern Greece. Mardonius, after failing to detach Athens by diplomacy, re-invaded Attica. But when the Peloponnesian states eventually mobilised, he chose southern Boeotia as more favourable ground for a decisive confrontation. After their defeat at Plataea (p. 25), the Persians evacuated European Greece, except for garrisons in Thrace and the Black Sea approaches. Meanwhile after some hesitation a League fleet crossed the Aegean and defeated the Persians at Mycale, provoking a second Ionian revolt. The subsequent capture of Sestos (479) and of Byzantium (478) brought operations by the Hellenic League to an end, and marks the lowest limit of what would normally be called the Persian Wars.

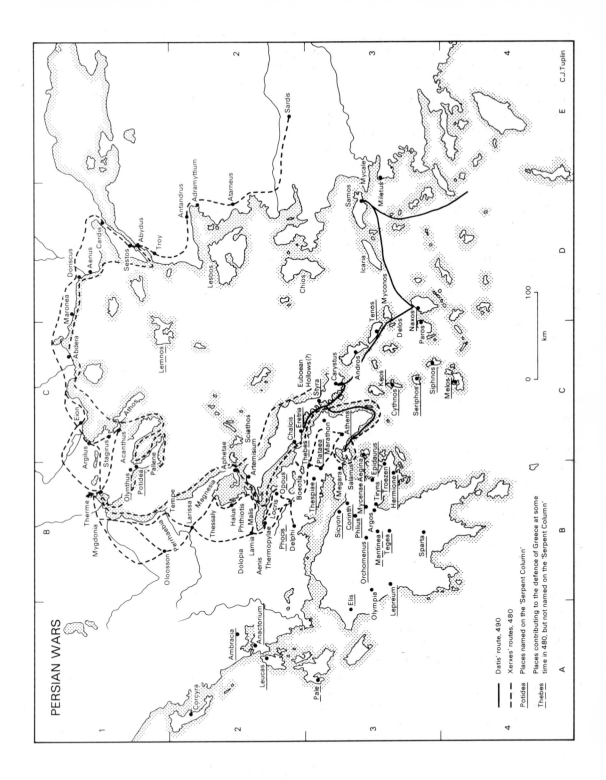

PERSIAN WARS

Datis' route, 490
Xerxes' routes, 480
● Potidea   Places named on the 'Serpent Column'
Thebes   Places contributing to the defence of Greece at some
         time in 480, but not named on the 'Serpent Column'

C.J.Tuplin

23

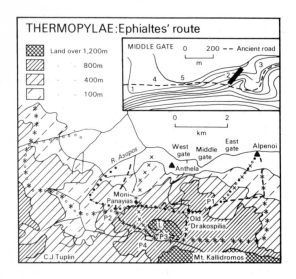

Thermopylae: Ephialtes' Route

The fighting in the Middle Gate near the Hot Springs [1] is straightforward: for two days the Greeks repelled assaults in front of the Phocian wall [5]; on the third day they pushed further west [4], but then retreated to a hillock west of the wall [3], and were annihilated by attacks from front and rear. The location of the Middle Gate is quite clear, thanks to identification of the wall [2]. The major topographical problem is identification of Ephialtes' route. Disagreement centres around four questions. Did the route reach high ground south west of Thermopylae directly, or via the Asopos Gorge, or by a long western detour? Did it pass north of Mount Lithiza, or south? Where did it descend to the coast? Where was the Phocian detachment? The map shows the route and Phocian position according to Grundy (....., P1), Munro (ooo, P2), Burn 1951 (xxxx, P3), Burn 1977 (***, P3), and Pritchett (---, P4).

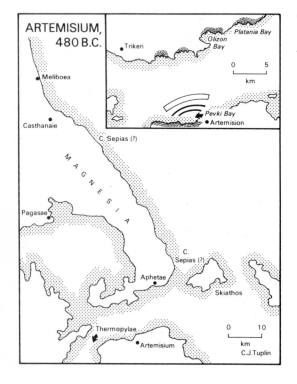

Artemisium, 480 BC

The Greek position at Pevki Bay is guaranteed by discovery of the Artemis shrine. Aphetae, the Persians' headquarters, was probably at Platania, though their fleet doubtless occupied several beaches (suitable areas are shaded on the inset map). The fighting involved two afternoon raids on Persian positions (not shown), and a full-scale Persian attack on Artemisium. Herodotus' account of the first engagement—the ships fighting in concentric circles, with the Greeks *inside*—is incredible, while of the last he says only that the Persians attacked in a crescent. It is crucially unclear how far north this encounter occurred. The map assumes a position near Pevki and, consequently, two Greek lines. Other related problems include the location of earlier Persian moorings 'between Casthanaie and Cape Sepias', and the timing and credibility of the attempted Persian circumnavigation of Euboea.

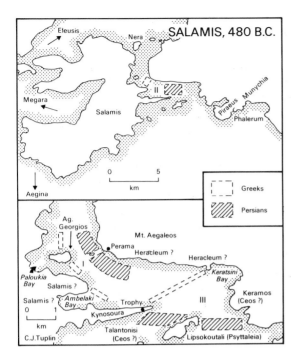

Salamis, 480 BC

All discussions revolve around crucial obscurities. (1) Was the Greek fleet largely in Ambelaki or Paloukia Bay? (2) Was the Persian fleet's dawn position (a) along the Attic shore facing Ambelaki and/or Paloukia [I], (b) across the strait from Kynosoura to the Attic shore [II], or (c) from Kynosoura towards Piraeus facing north [III]? (3) If (c), was the battle precipitated by the Persians sailing into the channel (and if so, was the eventual engagement of type I or II?), or by the Greeks coming out to a position across the channel entrance opposite the Persians [III]? The ancient battle monument on Kynosoura favours a southerly position, but does not decide other issues; and Xerxes' reported expectation that Psyttaleia (surely Lipsokoutali) would be near the battle could have been falsified in the event.

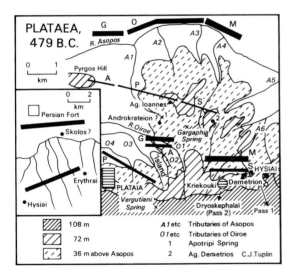

Plataea, 479 BC

Cavalry attacks and lack of water caused the Greeks to move from their initial position (inset) to the Ag. Demetrios-Pyrgos line (this location depends on the usual equation of Gargaphia with the modern Rhetsi springs). The Persians followed suit north of the Asopos. After 12 days during which the Persian cavalry harassed Greek water-carriers by the Asopos, cut supply lines over Dryoskephalai (day 8), and fouled Gargaphia (day 12), the Greeks moved south in some confusion. The positions of P indicated here, in front of Plataea, and of S, by a Demetrion (site fixed by the find-spot of inscriptions relating to Demeter) are fairly certain; that of A much less so. In their ensuing attack the two Persian wings were defeated and fled to the fort (M) or to Thebes (G), while the centre withdrew without engaging. The left wing of P, moving to support A, was severely mauled by Theban cavalry.

S: Spartans. P: Peloponnesians, Euboeans, NW Greeks, Aeginetans, Megarians. A: Athenians, Plataeans. M: Persians (under Mardonius). O: Medes, Bactrians, Indians, Sacae (under Artabazus). G: medizing Greeks.

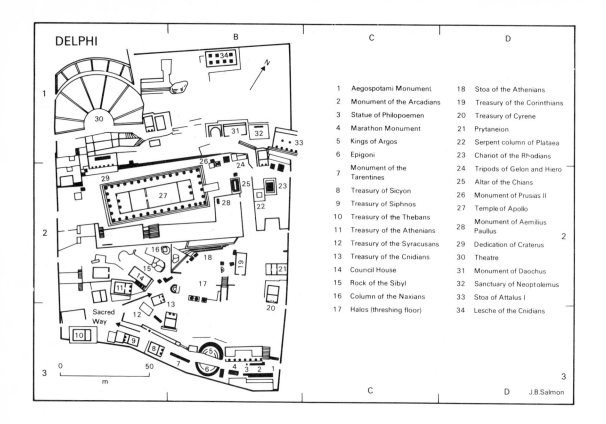

DELPHI

1 Aegospotami Monument	18 Stoa of the Athenians
2 Monument of the Arcadians	19 Treasury of the Corinthians
3 Statue of Philopoemen	20 Treasury of Cyrene
4 Marathon Monument	21 Prytaneion
5 Kings of Argos	22 Serpent column of Plataea
6 Epigoni	23 Chariot of the Rhodians
7 Monument of the Tarentines	24 Tripods of Gelon and Hiero
8 Treasury of Sicyon	25 Altar of the Chians
9 Treasury of Siphnos	26 Monument of Prusias II
10 Treasury of the Thebans	27 Temple of Apollo
11 Treasury of the Athenians	28 Monument of Aemilius Paullus
12 Treasury of the Syracusans	29 Dedication of Craterus
13 Treasury of the Cnidians	30 Theatre
14 Council House	31 Monument of Daochus
15 Rock of the Sibyl	32 Sanctuary of Neoptolemus
16 Column of the Naxians	33 Stoa of Attalus I
17 Halos (threshing floor)	34 Lesche of the Cnidians

J.B.Salmon

Delphi

The origins of the oracular cult of Apollo at Delphi are obscure. But its close association with the foundation of colonies in the west in the second half of the eighth century established a reputation which was maintained until a defeatist attitude was adopted to the invasion of Xerxes in 480. The present temple of Apollo (27) was built in the mid-fourth century; the expenses were met by contributions from the whole Greek world. Earlier temples on approximately the same site had been destroyed in 373 and 548. The earliest temple has not yet been traced, but already before the end of the seventh century Cypselus, tyrant of Corinth, built the first known treasury on the site (19). Numerous similar buildings followed, to house moveable dedications; there were already some half-dozen by the end of the sixth century. Other monuments in this panhellenic centre commemorated particular events. Like the treasuries,

they were placed beside the Sacred Way, along which worshippers climbed the steep path to the temple. The Serpent Column (22), dedicated by the combined Greek states after Plataea, was erected near the temple. Lower down, the intercity rivalries which led to many of the dedications are reflected in their locations: just beyond the entrance to the precinct are to be found the Spartan monument for Aegospotami (1), an Arcadian dedication of the fourth century (2), the Athenian monument for Marathon (4) and two Argive structures (5–6), while the Syracusan Treasury (12), built after the defeat of the Sicilian Expedition, faces the Athenian Treasury (11), erected nearly a century before. The changed political conditions of the late fourth century are reflected in the dedication of Craterus (29), which depicted his rescue of Alexander the Great during a lion hunt in Persia. The Halos (17) was the venue for a ritual associated with the cult. Nearly a kilometre away to the south east was the sanctuary of Athena.

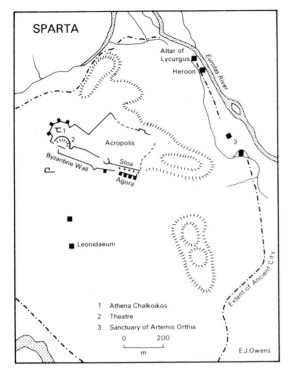

Sparta

Sparta's abnormal development had profound effects on the city itself. First, Spartans claimed that their soldiers were their walls, and although the city was partly walled in the fourth century, not until the second was it completely fortified. Thus Sparta for long remained a group of loosely-knit villages along the banks of the R. Eurotas. Second, there was no embellishment of the city, and the remains support Thucydides' remark that it possessed few public buildings.

Archaeologists have concentrated on the acropolis, where the site of the archaic temple of Athena Chalkioikos has been identified. The theatre is Hellenistic, as is the small temple to the south, wrongly identified as the 'tomb of Leonidas'. The stoa above the agora is Roman. East of the acropolis, close to the river, other monuments have been found: most important is the sanctuary of Artemis Orthia, where an early altar and temple have been identified. A theatre for spectators was added in the second century AD.

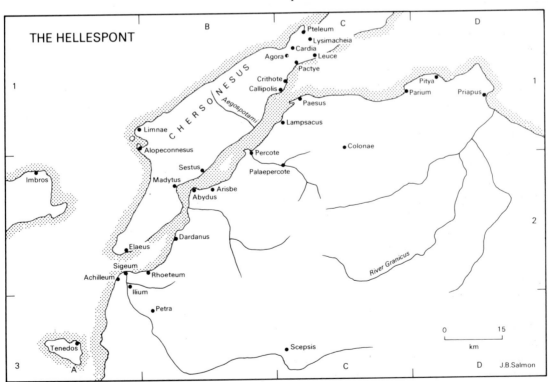

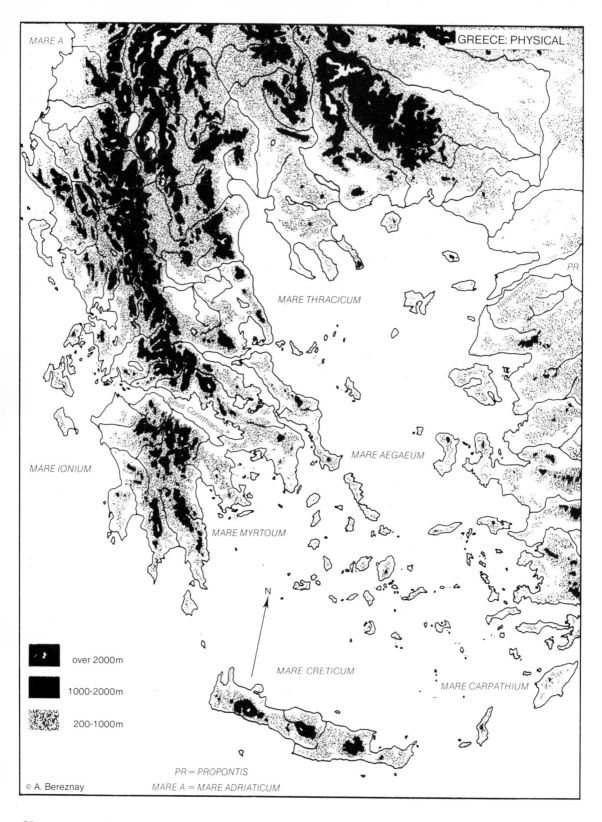

GREECE: PHYSICAL

MARE A

PR

Hellespontus

MARE THRACICUM

Sinus Corinthiacus

MARE IONIUM

MARE AEGAEUM

MARE MYRTOUM

N

MARE CRETICUM

MARE CARPATHIUM

over 2000m

1000-2000m

200-1000m

PR = PROPONTIS

MARE A = MARE ADRIATICUM

© A. Bereznay

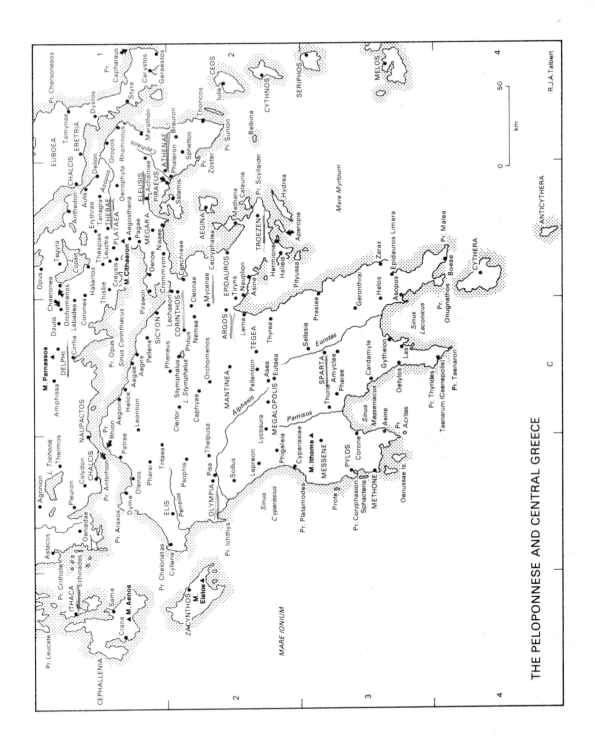

THE PELOPONNESE AND CENTRAL GREECE

R.J.A.Talbert

0   50
km

29

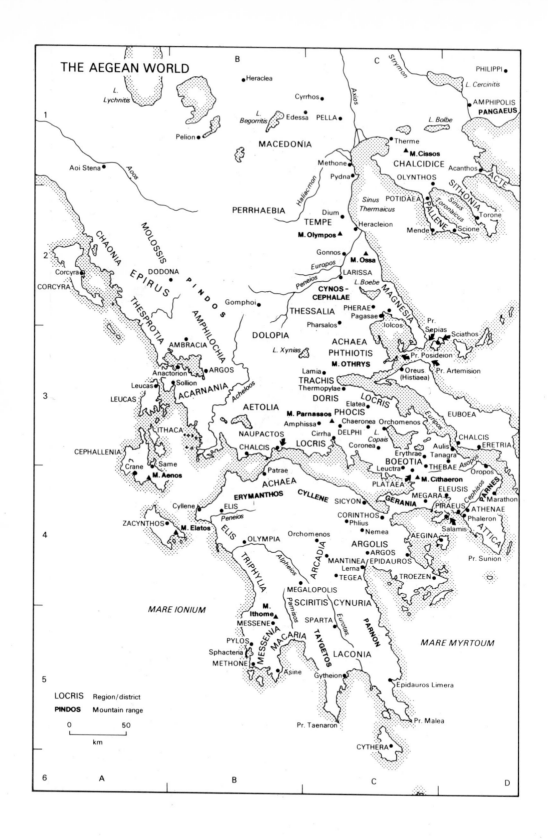

THE AEGEAN WORLD

PHILIPPI

L. Lychnitis

L. Cercinitis

Heraclea

AMPHIPOLIS

Cyrrhos

PANGAEUS

Axios

Strymon

L. Begorritis

Edessa   PELLA

L. Bolbe

Pelion

MACEDONIA

Therme

M. Cissos

Aoi Stena

Aoos

CHALCIDICE

Acanthos

ACTE

Methone

OLYNTHOS

SITHONIA

PERRHAEBIA

Pydna

POTIDAEA

Sinus
Thermaicus

PALLENE

Sinus
Toronaicus

Torone

Haliacmon

Dium

TEMPE

Heracleion

Mende

Scione

M. Olympos

MOLOSSIS

CHAONIA

Aoos

PINDOS

EPIRUS

DODONA

Gonnos

M. Ossa

Corcyra

Europos

LARISSA

CORCYRA

THESPROTIA

Gomphoi

CYNOS-
CEPHALAE

L. Boebe

Peneios

MAGNESIA

Pr.
Sepias

Sciathos

THESSALIA

PHERAE

Pr. Posideion

AMPHILOCHIA

AMBRACIA

DOLOPIA

Pagasae

Iolcos

Anactorion

ARGOS

L. Xynias

ACHAEA
PHTHIOTIS

Pr. Posideion

Leucas

Sollion

ACARNANIA

M. OTHRYS

Oreus
(Histiaea)

Pr. Artemision

LEUCAS

Acheloos

Lamia

TRACHIS

Thermopylae

LOCRIS

EUBOEA

AETOLIA

DORIS

Elatea

M. Parnassos

PHOCIS

Chaeronea

Orchomenos

Euripos

ITHACA

NAUPACTOS

Amphissa

DELPHI

*L.
Copais*

CHALCIS

CEPHALLENIA

CHALCIS

Cirrha

LOCRIS

Coronea

Erythrae

Aulis

ERETRIA

Crane

Same

Patrae

BOEOTIA

Tanagra

THEBAE

Asopos

Oropos

M. Aenos

ACHAEA

Leuctra

M. Cithaeron

PLATAEA

MEGARA

ELEUSIS

PARNES

Cyllene

ELIS

ERYMANTHOS

CYLLENE

SICYON

GERANIA

PIRAEUS

Cephisos

Marathon

ZACYNTHOS

Peneios

CORINTHOS

Phlius

Nemea

ATHENAE

Phaleron

M. Elatos

ELIS

Orchomenos

ARCADIA

AEGINA

Salamis

ATTICA

OLYMPIA

Alpheios

ARGOLIS

Pr. Sunion

TRIPHYLIA

MANTINEA

ARGOS

EPIDAUROS

Lerna

TEGEA

TROEZEN

MEGALOPOLIS

SCIRITIS

Parnisos

CYNURIA

MARE IONIUM

M.
Ithome

SPARTA

Eurotas

PARNON

MARE MYRTOUM

MESSENE

MESSENIA

LACONIA

PYLOS

MACARIA

TAYGETOS

Sphacteria

METHONE

Asine

Gytheion

Epidauros Limera

Pr. Malea

Pr. Taenaron

CYTHERA

LOCRIS   Region/district

PINDOS   Mountain range

0   50

km

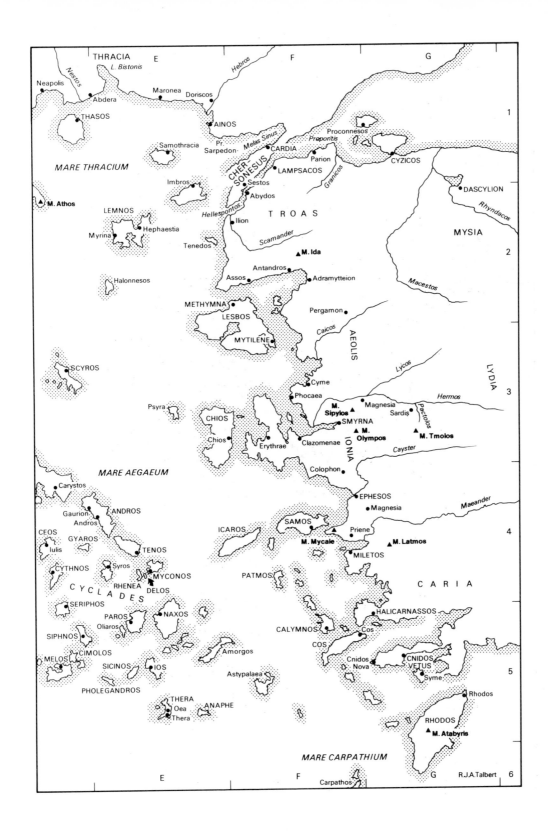

THRACIA

Nestos

L. Bistonis

E

Hebros

F

G

1

Neapolis

Abdera

Maronea

Doriscos

THASOS

AINOS

Pr. Sarpedon

Melas Sinus

CARDIA

Proconnesos

Propontis

CYZICOS

Samothracia

LAMPSACOS

Parion

Granicos

DASCYLION

MARE THRACIUM

CHER-SONESUS

Sestos

Rhyndacos

Imbros

Hellespontos

Abydos

MYSIA

M. Athos

LEMNOS

Myrina

Hephaestia

Ilion

TROAS

2

Tenedos

Scamander

M. Ida

Macestos

Halonnesos

Antandros

Adramytteion

Assos

METHYMNA

Pergamon

Caicos

AEOLIS

LESBOS

Lycos

LYDIA

MYTILENE

Hermos

3

SCYROS

Cyme

Phocaea

M. Sipylos

Magnesia

Sardis

Pactolos

Psyra

SMYRNA

CHIOS

M. Olympos

M. Tmolos

Chios

Erythrae

Clazomenae

IONIA

Cayster

MARE AEGAEUM

Colophon

Carystos

EPHESOS

Maeander

ANDROS

Magnesia

Gaurion

Andros

SAMOS

ICAROS

Priene

CEOS

GYAROS

M. Mycale

M. Latmos

4

Iulis

TENOS

MILETOS

CYTHNOS

Syros

MYCONOS

PATMOS

CARIA

RHENEA

DELOS

CYCLADES

SERIPHOS

PAROS

NAXOS

HALICARNASSOS

Oliaros

SIPHNOS

CALYMNOS

Cos

MELOS

CIMOLOS

COS

Cnidos

CNIDOS VETUS

SICINOS

IOS

Nova

SYME

5

Amorgos

Astypalaea

Syme

PHOLEGANDROS

THERA

Oea

ANAPHE

Rhodos

Thera

RHODOS

MARE CARPATHIUM

M. Atabyris

E

F

G

R.J.A.Talbert

6

Carpathos

31

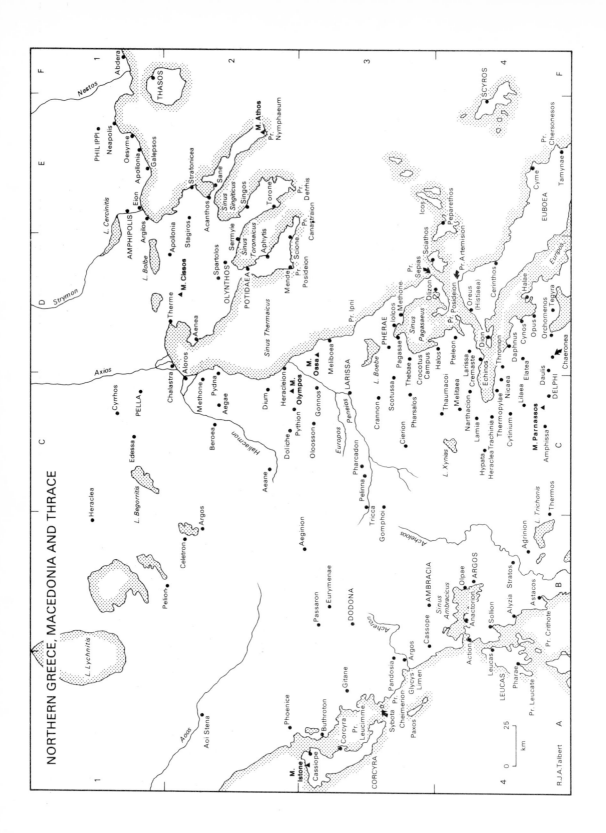

NORTHERN GREECE, MACEDONIA AND THRACE

R.J.A.Talbert

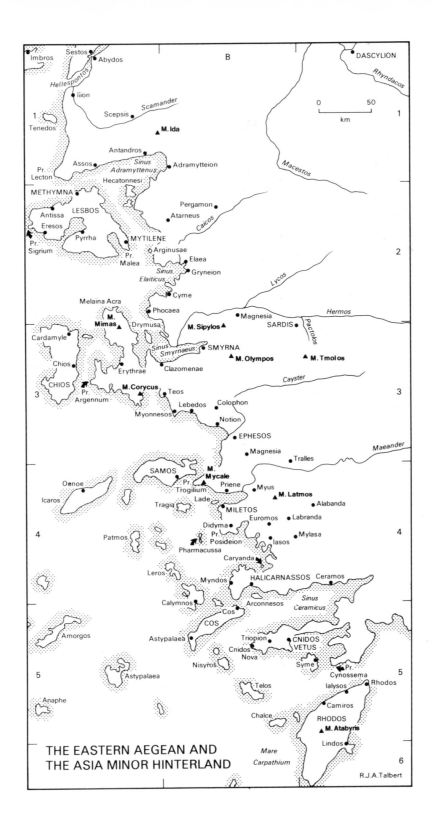

THE EASTERN AEGEAN AND
THE ASIA MINOR HINTERLAND

R.J.A.Talbert

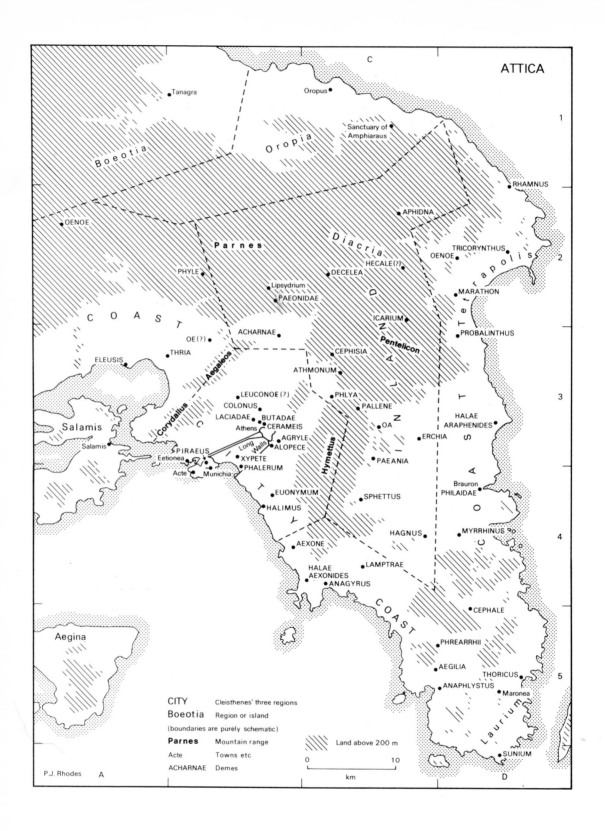

ATTICA

Tanagra

Oropus

Sanctuary of Amphiaraus

RHAMNUS

Boeotia   *Oropia*

OENOE

APHIDNA

Parnes   *Diacria*   OENOE   TRICORYNTHUS

PHYLE   DECELEA   HECALE(?)

Lipsydrium
PAEONIDAE   MARATHON

OE(?)   ACHARNAE   ICARIUM   PROBALINTHUS

Pentelicon

THRIA   CEPHISIA

ELEUSIS   ATHMONUM

Aegaleos

Salamis   LEUCONOE(?)   PHLYA

COLONUS   PALLENE   HALAE
LACIADAE   BUTADAE   ARAPHENIDES
Salamis   Athens   CERAMEIS   OA   ERCHIA

AGRYLE
Long   ALOPECE   PAEANIA
SPIRAEUS   *Walls*
Eetionea   XYPETE   PHALERUM
Acte   Munichia   Brauron
PHILAIDAE

EUONYMUM   SPHETTUS

HALIMUS   MYRRHINUS

HAGNUS

AEXONE   LAMPTRAE   CEPHALE

HALAE
AEXONIDES
ANAGYRUS   *COAST*   PHREARRHII

Aegina   AEGILIA
THORICUS
ANAPHLYSTUS   Maronea

Laurium

SUNIUM

CITY   Cleisthenes' three regions
Boeotia   Region or island
(boundaries are purely schematic)
Parnes   Mountain range
Acte   Towns etc
ACHARNAE   Demes   Land above 200 m

0   10
km

P.J. Rhodes

Attica

By the seventh century BC the whole of Attica (about 2,500 sq. km) belonged to the city state of Athens. Eleusis was the last area to be fully incorporated in the state. Salamis, acquired from Megara in the sixth century, Eleutherae (in the far north west, beyond Oenoe), acquired from Boeotia in the same century, and Oropia, disputed between Athens and Boeotia, were ruled as subject territory. By Cleisthenes' reforms of 508/7 Attica was organised in 139 demes. These were grouped to form ten tribes in such a way that each tribe comprised one *trittys* ('third') based on, but probably not wholly located in, each of the three regions, City, Coast and Inland. The demes forming a *trittys* were sometimes, but not always, a group of adjacent demes. These tribes and their subdivisions formed the basis of the army and of every aspect of Athenian public life. The Long Walls linking Athens to the harbour town of Piraeus were built in the mid-fifth century.

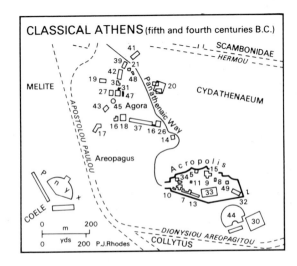

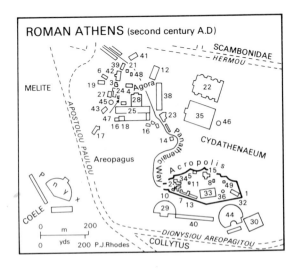

Classical and Roman Athens: Key

Buildings &c.

1	Aglaurus, cave of (new location)	26	Mint
2	Agrippa, monument of	27	New Bouleuterium
3	Apollo Patrous, temple of	28	Odeum of Agrippa
4	Ares, temple of	29	Odeum of Herodes Atticus
5	Arrhephori, house of	30	Odeum of Pericles
6	Arsenal (?)	31	Old Bouleuterium
7	Artemis Brauronia, sanctuary of	32	Pandion, shrine of (?)
8	Athena, altar of	33	Parthenon
9	Athena, site of old temple of	34	Propylaea
10	Athena Nike, temple of	35	Roman Agora
11	Athena Promachus, statue of	36	Rome and Augustus, temple of
12	Basilica	37	South Stoa
13	Chalcothece	38	Stoa of Attalus
14	Eleusinium	39	Stoa of the Basileus
15	Erechtheum	40	Stoa of Eumenes
16	Fountain houses	41	Stoa Poecile
17	Gaol	42	Stoa of Zeus
18	Heliaea	43	Strategeum (?)
19	Hephaesteum ('Theseum')	44	Theatre of Dionysus
20	Lawcourts (two small buildings replaced by one large)	45	Tholos
21	Leocoreum	46	Tower of the Winds
22	Library of Hadrian	47	Tribal Heroes, statues of (fourth-century location)
23	Library of Pantaenus	48	Twelve gods, altar of
24	Metroum	49	Zeus Polieus, shrine of (?)
25	Middle Stoa		

MELITE	Demes
Pnyx	Other ancient features
HERMOU	Modern streets

Athens

There is space here to show the centre of the city only. Athens, eight km from the sea, was occupied from the Neolithic period; a wall was built round the Acropolis in the Late Mycenaean period (thirteenth century BC). In classical Athens the Acropolis was the religious centre, where the principal temple of Athena stood (from the 440s/30s onwards, the Parthenon). The Areopagus was the meeting-place of the oldest council of state. In the sixth century the area to the north of it was cleared of private houses and graves, and became the Agora, the main square of the city; major civic buildings were erected on its west side in the fifth century. This may have been the original meeting-place of the assembly: the Pnyx was set out for the assembly in the fifth century.

In the Roman period a new market and the Library of Hadrian were built to the east of the Agora, and there was expansion further east in the 'City of Hadrian', an area occupied in classical times, but outside the classical city wall. Athens was sacked by the Persians in 480/79, by Sulla in 86 BC, by the Herulians in AD 267, and on various occasions thereafter. Although in prosperous times a greater area was occupied, a new wall after AD 267 enclosed simply the Acropolis and the area due north as far as the Roman market. The Parthenon, Erechtheum and Hephaesteum were all converted into Christian churches, and later the Parthenon became a mosque: that so much of them survives is due to this re-use.

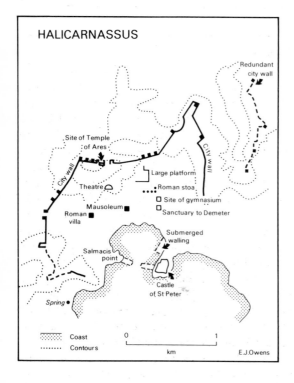

HALICARNASSUS

Redundant city wall

City wall

Site of Temple of Ares

City wall

Large platform

Theatre

Roman stoa

Site of gymnasium

Mausoleum

Sanctuary to Demeter

Roman villa

Submerged walling

Salmacis point

Castle of St Peter

Spring

Coast

Contours

0   1

km

E.J.Owens

Halicarnassus

Halicarnassus, occupying a naturally fortified position and with a good, sheltered harbour, was originally colonised by Dorians at the eastern promontory of the harbour (Zephyrion), where the ruined castle of St Peter now stands. Although by the classical period the town had expanded to include the western promontory (Salmacis), and the population had been increased by Ionian and native elements, Halicarnassus remained small until the accession of Mausolus to the satrapy of Caria in 377/6. Realising the advantages of the site, he chose it as his new capital, and transformed Halicarnassus into one of the most splendid cities in the ancient world. According to Vitruvius the buildings, rising on terraces, resembled the tiers of a theatre with the agora close to the shore, the Mausoleum on a broad avenue which ran across the middle of the city, and, dominating all, a temple to Ares on Göktepe. Due to continuous occupation throughout antiquity, only the walls and the sites of a few buildings remain. Thus many topographical details are problematic.

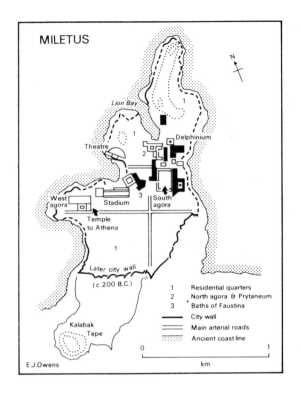

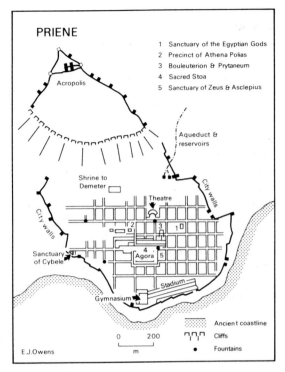

Miletus

Situated on a peninsula opposite the mouth of the R. Maeander, during the seventh and sixth centuries Miletus became an outstanding cultural and commercial centre. Traces of the extensive archaic city have emerged round Lion Bay and the Delphinium, on the theatre hill, around the temple to Athena, and as far south as the acropolis of Kalabak Tepe. Some parts evidently had a regular layout and basic amenities.

After its destruction by the Persians in 494 Miletus was rebuilt on a grid (only partially known). A large central area was reserved for future public use. In typical fashion the defences were not integrated with the street system, and main roads do not lead directly to the gates. Although the existing monuments are Hellenistic and Roman (the theatre dates to *c.* AD 100), several buildings, especially the northern agora, the Delphinium and the temple to Athena can be traced to the classical period, and the Prytaneum to even earlier. Silting of the R. Maeander eventually led to Miletus' decline.

Priene

Priene was always overshadowed by nearby Miletus and suffered even more than her from the silting of the R. Maeander. By the mid-fourth century the coast had so receded that the city was re-founded on a spur of Mount Mycale further downstream from its original site. It is remarkable for the application of a grid plan to a difficult, steeply sloping location, where the major arterial roads run east-west, while narrower streets, in places reduced to flights of steps, cross these at regular intervals to form rectangular blocks. Most public buildings are concentrated round the centrally sited agora and conform to the grid plan. Exceptionally the stadium, located at the lowest point in the city, is misaligned to take advantage of the level ground of the coast. The theatre— probably the best surviving Hellenistic example— is situated above the civic centre. Alexander, who made a visit here in 334, dedicated the temple to Athena. The terrain allowed water, conveyed by an aqueduct, to be piped throughout the city.

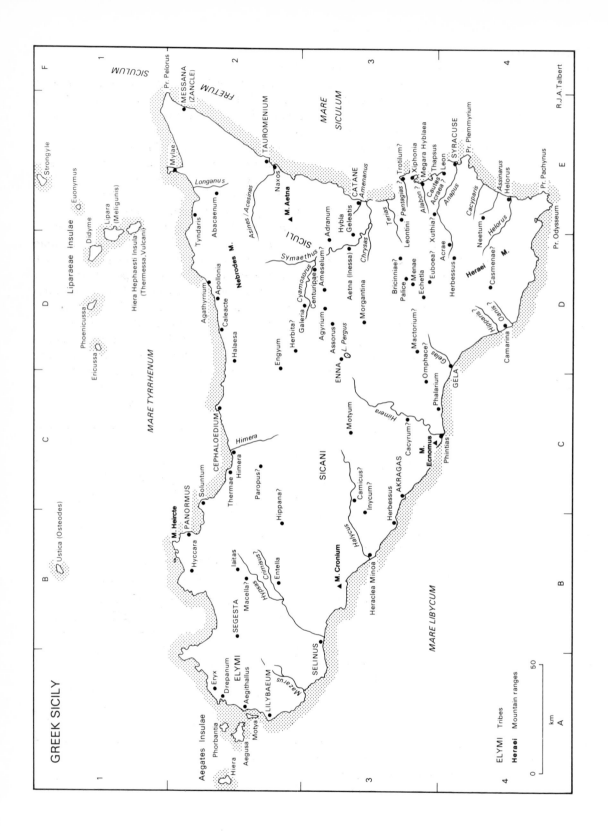

GREEK SICILY

Aegates Insulae

ELYMI   Tribes

Heraei   Mountain ranges

MARE TYRRHENUM

MARE LIBYCUM

MARE SICULUM

SICULUM FRETUM

Liparaeae Insulae

Strongyle

Euonymus

Didyme

Lipara (Meligunis)

Phoenicussa

Ericussa

Hiera Hephaesti Insula
(Thermessa, Vulcani)

Ustica (Osteodes)

Pr. Pelorus

MESSANA
(ZANCLE)

Mylae

Longanus

TAUROMENIUM

Agathyrnum

Tyndaris

Abacaenum

Apollonia

Asines / Acesines

Naxos

M. Aetna

Caleacte

Nebrodes M.

Halaesa

SICULI

Adranum

Hybla

Geleatis

Amenanus

CATANE

Engyum

Herbita?

Galeria

Cyamosorus

Centuripae

Ameselum?

Aetna (Inessa)

Symaethus

Chrysas

Tetas

Pantagias?

Trotilum?

Xiphonia

Megara Hyblaea

Leontini

Alabon?

Thapsus

Agyrium

Assorus

Morgantina

Bricinniae?

Palice

Menae

Echetla

Euboea?

Xuthia?

Acrae

Leon

Cauter?

Acraea?

SYRACUSE

Pr. Plemmyrium

ENNA

L. Pergus

Herbessus

Mactorium?

Herbessus

Neetum

Cacyparis

Pr. Pachynus

Pr. Odysseum

Pr. Piemmyrium

SICANI

Motyum

Himera

**M.
Ecnomus**

Omphace?

Phalarium

GELA

Gelas

Camarina

Hipparis

Oanis?

Casmenae?

Helorus

**Heraei
M.**

Assinarus

Helorus

Camicus?

AKRAGAS

Phintias

CEPHALOEDIUM

Himera

Himera

Thermae

Paropus?

Hippana?

Soluntum

PANORMUS

M. Heircte

Hyccara

Iaitas

Macella?

Hypsas

Crimisus?

Entella

SEGESTA

Halycus

Invycum?

M. Cronium

Heraclea Minoa

Eryx

Drepanum

Aegithallus

ELYMI

Motya

LILYBAEUM

Mazarus

SELINUS

Phorbantia

Aegusa

Hiera

R.J.A.Talbert

km

0   50

38

Greek Sicily

Sicily was one of the first areas colonised by Greeks from the latter part of the eighth century BC, in particular along its eastern and southern seaboards. The settlers' search for fertile agricultural land was amply rewarded, and a flourishing export trade to the Italian peninsula, north Africa and mainland Greece brought the leading communities an impressive level of prosperity. The character of their relations with native peoples varied, but the archaeological record shows how everywhere native territory was infiltrated by degrees, so that after *c.* 400 the tribes fade from the historical record.

Quite independently, Phoenicians were attracted to the far west of the island around the same time as Greeks reached the east. The first Phoenician base, on the tiny island of Motya, was perhaps intended as no more than a port of call on long-distance trading voyages. Thereafter, however (though the time-scale is obscure), cultivation of good land was the principal purpose of settlements at Panormus (Phoenician Ziz) and Soluntum, both perhaps dating from the seventh century; Motya was linked to the mainland by a causeway. These communities were independent of Carthage, and their relations with Greeks in the island remained generally excellent until around the end of the fifth century. Even later, when a Punic *epikrateia* comes to be recognised in treaties, it is best taken as a loose 'zone of influence', in no way presupposing a rigid barrier between the two races; while any notion that Carthage desired to further imperialistic ambitions in Sicily is misplaced.

Syracuse

The eighth century Corinthian settlement at Syracuse was originally confined to the island of Ortygia, which has a fresh water supply in the fountain of Arethusa, and sanctuaries of Apollo and Athena dating back at least to the sixth century. It must have been similarly early that the island became linked to the mainland by a causeway, and the adjacent area of Achradina (A on map) was settled, with agora, fortification wall, and the earliest cemeteries beyond. Later the city expanded into the districts of Temenites (TE), Neapolis (N), and Tyche (TY).

The siege by Athenian forces in 415/13 is narrated in detail by Thucydides: their bases were on the coast in the marshy area of Lysimeleia, on the bleak, waterless headland of Plemmyrium, and on the steep, uninhabited plateau of Epipolae, which dominates the city. But the Athenian plan to confine Syracuse within a wall running from Lysimeleia northwards (proceeding either north or north eastwards across Epipolae) was never completed; the Syracusans built three counter-walls to frustrate their attackers. The city together with Epipolae was ringed with fortifications by Dionysius I in the early fourth century, and a fortress built at Euryalus. Remains of the fine public buildings erected in Neapolis from the third century survive. Elsewhere modern occupation has limited investigation of the ancient city.

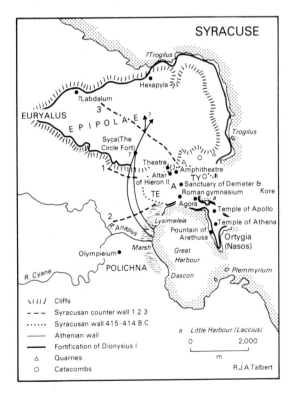

39

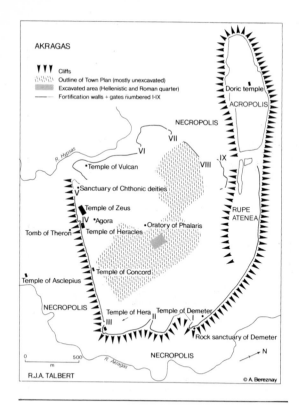

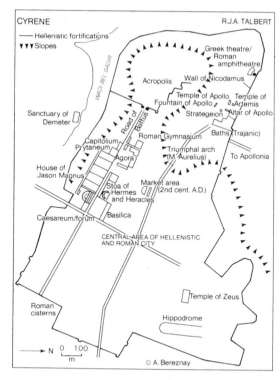

Akragas

Akragas, founded from Gela about 580 according to the tradition, was protected to the north by a long acropolis hill (the centre of the modern town), and to the south by a ridge below which ran the rivers Hypsas and Akragas. Polybius' description (9.27) rightly praises this splendid site. Strong fortification walls linking both natural features were built early to complete the city's defences. The extensive 'Hippodamian' street layout revealed by aerial photography may also date back to the sixth century. As a result of destruction suffered at successive stages in the city's history, the houses in the excavated area are only Hellenistic and Roman, yet are laid out on the original grid. Along the southern ridge was erected a series of temples and other sacred buildings, which testify to the citizens' ostentation and to the remarkable prosperity of their agriculture during the sixth and fifth centuries. The so-called Temple of Concord is notably well preserved thanks to former use as a Christian church.

Cyrene

Cyrene was founded from Thera in the late seventh century. It lies about eight km inland from the north African coast; a road led to its port, Apollonia, 19 km distant. The acropolis, where the original colonists may have settled, remains largely unexplored. A predominantly Roman city is visible today, though it retains the layout developed by Ptolemaic rulers, as well as some remodelled structures of the Hellenistic period. It was then that long fortification walls were built, encircling two hills which rise to 620 m in height, separated by a valley dropping away to the north west. The town of Shahat on the north east hill occupies much of the centre of ancient Cyrene. So excavation has been concentrated upon areas with no modern settlement, the sanctuary of Apollo and the south west hill. Both public buildings and private residences along the Road of Battus between the agora and the forum show the city to have been a flourishing Roman provincial capital. Widespread, fanatical damage in the course of the Jewish revolt of AD 115–17 was made good.

```
OLYMPIA                              B              C              D
River Kladeos                                                    1  Prytaneum
                                                                2  Philippeum
                                                                3  Leonidaeum
                                                                4  Pheidias' workshop
                                                                5  Palaestra
```

Olympia

The sanctuary of Zeus at Olympia, situated in a pleasant, wooded valley close to where the rivers Kladeos and Alphaeus meet, was one of the most famous shrines in Greece. In connection with the four-yearly games celebrated here the sanctuary was embellished by dedications of buildings, sculptures and other monuments.

The precinct itself, the Altis, stood at the foot of Kronos Hill and contained the major religious buildings. On its northern side were situated a temple of Hera with Zeus and a small metroon. The former was originally constructed of mud brick with wooden entablature and columns, although parts were later replaced in stone. The latter, built in the fourth century, honoured Rhea, mother of Zeus. The immense temple to Zeus stood on the southern side. Built *c.* 460 it housed Pheidias' great chryselephantine statue of the god. Other religious monuments within the precinct were the Philippeum, the circular building west of the Heraeum begun by Philip II of Macedon; the

mound covering the supposed tomb of Pelops; and an open-air altar in honour of Zeus.

Since the Altis was the gods' preserve, monuments associated with the administration of the site and the celebration of the games were located outside. To the west were the gymnasium and palaestra, the workshop of Pheidias (identified by tools and a cup bearing his name), priests' accommodation, baths, and the Leonidaeum, providing accommodation for distinguished visitors. To the east, the precinct was flanked by the stadium, which originally encroached upon it, the late fourth-century Echo Stoa (replacing a classical stoa), and the house constructed for Nero's visit. On the northern boundary a series of treasuries was situated, the majority dedicated by Greek cities in southern Italy and Sicily. Next to these Herodes Atticus provided a fountain house, the first at Olympia. The appeal of the sanctuary remained widespread until its enforced closure by Theodosius I at the end of the fourth century AD.

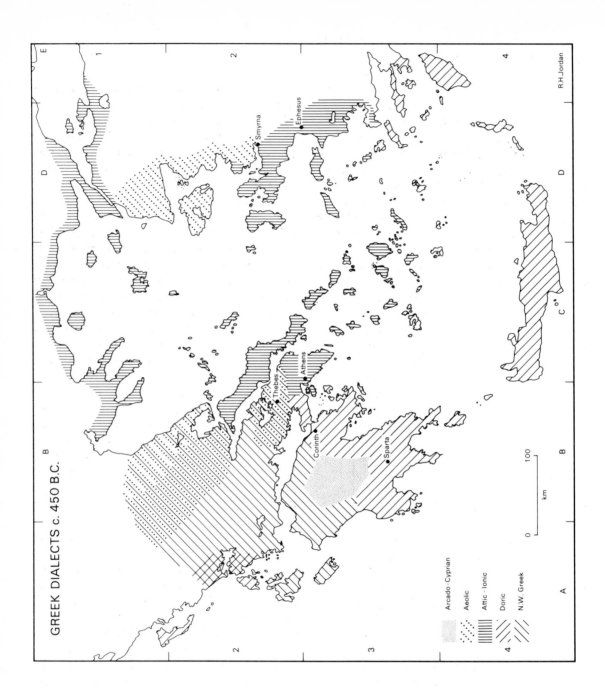

GREEK DIALECTS c. 450 B.C.

Smyrna
Ephesus
Thebes
Athens
Corinth
Sparta

Arcado-Cyprian
Aeolic
Attic-Ionic
Doric
N.W. Greek

0   100
km

R.H.Jordan

42

Greek Dialects *c.* 450 BC

In his *History* (7.57–8), Thucydides surveys the contingents from the various states and islands involved in the Athenian expedition against Syracuse, dividing them into three main groups—Dorian, Ionian and Aeolic. These three groups were living in clearly divided bands along the coast of Asia Minor in the classical period. So it was assumed that this triple division applied to the mainland as well, since the cities of the Asia Minor coast and islands were by tradition founded by cities or communities on the mainland.

In fact the linguistic relationships between the dialects on the mainland are much more complex. The dialect of Arcadia, for example, is closely related to that of Cyprus, suggesting that the island was colonised by speakers of an earlier form of Arcadian. Furthermore, the Greek discovered on the Linear B tablets from Pylos and elsewhere on the mainland is more closely akin to Arcadian than any other classical dialect. This leads to the supposition that a dialect of Greek from which Arcadian and Cyprian developed was at one time spoken over a much wider area in the Peloponnese.

Yet it was two different dialects, North West Greek and Doric, which predominated in the Peloponnese during the classical period, completely surrounding Arcadian. These two are closely related to each other, and North West Greek was spoken in classical times over a very wide area to the north of the Corinthian Gulf. The traditions concerning the Dorians and the speakers of North West Greek in the Peloponnese relate how they travelled to their later homes from the north in various groups, and the evidence of the dialects would seem to support this tradition in broad outline. A few traces of a pre-Doric dialect can be found in the inscriptions of some Doric areas. Thus we may suppose that the remote ancestors of the classical Doric and North West Greek speakers had once lived north of the Corinthian Gulf, perhaps not even along its northern shore, but across the high and wild land dominated by the Pindus mountain range.

The second of Thucydides' groups, the Ionian speakers, could be found in his lifetime in many of the coastal cities and islands round the Aegean. Thucydides states clearly an accepted historical fact of the time, that the Athenians were Ionians: for it was believed that the initial Ionian colonists of Asia Minor had set out from Athens. The evidence of inscriptions bears out the very close linguistic bond between the Attic speakers of Athens and the Ionians. Just how widespread the speakers of Ionic were on the mainland in the period before the arrival of the Dorians is a subject of much debate. Equally the precise relationship between Ionic and Arcado-Cyprian in this early period will almost certainly never be known.

Aeolic, the third of Thucydides' groups, is in many ways the most mysterious. In Asia Minor it formed the most northerly of the three dialect bands, and it is there that the inscriptions show it in its least contaminated form. Linguistic evidence from the two Aeolic areas on the mainland, Boeotia and Thessaly, strongly suggests that there the dialects had been infiltrated by a North West Greek dialect. This is particularly marked in Boeotian; in Thessalian the purer Aeolic is found naturally in the eastern part of the country.

All Greek dialects can be divided on linguistic grounds into two broad divisions usually called East and West Greek. This represents the most fundamental division and seems to have an historical significance, with the East Greek dialects—Attic-Ionic, Arcado-Cyprian and Aeolic—representing the Greek spoken in those areas of Greece prominent during the Mycenaean period. In contrast, the dialects of West Greek—Doric and North West Greek—represent those Greek speakers who came to their homes of the classical period after the collapse of the Mycenaean kingdoms.

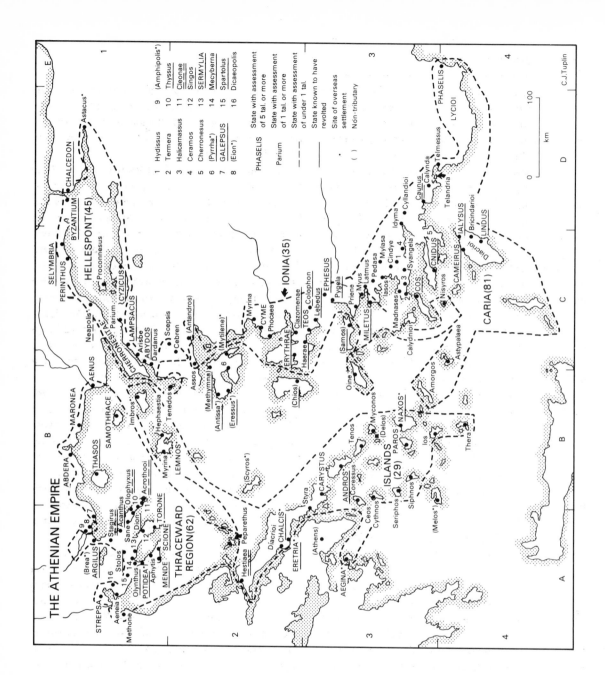

THE ATHENIAN EMPIRE

1 Hydissus
2 Termera
3 Halicarnassus
4 Ceramos
5 Cherronesus
6 (Pyrrha*)
7 GALEPSUS
8 (Eion*)
9 (Amphipolis*)
10 Thyssus
11 Cleonae
12 Singos
13 SERMYLIA
14 Mecyberna
15 Spartolus
16 Dicaeopolis

PHASELIS   State with assessment
             of 5 tal. or more

Parium   State with assessment
             of 1 tal. or more

             State with assessment
             of under 1 tal.

- - -   State known to have
             revolted

·   Site of overseas
             settlement

( )   Non-tributary

0   100
km

C.J.Tuplin

HELLESPONT (45)
IONIA (35)
CARIA (81)
THRACEWARD REGION (62)
ISLANDS (29)

44

The Athenian Empire

In 478 certain east Aegean members of the Hellenic League invited Athens to assume effective leadership of military action against Persia. The result was the alliance system commonly known as the Delian League. The name is modern, derived from the location of the treasury and of consultative meetings on Delos; contemporary parlance spoke simply of 'the Athenians and their allies'. Membership involved support of the League's military enterprises by provision of ships, or of money (tribute), in quantities determined by the Athenians. After 454 there were regular reassessments of tribute, theoretically every fourth year, but occasionally out of sequence (443 instead of 442, 428 and 425 instead of 426). The original membership and relative frequency of one or other type of contribution are obscure (Thucydides' valuation of the 'first tribute' at 460 talents being of uncertain import). However it is certain that choice or compulsion gradually made tribute payment the norm, so that by 431 only Chios and the cities of Lesbos were still furnishing ships (although Samos, which lost its fleet in 440/39, was paying war indemnity rather than tribute). By this time, too, Athenian official parlance was referring to 'the cities over whom the Athenians rule', and it had long been appropriate to speak of an Athenian Empire. Tribute is thus a central characteristic of the empire until its replacement in 413–10 by a 5 per cent import/export levy in the empire's harbours.

In 454 the treasury was moved to Athens, and a 1²/₃ per cent quota taken from tribute receipts for dedication to Athena began to be recorded on stone. The remains of these annual 'tribute lists' and of assessment lists from 425, 422 and (?)410 are the fundamental source for knowledge of the extent of the empire. Some 278 places are recorded as paying tribute at one time or another after 454/3 (32 for the first time in 429 or later); and a further 69 places can be named which were first assessed in 425 or later, but are not *known* to have paid. (The total number of such new assessments was certainly much larger.) For the location of all tribute payers and new assessments of 425 see the maps in R. Meiggs, *The Athenian Empire*.

The present map confines itself to states whose actual payments show an assessment of 1 talent or more at some date in the period 454/3 to 429/8, i.e. before pressures of war caused assessments to rise to much higher levels. A few places with lower assessments are also included for other reasons. The five tribute areas in which quotas are arranged in 442/38 (after which I and IV were amalgamated), together with the total number of actual paying states in each area (in brackets), are also shown. The wartime assessments introduced two new areas, *Actaean Cities* (the region between I and II), and *Euxine* (cities in the Crimea and on the west and south coasts of the Black Sea).

Two other features of the empire are illustrated. (1) Overseas settlement: here we may distinguish Thurii (see p. 84) and Amphipolis, which were indisputably colonies with minority Athenian participation, from the rest, which present problems of categorisation as between 'colony' and 'cleruchy'. (2) Revolt: the map shows places where revolt on one or more occasions is attested in literary sources, or by a conjunction of documents relating to organisation after revolt with evidence of non-payment in the quota lists. However it excludes cases where the hypothesis of revolt depends solely on the quota lists, e.g. Miletus (447, 445–3); Aegina (447); Cos (446–3); various islands which never appear in 453–50; 21 apparently regular payers in I, II and III which are absent on various occasions in 442–1, 439, 434, 432; some 20 places in III whose absence in 431 and later may be connected with the revolts of Potidaea, Spartolus and Olynthus; and over 25 Carian places absent in 441–39 and not recorded as paying after 443 at the latest.

45

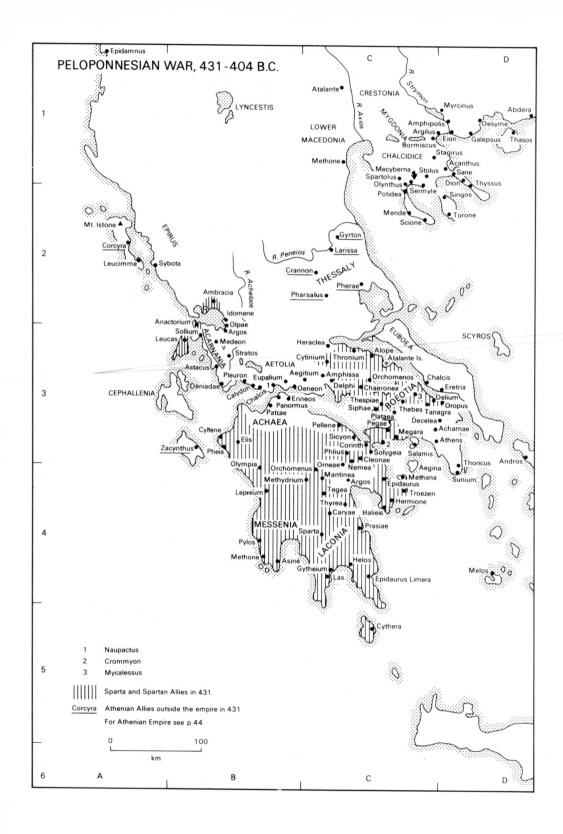

PELOPONNESIAN WAR, 431-404 B.C.

Epidamnus

Atalante

CRESTONIA

LYNCESTIS

Myrcinus

Abdera

LOWER
MACEDONIA

MYGDONIA

Amphipolis
Argilus
Bormiscus

Oesyme
Eion Galepsus Thasos

Methone

CHALCIDICE

Stagirus

Mecyberna Stolus
Spartolus
Olynthus Sermyle
Potidaea

Acanthus
Sane
Dion Thyssus
Singos

Mende
Scione

Torone

Mt. Istone

EPIRUS

Gyrton
Larissa

Corcyra

R. Peneios

Leucimme Sybota

Crannon
THESSALY

Pharsalus

Pherae

SCYROS

Ambracia

Idomene
Anactorium
Sollium Olpae
Argos
Leucas Medeon

Heraclea
Cytinium
Thronium
Alope
Atalante Is.

EUBOEA

Stratos

ACARNANIA

Astacus

AETOLIA

Aegitium Amphissa
Pleuron Eupalium Oeneon Delphi Chaeronea
Deniadae Calydon Erineos Thespiae
CEPHALLENIA Chalcis Panormus Siphae
Patrae

Orchomenos Chalcis
Eretria
Delium
Oropus
Thebes Tanagra
Decelea

ACHAEA

Cyllene

Zacynthus Pheia

Pellene
Sicyon
Corinth
Phlius
Orneae Nemea
Mantinea
Orchomenus Argos
Methydrium Tegea
Lepreum
Thyrea
Caryae

Plataea
Pegae
Megara
Acharnae
Athens

Sicyon
Cleonae
Solygeia
Salamis
Aegina

Methana
Epidaurus
Troezen
Hermione
Halieis

Andros

Thoricus
Sunium

Elis

Olympia

MESSENIA

Sparta
LACONIA

Pylos

Methone
Asine
Gytheium
Las

Prasiae

Helos
Epidaurus Limera

Melos

Cythera

1 Naupactus
2 Crommyon
3 Mycalessus

|||||| Sparta and Spartan Allies in 431

Corcyra Athenian Allies outside the empire in 431

For Athenian Empire see p.44

0   100
km

46

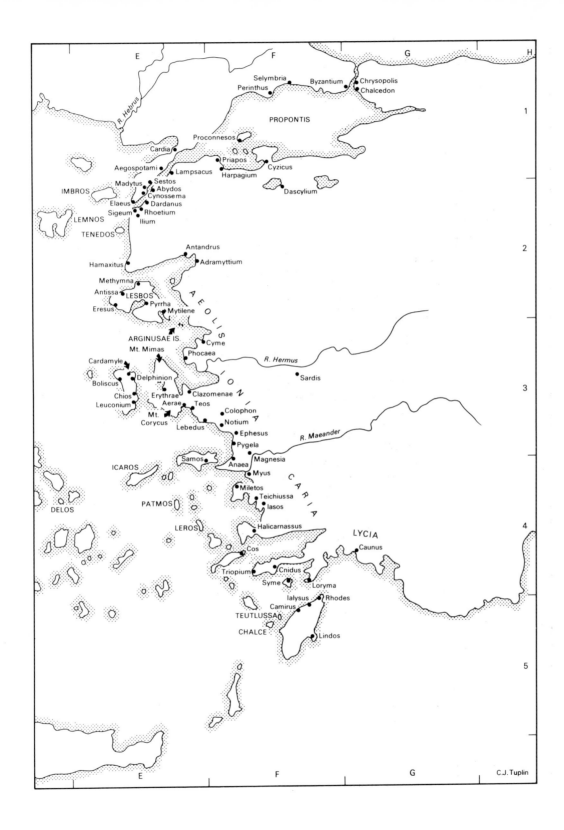

E F G H

Selymbria
Perinthus
Byzantium Chrysopolis
Chalcedon

PROPONTIS

1

Proconnesos
Cardia
Priapos
Aegospotami Lampsacus Cyzicus
Harpagium
Madytus Sestos
Abydos Dascylium
IMBROS Cynossema
Elaeus Dardanus
Sigeum Rhoetium
Ilium

LEMNOS

TENEDOS

2

Antandrus
Adramyttium
Hamaxitus
Methymna
A E O L I S
Antissa LESBOS
Eresus Pyrrha
Mytilene
ARGINUSAE IS.
Cyme
Mt. Mimas Phocaea
I O N I A R. Hermus
Cardamyle
Boliscus Delphinion Sardis
3
Chios Erythrae
Leuconium Aerae Clazomenae
Mt. Teos
Corycus Colophon
Lebedus Notium
Ephesus
R. Maeander
Pygela
Samos Magnesia
ICAROS Anaea
Myus
C A R I A
PATMOS Miletos
Teichiussa
Iasos
DELOS
LEROS Halicarnassus
LYCIA
4
Caunus
Cos
Triopium Cnidus
Syme Loryma
Ialysus Rhodes
Camirus
TEUTLUSSA
CHALCE Lindos

5

C.J. Tuplin

47

Peloponnesian War, 431–404 BC

The term Peloponnesian War (not actually used in surviving texts until the first century BC) designates the whole period from Sparta's declaration of war in 431—as supposed champion of the autonomy of the Greeks—until Athens' surrender and reduction to the status of a subject Spartan ally in 404. A single map can only 'illustrate' the fighting of this 27-year period by indicating the whereabouts of as many as possible of the places mentioned in the sources. Three phases can be discerned:

(1) 431–21, the 'Ten Years War' or 'Archidamian War' (an early, though inappropriate, term). During this period there was fighting in various theatres: Attica (regular Spartan invasions until 425); Peloponnese (Athenian maritime raids in 431, 430, 426; the introduction of garrisons in Pylos, Methone, Cythera in 425–4); central Greece (Spartan siege of Plataea, 429–7; Athenian attempts to capture Megara and various parts of Boeotia, 424); north west Greece (429–6) and Corcyra (427–5); 'Thraceward' region (431–29; 424–1); Lesbos (428–7); Sicily (427–4).

A major turning point was the Pylos campaign (425). After it, Sparta was not only under greater pressure at home; she had also to abandon invasions of Attica to protect the lives of 120 Spartiates taken prisoner. She was ready to negotiate a year's truce in 423–2, and a 50-years peace in 421, when Brasidas' successful encouragement of rebellion among Athens' Thraceward allies provided something of a position of strength from which to do so. The resultant 'Peace of Nicias', accompanied as it was by a defensive alliance, required each side to surrender certain territorial gains (chiefly in the Peloponnese and Thrace) and all prisoners taken. But the territorial requirements were never properly implemented, and the peace was a very tense one from the outset.

(2) 421–13, an interlude—lasting until Sparta's occupation of Decelea in northern Attica—which Thucydides insisted was mostly no better than a 'suspicious truce' and therefore really part of the war. There was sporadic fighting in Thrace. Active hostility between Athens and Sparta appears in two main areas: Sicily, where resistance to Athens' major onslaught against Syracuse came to be directed by the Spartan Gylippus (415–13); Peloponnese, where Athens' defensive alliance with three anti-Spartan states, Argos, Mantinea, and Elis (420), led to military operations, including some direct action against Sparta or her unequivocal allies—incursions from Pylos (419 onwards); capture of Orchomenus (418) and Orneae (416/15); siege of Epidaurus (418–17); battle of Mantinea (418); maritime attacks on eastern Laconia (414).

(3) 413–04, the 'Decelean War' (cf. above), or 'Ionian War', because it was mostly fought out along the coasts from Byzantium to Rhodes. Both names underline crucial differences from the first period, when Sparta had not attempted either to *occupy* Attica, or, normally, to encourage or exploit disorder in the eastern Aegean or Black Sea approaches. The latter development was now prompted by over-optimistic expectations after Athens' Sicilian disaster. Another vital new element is Persian co-operation with Sparta. For five years this did not prevent Athenian recovery—in 410–08 especially. Only after the arrival of the Great King's son, Cyrus, in 407 was Persian wealth used effectively, at least whenever Lysander was in office as navarch (407 and 405–4). The change is well illustrated by the contrast between Sparta's hesitant reaction to loss of a fleet at Cyzicus (410), and the immediate replacement of the losses at Arginusae (406) with the ships which destroyed Athenian naval power at Aegospotami (405).

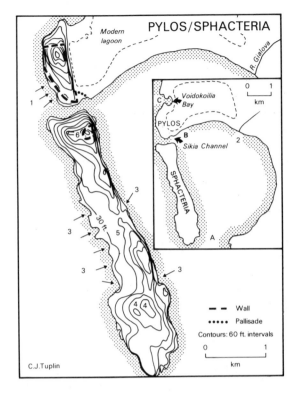

PYLOS/SPHACTERIA

Modern lagoon

R. Gialova

Voidokoilia Bay

PYLOS

Sikia Channel

SPHACTERIA

- – – Wall
- ····· Pallisade

Contours: 60 ft. intervals

0   1
km

C.J.Tuplin

Pylos/Sphacteria

Five stages can be discerned in the events of 425 described by Thucydides (4.2-6, 8-23, 26-41). (1) The fortification of Pylos (?two stone walls and a palisade), and its occupation by a small Athenian force. (2) The encampment of Spartan land and naval forces around R. Gialova, and the installation of 420 hoplites on Sphacteria. Allegedly the Spartans intended to block the harbour entrances, i.e. either A and B, or B and C. In context Thucydides' words must refer to A/B, but unless the text is emended the reported dimensions of the entrances will only fit B/C. The tactical value of the plan, which was not carried out, is in any case dubious. (3) Two days of unsuccessful seaborne attacks on Pylos [1]. (4) A Spartan naval defeat in the harbour [2]. (5) The Athenian landings on Sphacteria [3]: a first wave disposed of southern outposts [4]; a second forced the main body [5] to retreat to the fort on Mount Elias [6], where it surrendered after some Messenians scaled the western cliffs.

The Bosporan Realm and its Neighbours

By the fifth century Panticapaeum had emerged as the leading Greek settlement on the Cimmerian Bosporus. Power was seized here *c.* 480 by Archaeanax. His descendants (of whom nothing is known) were displaced *c.* 438 by Spartocus, whose family was to maintain its rule in Bosporus till the late second century. To the west the Spartocids eventually secured control of the major port of Theodosia, even though Heraclea Pontica came to the latter's defence. Eastwards they sought control first of the Taman peninsula, and then gradually of the Maeotian tribes up the eastern shore of the Sea of Azov—objectives brought to completion during the reign of Paerisades II (344–11), when the Bosporan realm reached its zenith.

Various circumstances enabled the Spartocids to maintain their rule for an exceptionally long span by Greek standards. Not only did the family continue to produce suitably strong, long-lived successors over generations. In addition, even though the state was run entirely at their personal whim, they exercised moderation, causing little friction at home, and abroad shunning any reckless expansion such as came to harm many Greek tyrannies. Above all, however, the state was unusually wealthy. Since both rulers and ruled benefited, the poverty and consequent tensions common elsewhere were absent, and there was unanimous recognition that continued prosperity rested upon the maintenance of peace and stability.

Bosporan wealth derived principally from fish (herring, sturgeon, tunny), vines, and above all, corn. The latter was both grown locally, and brought from the plains of south Russia for export all over the Greek world. Well into the third century at least, Bosporus was the largest single supplier of corn to mainland Greece, especially to Athens, whose merchants enjoyed preferential treatment during the late fifth and fourth centuries. Wine was also made, and fish salted, on a significant scale, as shown by excavation of wine-making establishments and pickling vats, notably at Tyritace and Myrmecium.

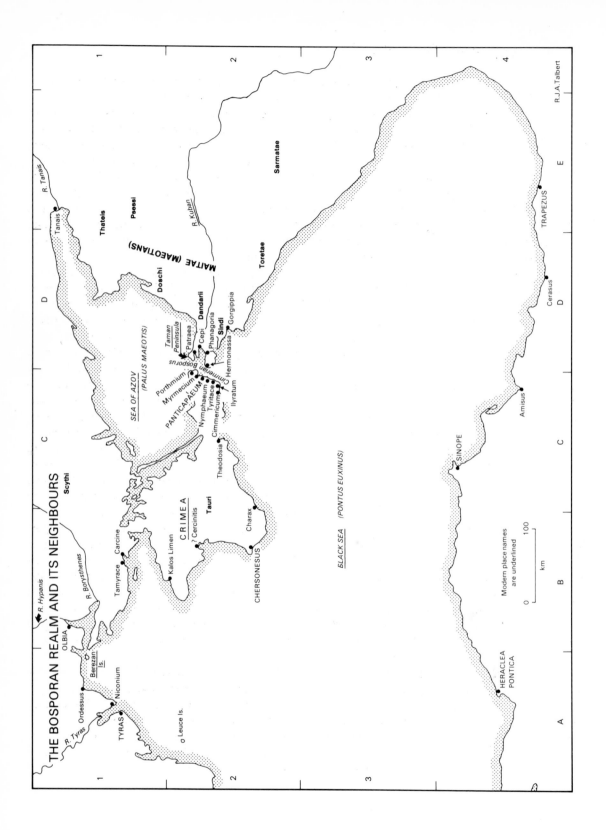

THE BOSPORAN REALM AND ITS NEIGHBOURS

R. Hypanis

Scythi

OLBIA

Berezan Is.

R. Borysthenes

Tamyrace
Carcine

Kalos Limen

CRIMEA

Cercinitis

Tauri

CHERSONESUS

Charax

Theodosia

Cimmericum

PANTICAPAEUM

Myrmecium

Porthmium

Nymphaeum

Tyritace

Ilyratum

Cimmerian Bosporus

Bosporus

Patraea

Taman Peninsula

Cepi

Phanagoria

Hermonassa

Gorgippia

Sindi

Dandarii

Doschi

MAIATAE (MAEOTIANS)

Thateis

Psessi

Toretae

Sarmatae

Tanais

R. Tanais

SEA OF AZOV
(PALUS MAEOTIS)

Niconium

TYRAS

Ordessus

R. Tyras

Leuce Is.

BLACK SEA   (PONTUS EUXINUS)

HERACLEA PONTICA

SINOPE

Amisus

TRAPEZUS

Cerasus

R. Kuban

Modern place names
are underlined

0   100
km

R.J.A.Talbert

50

Trade in the Classical Greek World

The pattern of Greek trading in and around the Mediterranean was largely determined by the need tŏ secure certain basic supplies—foodstuffs, timber, and metals above all. Some overseas settlements were primarily commercial in aim—Pithecussae and Sinope for iron, for example, Al Mina for north Syrian metal ores, Massilia at the end of an overland river-route for tin from the north. The Pontic settlements, major sources of fish and grain, are termed *emporia* by Herodotus. Settlements with a more generally commercial purpose were Gravisca in Etruria and Naucratis in the Nile Delta.

Except for certain basic metals, however, trade was a marginal activity for the Greek world. The climatic homogeneity of much of the Mediterranean meant that most agricultural products could be obtained locally everywhere. So only regional wines of high quality, for instance, were worth exporting. Those of Thasos, Chios, and Lesbos had the highest reputation; Massilia sold its local product to enthusiastic Gauls who did not cultivate the vine. Athens and Egypt, too, seem to have been major customers for fine wine. Specialities exported by them in return were olive oil and fine pottery from Athens, grain, linen and papyrus from Egypt.

Corn was the principal exception to local availability. Most mainland and Aegean states imported some grain. South Italy, Sicily and Egypt supplied the Peloponnese. By the mid-fifth century Athens was heavily dependent on imported corn, obtained mainly from Thrace and south Russia.

Manufacture was on a small scale, and also mainly for local consumption. Individual traders travelled from port to port, buying and selling piecemeal. Pottery provides most of the evidence. Graffiti on Athenian pottery give some indications of traders to the west placing 'bulk' orders, but with the exception of the workshop of Nikosthenes there is not yet evidence of work being produced to specification to meet the taste of a particular market. Current research indicates that in the late fifth and fourth centuries Attic black glaze pottery was carried by Phoenician traders to much of the south and east Mediterranean.

In general, long voyages across the open sea were avoided. Some towns, like the Adriatic settlements, therefore became important as stepping stones, others because they commanded straits like the Bosporus, or lay on an isthmus. Corinth is the prime example of the latter type, though Athens also brought in goods by way of Euboea as well as Piraeus. Towns at or near river mouths—Massilia, Spina, Istrus, Olbia—traded up the rivers with their hinterland.

So far as any one Greek city was concerned, much of its trade might be in the hands of non-citizens, either resident (metics), or in passage. Instances of state intervention to control production or trade are few, and confined to staple products. The Attic silver mines were state owned, but leased to private concessionaires. In the early fourth century the towns of Ceos legislated to confine the export of *miltos* (red ochre) to vessels designated by Athens. The Thasians regulated the wholesale purchase and retail sale of their wines, but were evidently able to ban only Thasian vessels from importing foreign wines to the neighbouring mainland. In the fifth century Athens was sufficiently powerful to compel corn ships from the Black Sea to unload at Piraeus, and to limit the quantity re-exported; other states could import corn from Byzantium only on licence from Athens. In the fourth century by contrast, while restrictions were imposed on corn dealing in Attica, imports could only be encouraged indirectly, either by regulations on loans for mercantile ventures, or by offering incentives both to shippers and to foreign rulers able to control exports from their own territories.

Apart from the Greeks, Phoenicians were the main traders, covering the southern Mediterranean especially. From early in the fifth century the Phoenician settlement at Carthage virtually monopolised trade with Sardinia, western Sicily, southern Spain, and much of north Africa; it also controlled the Atlantic tin route.

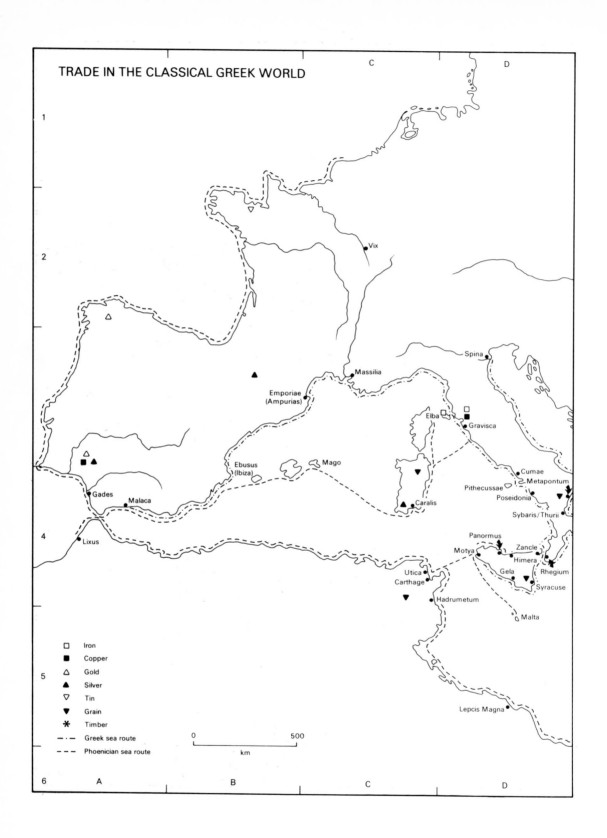

TRADE IN THE CLASSICAL GREEK WORLD

□	Iron
■	Copper
△	Gold
▲	Silver
▽	Tin
▼	Grain
✳	Timber
—·—·	Greek sea route
— — —	Phoenician sea route

0   500
km

Vix
Spina
Massilia
Emporiae
(Ampurias)
Elba
Gravisca
Ebusus
(Ibiza)
Mago
Caralis
Cumae
Metapontum
Pithecussae
Poseidonia
Sybaris/Thurii
Gades
Malaca
Panormus
Zancle
Motya
Himera
Rhegium
Lixus
Gela
Utica
Syracuse
Carthage
Hadrumetum
Malta
Lepcis Magna

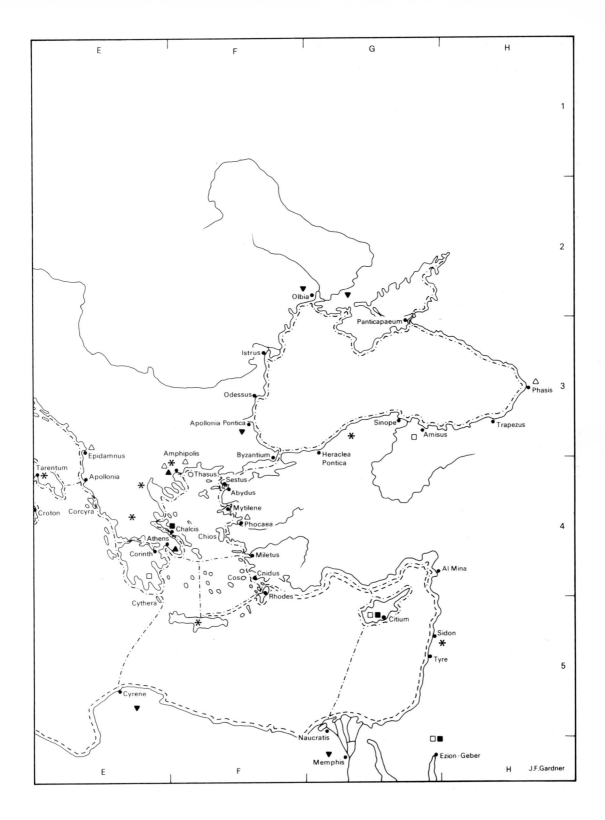

E · · · · · · · · · · · · · · · F · · · · · · · · · · · · · · · G · · · · · · · · · · · · · · · H

1

2

Olbia
▼

▼

Panticapaeum

Istrus

Phasis △

Odessus

Apollonia Pontica
▼

Sinope
Amisus □

Trapezus

3

Byzantium

Heraclea
Pontica

✳

Epidamnus △

Tarentum
✳

Amphipolis
△ ✳ △
▲ ○ Thasus
Sestus
Abydus

Al Mina

Apollonia

Croton   Corcyra

✳

Mytilene
Phocaea △

Chalcis ■
Athens
▲
Corinth   Chios

Miletus

4

□

Cythera

Cnidus
Cos ○
Rhodes ○

□ ■ Citium

Sidon
✳

Tyre

5

✳

Cyrene
▼

Naucratis

□ ■

Memphis ▼

Ezion-Geber

E · · · · · · · · · · · · · · · F · H   J.F.Gardner

53

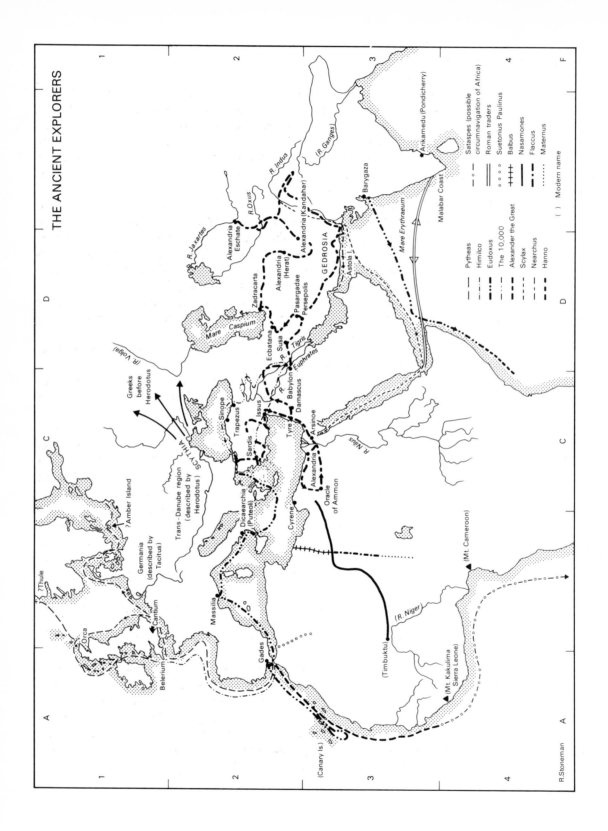

THE ANCIENT EXPLORERS

Pytheas
Himilco
Eudoxus
The 10,000
Alexander the Great
Scylax
Nearchus
Hanno

Sataspes (possible
circumnavigation of Africa)
Roman traders
Suetonius Paulinus
Balbus
Nasamones
Flaccus
Maternus

( ) Modern name

R.Stoneman

The Ancient Explorers

From early times Greeks were acquainted with, or at the least aware of, their neighbours to the east and north east. Voyages to these regions—presumably for trading—are reflected in the legend of the Argonauts, in the exploits attributed to Aristeas of Proconnesus, and in the mythical wanderings of Io recounted in Aeschylus, *Prometheus Bound*. Her route takes in Scythians, Chalybes and Amazons to the north; next the Caucasus, Cimmerii and the Bosporus; then Asia, haunt of the fabulous Graeae, the mute hounds of Zeus, and the one-eyed Arimaspians. Thereafter she turns south to the Aethiopes and the R. Nile.

In the fifth century Herodotus made extensive researches on Egypt, Scythia, the Persian empire, and India, some of them by personal observation. His only Greek predecessor was Scylax of Caryanda, who in a voyage of coastal exploration undertaken *c.* 510 for the Great King Darius set off from near Attock on the R. Indus and sailed as far as Arsinoe. Before Scylax, two Carthaginians, Himilco (*c.* 525) and Hanno (*c.* 500), had sailed respectively to right and left out of the Pillars of Hercules (Straits of Gibraltar). Himilco reached Brittany, but probably did not go as far as Britain. From the account in Polybius it would seem that Hanno reached Sierra Leone, or possibly even Cameroon. This is further than any other traveller before the Middle Ages, unless the report in Herodotus be accepted of a circumnavigation of Africa by a Persian named Sataspes during the reign of Xerxes (486–65).

It is appropriate to mention here the March of the Ten Thousand led by Cyrus the Younger, which forms the subject of Xenophon's *Anabasis* (see p. 58). His march seems to have been emulated in part by Alexander the Great, who crossed the Hellespont in 334 to begin his remarkable campaign of conquest of the Persian empire (see pp. 64–5). Alexander's expedition included a geographer and other scientific staff, and aimed to record scientific information as well as to make conquests. In 329 he passed the 'Caspian Gates' and entered hitherto unexplored territory. He was in central Asia and northern India until 326. His admiral Nearchus was despatched down the R. Indus to seek a sea route back to Persia, while Alexander led his army through the burning Gedrosian desert of south Iran, finally reaching Susa in 324.

The British Isles were visited *c.* 310 by Pytheas, a captain from Massilia, who sailed north out of the Pillars of Hercules. Though he is mentioned by Dicaearchus and Strabo, most of our information comes from Diodorus and Pliny. Besides apparently circumnavigating Britain he sailed into the North Sea, reporting a condition where sea and air merge in a kind of jelly (a thick fog plus floating ice?). His tantalising island, Ultima Thule, has been variously identified as Iceland or part of the Norwegian coast.

In the late first century BC Eudoxus of Cyzicus made two voyages to India, on the second of which he was blown down the African coastline. According to Strabo, this experience prompted him to try the circumnavigation the other way. Here he was driven aground by the north east trade wind and turned back; but after reaching the Canary Islands the expedition was lost, from causes unknown.

Several ancient explorers penetrated the Sahara desert. Herodotus records one journey through it by five men of the Berber tribe of the Nasamones. But this lead was hardly followed until Roman times. Then, in 19 BC, Cornelius Balbus, proconsul of Africa, explored south into the desert. In the late first century AD another proconsul, Septimius Flaccus, made a three-month march inland, while Julius Maternus at some unknown date extended the route to the Sudan. In AD 42 Suetonius Paulinus crossed the Atlas. But in general Romans were not prompted by such scientific curiosity as Greeks. Much ancient geographical knowledge is diluted and distorted in mediaeval travellers' tales, until the fashion for pilgrimage again opened distant lands as objects of interest, this time to north west Europeans.

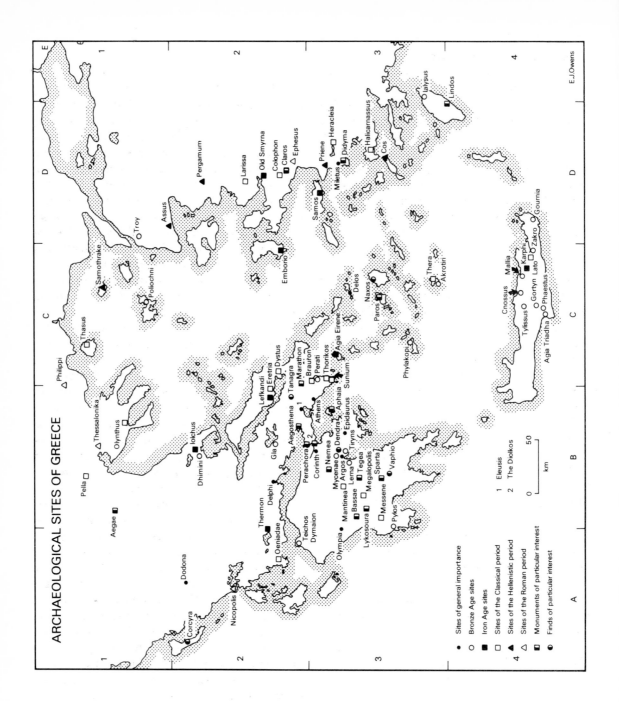

ARCHAEOLOGICAL SITES OF GREECE

Corcyra
Nicopolis
Dodona

Aegae

Pella
Philippi
Thessalonika
Olynthus
Thasus
Samothrake
Poliochni
Troy
Assus
Pergamum

Dhimini
Iolchus
Larissa
Old Smyrna
Colophon
Claros
Ephesus

Thermon
Oeniadae
Delphi
Gla
Lefkandi
Eretria
Dystus
Tanagra
Marathon
Brauron
Perati
Thorikos
Agia Eirene
Priene
Heracleia
Samos
Miletus
Didyma
Halicarnassus
Cos

Teichos Dymaion
Aegosthena
Perachora
Corinth
Mycenae
Argos
Lerna
Tiryns
Athens
Dendra
Epidaurus
Aphaia
Sunium
Naxos
Paros
Delos
Thera
Akrotiri

Ialysus
Lindos

Olympia
Mantinea
Nemea
Tegea
Bassae
Megalopolis
Sparta
Phylakopi

Lykosoura
Messene
Pylos
Vaphio

Eleusis
The Diolkos

Crossus
Mallia
Tylissus
Gortyn
Lato
Karphi
Zakro
Gournia
Agia Triadha
Phaestus

1 Eleusis
2 The Diolkos

0   50
km

- Sites of general importance
○ Bronze Age sites
■ Iron Age sites
□ Sites of the Classical period
▲ Sites of the Hellenistic period
△ Sites of the Roman period
▣ Monuments of particular interest
◕ Finds of particular interest

E.J.Owens

56

Archaeological Sites of Greece

In the latter part of the nineteenth century Heinrich Schliemann's interest in Homer, and his desire to uncover Priam's Troy, laid the foundation for modern archaeology in the Aegean. His excavations at Hissarlik generated interest which led to the discovery of other great prehistoric sites. Archaeology has since come to illuminate all aspects of ancient Greek history and culture. Thus, even when written records are available, archaeology can supplement and complement their evidence, or indeed provide primary information, if the documents are deficient.

Because of the abundance of archaeological evidence, and the fact that almost every place in Greece can be regarded as an archaeological site, the choices for this map are difficult to make. Its aim is twofold: first, to indicate the most important and impressive sites and monuments of the Aegean; second, to show where the most significant contributions to our understanding of ancient Greece have been made.

Four broad categories of site may be identified. First, those places which have immensely furthered our knowledge, most notably perhaps of architecture—among them, Athens (inhabited from Neolithic times); the great sanctuaries of Olympia, Delphi and Dodona; and the cities of Delos and Miletus. Although the most impressive remains from the latter two date to Hellenistic and Roman times, their archaeological importance extends beyond their standing monuments.

Second, sites which illustrate the major historical periods of Greece from the Bronze Age to the Roman era. Among Bronze Age sites are not only great palaces, but also the important towns of Dimini, Poliochni and Akrotiri, the impressive villa of Aghia Triada, the cemetery of Perati, and the fort at Teichos Dymaion. Iron Age sites include the incipient *polis* of Emborio on Chios;

Old Smyrna, where fortifications have been found; and Lefkandi, the excavation of which is substantially changing the present picture of the Dark Age. The sites of the classical to Roman periods mostly illustrate cities or aspects of their architecture. Thus Thorikos is a fine example of an industrial town of the classical period. Olynthus reveals the nature of a residential district of a regularly planned town, while Priene (see further p. 37) illustrates not only a medium-sized Hellenistic city, but also the application of a grid plan to a steeply sloping location. Substantial fifth-century houses have come to light at Dystus. Roman towns and monuments are represented by the sites of Philippi and Ephesus.

Third, specific monuments. For example, the pleasantly situated temple at Nemea; the fortifications of Aegosthena; the remains of the *diolkos* at the isthmus of Corinth, along which ships were dragged to avoid the long and hazardous journey around the Peloponnese; the water installations at Perachora; the oracular shrine at Claros; the temple to Artemis at Brauron, where wooden artefacts have come to light; the recently discovered tomb of Philip II of Macedon at Aegae; and the ancient marble quarries on Paros.

Fourth, sites where important or unusual finds have been made. A substantial number of fourth-century terracotta figurines were found in graves at Tanagra. A complete set of Bronze Age armour came to light at Dendra in the Argolid. The restored pediment of the archaic temple of Artemis is housed in the Corfu museum. On Naxos a colossal, unfinished statue of the seventh century, still attached to the living rock by its back, shows the method by which large sculpture was produced. Two gold cups, fashioned by Cretan smiths and decorated with complementary narrative scenes, were discovered at Vaphio.

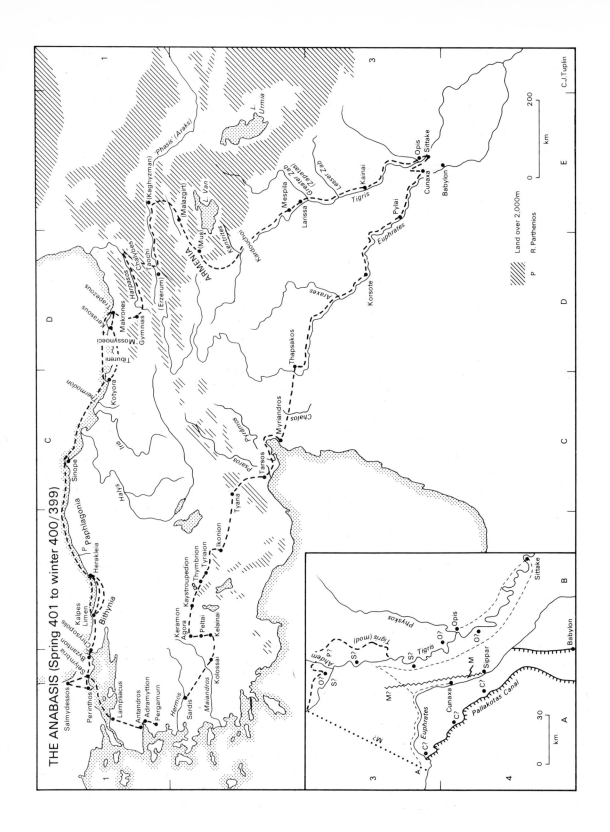

THE ANABASIS (Spring 401 to winter 400/399)

Land over 2,000m
P   R. Parthenios

km
0   200

Bithynia
Salmydessos
Selymbria
Byzantion
Chrysopolis
Perinthos
Lampsacus
Antandros
Adramyttion
Pergamum
Hermos
Sardis
Maiandros
Kolossai
Kelainai
Peltai
Keramon Agora
Kaystroupedion
Thymbrion
Tyriaion
Ikonion
Tyana
Tarsos
Psaros
Pyramos
Myriandros
Chalos
Thapsakos
Araxes
Korsote
Euphrates
Pylai
Cunaxa
Babylon
Sittake
Opis
Kainai
Tigris
Greater Zab (Zapatas)
Lesser Zab
Mespila
Larissa
Kardouchoi
ARMENIA
(Mus)
Kentrites
(Malazgirt)
(Kaghyzman)
'Phasis' (Araks)
L. Van
L. Urmia
(Erzerum)
Taochi
Chalybes
Harpasos
Makrones
Mossynoeci
Gymnias
Tibareni
Kerasous
(Trapezous)
Thermodon
(Kotyora)
Halys
Iris
Sinope
Herakleia
Kalpes Limen
P Paphlagonia

C.J.Tuplin

58

km
0   30

Ahdem
O?
S?
Euphrates
C?
M?
M?
S?
Tigris (mod)
Physkos
Opis
O?
O?
M?
Sippar
M
Cunaxa
C?
C?
Pallakotas Canal
Babylon
Sittake

The Anabasis

The map shows the routes taken by Cyrus' rebel army from Sardis to Cunaxa, where it was defeated by Artaxerxes; by the Greek and non-Greek remnants, marching separately, from Cunaxa to the R. Zab, where the Greek generals were treacherously murdered by Tissaphernes; and by the Greeks from the R. Zab to Byzantium, eastern Thrace and Aeolis. There are two problematic sections.

(1) *Cunaxa to Opis.* The Greeks marched north/ north east for three days, stopped for over three weeks negotiating with the Persians and vainly waiting for Tissaphernes to escort them back to the Aegean, then marched to the Median Wall in three days, to the R. Tigris at Sittake in another two days, and up its east bank to the R. Physkos and Opis in a further four days. The location of all the named points is controversial: some have even suggested that Xenophon carelessly interchanged Opis and Sittake! The inset illustrates Barnett's solution: Cunaxa = Nuseffiat, Median Wall = Nebuchadnezzar's Opis-Sippar fortifications (partly preserved between Sippar and Nuseffiat), Sittake = Humaniye (near Azizye), R. Physkos and Opis = R. Diyala and a site at its junction with the Tigris. Other suggestions are shown for comparison as C?, M?, S?, P?, O?. A represents 'Artaxerxes' Ditch', part of a northern fortification line between the rivers, crossed two days before the battle.

(2) *Mespila (Nineveh)-Trapezus*, a march of three-and-a-half months, the course of which depends on deciding where the Greeks crossed or marched along the rivers Kentrites, Teleboas, Euphrates, 'Phasis' (i.e. Araks) and Harpasos. There is nothing in the sources to help except the record of distances (in days and *parasangs*, rather inexact measurements), general descriptions of terrain, and a scatter of tribal names, valueless in themselves. The solution shown is that of Lehmann-Haupt. Most others are generally similar: they tend to reduce or eliminate the detour to Malazgirt and Kaghyzman, but the final section from the upper Harpasos is common to all. The only radical alternative would be a route following a wide westerly arc from Muş to Gymnias.

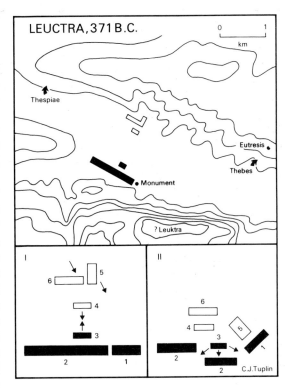

LEUCTRA, 371 B.C.

Leuctra, 371 BC

The approximate location is established by the Theban battle monument. Combination of the individually incomplete ancient accounts of the battle reveals three key points:

(a) The Spartan cavalry [3] was placed opposite the enemy's initial position and therefore (contrary to normal practice) in front of the infantry, part of which it fouled and put out of action when easily defeated by the Boeotian cavalry [4] (Phase I).

(b) The Spartan King Cleombrotus attempted to counter a diagonal Boeotian advance by swinging his right wing forward, but could not complete the move before the arrival of the Thebans, spearheaded by the Sacred Band (front left).

(c) The 50-deep Theban hoplite contingent [5] crushed the isolated Lacedaemonians [1] (especially the Spartiate entourage of Cleombrotus), while the other Boeotians [6] and the Peloponnesians [2] remained unengaged (Phase II, actually almost simultaneous with Phase I).

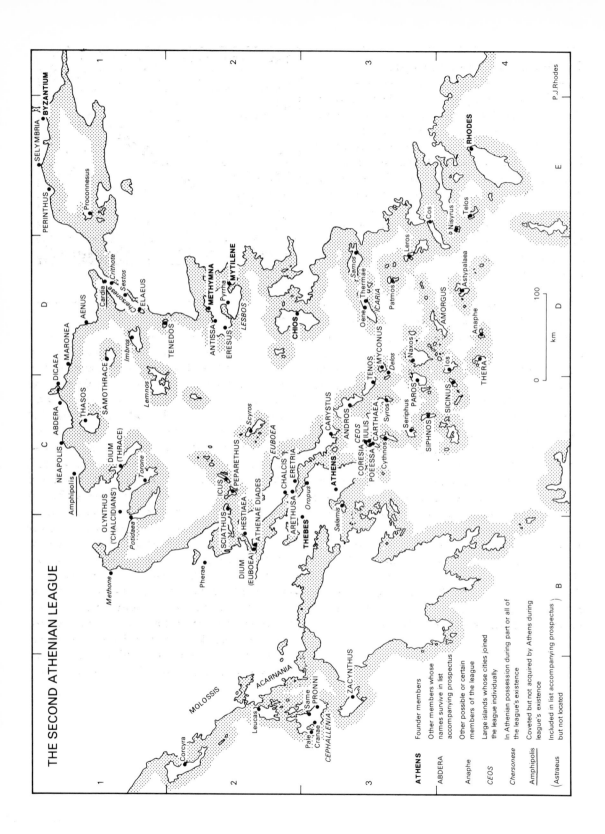

THE SECOND ATHENIAN LEAGUE

ATHENS Founder members

ABDERA Other members whose names survive in list accompanying prospectus

Anaphe Other possible or certain members of the league

CEOS Large islands whose cities joined the league individually

Chersonese In Athenian possession during part or all of the league's existence

Amphipolis Coveted but not acquired by Athens during league's existence

(Astraeus) Included in list accompanying prospectus but not located

P.J.Rhodes

The Second Athenian League

In 378/7, exactly 100 years after the founding of the Delian League, the Second Athenian League was founded. We possess its prospectus, a decree of the Athenian assembly which states defence of the freedom of Greek and barbarian states against Spartan imperialism as the League's purpose; all states outside Persia's domains are invited to join on stated terms, designed to protect members against the encroachments on their freedom which Athens had practised in the Delian League. Appended to the decree is a list of members, to which additions were made on various occasions between 377 and *c.* 375, but not thereafter.

The League was never as large or as prosperous as the Delian League, but fear of Sparta, and Athens' promises of good behaviour, won it widespread support in the 370s, mostly among former members of the Delian League. However, at the battle of Leuctra in 371 Sparta was decisively beaten by Thebes, and the threat of Spartan imperialism was destroyed. In the 360s Athens turned to supporting Sparta against Thebes; the cities of Euboea left the League with Thebes. In the Aegean Athens began making conquests and planting settlements, and broke some of the promises made at the League's foundation. Some members, especially in the south east Aegean, left the League as a result of the Social War of 356–5, but certain former members rejoined when they felt threatened by the growing power of Philip of Macedon. After his victory over Athens and Thebes at Chaeronea in 338, Philip organised the mainland Greeks in the League of Corinth, and the Second Athenian League ceased to exist.

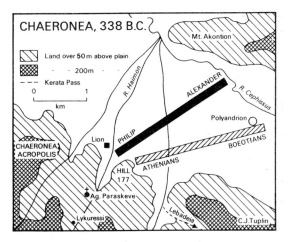

Chaeronea, 338 BC

The relative positions of Athenian and Boeotian hoplites, Philip and Alexander are clear, and an eastern limit for the battlefield is provided by the Macedonian *polyandrion* and the Greeks' withdrawal to Lebadeia. The identity of the 254 skeletons under the Lion monument is too uncertain for them to help topographically; but the R. Haimon, near which some of the Greeks camped, must be west of Hill 177, which favours location of the Greek left near that hill rather than at the end of the Lebadeia road. Both Macedonian wings routed the enemy, with Alexander achieving the first breakthrough. However a more precise picture depends on whether he was leading the Companion Cavalry, and whether Polyaenus is reliable in his report of a deliberate retreat by the Macedonian right, which tempted the Athenians into disastrous pursuit. These problems are linked, for if Alexander led a cavalry charge (the normal view), Polyaenus must be used to explain why there was a gap in the Greek line for him to attack.

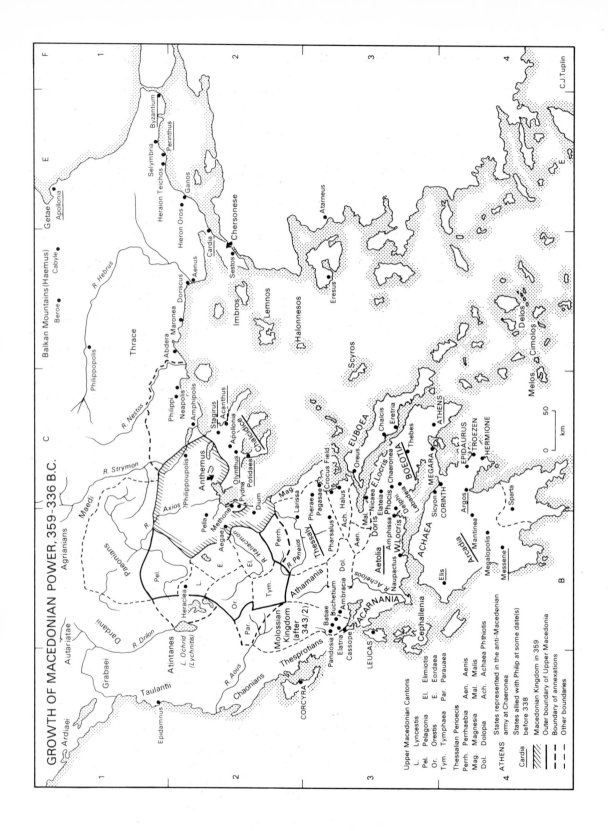

GROWTH OF MACEDONIAN POWER, 359-336 B.C.

C.J.Tuplin

Upper Macedonian Cantons

L.   Lyncestis
Pel. Pelagonia   El. Elimiotis
Or.   Orestis   E.   Eordaea
Tym. Tymphaea   Par. Parauaea

Thessalian Perioecis

Perrh. Perrhaebia   Aen. Aenis
Mag.   Magnesia   Mal. Malis
Dol.   Dolopia   Ach. Achaea Phthiotis

ATHENS   States represented in the anti-Macedonian
4   army at Chaeronea

Cardia   States allied with Philip at some date(s)
         before 338

– – –   Outer boundary of Upper Macedonia
– – – –   Boundary of annexations
– – – –   Other boundaries

km   0   50

The Growth of Macedonian Power, 359–336 BC

The growth of Macedonian power involves two distinct phenomena.

(1) *The extension of the Macedonian Kingdom proper.* This was achieved partly by the imposition of unprecedentedly firm control on the Upper Macedonian cantons, and partly by actual annexation of adjacent non-Macedonian territory. The scale of such annexations is debatable. The map registers the acquisition of the region up to Lake Ochrid (358), Pydna (357), the Strymon-Nestos area (356), Methone (354), Perrhaebia (352), and Parauaea (?351). Some would add Paeonia (356), and all of Chalcidice (348). The alternative view is that Paeonia simply became a vassal principality and that, although the land of Potidaea and Olynthus (cities destroyed in 356 and 348) was occupied by Macedonians, the surviving cities of Chalcidice became Philip's allies. At least one Macedonian cavalry squadron was named after a Chalcidian town—Apollonia.

(2) *The acquisition of effective control in areas outside the Kingdom.* Here three phenomena may be distinguished.

(i) The imposition of vassal status on tribal areas: Paeonians (356: see above); Dardanians (345); Odrysian Thracians under Cetriporis (towards R. Nestos: 356), Amadocus (between R. Nestos and R. Hebros: 352), and Cersobleptes (beyond R. Hebros: 352); the Molossian kingdom (*c.* 351–43/2: it is not clear what implications Molossian vassaldom had for the kingdom's allies among the Chaonians and Thesprotians); (?)Getae under Cothelas (*c.* 341); Scythians under Atheas (340). It is unlikely that the Agrianes were vassals, and the evidence that some or all of the Grabaei, Autariatae and Ardiaei were in that category is weaker than sometimes suggested. The Talauntii certainly were not vassals. The situation in Thrace after 342/1 is uncertain: some believe that a tribute-paying province stretching north to the Balkan Mountains (Haemus) was established under a Macedonian *strategos* (an office first attested under Alexander).

(ii) Thessaly: Philip's suppression of Pherae in 352 was followed by his acclamation as *archon* of the Thessalian League, an extraordinary position for a Macedonian king, in virtue of which he could receive taxes, command military support, and generally control the cities as he saw fit; after 344 the ancient office of tetrarch was revived to assist the process. The status of the *perioecis* (areas theoretically dependent on individual cities) is debatable: Perrhaebia and Magnesia were annexed in 352, but it is not clear whether the non-annexed areas (including Magnesia after 346) were subject to Philip as *archon* directly, or via the cities.

(iii) Other Greek states: Philip's alliances with several states between 359 and 338 may in varying degrees be construed as expressions of his growing power, and the same goes for his more or less open interferences in the politics of Euboea, Megara and the Peloponnese after 346, and his addition of certain small Greek towns to the Molossian kingdom in 343/2. But the chief expression and instrument of hegemony is the Corinthian League of 338, an organisation which involved assertions of Greek autonomy (but also the outlawing of socio-economic revolution); freedom from tribute and garrisons (except in Ambracia, Corinth and Thebes); the right of deliberation in League synods (albeit occasional and carefully orchestrated); and the obligation to provide military support for the projected Persian expedition. In default of appreciable precise evidence, the League must be presumed to have included all mainland and Aegean Greek states which were neither part of Macedonia nor in Persian hands; the only known exception is Sparta.

It should be stressed that, notwithstanding the erection of a farflung Macedonian *Reich*, the fundamental fact of Macedonian power remained the military potential of Macedonia itself, and the chief development here was the creation of a well-disciplined infantry force. In this context the use of population transfers to alter settlement patterns and create the appropriate human raw material was vital, but the general references in the sources do not permit any precise description of the process.

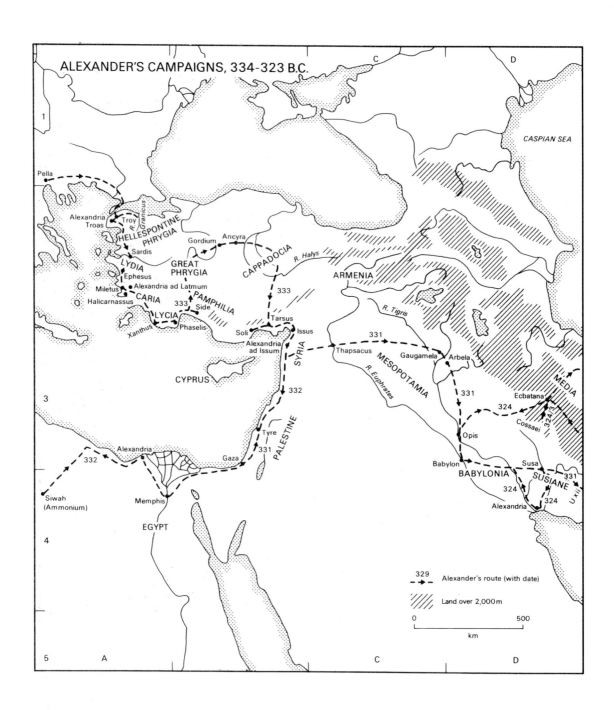

ALEXANDER'S CAMPAIGNS, 334-323 B.C.

CASPIAN SEA

Pella

Alexandria
Troas
Troy
R. Granicus
HELLESPONTINE
PHRYGIA
Sardis
LYDIA
Ephesus
Miletus
Alexandria ad Latmum
Halicarnassus
CARIA
LYCIA
Xanthus
Phaselis
333
Side
PAMPHILIA
Gordium
Ancyra
GREAT
PHRYGIA
CAPPADOCIA
R. Halys
333
Soli
Tarsus
Alexandria
ad Issum
Issus
ARMENIA
R. Tigris
331
Thapsacus
Gaugamela
Arbela
MEDIA
Ecbatana
324
Cossaei
324
331
Opis
SYRIA
MESOPOTAMIA
R. Euphrates
CYPRUS

332
Tyre
331
Gaza
PALESTINE
Babylon
Susa
331
BABYLONIA
SUSIANE
Uxii
324
324
Alexandria

Alexandria
332

Siwah
(Ammonium)
Memphis
EGYPT

329
Alexander's route (with date)

Land over 2,000m

0   500
km

64

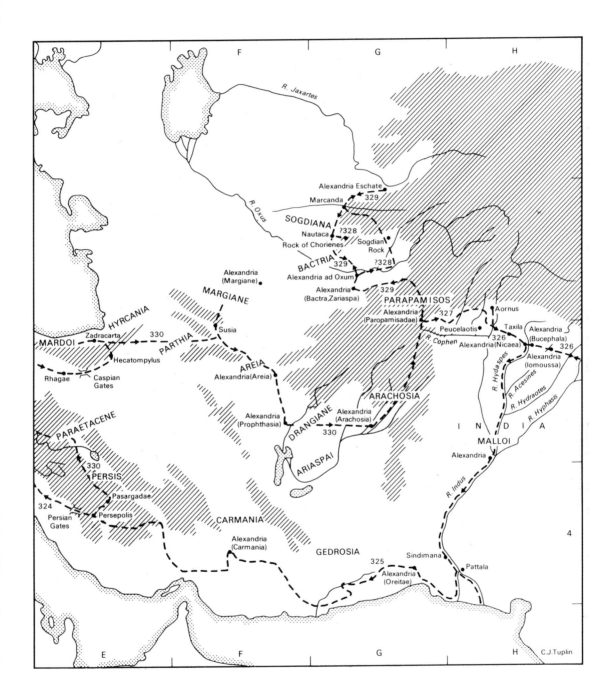

R. Jaxartes

R. Oxus

Alexandria Eschate
Marcanda
329

SOGDIANA

?328
Nautaca
Rock of Chorienes   Sogdian
                      Rock

BACTRIA   329   ?328

Alexandria ad Oxum

Alexandria   329
(Bactra,Zariaspa)   PARAPAMISOS

Alexandria
(Margiane)

MARGIANE

Alexandria   327   Aornus
(Paropamisadae)
                    Peucelaotis   Taxila
HYRCANIA   Alexandria
                                           326   (Bucephala)
MARDOI Zadracarta   330   PARTHIA   Susia   Alexandria(Nicaea)   326
         Hecatompylus   R. Cophen   Alexandria
                                  AREIA   (Iomoussa)
Rhagae   Caspian   R. Hydaspes
          Gates   Alexandria(Areia)   R. Acesines
                                                                   R. Hydraotes
                                    ARACHOSIA   I N D I A   R. Hyphasis
PARAETACENE   Alexandria   Alexandria
                     (Prophthasia)   (Arachosia)
          330   DRANGIANE   MALLOI
    PERSIS   330
         Pasargadae   Alexandria
324   ARIASPAI
Persian   Persepolis
Gates   CARMANIA
                                                      R. Indus
                    Alexandria
                    (Carmania)   GEDROSIA
                                              325   Sindimana
                                                          Pattala
                                    Alexandria
                                    (Oreitae)

4

E   F   G   H   C.J.Tuplin

Alexander's Campaigns, 334–23 BC

The map illustrates Alexander's movements between the departure from Pella in 334 and his death at Babylon in 323. The general picture of his progress is not in doubt—334–1: Asia Minor, Levant; 331–30: Mesopotamia, Iran, Afghanistan; 329–7: Afghanistan, Soviet Central Asia; 327–5: Pakistan, India; 325–3: Iran, Mesopotamia. However lack of precise ancient evidence, conflict between different sources, and differences of opinion about logistical probabilities can render exact identification of the routes followed controversial. Sections where even a small scale map must reflect a disputed interpretation include Ancyra–Tarsus; Tyre–Thapsacus (the site of the latter is a notorious crux); Ecbatana–Rhagae; Zadracarta–Alexandria in Areia (= Herat); Herat–Alexandria in Arachosia (= Kandahar); movements either side of the R. Oxus in 328 (in particular, did Alexander actually visit Alexandria in Margiane (= Merv)?; Pattala–Alexandria in Carmania.

The campaigns fall into four periods.

(1) The war against Darius, ending in 330 with the latter's murder as he fled east from Rhagae. Though Alexander had claimed the Persian throne in 332, and had been hailed as 'King of Asia' by his army after Gaugamela, with Darius' opportune death such claims became a reality; further fighting would be against usurpers—like Darius' killer Bessus, who adopted the upright tiara of an Achaemenid king—and against recalcitrant 'subjects'. The reduction of Darius to the level of an expendable fugitive was principally achieved by three set-piece battles: at the R. Granicus (334: the attempt by Asia Minor forces to contain the invader); Issus (333: Darius' first personal appearance, and a defeat even though he first out-manoeuvred Alexander strategically); and Gaugamela (331: the defeat which exposed the empire's Mesopotamian and Iranian heartland). The delay between Issus and Gaugamela, which gave Darius another chance, was due to the time expended on the sieges of Tyre (p. 68) and Gaza, and the occupation of Egypt—diversions necessitated by Alexander's strategy of neutralising the Persian navy by control of its bases.

(2) In 330–27 Alexander slowly asserted control in the eastern satrapies against resistance from Satibarzanes, his own appointee as satrap of Areia; Bessus, satrap of Bactria and would-be Great King; and Spitamenes, leader of a rebellion in initially submissive Sogdiana. This occupied Alexander's attention for 18 months of hard and ill-documented campaigning in alternately mountainous and desert terrain. His successes in this period disposed of all concerted Iranian nationalist opposition to the foreign King of Kings. The next time there was trouble in Bactria, in 325, it came from discontented Greek mercenaries who disliked being settled in such an un-Greek environment.

(3) In 327 Alexander crossed into India (mostly staying within Pakistan in modern terms), capturing the apparently impregnable Aornus rock (Pir-Sar) early on, and then eliminating the resistance of King Poros at the R. Hydaspes (p. 69). Further advance eastwards stopped at the R. Hyphasis, when the army refused to endorse a decision to make for the R. Ganges. Instead Alexander set off down the R. Indus to subdue the tribes of its middle and lower reaches, which he did with considerable bloodletting. Return to the empire's centre along the coasts of Baluchistan and Iran became impossible when monsoons delayed the fleet, so Alexander had to cross the Gedrosian desert, losing up to three-quarters of his army to hunger and thirst in the process.

(4) 324–3 saw him back in Babylonia, and largely inactive militarily, except for a winter campaign against the Cossaei, and the preparations for an expedition to Arabia which his death forestalled.

RIVER GRANICUS, 334 B.C.

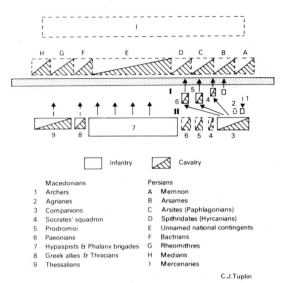

	Infantry		Cavalry

	Macedonians		Persians
1	Archers	A	Memnon
2	Agrianes	B	Arsames
3	Companions	C	Arsites (Paphlagonians)
4	Socrates' squadron	D	Spithridates (Hyrcanians)
5	Prodromoi	E	Unnamed national contingents
6	Paeonians	F	Bactrians
7	Hypaspists & Phalanx brigades	G	Rheomithres
8	Greek allies & Thracians	H	Medians
9	Thessalians	I	Mercenaries

C.J.Tuplin

ISSUS, 333 B.C.

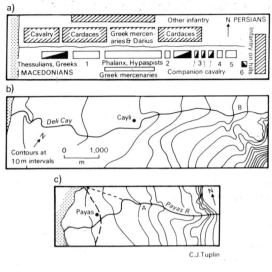

C.J.Tuplin

River Granicus, 334 BC

There is fundamental conflict between the main accounts. In Arrian Alexander fights his way across the river against Persian cavalry ranged on the east bank, while in Diodorus he makes an unopposed dawn crossing and fights a 'normal' engagement in the plain east of the river. Arrian's somewhat more circumstantial account is perhaps the lesser of two evils, though Diodorus supplies the Persian dispositions. There are two phases: first, the crossing, with two cavalry attacks on the Macedonian right, the second co-ordinated with infantry advance; second, the annihilation of the Persians' Greek mercenaries in the plain (not shown). The limited extent of the areas where crossing was unimpeded by either high banks or trees, or both, may explain Alexander's 'oblique' line of attack and his ultimate success (the very localised fighting neutralising Persian numerical advantage). But the process can only be represented schematically, since precise topographical information is lacking; possibly it is no longer even obtainable, as the river may have shifted course.

Issus, 333 BC

(a) represents schematically one interpretation of the final pre-battle dispositions recorded in Arrian. [1: Thracian javelineers, Cretan archers; 2: archers; 3: *prodromoi*, Paeonians; 4: archers, Agrianians; 5: Greek mercenaries; 6: small cavalry unit.] The Macedonian centre/right routed the enemy—the first breakthrough being led by Alexander against the Cardaces—while the left checked the Persian cavalry. Detailed reconstruction is difficult, not least as regards the initial Macedonian attack. A crucial problem here is the identification of the R. Pinarus. It seems most likely to have been either the Deli Cay (30 km north of Iskenderun), or the Payas (20 km north), where coastline and riverbed may have changed: see broken lines in (c). The Payas fits various reported distances less badly, but steep banks above A preclude the initial Macedonian cavalry charge implied by the sources—and indeed *any* orderly cavalry advance. So either the battle occurred on the Deli (between B and the sea), or infantry brigades opened the attack.

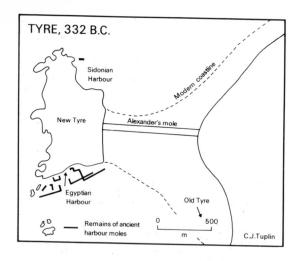

TYRE, 332 B.C.

Sidonian Harbour

New Tyre

Alexander's mole

Modern coastline

Egyptian Harbour

Old Tyre

Remains of ancient harbour moles

0   500

m

C.J.Tuplin

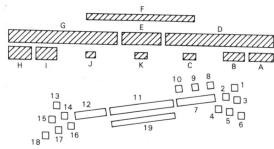

GAUGAMELA, 331 B.C.

Macedonians
1   Mercenary cavalry
2   Prodromoi
3   Paeonians
4   Agrianians
5   Archers
6   Mercenary infantry
7   Alexander with Companion cavalry
8   Thracian javelineers
9   Cretan archers
10 Agrianians
11 Hypaspists & Phalanx bridges
12 Thessalian cavalry
13 Mercenary cavalry
14 Greek cavalry
15 Odrysian cavalry
16 Thracian javelineers
17 Cretan archers
18 Mercenaries
19 Second line infantry

C.J.Tuplin

Persians
A   Bactrian cavalry
B   Scythian, Massagetic cavalry
C   Chariots
D   Bactrians, Dahae, Arachosians, Susians, Persians, Cadusians (mostly cavalry)
E   Darius with Persian 'Kinsmen' & melophoroi, Indians, 'transplanted Carians', Mardian archers, Greek mercenaries
F   Reserve infantry (Uxians, Babylonians, Sitacenians, Red Sea men, Syrians, Mesopotamians, Medes
G   Parthians, Sacae, Tapurians, Hyrcanians, Albanians, Sacesinians (all cavalry)
H   Armenian cavalry
I   Cappadocian cavalry
J   Chariots
K   Chariots & elephants

Tyre, 332 BC

The sources are only in broad agreement, and none provides enough incident for a siege of seven months. Initial Macedonian attempts to provide a platform for siege engines by constructing a mole encountered the insuperable difficulty of protecting the workmen against Tyrian attacks from the walls and from ships. Alexander's acquisition of 224 ships from Cyprus, Phoenicia, Rhodes, Cilicia and Lycia was crucial. The Tyrian fleet was then confined to harbour; a small sortie from the north, Sidonian, harbour failed. The mole was completed—though in the event its role was largely diversionary—and a successful assault was mounted. Two ship-borne engines inflicted sufficient damage for an assault party under Alexander to seize a stretch of wall (?adjacent to the south harbour), while the fleet broke into the harbours. However the puzzle of why this attack succeeded when others had failed is never properly solved by any source.

Gaugamela, 331 BC

To quote Brunt, 'The diversity of modern accounts . . . shows that agreement . . . has not been attained and suggests that it is unattainable'. This entirely schematic plan shows the position just before first contact. The dispositions are from Arrian. The oblique Macedonian line, position of the wings, and extent of the Persian overlap, are arguable. Thereafter three stages may be identified:

(1) The Macedonian right [1–6] stalls attack by Darius' left wing [A, B, parts of D], while light-armed troops [8–10] neutralise a chariot attack [C].

(2) The Companions and infantry phalanx [7, 11] rout the now exposed Persian left/centre [rest of D, E]; Darius flees; the extreme left panics.

(3) The Macedonian left and left-centre phalanx comes under severe pressure: some Persian cavalry may have got through it, or around it, to the baggage camp. But apparently the phalanx holds its own unaided, since the Companions and other cavalry [7, 1] moving behind the lines encounter retreating Parthian cavalry. Controversy attaches particularly to this entire last stage of the battle.

RIVER HYDASPES, 326 B.C.

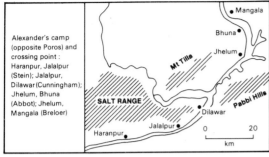

Alexander's camp (opposite Poros) and crossing point: Haranpur, Jalalpur (Stein); Jalalpur, Dilawar (Cunningham); Jhelum, Bhuna (Abbot); Jhelum, Mangala (Breloer)

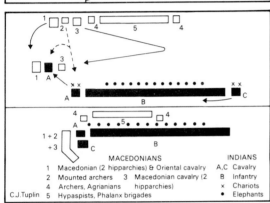

MACEDONIANS

1 Macedonian (2 hipparchies) & Oriental cavalry
2 Mounted archers
3 Macedonian cavalry (2 hipparchies)
4 Archers, Agrianians
5 Hypaspists, Phalanx brigades

INDIANS

A,C Cavalry
B Infantry
x Chariots
• Elephants

C.J.Tuplin

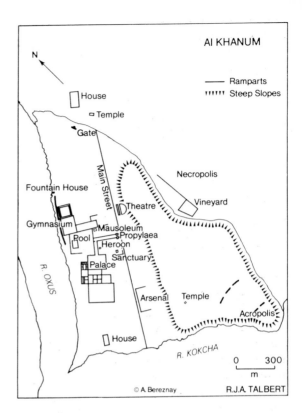

AI KHANUM

—— Ramparts
ɪɪɪɪɪɪ Steep Slopes

© A. Bereznay   R.J.A. TALBERT

River Hydaspes, 326 BC

The map illustrates (a) Alexander's surprise river crossing, for which Stein's location is generally preferred; and (b) the subsequent decisive battle. Poros' dispositions derive from Arrian; Alexander's are nowhere properly described. The extent of Indian overlap is debatable.

Alexander's initial cavalry victory drove the Indian horse onto the infantry line, and caused the elephants/infantry to attempt a leftward counter-movement. The Indian left's co-ordination was thus broken, and it was exposed to the Macedonian infantry, which pelted the elephants with missiles and then mounted a crushing mass charge. The chief problem is unit 3, which made for the Indian right but still participated in the cavalry battle. Probably it doubled back as shown, but some believe that Poros transferred his right-wing cavalry to the left—as is likely in any case—and that unit 3 followed them behind the Indian lines and attacked as they reached their goal.

Ai Khanum

The site of Ai Khanum ('Lady moon') takes its name from the nearby village in a remote frontier region where Afghanistan borders the USSR. Discovered by accident, it has been excavated by a French archaeological mission since 1965 to uncover the first evidence (beyond coins) of Greco-Bactrian civilisation. The city was most probably founded either by Alexander or Seleucus, and flourished for nearly 200 years until its violent destruction at the hands of nomadic invaders in the late first century BC. Its situation at the confluence of the Oxus and Kokcha was well chosen, with an acropolis rising to 60 metres reinforced by ramparts, especially to the exposed north east. The best residential area (to the south west) and the city's extensive public buildings were concentrated in the flat area between the left bank of the R. Oxus and a straight main street running below the acropolis. Throughout there appears a revealing blend of Oriental influence and traditional Greek elements.

69

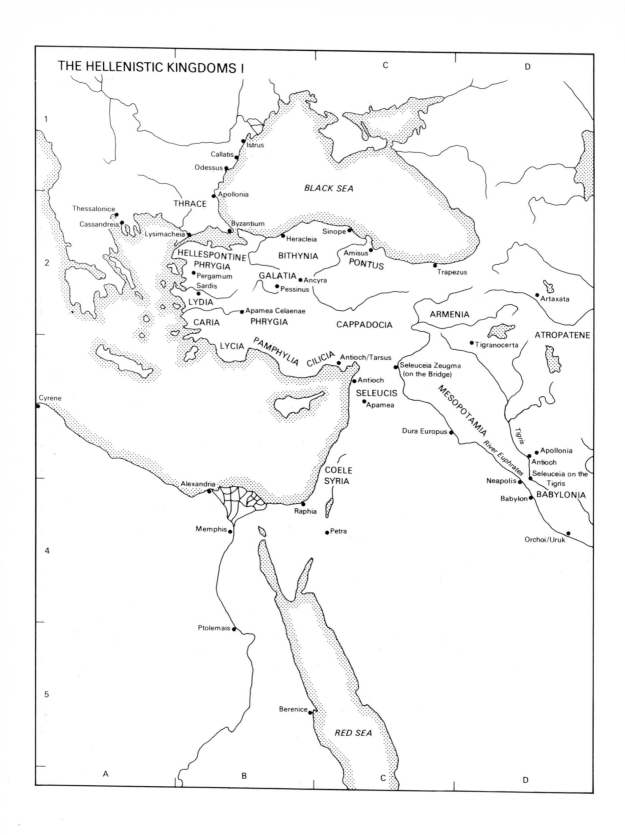

THE HELLENISTIC KINGDOMS I

Istrus
Callatis
Odessus
Apollonia
THRACE
Thessalonice
Cassandreia
Lysimacheia
Byzantium
BLACK SEA
Heracleia
Sinope
HELLESPONTINE
PHRYGIA
BITHYNIA
Amisus
PONTUS
Pergamum
GALATIA
Ancyra
Trapezus
Sardis
Pessinus
Artaxata
LYDIA
ARMENIA
CARIA
Apamea Celaenae
PHRYGIA
ATROPATENE
CAPPADOCIA
Tigranocerta
LYCIA
PAMPHYLIA
CILICIA
Antioch/Tarsus
MESOPOTAMIA
Cyrene
Antioch
Seleuceia Zeugma
(on the Bridge)
SELEUCIS
Apamea
Dura Europus
River Euphrates
Tigris
Apollonia
Antioch
Seleuceia on the
Tigris
Neapolis
Alexandria
COELE
SYRIA
Babylon
BABYLONIA
Raphia
Memphis
Petra
Orchoi/Uruk

Ptolemais

Berenice
RED SEA

A   B   C   D

70

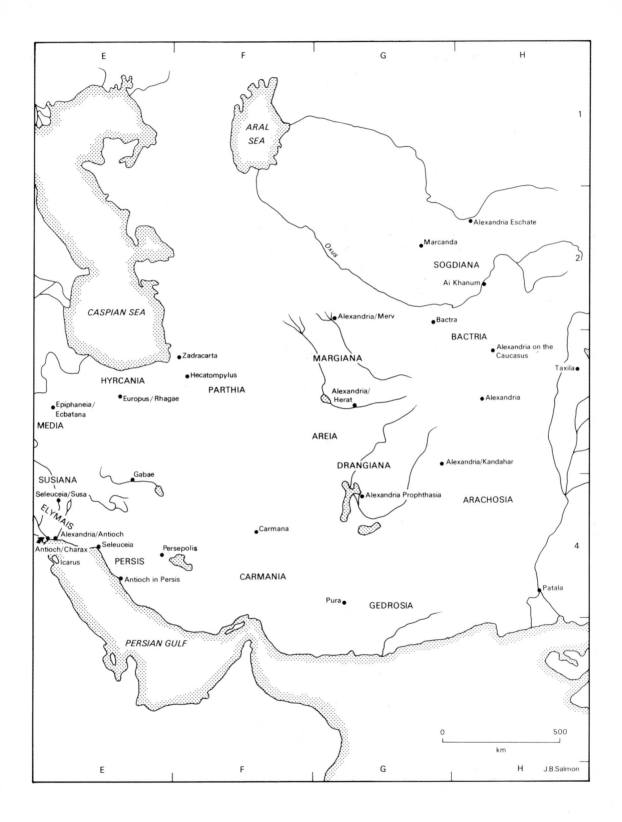

ARAL
SEA

E   F   G   H

1

• Alexandria Eschate

• Marcanda

SOGDIANA

2

Ai Khanum •

CASPIAN SEA

• Alexandria/Merv

• Bactra

BACTRIA

• Zadracarta

MARGIANA

• Alexandria on the
Caucasus

Taxila •

• Hecatompylus

• Alexandria

HYRCANIA

PARTHIA

• Europus / Rhagae

Alexandria/
Herat

• Epiphaneia/
Ecbatana

AREIA

MEDIA

DRANGIANA

• Alexandria/Kandahar

Gabae

SUSIANA

Seleuceia/Susa

Alexandria Prophthasia

ARACHOSIA

ELYMAIS

Alexandria/Antioch

Antioch/Charax

Seleuceia

• Carmana

Persepolis

4

Icarus

PERSIS

• Antioch in Persis

CARMANIA

Patala

Pura •

GEDROSIA

PERSIAN GULF

0   500

km

E   F   G   H   J.B.Salmon

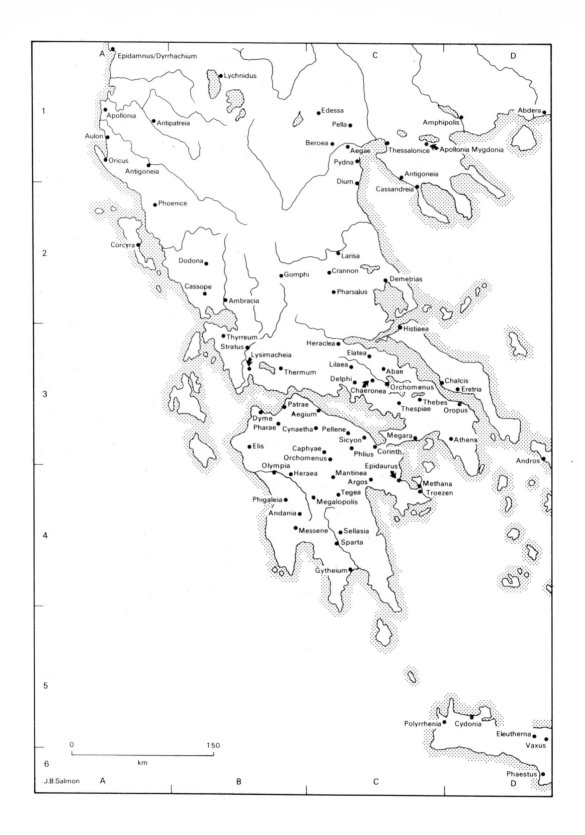

A · Epidamnus/Dyrrhachium

C

D

• Lychnidus

1

Apollonia •
• Edessa
• Antipatreia
Pella •
Amphipolis
• Abdera
Aulon •
Beroea •
Thessalonice
Apollonia Mygdonia
Oricus •
Aegae •
• Antigoneia
Pydna •
Antigoneia •
• Phoenice
Dium •
Cassandreia •

2
Corcyra •
• Larisa
• Dodona
• Crannon
• Demetrias
• Cassope
• Gomphi
• Ambracia
Pharsalus •

• Histiaea
• Thyrreum
Heraclea •
Stratus •
Elatea •
Lysimacheia
Lilaea •
• Abae
• Chalcis
• Thermum
Delphi •
Orchomenus
• Eretria
Chaeronea •
Thebes •
3
Patrae •
Aegium •
Thespiae •
Oropus •
Dyme •
Pharae •
Cynaetha •
Pellene •
Megara •
Sicyon •
• Athens
• Elis
Caphyae •
Phlius •
Corinth •
Orchomenus •
Epidaurus
Andros
Olympia •
Heraea •
Mantinea •
Methana
Argos •
Troezen
Phigaleia •
Tegea •
Andania •
Megalopolis •

4
Messene •
Sellasia •
Sparta •

Gytheium •

5

Polyrrhenia •
• Cydonia
Eleutherna •
• Vaxus

0   150

km
6
J.B.Salmon   A   B   C   D

Phaestus •

72

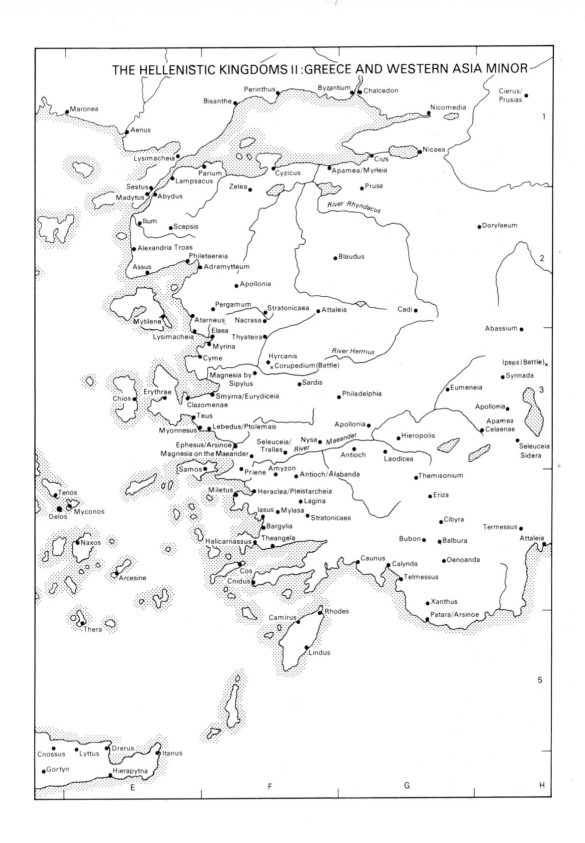

THE HELLENISTIC KINGDOMS II: GREECE AND WESTERN ASIA MINOR

Maronea

Perinthus · · Byzantium
Bisanthe · · · Chalcedon · Cierus/Prusias
Aenus · Nicomedia

1

Lysimacheia · · Cius · Nicaea
Parium · Cyzicus · Apamea/Myrleia
Lampsacus · Zelea · Prusa
Sestus · · Dorylaeum
Madytus · Abydus · River Rhyndacus
Ilium · Scepsis

2

Alexandria Troas · Blaudus
Philetaereia
Assus · Adramytteum
Apollonia · Abassium
Pergamum · Stratonicaea
Mytilene · Nacrasa · Attaleia · Cadi
Atarneus
Elaea · Thyateira
Lysimacheia · Myrina
Cyme · Hyrcanis · River Hermus · Ipsus (Battle) ×
Corupedium (Battle) × · Synnada
Magnesia by Sipylus · Sardis
Chios · Erythrae · Smyrna/Eurydiceia · Philadelphia · Eumeneia

3

Clazomenae · Apollonia
Teus · Apamea
Myonnesus · Apollonia · Celaenae
Lebedus/Ptolemais · Hieropolis · Seleuceia Sidera
Ephesus/Arsinoe · Seleuceia/Tralles · Nysa · Maeander River
Magnesia on the Maeander · Antioch · Laodicea
Samos · Priene · Amyzon
Antioch/Alabanda · Themisonium
Miletus · Heraclea/Pleistarcheia · Eriza
Tenos · Lagina
Myconos · Iasus · Mylasa · Stratonicaea
Delos · Bargylia · Cibyra · Termessus
Naxos · Theangela · Bubon · Balbura · Attaleia
Halicarnassus · Caunus · Oenoanda
Arcesine · Cos · Calynda
Cnidus · Telmessus
Xanthus

5

Camirus · Rhodes · Patara/Arsinoe
Thera
Lindus

Cnossus · Lyttus · Drerus · Itanus
Gortyn · Hierapytna

E   F   G   H

73

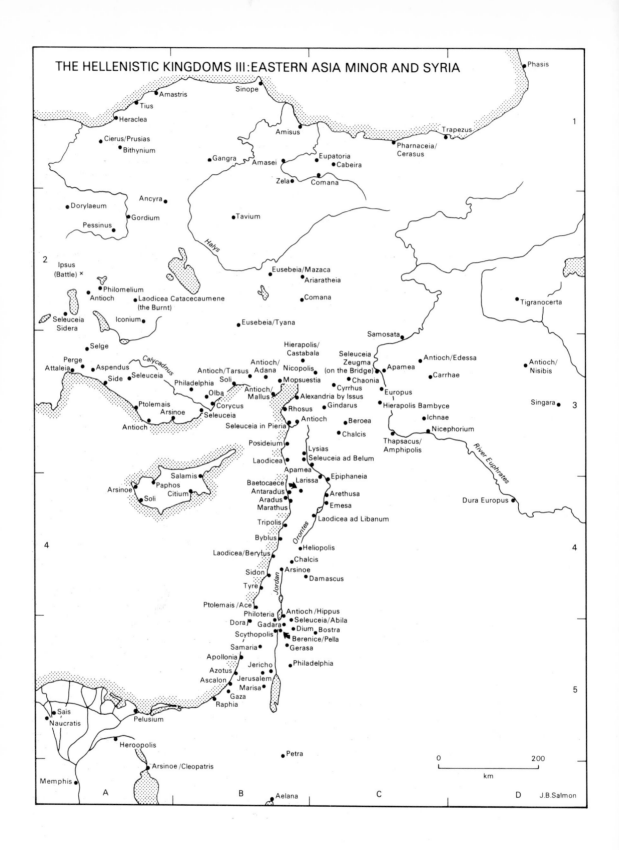

THE HELLENISTIC KINGDOMS III: EASTERN ASIA MINOR AND SYRIA

Phasis

1

Amastris
Sinope
Tius
Heraclea
Trapezus
Amisus
Pharnaceia/
Cierus/Prusias
Cerasus
Bithynium
Gangra
Eupatoria
Amasei
Cabeira
Zela
Comana

Ancyra
Dorylaeum
Gordium
Tavium
Pessinus
Halys

2
Ipsus
(Battle) ×
Eusebeia/Mazaca
Ariaratheia
Philomelium
Antioch
Laodicea Catacecaumene
Comana
(the Burnt)
Tigranocerta
Seleuceia
Sidera
Iconium
Eusebeia/Tyana

Selge
Samosata
Hierapolis/
Castabala
Seleuceia
Antioch/Edessa
Antioch/
Perge
Zeugma
Apamea
Nisibis
Attaleia
Aspendus
Antioch/Adana
Nicopolis
(on the Bridge)
Carrhae
Side
Seleuceia
Tarsus
Chaonia
Philadelphia
Soli
Mopsuestia
Cyrrhus
Europus
Olba
Antioch/
Alexandria by Issus
Hierapolis Bambyce
Singara
3
Ptolemais
Mallus
Gindarus
Corycus
Rhosus
Ichnae
Arsinoe
Seleuceia
Antioch
Beroea
Nicephorium
Antioch
Seleuceia in Pieria
Chalcis
Thapsacus/
Amphipolis
Posideium
Laodicea
Lysias
Seleuceia ad Belum
River Euphrates
Salamis
Apamea
Epiphaneia
Arsinoe
Paphos
Larissa
Baetocaece
Antaradus
Arethusa
Citium
Soli
Aradus
Emesa
Marathus
Laodicea ad Libanum
Dura Europus
Tripolis
Orontes
4
Byblus
4
Heliopolis
Laodicea/Berytus
Chalcis
Sidon
Arsinoe
Tyre
Damascus
Jordan
Ptolemais/Ace
Philoteria
Antioch/Hippus
Dora
Gadara
Seleuceia/Abila
Scythopolis
Dium
Bostra
Samaria
Berenice/Pella
Gerasa
Apollonia
Jericho
Azotus
Philadelphia
Ascalon
Jerusalem
Marisa
5
Gaza
Raphia
Sais
Naucratis
Pelusium

Heroopolis
Petra
0
200
Arsinoe/Cleopatris
km
Memphis
A
B
C
D
J.B.Salmon
Aelana

74

The Hellenistic Kingdoms

While Alexander greatly increased the scale of the Greek world, the successor kingdoms never quite achieved stability in their inheritance. The Ptolemaic dynasty in Egypt was both the first to be securely established and the last to fall, when Augustus defeated Antony and Cleopatra in 30 BC. Antigonus Monophthalmus gained control of Syria and Asia Minor, but lost it at Ipsus in 301; his descendants did not establish a secure hold in the Hellenistic world until a quarter of a century later, when Antigonus Gonatas gained Macedon. The dynasty finally fell after defeat by the Romans at Pydna in 168. The foundation of the Seleucid dynasty was laid by Seleucus in the eastern part of Alexander's realm while Syria was controlled by Antigonus Monophthalmus. Seleucus and Lysimachus, then in command of Thrace, defeated Antigonus at Ipsus; Lysimachus won Asia Minor and Seleucus north Syria. Twenty years later Seleucus defeated Lysimachus at Corupedium and gained Asia Minor. The Attalid dynasty of Pergamum remained a minor power until the Seleucids were excluded from Asia Minor, following the Roman victory over Antiochus III at Magnesia-by-Sipylus in 190.

A major feature of the period was the foundation of new cities, often with dynastic names. The trend, begun by Alexander, was continued especially by the Seleucids. Cities reinforced royal control, and offered familiar institutions to the Greek and Macedonian settlers who fulfilled a key military and administrative role. Many native settlements were eventually granted city status. Cities enjoyed a theoretical independence, though in practice they generally recognised that their interests coincided with those of the kings. Even in the Greek homeland new cities such as Demetrias, and Lysimacheia in the Thracian Chersonese, were founded by the kings, or old cities were strengthened, to secure control of strategically vital regions. By contrast, the Ptolemies' control of Egypt was secure enough to make new cities superfluous; their only foundation was the early one of Ptolemais.

The Seleucids' realm cannot be accurately defined at any stage. Once established in north Syria, they secured it with numerous city foundations in what came to be known as the Seleucis. This controlled communications either side of the desert between Coele Syria and Mesopotamia, both with Egypt and further east along the rivers Tigris and Euphrates. It also gave Seleucus his only westward sea communications; when he gained Asia Minor it became less exposed on the periphery of the realm, but Seleucid control in Asia Minor was only ever partial. The Ptolemies maintained possessions in the south, while independent states were strung along the north coast. The Galatians were gradually restricted to what came to be known as Galatia; and the Attalids were independent long before they profited from the Roman desire to exclude the Seleucids. Rebels exploited the difficulty of maintaining control over the enormous realm, and kings faced attempts at secession both in Asia Minor and in the 'Upper Satrapies' beyond Seleuceia on the Tigris. Seleucus I had already yielded the easternmost portions of Alexander's conquests to Chandragupta, while royal subordinates later seceded in Bactria and Parthia. Antiochus III restored control briefly. But pressure from the Parthians combined with that of Rome to squeeze the Seleucids into north Syria, where they were finally suppressed by Pompey.

The power of the Ptolemies was based on the wealth of Egypt; but in the late fourth and third centuries they enjoyed widespread possessions in southern Asia Minor, the Aegean and even mainland Greece. Despite his failure to participate at Ipsus—indeed perhaps because of it—Ptolemy I profited by seizing Coele Syria; the area was disputed with the Seleucids in various 'Syrian Wars' until Antiochus III gained it, along with a problematic relationship with the Jews, in 200. Major internal difficulties, created both by rebellious Egyptians and by dynastic disputes, prevented the Ptolemies from playing a significant positive role in the Mediterranean world in the second century.

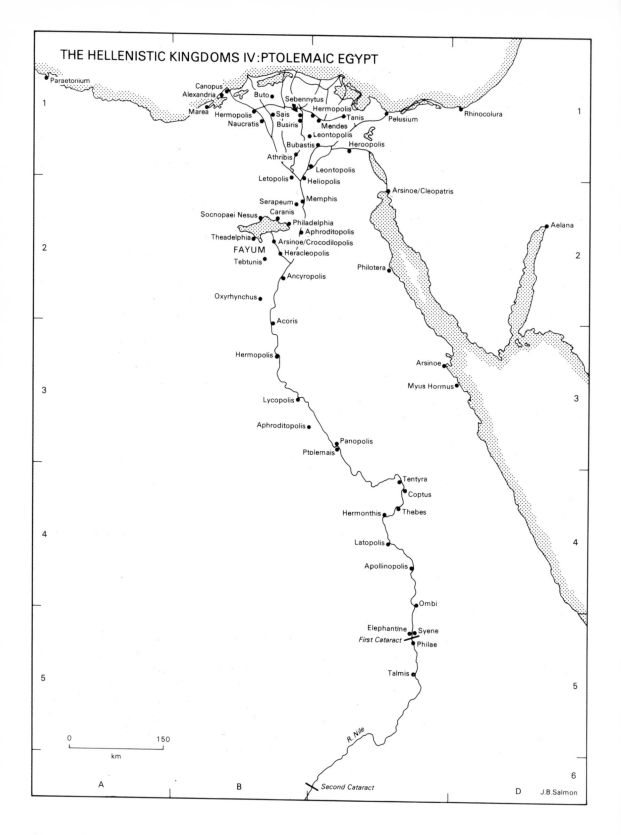

THE HELLENISTIC KINGDOMS IV: PTOLEMAIC EGYPT

Paraetonium

Canopus
Alexandria
Marea
Hermopolis
Naucratis
Buto
Sebennytus
Hermopolis
Sais
Busiris
Mendes
Tanis
Pelusium
Rhinocolura
Leontopolis
Bubastis
Heroopolis
Athribis
Leontopolis
Letopolis
Heliopolis
Arsinoe/Cleopatris
Serapeum
Memphis
Socnopaei Nesus
Caranis
Philadelphia
Theadelphia
Aphroditopolis
Arsinoe/Crocodilopolis
FAYUM
Heracleopolis
Tebtunis
Ancyropolis
Philotera
Oxyrhynchus
Aelana
Acoris
Hermopolis
Arsinoe
Lycopolis
Myus Hormus
Aphroditopolis
Panopolis
Ptolemais
Tentyra
Coptus
Hermonthis
Thebes
Latopolis
Apollinopolis
Ombi
Elephantine
Syene
First Cataract
Philae
Talmis
R. Nile

0   150
km

A   B   D   J.B.Salmon

Second Cataract

76

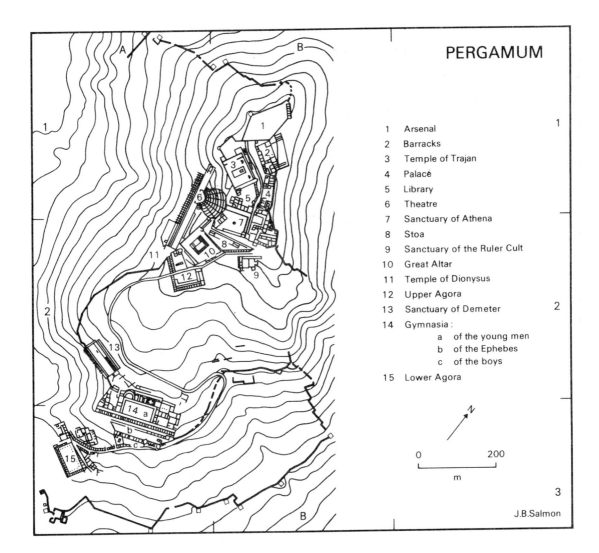

PERGAMUM

1 Arsenal
2 Barracks
3 Temple of Trajan
4 Palace
5 Library
6 Theatre
7 Sanctuary of Athena
8 Stoa
9 Sanctuary of the Ruler Cult
10 Great Altar
11 Temple of Dionysus
12 Upper Agora
13 Sanctuary of Demeter
14 Gymnasia:
    a of the young men
    b of the Ephebes
    c of the boys
15 Lower Agora

0   200

m

J.B.Salmon

Pergamum

Lysimachus, when he controlled Asia Minor, left Philetaerus in charge of his treasury at Pergamum and enabled him to lay the foundations for the Attalid dynasty. It increased its status with the defeat of the Galatians of central Asia Minor by Attalus I in the 230s. Pergamum, built on a steep rocky hill, reflects both its standing as a royal capital, and what was expected of a well-appointed Hellenistic city. The gymnasium, with its three sections (14a–c), was the largest in the Greek world. The arsenal (1), barracks (2), and palace (4) were situated appropriately at the top of the hill. The library (5) shows the Attalids as patrons of learning, while the sculptural decoration of the Great Altar of Zeus (10), depicting the battle between Gods and Giants, symbolises the victory over the Galatians.

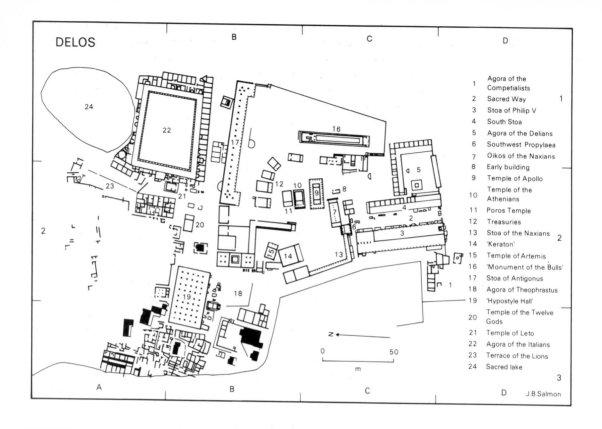

1	Agora of the Competialists
2	Sacred Way
3	Stoa of Philip V
4	South Stoa
5	Agora of the Delians
6	Southwest Propylaea
7	Oikos of the Naxians
8	Early building
9	Temple of Apollo
10	Temple of the Athenians
11	Poros Temple
12	Treasuries
13	Stoa of the Naxians
14	'Keraton'
15	Temple of Artemis
16	'Monument of the Bulls'
17	Stoa of Antigonus
18	Agora of Theophrastus
19	'Hypostyle Hall'
20	Temple of the Twelve Gods
21	Temple of Leto
22	Agora of the Italians
23	Terrace of the Lions
24	Sacred lake

J.B.Salmon

Delos

The earliest known temple (11) on the tiny Aegean island of Delos is as late as the sixth century; but other buildings (7, 8) on the site reflect a much earlier origin for the cult of Apollo here. A huge marble statue of kouros type, made in the early sixth century, stood in the open air against the north wall of the Oikos (House) of the Naxians (7); and a terrace which looked over the approach from the north was embellished by a series of marble lions (23). When the Delian League was founded, a new temple (9) was begun; but it was not completed until Hellenistic times, perhaps because of the removal of the treasury of the League to Athens in 454. A third temple (10) was constructed by the Athenians during the Peloponnesian War, and the island was ritually purified. But there was never a large temple on the site. Since the whole island was thought to be sacred, the sanctuary was not clearly defined. Other deities besides Apollo had temples,

among them his sister Artemis (15), and their mother Leto (21). A sacred dance was performed in front of the Keraton (14).

The fourth century saw little development; but during the Hellenistic period the first major structures were erected. Kings of the Antigonid dynasty of Macedon constructed two stoas (3, 17), and an Antigonus (probably Gonatas) built what is known from part of its decoration as the Monument of the Bulls (16) to house a ship dedicated in memory of a naval victory. The numerous agoras (1, 5, 18, 22) reflect the Hellenistic development of Delos as a commercial centre, and the 'Hypostyle Hall' (19) may have been connected with similar activity. Structures for other deities, often showing the cosmopolitan origins of the traders who frequented the island, were to be found elsewhere; and especially to the south of the main sacred area there were residential quarters.

Major Cult Centres of the Classical World

No maps can show the complexities of religion in the classical world. Personal beliefs defy geography, and polytheism itself took many forms. There were cults of most of the Olympian gods in every great city and in many lesser ones. The maps here present a selection of major shrines, oracles, and centres of worship, all notable for political or literary reasons. Cults of heroes, and places merely mentioned in the legends associated with deities, are generally excluded except for the cult of the 'demi-god' Heracles, and the special case of the oracle of the seer Amphiaraus. No attempt has been made to mark all shrines known in major centres of population, such as Rome, Ostia or Athens. It should be recognised that cult was also paid everywhere to numerous local heroes—such as Oedipus at Colonus, or Neoptolemus at Delphi, to name but two prominent in the literary tradition.

The picture which emerges cannot reveal the numerically dominant cult in particular areas. The cults of Iuppiter and Mars, for example, were in fact predominant throughout Italy. Equally it has not proved possible to trace on the maps the rise and decline of different sites. For instance, the Olympic Games are important from the earliest historical times, while the mysteries of the Cabiri on Samothrace only assume significance first in the fourth century, and reach their heyday much later; the latter point applies also to the sites of the Asia Minor coast. The emphasis in these maps is on cults vigorous in the classical period.

The map of the Aegean World attempts to show, within the constraints of present knowledge, four principal features as follows: cults, festivals and sites of panhellenic importance (oracles, games, mysteries); cults of unusual interest owing to the nature of their ritual (Brauron, Eleusis, Artemis Orthia at Sparta, Lebadea); cults where the archaeological evidence is especially illuminating or interesting (Bassae, Aegina); the legendary dwelling places of the gods, important in literary sources. In most of the cults, the ritual included an annual festival, often with races or other games. Where the names of the festivals do not echo that of

the god honoured, they may be traced through the works cited in the 'Suggestions for Further Reading'. It should be noted that because of the strong Minoan-Mycenaean heritage, *Cretan* gods and cults differ from those of the mainland. Most Cretan gods, however, came to be identified with counterparts from the latter group in the classical period. The cults shown in Sicily and south Italy reflect some of the vigorous temple building of the tyrants of the sixth and fifth centuries BC. It is hard to tell how far the sites of temples there continue the traditional cult sites of pre-Greek times.

In some parts of the ancient world major cult centres were so few that no attempt has been made to map these areas. For the western provinces of the Roman Empire, the table in R. MacMullen, *Paganism in the Roman Empire*, p. 6, shows that—apart from Iuppiter, whose cult was pre-eminent here—the most popular gods in dedicatory inscriptions were as follows, in descending order of frequency:

Gaul and Germany: Mercury, Mars, Apollo, Hercules, Mithras/Sol, Fortuna, Cybele, Silvanus;

North Africa: Mercury, Liber, Fortuna, Mars, Venus, Hercules, Aesculapius, Silvanus;

Italy (apart from Rome and Ostia): Hercules, Mercury, Fortuna, Silvanus, Diana, Isis/Serapis, Mithras/Sol, Venus, Mars;

North-central provinces: Silvanus, Mithras/Sol, Diana, Hercules, Liber.

Further complication was caused by the tendency to identify gods of one people with those of another (syncretism). Greeks gave the names of their Greek gods to the deities whose cults they encountered in Egypt; Romanised Celts identified their own gods with those of the Romans, or combined two names of originally separate divinities (like Mars Segomo). The most important series of identifications—the *interpretatio romana* of the main Greek deities—appears on p. 81.

Many gods appear in the same form in Greek and Latin: for example, Apollo (Phoebus), Cybele, Hecate, Isis, Uranus. For some Roman gods—such as Ianus and Iuturna—no Greek equivalent was found.

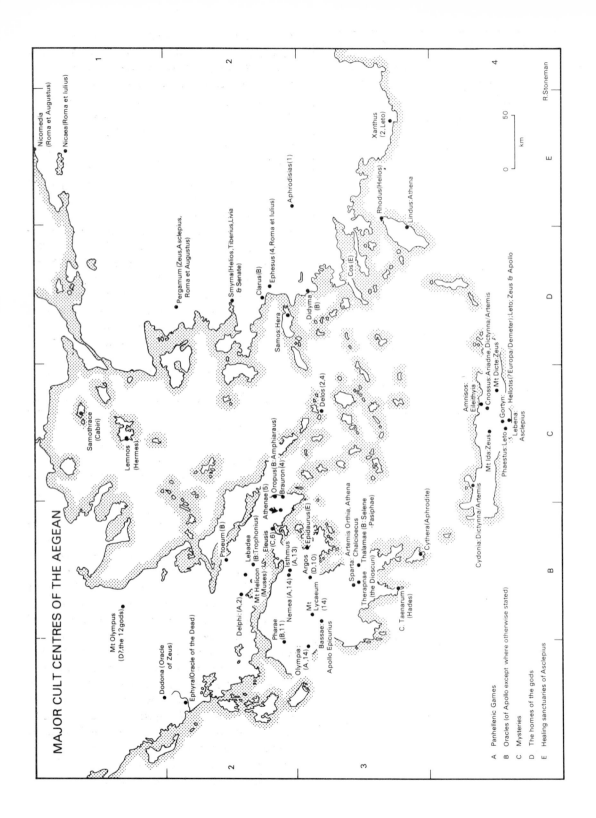

MAJOR CULT CENTRES OF THE AEGEAN

A Panhellenic Games
B Oracles (of Apollo except where otherwise stated)
C Mysteries
D The homes of the gods
E Healing sanctuaries of Asclepius

Nicomedia
(Roma et Augustus)
Nicaea(Roma et Iulius)

Xanthus
(2, Leto)

Aphrodisias(1)

Rhodus(Helios)
Lindus:Athena

Pergamum (Zeus,Asclepius,
Roma et Augustus)

Smyrna(Helios, Tiberius,Livia
& Senate)

Clarus(B)

Ephesus (4, Roma et Iulius)

Samos:Hera

Didyma
(B)

Cos (E)

Samothrace
(Cabiri)

Lemnos
(Hermes)

Delos (2,4)

Amnisos:
Eileithyia

Cnossus:Ariadne,Dictynna/Artemis
Mt Dicte:Zeus

Mt Ida:Zeus

Phaestus: Leto;   Gortyn:
Lebena: Heliotis(?Europa/Demeter);Leto; Zeus & Apollo
Asclepius

Cydonia:Dictynna/Artemis

Mt Olympus
(D?,the 12 gods)

Dodona (Oracle
of Zeus)

Ephyra(Oracle of the Dead)

Delphi: (A.2)

Ptoeum(B)

Lebadea
(B:Trophonius)

Mt Helicon
(Muses)

Eleusis
(C.6)

Isthmus'
(A.13)

Oropus(B: Amphiaraus)

Athenae(5)
Brauron(4)

Epidaurus(E)

Sparta: Artemis Orthia, Athena
Chalcioecus

Thalamae (B: Selene
-Pasiphae)

Cythera (Aphrodite)

Pharae
(B.11)

Nemea (A.14)

Argos
(D.10)

Mt
Lycaeum
(14)

Therapnae
(the Dioscuri)

Olympia:
(A.14)

Bassae:
Apollo Epicurius

C. Taenarum
(Hades)

R.Stoneman

0   50
km

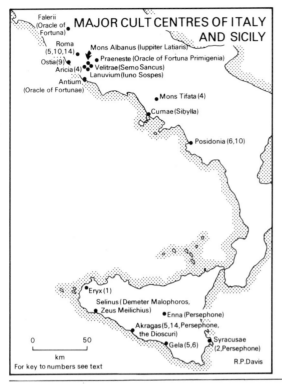

MAJOR CULT CENTRES OF ITALY AND SICILY

Falerii (Oracle of Fortuna)
Roma (5,10,14)
Ostia (9)
Aricia (4)
Antium (Oracle of Fortunae)
Mons Albanus (Iuppiter Latiaris)
Praeneste (Oracle of Fortuna Primigenia)
Velitrae (Semo Sancus)
Lanuvium (Iuno Sospes)
Mons Tifata (4)
Cumae (Sibylla)
Posidonia (6,10)
Eryx (1)
Selinus (Demeter Malophoros, Zeus Meilichius)
Enna (Persephone)
Akragas (5,14, Persephone, the Dioscuri)
Gela (5,6)
Syracusae (2, Persephone)

0   50
km
For key to numbers see text

R.P.Davis

The Great Olympians (numbered as on both maps opposite): 1. Aphrodite = Venus; 2. Apollo = Apollo; 3. Ares = Mars; 4. Artemis = Diana; 5. Athene = Minerva; 6. Demeter = Ceres; 7. Dionysus (Iacchus, Bacchus) = Liber Pater (Bacchus); 8. Hades (Pluton) = Dis (Pluto); 9. Hephaestus = Volcanus; 10. Hera = Iuno; 11. Hermes = Mercurius; 12. Hestia = Vesta; 13. Poseidon = Neptunus; 14. Zeus = Iuppiter.

Other deities: Amphitrite = Salacia; Asklepios = Aesculapius; Charites = Gratiae (the Graces); Cronos = Saturnus; Eileithyia = Lucina; Enyo = Bellona; Eōs = Aurora (Dawn); Erinyes = Furiae (the Furies); Erōs = Cupidus; Gaia = Tellus (Earth); Hebe = Iuventas; Helios = Sol (Sun); Hygieia = Salus (Health); Leto = Latona; Moirae = Fata *or* Parcae (the Fates); Nike = Victoria; Pan = Faunus; Persephone (Kore) = Proserpina (Libera); Satyres = Satyres, Fauni *or* Sileni; Selene = Luna (Moon); Silenus = Silvanus; Tyche = Fortuna.

Heroes: Aias = Aiax; Hekabe = Hecuba; Heracles = Hercules; Odysseus = Ulixes.

ALEXANDRIA

0   1,000
m

1	Lighthouse	11	Theatre
2	Cape Loxias	12	Caesareum/Sebasteum
3	Royal Harbour	13	Emporium
4	Antirrhodus	14	Dockyards
5	Timonium	15	Serapeum, 'Pompey's Pillar' (Column of Diocletian)
6	Great Harbour	16	Small Late Roman Theatre
7	Heptastadium	17	Cemeteries
8	Cibotus Harbour	18	
9	Eunostus Harbour		
10	Palaces, Museum, Tomb of Alexander & the Ptolemies		

J.B.Salmon

Alexandria

Alexandria was Alexander's first foundation; it soon became the capital of the Ptolemies. The Heptastadium joined the island of Pharos to the mainland and created two main harbours. The royal palaces, the tomb of Alexander and the museum and library were all to be found in the same region of the city: from the latter two institutions those attracted by Ptolemaic patronage led the intellectual life of the Hellenistic world. Alexandria's commercial significance is shown by the emporium, with its customs and warehouses. Very little, however, has been uncovered, although cemeteries to east and west presumably define the area inhabited by the mixed Greek, Jewish and Egyptian population. The Serapeum is known from excavation; the site of the Caesareum, later the Sebasteum (Augusteum), was marked by two obelisks removed in the nineteenth century to London (Cleopatra's Needle) and New York. But in general our knowledge of the Ptolemaic city still depends mainly on Strabo's description.

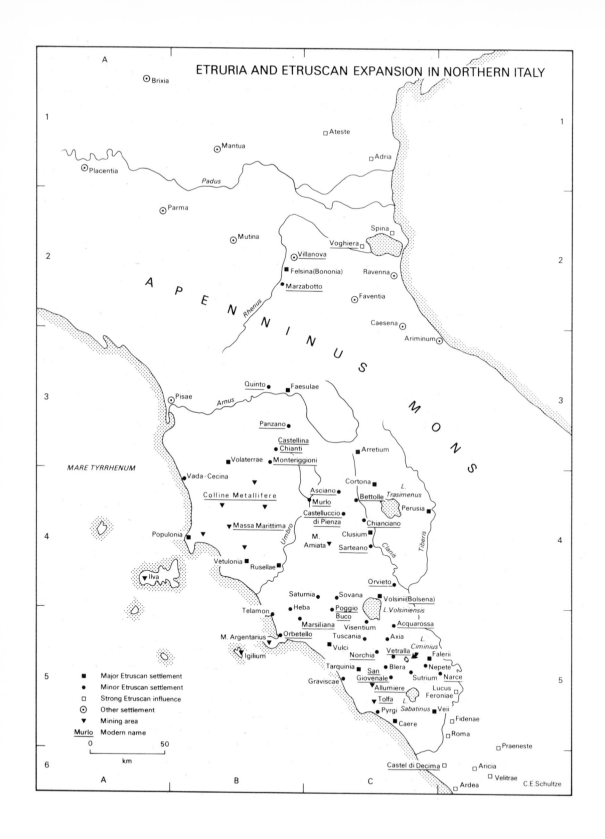

ETRURIA AND ETRUSCAN EXPANSION IN NORTHERN ITALY

⊙ Brixia

☐ Ateste

⊙ Mantua

☐ Adria

⊙ Placentia

Padus

⊙ Parma

Spina

⊙ Mutina

Voghiera ☐

⊙ Villanova

■ Felsina(Bononia)

Ravenna ⊙

■ Marzabotto

Rhenus

Faventia ⊙

A P E N

Caesena ⊙

N I N U S

Ariminum ⊙

Quinto ● ■ Faesulae

Pisae ●

Arnus

M O N S

Panzano ●

Castellina ● Chianti

■ Arretium

MARE TYRRHENUM

Volaterrae ● ● Monteriggioni

Cortona ●

L.

Vada - Cecina ●

Trasimenus

▼

Asciano ●

Bettolle ●

▼ Murlo

● Perusia

Colline Metallifere

Castelluccio ● di Pienza

● Chianciano

▼

Umbro

M. ▼ Clusium ☐

▼ Massa Marittima

Amiata ▼ Sarteano ●

Clanis

Tiberis

Populonia ■ ▼

Vetulonia ■ ● Rusellae

● Orvieto

▼ Ilva

Saturnia ● ● Sovana

Volsinii(Bolsena) ■

Telamon ● ● Heba

● Poggio Buco

L.Volsiniensis

Marsiliana ● ● Visentium

● Acquarossa

M. Argentarius ● Orbetello

Tuscania ●

● Axia

L.

▽ Igilium

● Vulci

Norchia ● Vetralla

Ciminius

● Falerii

Tarquinia ■

San Blera ● ● Nepete

Graviscae ● Giovenale ●

Sutrium ● Narce

Allumiere ●

Lucus Feroniae ☐

▼ Tolfa

L.

● Pyrgi ● Axia

Sabatinus

■ Veii

● Caere

☐ Fidenae

☐ Roma

☐ Praeneste

■ Major Etruscan settlement

● Minor Etruscan settlement

☐ Strong Etruscan influence

⊙ Other settlement

▼ Mining area

Murlo Modern name

Castel di Decima ☐

☐ Aricia

0   50

☐ Velitrae

km

C.E.Schultze

☐ Ardea

A   B   C

Etruria and Etruscan Expansion in Northern Italy

Etruria proper is bounded by the rivers Arnus and Tiber and stretches from the Tyrrhenian Sea to the Apennines. Much of the terrain—like the Colline Metallifere and Mons Amiata—is mountainous, or at least hilly. The volcanic activity which created Lake Volsiniensis and other crater lakes also formed soft tufa rock which breaks down easily to form a fertile soil. There are alluvial river valleys and small coastal plains. In classical times, at Veii and elsewhere irrigation improved natural fertility. There were easy communications by sea and along the navigable Arnus and Tiber; many smaller rivers, too, linked inland towns to the coast. An important route was provided by the Clanis and Tiber: it joined the northern and southern cities, and through Rome or Praeneste gave access to the Liris-Volturnus route into Campania. Northwards, a route led from the mid-Arnus over the Apennine watershed to the Rhenus, and thence to Felsina and the Po. Mineral deposits exploited from the Bronze Age explain early Etruscan prosperity. Ilva (Elba) produced iron, Volaterrae copper, Tolfa iron and copper, while the Colline Metallifere yielded copper, silver, and lead.

Etruscan civilisation flourished from the eighth century and reached its height in the sixth century. Its heartland roughly corresponds with the southern area of Villanovan influence—an Iron Age culture (900–700) named after Villanova, near Felsina, where the first finds were made. While Villanovans played an important formative role, other influences, too, moulded Etruscan civilisation, especially from the east. In the seventh century Etruscan city-states developed, typically consisting of a planned urban centre, with an agricultural hinterland and a cluster of satellite towns. In addition to alliances, a loose confederation of 12 cities—the 'Etruscan dodecapolis'—is recorded, probably religious rather than political in character. Within communities a wealthy elite controlled a large class of dependants. South Etruria developed first, with the growth of towns such as Tarquinia, Caere, Vulci and Veii: lying on accessible trading routes, these centres achieved a high degree of skill in metal-working, pottery, and other crafts. More northerly inland towns like Clusium soon followed. Later their flourishing agriculture enabled them to remain prosperous after the coastal towns had started to decline in the fifth century.

Etruscans crossed the Apennines to settle in the Po valley, where their most important towns were Felsina, Marzabotto and Mantua. Down to the fourth century there was also considerable interchange with other communities both north and south of the Po, and along the Adriatic coast. In the fifth century Adria and especially Spina became major centres for trade with Greece. Southwards, Etruscans settled at Capua and elsewhere in Campania as far as the Salernum area (see p. 115). Sources mention a dodecapolis in both the Po area and Campania. Despite the difficulties which the story raises, it reflects a strong tradition about the scope of Etruscan power. Notable influence in Latium is best documented for Rome: an Etruscan dynasty ruled here from the late seventh century, and constitutional, religious, and artistic influences are clear. Remains from Praeneste and other Latin towns similarly reflect close links.

Etruscan sea-power brought contact with Corsica, Sardinia and the Phoenicians. Commercial and military alliances were made between Etruscans and Carthaginians, who shared a common interest in resisting Greek penetration of the Western Mediterranean. Nonetheless Etruscans traded extensively with Greeks, as well as developing and transmitting an alphabet derived from that used by the Greeks of Cumae in the eighth century.

From the late sixth century Etruscan power began to decline, with the fall of the Etruscan dynasty at Rome, and defeats by Latins and Cumaeans at Aricia c. 504, and by the Syracusans off Cumae in 474. In the north, Celts pressed on the Po area in the later fifth century, and reached north Etruria in the fourth century. Finally Rome took the offensive. Veii fell first, in 396; with the conquest of Falerii in 241, the whole of Etruria was under Roman domination.

EARLY ITALY

RAETI
CARNI

Comum
Mediolanum
CENOMANI
Brixia
Verona
VENETI
HISTRI
INSUBRES
Ateste
Mantua
Atria
LIGURES
FRINIATES
Padus
LINGONES
Spina
APUANI
Felsina
(Bononia)
BOII
Marzabotto
Ravenna
INGAUNI

Fanum
Novilara
SENONES
Ancona
UMBRI
Numana
Arretium
Iguvium
PICENTES
Murlo
Populonia
ETRUSCI
Clusium
Vetulonia
Tuder
Asculum
Campovalano
Volsinii
Interamna
Penna Sant'Andrea
Reate PRAETUTTII
Aleria
Vulci
SABINI
VESTINI
Tarquinii
Falerii
PAELIGNI
Capestrano
Gravisca
FALISCI
Cures
Allia
2 MARRUCINI
Caere
1
Tibur
AEQUI
Sulmo
FRENTANI
Rome
MARSI
Arpinum
4
Teanum Apulum
LATINI
HERNICI
3 Anagnia
Aufidena
5 Luceria Arpi Sipontum
Antium
VOLSCI AURUNCI
CARRICINI
DAUNI APULI Salapia
Tarracina
(OSCI) 6
PENTRI
SAMNITES
Aequum Canusium
Suessa Aurunca
SIDICINI
Cales
Tuticum Rubi Barium
Cumae
Capua
7 Caudium
Malventum
Melfi PEUCETII
Pithecusae
CAMPANI
Abella HIRPINI
Rossano di
Gnathia
Brundisium
CAUDINI
LUCANI
Vaglio
IAPYGES
MESSAPII
Lupiae
Pontecagnano
Sala
Tarentum
Manduria
Rudiae
Posidonia(Paestum)
Consilina OENOTRI
Metapontum
Uzentum
Velia
ITALIOTES
Thurii
Croton
Consentia
Hipponium
BRUTTII
ITALIOTES
Locri
Rhegium

Legend

DAUNI   6th-5th century peoples
RAETI   4th-3rd century peoples
□   Greek colony
●   Major settlement
Brixia Ancient name
Murlo   Modern name
+   Battle - Roman defeat

1 Veii
2 Corfinium
3 Praeneste
4 Pietrabbondante
5 Larinum
6 Teanum Sidicinum
7 Suessula

0   100
km

C.E.Schultze

Early Italy

Italy in the early historical period presented a diversity of peoples, with different languages, cultures, and levels of civilisation. From the fifth century, population movements, invasions and resettlement created considerable flux. Moreover, on the southern and western coasts, good communications by sea and land, together with the presence of foreign settlers and traders, contributed to the spread and exchange of cultural influences. The eastern side, with less favourable terrain and poorer communications—no navigable rivers or good harbours—was less affected by such development, while the Apennines limited westward contact. Impact from overseas is clear: from Carthaginians based in Corsica, Sardinia and Sicily; from Greeks (Italiotes), who since the eighth century had colonised the coast from Cumae to Tarentum (*Magna Graecia*) as well as Sicily; from Illyrians, known as Iapyges, who settled first in the heel of Italy and then spread north; and from Gauls, Celtic-speaking invaders from beyond the Alps.

In the north, from the fifth century Gallic tribes occupied the area which Romans called *Gallia Cisalpina*. The Insubres and Cenomani settled north of the R. Padus (Po): these Transpadane Gauls greatly influenced their neighbours the Veneti and Raeti, and also mingled with Ligurian tribes to the west. South of the river, the powerful Boii around Bononia, together with their kin the Lingones, ended Etruscan control of the Po valley area. The most southerly group, the Senones, occupied the Adriatic coastal region later known as *Ager Gallicus*. Celtic incursions reached Etruria, Latium and, in 390, Rome itself. Even when settled, the Gauls were widely regarded as a threat until the early second century—a factor which contributed to the establishment of Roman hegemony in Italy. In the north western Apennines lived the Ligures, a tough, semi-civilised people; only the coastal tribes enjoyed significant prosperity.

In peninsular Italy, the Etruscans, powerful until the fifth century, spread their civilisation to the Po area and Campania (see p. 82). East of Etruria, the Umbrian tribes formed a cultural, but not a political, unity. Picenum on the Adriatic was another region with a distinctive culture, but ethnically mixed, including a strong Sabellic (Oscan-speaking) element. The Praetuttii, too, were Sabellic. On the west coast, Rome's immediate neighbours were her kin the Latins; they and the Hernici were her earliest allies against fifth century incursions upon Latium by the Umbrian-speaking Aequi and Volsci. There were also early contacts with the Sabini, along the salt-route from the sea to their inland villages. The Aurunci were the last remaining element of the originally widespread Osci, overrun by more powerful neighbours. Italic peoples of the mid-Apennine area encountered by Rome in the fourth century were the Vestini, Marrucini, Paeligni and Frentani: all were Oscan-speakers living under various forms of tribal organisation, as did the Umbrian-speaking Marsi.

From the late fifth century the Sabellic tribes of the southern Apennines expanded notably. After the collapse of Etruscan power in Campania, cities such as Capua and Cumae were taken over and adopted Oscan speech. However the Sabellic invaders—thereafter known as Campanians—became completely urbanised under a city-state organisation, as had the Sidicini. In the fourth century they in turn were threatened by their Samnite kin, the warlike Oscan tribal confederation of the Apennine uplands—Caudini, Carricini, Pentri and Hirpini, the two last being the most powerful. East of the Apennines, the Dauni and Peucetii had developed a distinctive culture. When Sabellic penetration occurred there too, it was the northern peoples, the Apuli, who became the most Oscanised; the Messapii retained an Illyrian-type language. Further south west, the Oscan-speaking Lucani similarly overran and mingled with the Oenotri in the fifth century, as well as attacking several Greek cities. The toe of Italy was occupied by the tribal federation of the Bruttii, who were an offshoot of the Lucani: yet they never entirely dominated the Greek settlers there.

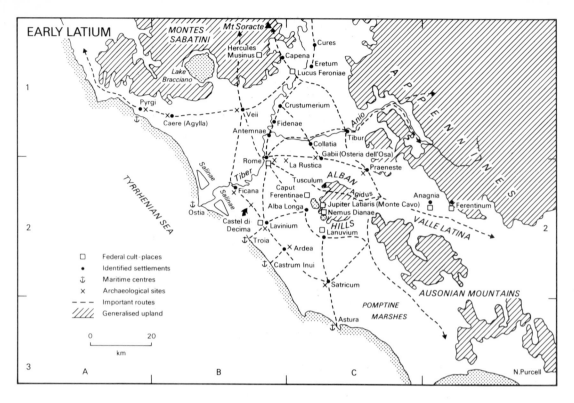

Federal cult-places
Identified settlements
Maritime centres
Archaeological sites
Important routes
Generalised upland

0   20
km

N.Purcell

Early Latium

Between the steep scarp of the Appennine ridges and the outlying Ausonian mountains, the Valle Latina provides an excellent low level inland route north from Campania. It debouches into a wide plain from which rise two large volcanic uplands, the Monti Sabatini and the Alban hills. Between these flow the perennial and navigable Tiber, and its tributary the Anio, whose headwaters form a rare east-west route across the mountain spine of the peninsula. A relatively heavy rainfall has furrowed the sides of the volcanoes with a radial pattern of deeply incised gullies, between which are many defensive sites. In the eighth to sixth centuries these were occupied by the numerous small agricultural settlements of an Italic people whose copious archaeological remains are now usually called Latial. Over the last twenty years it has become clear from sites like Castel di Decima and Osteria dell' Osa that their society was prosperous and complex, as well as distinct from the Hellenised Etruscans to the north and in Campania, and from the other Italic peoples.

Near the Tiber—which served both as a route to the interior and as port of entry for overseas cultural influences—the terrain is flatter, though not very fertile. This is the distinctive landscape of the Roman Campagna, an area virtually uninhabited in large tracts almost within living memory, but in the imperial period the teeming hinterland of Rome: it was crisscrossed by a network of local and long-distance roads, which gave access to suburban communities, dormitory towns, villas and horticultural areas (see p. 122). This unique human landscape was the product of Rome's astonishing success as an imperial capital. Her cultural and political achievement was founded upon her nodal position on the navigable Tiber: in the Latial period this had given her the hegemony of the towns of the region, as well as a prosperity which even in the sixth century made her one of the larger cities of the western Mediterranean.

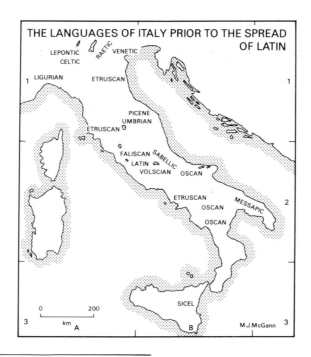

THE LANGUAGES OF ITALY PRIOR TO THE SPREAD OF LATIN

The Languages of Italy Prior to the Spread of Latin

It is impossible to represent accurately with clear cut boundaries the languages spoken in Italy at a precise date. With the exception of Latin, our knowledge of the languages of ancient Italy derives mainly from inscriptions (most of which cannot be dated precisely), and in a much lesser degree from proper names and a few individual words (glosses) preserved by classical writers. Not only is this latter evidence, too, chronologically ill-defined; it also does not necessarily provide accurate information about *speech* communities. The map therefore must confine itself to illustrating the linguistic diversity of Italy and Sicily before the rise of Rome and the accompanying spread of Latin.

Several of the languages of ancient Italy—including Latin—belong to the linguistic group called Indo-European. In ancient times such Indo-European languages were spoken in areas as far apart as Ireland and India. They share certain features usually held to point to a common origin in a language not directly attested (termed proto-Indo-European). From it, through a process of differentiation, the historically attested Indo-European languages derive.

Latin was originally the language of the city of Rome and, with some dialectal differences, of the region of Latium. Very similar to Latin is the language of some inscriptions from Falerii, north of Rome. Known as *Faliscan*, it shows in addition some influence from *Etruscan*, the language of Etruria, which is attested also in the north east of the peninsula and in Campania. Etruscan is almost certainly a non-Indo-European language. It is represented by a large number of texts, most of which are short, and consist of proper names and recurring formulae; these can be understood. However, the much smaller number of longer texts cannot yet be translated with confidence.

A language scantily attested through proper names and glosses in the region of Liguria, north of Etruria, has been called *Ligurian*. *Celtic* (an Indo-European language) was introduced to Italy by settlers who established themselves in the north Italian plain and were called Galli by the Romans. From an area further north come inscriptions in an apparently Indo-European language called

Lepontic. In north east Italy are attested *Raetic*, of uncertain classification; *Venetic*, Indo-European, and showing similarities to Latin; and, as has been noted, *Etruscan*. From further south, in Picenum, comes a number of inscriptions in a language, or possibly two languages, of obscure classification, which is best called *Picene* (or *North* and *South Picene*).

From Iguvium in Umbria (east of Etruria) come substantial religious inscriptions written in an Indo-European language which is taken to be representative of the whole region and is termed *Umbrian*. Closely related to it is *Oscan*, the dominant language of southern Italy before the Roman conquest. In central Italy various languages are attested—the *Sabellic* group and *Volscian*. These show similarities to Oscan and Umbrian, and with them form the so-called *Osco-Umbrian* group of languages.

A language attested in the heel of Italy, *Messapic*, has been seen as having Balkan connections. Some inscriptions from the east of Sicily are in a language called *Sicel*. In addition to these languages, *Greek* was spoken and written in many places in southern Italy and Sicily.

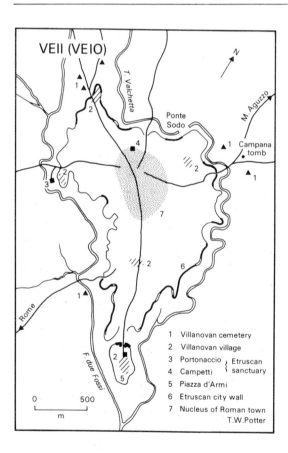

1 Villanovan cemetery
2 Villanovan village
3 Portonaccio ⎱ Etruscan
4 Campetti ⎰ sanctuary
5 Piazza d'Armi
6 Etruscan city wall
7 Nucleus of Roman town

T.W.Potter

Veii

The site of Veii lies 16 km to the north of the centre of Rome, a proximity that was bound to bring this leading Etruscan city into conflict with an expanding young republic. Veii originated as a series of Villanovan villages, probably founded in the ninth century BC; they were dispersed around a great plateau, strongly protected by river valleys. These villages eventually coalesced to form the Etruscan settlement. Regular streets, houses and a sanctuary were laid out in the sixth century on the Piazza d'Armi, but the rest of the Etruscan city grew up in a haphazard way. Though massive town defences were provided in the fifth century, the city lapsed into obscurity after Veii's defeat by Rome in 396.

As a community which possessed a forum, theatre, baths and the *schola* of a *collegium* (the three latter structures known through inscriptions), Veii was later accorded municipal status under Augustus. But it had been bypassed by the new Roman road system, and supported only a small population. Veii was nevertheless one of the many major Etruscan cities which remained in occupation well into the imperial period, and often into medieval and modern times.

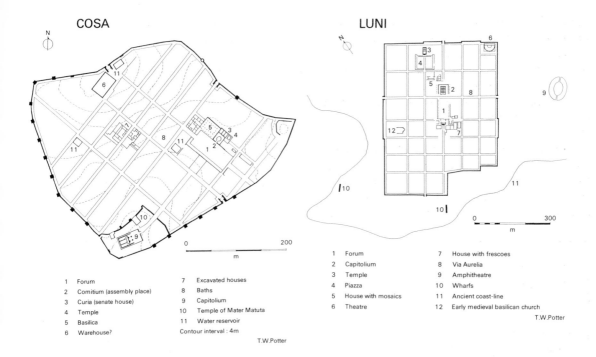

COSA

1 Forum
2 Comitium (assembly place)
3 Curia (senate house)
4 Temple
5 Basilica
6 Warehouse?
7 Excavated houses
8 Baths
9 Capitolium
10 Temple of Mater Matuta
11 Water reservoir
Contour interval : 4m

T.W.Potter

LUNI

1 Forum
2 Capitolium
3 Temple
4 Piazza
5 House with mosaics
6 Theatre
7 House with frescoes
8 Via Aurelia
9 Amphitheatre
10 Wharfs
11 Ancient coast-line
12 Early medieval basilican church

T.W.Potter

Cosa

The Latin colony of Cosa was founded in 273 BC in the territory of the Etruscan city of Vulci. Strongly positioned on a limestone hill overlooking the Tyrrhenian Sea, it has been extensively excavated. The walls enclosed some 13.35 hectares of undulating terrain, which dictate the irregular shape of the defences. There were numerous towers along the more vulnerable west and south sides, which face the sea; and, as was customary in Italic towns, there were three gates. Inside the walls, the streets divided the town into a series of rectangular blocks. The irregularity of the contours ensured that the forum and associated buildings (which represent at least five main phases of construction) lay somewhat off centre; while the Capitolium was situated within its own defences on an eminence to the south west. Houses are attested in nearly every block: excavation shows them to have consisted of rooms laid out around a central court. Water storage tanks are also a conspicuous feature of the site.

Luna

The Roman colony of Luna (Luni) is situated on low-lying flat ground, close to the ancient coastline of the Tyrrhenian Sea and overshadowed by hills containing the imperial marble quarries of Carrara. Founded early in the second century BC and made a *colonia* under Augustus, the site was not finally abandoned until the thirteenth century AD. The town plan as demarcated by its wall is a rectangle, within which was a regular grid of streets. Public buildings identified include a forum—centrally placed, as was customary—the Capitolium, and a covered theatre. Richly decorated private houses have also been excavated. Outside the town was an amphitheatre; there are traces of wharfs too. These port facilities were of particular importance for the export of marble, cheese and other goods, as well as for the import of items such as oil and wine from Spain, north Africa and elsewhere. Although the forum was out of use by *c.* AD 400, the long-distance trading contacts remained active till much later.

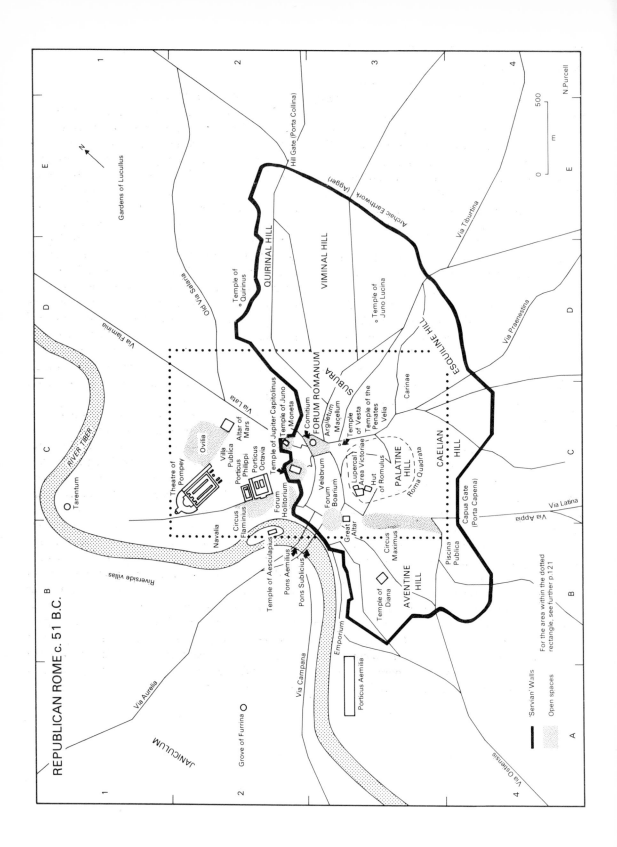

REPUBLICAN ROME c. 51 B.C.

N. Purcell

0   500
m

'Servian' Walls

Open spaces

For the area within the dotted rectangle, see further p.121

JANICULUM

Grove of Furina

Via Aurelia

Via Campana

Emporium

Porticus Aemilia

Via Ostiensis

Via Appia

Via Latina

Capua Gate (Porta Capena)

Piscina Publica

Circus Maximus

AVENTINE HILL

Temple of Diana

Pons Subicius

Pons Aemilius

Temple of Aesculapius

Navalia

Circus Flaminius

Riverside villas

RIVER TIBER

Tarentum

Theatre of Pompey

Ovilia

Villa Publica

Porticus Philippi

Porticus Octavia

Altar of Mars

Forum Holitorium

Forum Boarium

Great Altar

Velabrum

Lupercal

Area Victoriae

Hut of Romulus

PALATINE HILL

Roma Quadrata

CAELIAN HILL

Temple of Jupiter Capitolinus

Temple of Juno Moneta

Comitium

FORUM ROMANUM

Argiletum

Macellum

Temple of Vesta

Temple of the Penates

Velia

Carinae

SUBURA

ESQUILINE HILL

Via Lata

Via Flaminia

Old Via Salaria

Gardens of Lucullus

Temple of Quirinus

QUIRINAL HILL

VIMINAL HILL

Temple of Juno Lucina

Hill Gate (Porta Collina)

Archaic Earthwork (Agger)

Via Tiburtina

Via Praenestina

Republican Rome

Streams draining into the R. Tiber have cut deep, steep-sided valleys into gently sloping beds of volcanic tufa and calcareous freshwater deposits to form long projecting spurs and isolated hills. The gullies between these were much deeper before the centuries of continuous urban occupation partly obliterated them. The valley floors were very ill-drained, so that in the eighth and seventh centuries BC it was the tops which formed the sites for a number of nucleated village settlements. The Romans believed that the one on the Palatine Hill—which they called Roma Quadrata, or 'Square Rome'—was the most ancient. In affirming its primacy they could show huts and other genuine remains of the prehistoric period. They also believed in an ethnic difference between the inhabitants of the hills.

Archaeology and the Roman tradition alike confirm the unification of these settlements into one large and urbanised unit around the end of the seventh century. In the sixth century Rome was a city of importance, with fortifications and public monuments comparable to those of any contemporary Mediterranean city—above all the great temple of Jupiter on the Capitol. The Tiber had been bridged by this time: indeed it was the presence of the bridge which brought about the accumulation of the island in the river, not the island which made possible the bridge. In affording a highway to the interior as well as an extended, safe harbour along its banks, the Tiber was essential to the development of Rome: it made the city a great port and the place of contact between the Mediterranean maritime world and the peoples of peninsular Italy. Close to the river grew up the markets of the city and an emporium which attained its greatest elaboration in the second century BC with the building of the enormous Porticus Aemilia.

The valleys between the hills became densely packed with Rome's rapidly swelling population, but the hilltops—cooler in summer—remained the preserve of the wealthy, particularly the Palatine and the Carinae spur of the Esquiline. By the end of the Republic the built-up area had virtually filled the walls of the Middle Republican period (last renewed in the 80s), and was spreading out onto the Campus Martius and beyond the Capena Gate. But the meadows of the two Tiber meanders were still too wet for development, and Transtiberim only became populous in the Augustan period. However from the third century onwards the open spaces of the Campus Martius—scene of popular assemblies at muster-time or elections—were rapidly made monumental along Hellenistic lines. A succession of triumphing commanders right down to Augustus built here great porticoes, temples, and finally theatres.

Although from the earliest times the same spirit of display had sprinkled the city with fine temples, it was only in the last years of the Republic that Rome's architecture, even in the Campus Martius or Forum Romanum, once again came to compare with that of the Greek East. From the third century onwards much money had regularly been channelled into utilitarian projects such as aqueducts and roads, but the city remained under-provided with amenities, and its appearance was generally shabby until the Augustan age. Such open spaces as the Circus Flaminius and Circus Maximus, for example, did not acquire their monumental definition until quite late. The survival of so large a population in so cramped and unhealthy a position must always have been precarious; without the river, and later the assistance of the aqueducts, it would have been impossible.

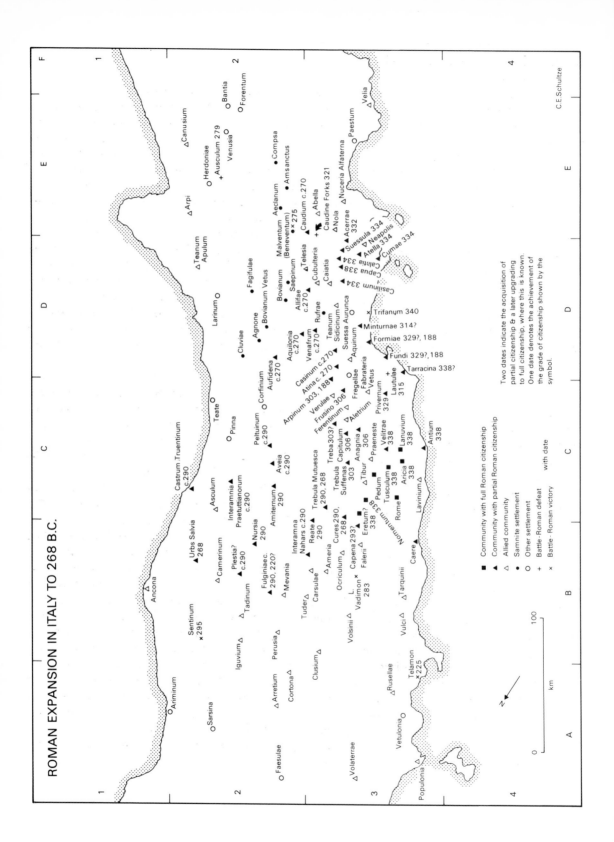

ROMAN EXPANSION IN ITALY TO 268 B.C.

Ariminum

Sarsina

Faesulae

Vetulonia

Populonia

△Volaterrae

Telamon
× 225

Rusellae△

△Arretium
Cortona△

Clusium△

Iguvium△

Perusia△

Volsinii△

L.
Vadimon × 283

Faleri△

Vulci△

Caere○

△Tarquinii

Ancona △

Castrum Truentinum
c.290

△Camerinum

△Tadinum

Sentinum
× 295

Urbs Salvia
▲ 268

△Asculum

Interamnia ▲
Praetuttianorum
c.290

Nursia
▲ 290

Fulginiae c.
290, 220?

△Mevania

△Tuder

Carsulae△

Ocriculum△

Capena 293?▲

Amiterium
290

Interamna
Nahars c.290

Reate ▲
290

△Ameria

Cures 290,
268 △

Eretum?
338 ▲

Nomentum 338 ▲

Rome ●

Teate○

Pinna○

Peltuinum
c.290

Aveia
c.290

Trebula Mutuesca
290, 268

Trebula
Suffenas
303

Treba 303?△

△Tibur
303

Anagnia
306

Praeneste○

Pedum
338

Tusculum△

Aricia
▲ 338

Lavinium△

Corfinium○

Aufidena
c.270

Atina c. 270

Arpinum
303, 188 ▲

Venulae▽

Frusino 306▽

Ferentinum ▽

△Aletrium

Velitrae
▲ 338

Lanuvium
▲ 338

Antium
■ 338

Cluviae ●

Agnone ●

Larinum○

Fagifulae ●

Bovianum Vetus ●

Casinum c. 270 ▲

Teanum
Sidicinum △

Suessa Aurunca △

Fregellae○

Fabrateria
Vetus ▽

Privernum
▲ 329

Lautulae
+ 315

Teanum
Apulum △

Bovianum ●

Saepinum△

Allifae
c.270

Rufrae ▲

Aquilonia
c.270

Venafrum
c.270

Aquinum △

Minturnae 314? ▲

Formiae 329?, 188 ▲

Fundi 329?, 188 ○

Tarracina 338? +

Trifanum 340 ×

Arpi △

Herdoniae △

Ausculum 279
+

Venusia ○

Malventum ●
(Beneventum)

× 275

Aeclanum ●

Amsanctus ●

Compsa ●

Telesia △

Cubulteria ▲

Caiatia △

Casilinum 334 ▲

Capua 338 ▲

Calatia 334 ▲

Caudium c.270 △

Caudine Forks 321

Abella △

Nola △

Acerrae
332

Suessula 334 ▽

Neapolis ▽

Atella 334 ▽

Cumae 334 ▽

Nuceria Alfaterna ○

Paestum ○

Velia ○

Bantia ○

Forentum ○

Canusium △

C.E.Schultze

Two dates indicate the acquisition of
partial citizenship & a later upgrading
to full citizenship, where this is known.
One date denotes the achievement of
the grade of citizenship shown by the
symbol.

■ Community with full Roman citizenship

▲ Community with partial Roman citizenship

△ Allied community

▽ Samnite settlement

○ Other settlement

+ Battle - Roman defeat

× Battle - Roman victory   with date

N

km

0   100

Roman Expansion in Italy to 268 BC

Roman expansion began in the regal period with the annexation of smaller neighbouring settlements. Their inhabitants became Roman citizens, enrolled in the four urban and seventeen rural tribes (local areas of domicile) which were in existence by 495. Down to the early fourth century Rome was occupied in holding her own in Latium, and in co-operating with her Latin and Hernican neighbours to resist incursions from Aequi and Volsci. Expansion took the form of colonisation jointly with the Latins (see pp. 94–5). The conquest of Etruscan Veii in 396 (see p. 82) greatly increased Roman territory: the land was allotted in viritane grants to individual Roman citizens, who were enrolled in four new tribes in 387. The capture of Rome by the Gauls in 390 slowed progress; but two new tribes were created in 358, and Rome had recovered by the mid-fourth century.

After victory over Latins, Campanians, Volscians and others in the 'Latin war' (340–38), the increasing size of the territory under Rome's influence led to new forms of association and control, not necessarily entailing Roman annexation, settlement or even administration—for which, in any case, she was not equipped. Certain existing communities were incorporated as *municipia*: their inhabitants became Roman citizens, liable to military service and taxation. In recompense *municipia* enjoyed local autonomy and retained their laws, customs and identity. There were two grades: in the more privileged, the inhabitants were *cives Romani optimo iure* (Roman citizens with full rights), wholly equal to existing Roman citizens and enrolled in Roman tribes; in the less privileged, they were *cives sine suffragio* (citizens without vote), partial citizens, possessing the same rights in private law, but unable to vote or hold office at Rome. Full citizenship was granted initially just to selected Latin-speaking communities; more distant or less cultured peoples first received partial citizenship, and were upgraded later. Some Sabine towns were the first non-Latins to benefit thus in 268.

Other states became allies (*socii* or *foederati*) on signing a bilateral treaty (*foedus*) with Rome. This defined their duties and privileges, which varied greatly. Though in theory independent and self-governing, most allies were really more or less subordinate to Rome. Their chief duty was to provide troops; they did not pay Roman taxes. However, since treaties were often imposed by Rome after conquest—which usually also entailed confiscation of territory—the provision of troops from a reduced economic base could prove onerous. Allied communities were very diverse in origin and social organisation: Greek city states, Italian towns, tribal peoples. Those whose status is firmly attested or fairly certain are shown here; doubtless there were many more by the mid-third century.

After 338, the last power to resist Roman control of the peninsula was the Samnite tribal confederation of the southern Apennines. Rome recognised a Samnite sphere in a treaty of 354, and despite hostilities in 343–1, the Samnites were Rome's allies again by the time of the 'Latin war' of 340–38. However Rome's continuing expansion, and especially the foundation of Fregellae (328), provoked lengthy second and third Samnite wars (327–04, 298–90). The Samnites had Etruscan, Umbrian and Gallic allies, so that Rome was often fighting on two fronts. Victory at Sentinum (295) gained her northern central Italy, and by 290 the defeated Samnites were forced into a Roman alliance, losing much territory. Colonisation and viritane grants continued meanwhile, with new tribes being created in pairs in 332, 318, 299 and 241, bringing the tribal total to 35. Finally, in the Pyrrhic war (280–72) the Tarentines, other south Italians, and Samnites, with help from Pyrrhus of Epirus, made a last unsuccessful stand against Rome. Thus under one form or another the peninsula south of Ariminum was now subject to her; the process of assimilation and romanisation continued.

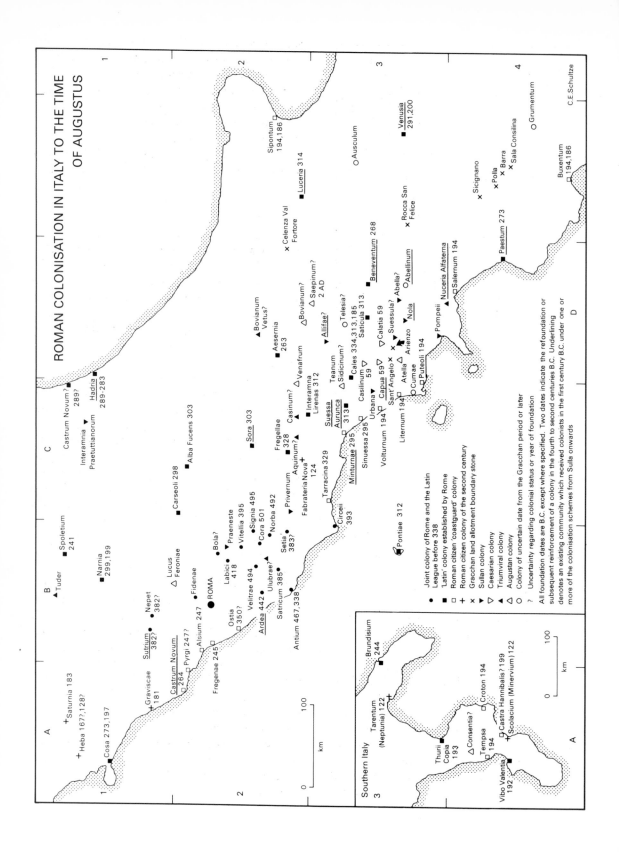

ROMAN COLONISATION IN ITALY TO THE TIME OF AUGUSTUS

C.E.Schultze

Legend:

- Joint colony of Rome and the Latin League before 338
- 'Latin' colony established by Rome
- Roman citizen 'coastguard' colony
- Roman citizen colony of the second century
- Gracchan land allotment boundary stone
- Sullan colony
- Caesarian colony
- Triumviral colony
- Augustan colony
- Colony of uncertain date from the Gracchan period or later
- ? Uncertainty regarding colonial status or year of foundation

All foundation dates are B.C. except where specified. Two dates indicate the refoundation or subsequent reinforcement of a colony in the fourth to second centuries B.C. Underlining denotes an existing community which received colonists in the first century B.C. under one or more of the colonisation schemes from Sulla onwards

Main map labels:
Cosa 273,197 · Heba 167?,128? · Saturnia 183 · Graviscae 181 · Castrum Novum 264 · Pyrgi 247? · Alsium 247 · Fregenae 245 · Tuder · Spoletium 241 · Narnia 299,199 · Lucus Feroniae · Fidenae · Nepet 382? · Sutrium 382? · Ostia 350? · Ardea 442 · ROMA · Bola? · Labici 418 · Praeneste · Velitrae 494 · Vitellia 395 · Signia 495 · Cora 501 · Norba 492 · Ulubrae? · Satricum 385 · Setia 382? · Antium 467,338 · Circeii 393 · Pontiae 312 · Tarracina 329 · Privernum · Fabrateria Nova 124 · Aquinum? · Fregellae 328 · Casinum? · Interamna Lirenas 312 · Venafrum · Sora 303 · Carseoli 298 · Alba Fucens · Interamnia Praetuttianorum · Hadria 289-283 · Castrum Novum? 289? · Aesernia 263 · Bovianum Vetus? · Bovianum? · Saepinum? 2 AD · Telesia? · Allifae? · Teanum Sidicinum? · Cales 334,313,185 · Saticula 313 · Calatia 59 · Suessula? · Abella? · Abellinum · Casilinum? · Sant'Angelo · Atella · Arienzo · Nola · Capua 59 · Urbana 59 · Suessa Aurunca 313 · Sinuessa 295 · Minturnae 295 · Volturnum 194 · Liternum 194 · Puteoli 194 · Cumae · Pompeii · Nuceria Alfaterna · Salernum 194 · Benevantum 268 · Celenza Val Fortore · Luceria 314 · Sipontum 194,186 · Ausculum · Rocca San Felice · Venusia 291,200 · Paestum 273 · Sicignano · Polla · Barra · Sala Consilina · Grumentum · Buxentum 194,186

Southern Italy

Brundisium 244 · Tarentum (Neptunia) 122 · Thurii Copia 193 · Consentia? · Tempsa 194 · Croton 194 · Castra Hannibalis? 199 · Scolacium (Minervium) 122 · Vibo Valentia 192

94

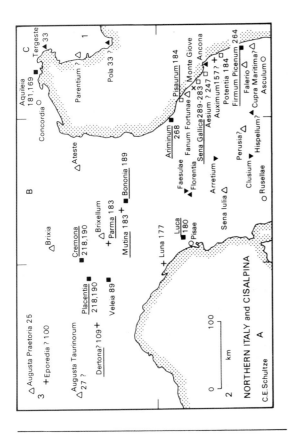

Augusta Praetoria 25
3
+ Eporedia ? 100

△ Augusta Taurinorum
△ 27 ?

Dertona? 109 +

■ Placentia
218,190

■ Veleia 89

△ Brixia

Cremona
218,190

△ Brixellum
+ Parma 183

Mutina 183 + ■ Bononia 189

+ Luca 177

Luca
■ 180

○ Pisae
○ Pisae

Sena Iulia △

B

Concordia ○

C

Tergeste ▲ 33

Aquileia
181,169

Parentium ? △

△ Ateste

Pola 33 ? ◀

1

Pisaurum 184
Ariminum ▲
268 Fanum Fortunae △
Faesulae Sena Gallica 289-283 □
△ × Monte Giove
Florentia Aesium ? 247 □ Ancona
Arretium ▼ Auximum157 ? + □
Perusia? Potentia 184 □
Clusium ▼ Firmum Picenum 264
○ Rusellae Falerio △
Hispellum? Cupra Maritima? △
Asculum ○

100

km

0

2

NORTHERN ITALY and CISALPINA

A

C.E.Schultze

Roman Colonisation

In Roman terms, to found a colony was to establish a self-governing civic community with its own laws, magistrates and administration. The necessary land was acquired by conquest and expropriation of the former inhabitants. An urban centre was built to a more or less standard pattern, as at Cosa (p. 89). In addition to residential areas this included temples, market, assembly area and public buildings, like senate house, court, treasury. Some inhabitants lived within the walls, others settled in the *territorium* beyond. All were allotted plots of ground, as well as sharing rights over common land.

Down to 338 Rome established colonies jointly with her fellow members of the Latin League (*Priscae Latinae Coloniae*). The colonists held the citizenship of their new community, which was a Latin city like any existing League member. After the League's dissolution, Rome continued to found similar colonies (as first at Cales in 334), which likewise possessed Latin status, although the settlers were no longer necessarily Latin by origin, nor were such colonies sited within the geographical area of Latium. These communities (*Coloniae Latinae*) often consisted of some 4,000 families. Rome also founded 'citizen' colonies (*Coloniae civium Romanorum*), whose inhabitants retained Roman citizenship: these were much smaller, with only 300 families, who were allotted tiny plots of land. They are often referred to as 'maritime' or 'coastguard' colonies, since their function was to protect coasts. After the second Punic war, with more confiscated land available, and a higher value set on Roman citizenship, citizen colonies of a new type came to be established: they were sited inland, and larger, with several thousand settlers who received bigger plots. Saturnia (183) conformed to this pattern; the few Latin colonies of the second century are similar.

Foundations then ceased for over 50 years. In the Gracchan period, however, colonisation and viritane allotment—the grant of plots to individual settlers without establishing any centre—were resumed. Next, after the Social war (91–89), the nature of colonisation changed. First century programmes involved the dispatch of new settlers (often veterans) to existing communities. Where insufficient public land was available, what was required had to be bought, or was confiscated as a consequence of civil war. By this period colonisation and land settlement generally had become important forms of political patronage.

Colonies fulfilled several major functions. They were often sited at strategic points or on main lines of communication: thus Fregellae (328) controlled a crossing of the R. Liris and threatened Samnium, while Cremona and Placentia (218) thrust into Gallic territory. Colonies could be used to dominate a hostile area: Venusia (291) split up the Hirpini and Lucani after the third Samnite war. Colonial institutions and language helped the process of romanisation. Above all, colonies formed an important reserve of manpower, since land grants to the poor who were not liable for military service (*proletarii*) transformed them into *assidui* who were so liable.

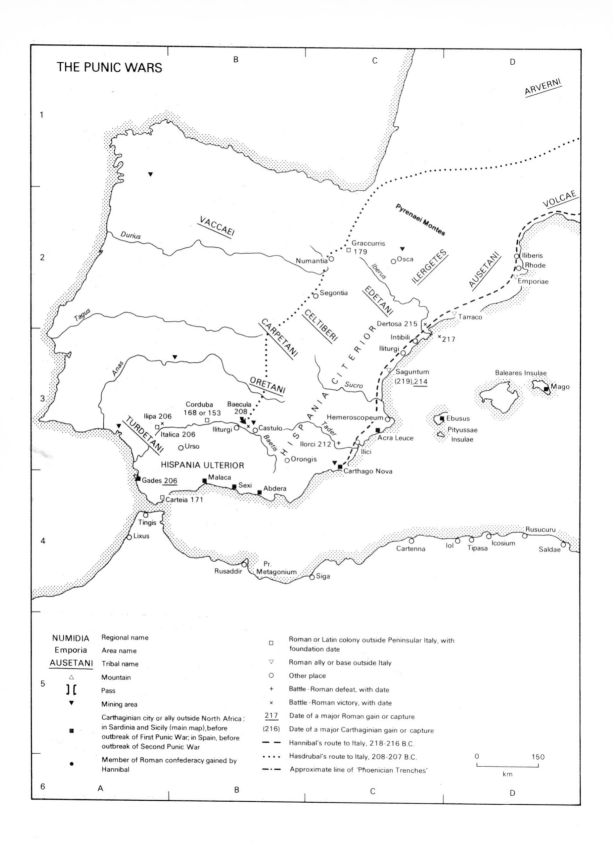

THE PUNIC WARS

ARVERNI

B · C · D

1

VACCAEI

Durius

Pyrenaei Montes

VOLCAE

2 · Numantia○ · Graccurris □ 179 · ○ Osca · ILERGETES · AUSETANI · ○ Iliberis · ○ Rhode · ▽ · Emporiae

Iberus

Segontia○

CARPETANI · CELTIBERI · EDETANI · Dertosa 215 × · × Tarraco · × 217

Tagus

Intibili
Iliturgi
Saguntum
(219),214

ORETANI · *Sucro* · Baleares Insulae · ■ Mago

3 · Corduba 168 or 153 · Baecula 208 · Hemeroscopeum

Ilipa 206 · TURDETANI · □ Italica 206 · ○ Iliturgi · Castulo · *Tader* · + · ■ Ebusus · Pityussae Insulae

○ Urso · Ilorci 212 · ● Ilici · ■ Acra Leuce

Baetis · ○ Orongis

HISPANIA ULTERIOR · ■ Carthago Nova

Gades 206 · ■ Malaca · ■ Sexi · Abdera

□ Carteia 171

Tingis○

4 · ○ Lixus · ○ Cartenna · ○ Iol · ○ Tipasa · ○ Icosium · Rusucuru · ○ Saldae

Rusaddir○ · Pr. Metagonium · ○ Siga

5

6 · A · B · C · D

96

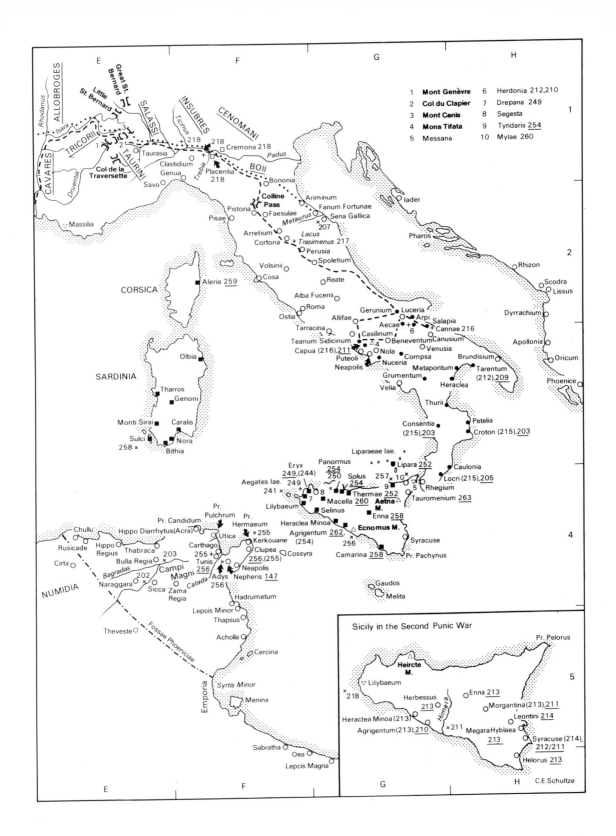

E

ALLOBROGES

Rhodanus

Isara

CAVARES

TRICORII

SALASSI

TAURINI

Great St. Bernard

Little St. Bernard

1 Mont Genèvre
2 Col du Clapier
3 Mont Cenis
4 Mons Tifata
5 Messana

6 Herdonia 212,210
7 Drepana 249
8 Segesta
9 Tyndaris 254
10 Mylae 260

Col de la Traversette

Druentia

Genua

Savo

Taurasia

Clastidium

Ticinus

Placentia 218

Trebia

+ 218

Cremona 218

INSUBRES

CENOMANI

Padus

BOII

Bononia

Massilia

Pistoria

Pisae

Colline Pass

Faesulae

Arretium

Cortona

Metaurus

Ariminum

Fanum Fortunae

Sena Gallica

× 207

Lacus Trasimenus 217

Perusia

Spoletium

Volsinii

Cosa

Reate

Alba Fucens

Roma

Ostia

Allifae

Tarracina

Teanum Sidicinum

Capua (216),211

Puteoli

Neapolis

Casilinum

△ 4

Beneventum

Nola

Nuceria

Compsa

Grumentum

Velia

Gerunium

Luceria

Arpi

Aecae

+ 6

Salapia

Cannae 216

Canusium

Venusia

Metapontum

Heraclea

Thurii

Consentia (215),203

Croton (215),203

CORSICA

Aleria 259

SARDINIA

Olbia

Tharros

Genoni

Monti Sirai

Caralis

Sulci

258 ×

Nora

Bithia

Iader

Pharos

Rhizon

Scodra

Lissus

Dyrrachium

Apollonia

Brundisium

Tarentum (212),209

Phoenice

Oricum

Petelia

Liparaeae Iae.

Eryx 249,(244)

Panormus 254

Lipara 252

Caulonia

Solus 254

257 × 10

Locri (215),205

Aegates Iae. 249

250

9

Rhegium

241 ×

7

8

Thermae 252

Aetna M. △

Tauromenium 263

Pr. Pulchrum

Lilybaeum

Macella 260

Selinus

Enna 258

Messana

Chullu

Pr. Candidum

Pr. Hermaeum

Utica

× 255

Heraclea Minoa

Agrigentum (254)

Ecnomus M. △

Syracuse

Rusicade

Hippo Diarrhytus (Acra)

Kerkouane

256

Hippo Regius

Thabraca

203

Carthago 255 +

Clupea 256,(255)

Cossyra

Camarina 258

Pr. Pachynus

Cirta

Bulla Regia

Tunis 256 ×

Bagradas

Campi Magni 256

Adys 256

Neapolis

Nepheris 147

NUMIDIA

202

Naraggara

Sicca

Zama Regia

Catada

Gaudos

Melita

Theveste

Fossae Phoeniciae

Hadrumetum

Lepcis Minor

Thapsus

Acholla

Cercina

Emporia

Syrtis Minor

Meninx

Sabratha

Oea

Lepcis Magna

Sicily in the Second Punic War

Pr. Pelorus

Heircte M. △

Lilybaeum ▽

× 218

Herbessus 213

Heraclea Minoa (213)

Agrigentum (213),210

× 211

Himera

Enna 213

Morgantina (213),211

Leontini 214

Megara Hyblaea 213

Syracuse (214), 212/211

Helorus 213

C.E.Schultze

E

F

G

H

The Punic Wars

Rome's struggle with Carthage for supremacy in the western Mediterranean was fought out in the three Punic wars of 264–41, 218–01, and 149–6. At the outbreak of the first Rome was the chief city of Italy, while Carthage, as a wealthy maritime power, dominated western Mediterranean trade in metals and other commodities, and had dependencies and trading posts in Africa, Spain, Corsica, Sardinia and western Sicily. The initial encounter occurred in Sicily, when Rome agreed to help the Mamertini of Messana against the Carthaginians. However her aims soon expanded to include the expulsion of the Carthaginians from the entire island. This required her to become a naval power, building ships and drawing heavily upon her own and her allies' manpower. Despite the failure of Regulus' expedition to Africa (256–5), and serious losses at sea, Rome did persist with this policy. From the Carthaginian viewpoint there was no value in continuing the struggle for Sicily indefinitely; after a defeat off the Aegates Islands in 241 Carthage therefore made peace, agreeing to evacuate Sicily and pay an indemnity. In 238 Rome next took advantage of internal difficulties at Carthage to force the cession of Sardinia too; subjugation of native populations there and in Corsica occupied much of the following decade.

The Carthaginians meanwhile concentrated on extending their empire in Spain, until they dominated the south and east coastal area from the R. Baetis to the R. Iberus (Ebro), and had some control over the tribes of the hinterland. An excuse for Rome to intervene came in 218 when Saguntum, a city friendly to her, was captured by Hannibal. He then marched swiftly upon Italy, hoping that a rapid series of successes would win over Rome's allies. He inflicted several severe defeats upon the Romans, culminating in that at Cannae in 216. Although much of southern Italy then joined Hannibal, he was nonetheless unable to undermine Rome's power base in central Italy, or to make effective use of his Gallic allies in the north.

Rome meanwhile avoided major confrontations—the so called 'Fabian' strategy, named after the general Fabius Cunctator. Moreover Roman determination to remain engaged in Spain constantly required Carthage to divert resources there, so that Hannibal never received the reinforcements which might have enabled him to force a decisive battle and break the deadlock. An alliance between Carthage and Macedon in 215 had no more than a slight diversionary effect. The turning point of the war only came in 211 with the Romans' recapture of Capua and Syracuse. It gradually became clear that despite the setbacks which Rome had suffered, Hannibal could not hold his gains in Italy in the long term. Hasdrubal's attempt to reinforce him from Spain resulted in a defeat at the R. Metaurus in 207. In 203 Hannibal finally left Italy. In the same year Scipio Africanus, who had overcome the Carthaginians in Spain between 210 and 206, began operations in Africa itself. In 202 he defeated Hannibal at Zama. Peace terms included Carthaginian evacuation of Spain, payment of a large indemnity, and rewards for Rome's African ally, Massinissa of Numidia.

Over the next 50 years Carthage continued to prosper, though her scope for territorial expansion was severely restricted. In Africa she had secure possession only of the land within the 'Phoenician Trenches', whose exact position is uncertain. Not only was the territory beyond disputed with Massinissa; Rome also tacitly encouraged him to encroach on important Carthaginian possessions such as the Emporia district. In 149, seizing the chance offered by Carthaginian hostilities against Massinissa and the voluntary surrender of Utica, Rome declared war. All the fighting took place at Carthage and in its hinterland. Punic resistance was stiff: only in 146, when the siege had been made effective by the building of walls and ditches, and by a mole blocking the harbour mouth, did the city fall to Scipio Aemilianus. It was then totally destroyed.

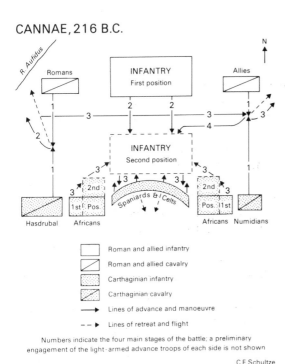

CANNAE, 216 B.C.

Roman and allied infantry
Roman and allied cavalry
Carthaginian infantry
Carthaginian cavalry
Lines of advance and manoeuvre
Lines of retreat and flight

Numbers indicate the four main stages of the battle; a preliminary
engagement of the light-armed advance troops of each side is not shown

C.E.Schultze

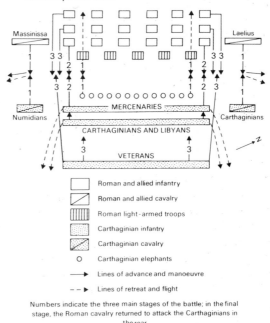

ZAMA, 202 B.C.

Roman and allied infantry
Roman and allied cavalry
Roman light-armed troops
Carthaginian infantry
Carthaginian cavalry
Carthaginian elephants
Lines of advance and manoeuvre
Lines of retreat and flight

Numbers indicate the three main stages of the battle; in the final
stage, the Roman cavalry returned to attack the Carthaginians in
the rear

C.E.Schultze

Cannae, 216 BC

The battle of Cannae was fought on 2 August 216. The terrain, on the right bank of the R. Aufidus, is fairly smooth and slopes down towards the sea. Roman and allied forces were 6,000 cavalry, 55,000 infantry, and 15,000 light armed troops; the corresponding numbers on Hannibal's side were approximately 10,000, 30,000 and 10,000. After preliminary skirmishing by light armed troops, the cavalry forces met (stage 1). Hasdrubal on the Punic left wing routed the Roman cavalry facing him (2), and then crossed behind the Roman infantry to help against the allied cavalry (3). The Roman infantry was advancing (2) to attack Hannibal's centre, deployed in a thin line thrust forward in crescent formation (3). Meanwhile Hannibal's Africans, stationed to the left and right, executed a turn which brought them up facing the Roman flanks: they then attacked from either side as the Spaniards and Celts fell back (3). The Romans could not redeploy, and their defeat was completed when Hasdrubal's cavalry returned and fell upon them from the rear (4).

Zama, 202 BC

The battle of Zama was fought in autumn 202; the exact site is unknown. The Romans under Scipio Africanus had 23,000 infantry and 6,000 cavalry, while Hannibal had some 36,000 infantry and 4,000 cavalry. In the first stage Scipio placed his light armed troops to face the charge of Carthaginian elephants (1). Retreat routes were left for the troops by arranging the maniples of the three lines of Roman infantry in rows rather than in the usual chessboard formation. Meanwhile, when the cavalry on each wing engaged (1), the Carthaginians were pursued off the field. Then the front line of Roman infantry successfully attacked Hannibal's first two lines (2), who retreated to the flanks with heavy losses. While the Roman front line closed up, Scipio brought in his second and third lines, who engaged Hannibal's third-line veterans, hitherto kept in reserve (3). Finally the Roman cavalry returned from pursuit, and from the rear massacred the Carthaginians. Roman losses were slight.

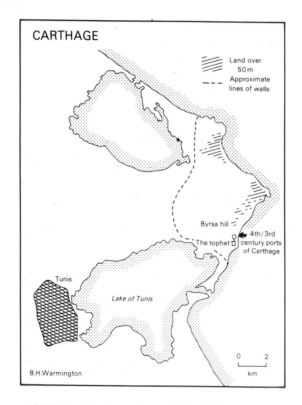

CARTHAGE

Land over
50 m
Approximate
lines of walls

Byrsa hill

The tophet

4th/3rd
century ports
of Carthage

Tunis

Lake of Tunis

0   2
km

B.H.Warmington

Carthage

Carthage, just north of modern Tunis, was founded by Phoenicians—in 814 BC according to tradition. It emerged as the largest Phoenician settlement in the west during struggles with the Greeks of Sicily. From the fifth century it controlled an empire dominating the coasts of north Africa, Spain, Sardinia and western Sicily. Its wealth came from metals and agricultural trade.

As the plan indicates, little is known of the layout of Phoenician Carthage, which was destroyed by Rome in 146 BC and then built over a century later. The original settlement has usually been located in the area of the *tophet*, or sacrificial burial ground, and the nearby hill identified with the ancient citadel known as Byrsa. Recent excavations, however, reveal that the visible Phoenician ports date from the fourth century BC at the earliest, and that the whole area including the Byrsa hill may represent a relatively late extension of an early area of settlement which has yet to be exactly located.

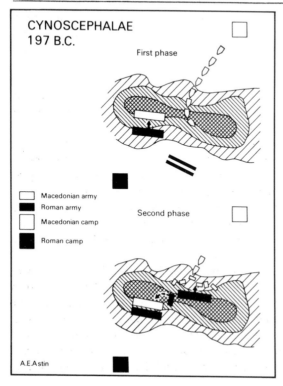

CYNOSCEPHALAE
197 B.C.

First phase

Macedonian army
Roman army
Macedonian camp
Roman camp

Second phase

A.E.Astin

Cynoscephalae, 197 BC

Cynoscephalae was in southern Thessaly, near Scotussa; the exact site is unknown. The Macedonian and Roman armies, commanded respectively by Philip V and T. Flamininus, were marching west from Pherae but were concealed from each other by hills. In wet and misty conditions Philip encamped his army and sent a covering screen to occupy a rugged ridge between him and the Romans. Flamininus, encamped south of it but uncertain of Philip's whereabouts, sent out cavalry and light armed troops to reconnoitre. A clash ensued; each side summoned reinforcements. Encouraged by news of successes, Philip now decided to deploy his main army on the ridge; meanwhile a covering action by Aetolian cavalry gave Flamininus time to draw up his army below. He at first attacked with his left flank, but it had little success against the Macedonian right. Observing that the Macedonian left had been delayed and was only beginning to move into position, Flamininus next attacked with his right, which gained the heights and routed the opposing left before it could be deployed. Part of the Roman army then wheeled round against the flank and rear of the Macedonian right, whose close-order phalanx formation was too inflexible to enable it to meet the double attack. Philip was crushingly defeated.

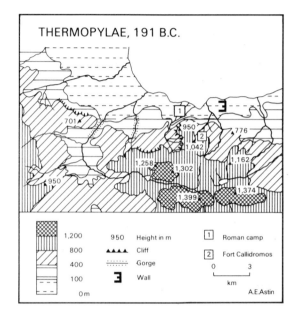

THERMOPYLAE, 191 B.C.

▨	1,200	950	Height in m	1 Roman camp
▥	800	▲▲▲▲ Cliff		2 Fort Callidromos
	400	⋯⋯ Gorge		0 3
	100	⌇ Wall		km
	0 m			A.E.Astin

Thermopylae, 191 BC

To minimise the disparity between his force of little more than 10,000 and the Roman army of about 22,000, Antiochus III occupied the pass of Thermopylae. He held the so-called East Gate, where he built a substantial wall. The Romans under M'. Acilius Glabrio encamped near the hot springs. When they assaulted Antiochus' position, they were forced to narrow their front and to attack up a slope; they also suffered from missiles directed from higher ground to their right. Meanwhile, however, two Roman detachments had been sent against three forts which guarded mountain paths around the pass itself. One detachment made little progress, while the other, under M. Porcius Cato, for a time lost its way. Yet eventually Cato's 2,000 men routed the Aetolian garrison of Fort Callidromos, and then moved down behind Antiochus' line. The alarm caused by their sudden appearance soon led to a rout.

The Roman Empire in 60 BC

Rome's acquisition of an empire was a slow, haphazard process, and her involvement in its administration always remained limited. Communities continued to manage their local affairs. Not until the 220s were Rome's first gains—Sicily and Sardinia/Corsica—organised, and arrangements made for each to become the regular, annual *provincia* (or 'sphere of action') of a praetor. Two more such praetorships were created for 'Further' and 'Nearer' Spain in 198/7. But none was added for Macedonia (whose governor also had the oversight of Achaea or southern Greece), or Africa, both annexed in 146, or for Asia, organised in the 120s, or Gallia Transalpina, to which a governor was being sent regularly by 100. It was therefore necessary for promagistrates to fill these posts, and indeed from the late second century this became the normal practice for all provincial governorships. *Provincia* now comes to have the specific connotation of an administered territory overseas. A governor was sent regularly to Gallia Cisalpina from around Sulla's time. Cyrene and Crete, annexed respectively in 74 and 67, were governed as a single province. In the 60s Pompey's eastern conquests added vast areas—Bithynia/Pontus, Cilicia and Syria.

To the end of the Republic, Rome's hold over most provinces was patchy, and their frontiers generally ill-defined. In the case of Illyricum Rome even laid claim to the coastal strip, yet seldom sent a governor. In many regions definition of frontiers had little significance when these adjoined the territories of 'client kings', local rulers recognised by

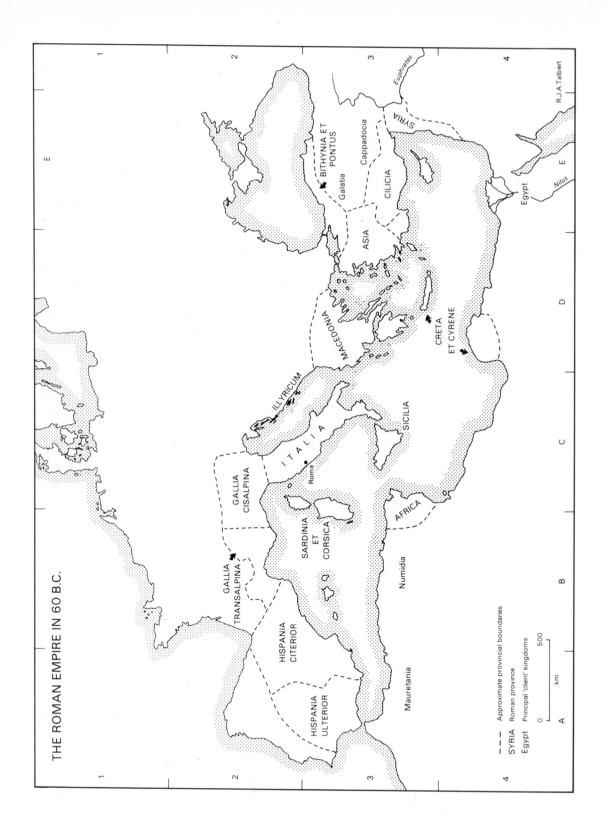

THE ROMAN EMPIRE IN 60 B.C.

BITHYNIA ET
PONTUS

Galatia

Cappadocia

SYRIA

ASIA

CILICIA

Euphrates

Egypt

Nilus

R.J.A.Talbert

MACEDONIA

CRETA
ET CYRENE

ILLYRICUM

I T A L I A

SICILIA

GALLIA
CISALPINA

Roma

SARDINIA
ET
CORSICA

AFRICA

Numidia

GALLIA
TRANSALPINA

HISPANIA
CITERIOR

Mauretania

HISPANIA
ULTERIOR

– – –   Approximate provincial boundaries

SYRIA   Roman province

Egypt   Principal 'client' kingdoms

0   500
km

Rome and willing to serve her in return for the benefits of freedom and protection. The most important such friendly states during the late Republic (in Africa and Asia Minor) are marked.

Roman Campaigns of 49–30 BC

After he had crossed the R. Rubicon into Italy in January 49 it took Julius Caesar five years of intermittent campaigning to achieve control of the Roman world. He gained Italy itself in two months, since a Pompeian stand at Corfinium proved short lived. However Pompey, with further forces, escaped to Greece via Brundisium. Because Caesar lacked a fleet, he delayed pursuit, and instead turned west to Spain where he brilliantly dislodged superior Pompeian forces from an entrenched position at Ilerda, and then marched south to accept the surrender of Corduba. Massilia, too, yielded after a five months' blockade, and a threatened mutiny of four legions at Placentia was swiftly averted.

In 48 Caesar crossed to Epirus. After a blockade of Pompey's army at Dyrrhachium had failed, he made for Thessaly, where he routed the superior enemy forces at Pharsalus (see p. 105). Pompey fled to Egypt, only to be assassinated on arrival there. Caesar followed, but roused such hostility by his plan to gain control of Egypt, that he found himself besieged in the palace quarters of Alexandria during winter 48/7, and was only able to recover the situation in spring 47, when Ptolemy XIII was defeated and Cleopatra (now Caesar's mistress) was made effective ruler. Soon afterwards he dashed to crush the imminent threat to Asia Minor posed by Pharnaces of Bosporus, which he accomplished in a lightning five days' campaign at Zela.

After some months in Italy Caesar returned to campaigning in late 47, since Pompeian forces in Africa, supported by King Juba of Numidia, had grown alarmingly in strength. Caesar risked a winter campaign to crush them, and after early difficulties at Ruspina did so successfully within four months. The final battle, at Thapsus, turned into a massacre. Pompey's sons, however, regrouped their forces in southern Spain, where Caesar faced them in March 45. The battle at Munda was his hardest won victory, but its outcome proved decisive. Pompeian casualties were heavy, and of the leaders only Sextus Pompeius survived. The campaigns against Dacia and Parthia planned by Caesar for 44 were forestalled by his assassination.

After the dictator's death civil war resumed, this time between his supporters and his assassins. In 43 heavy fighting occurred in Cisalpine Gaul, where the governor, Decimus Brutus, was first besieged in Mutina by Antony; the latter was then defeated by the forces of the consuls and Octavian at both Forum Gallorum and Bononia. However, Antony, Octavian and Lepidus came together to form the Second Triumvirate. Meanwhile the assassins M. Brutus and Cassius consolidated their hold on the east, but were faced and beaten by Antony and Octavian in two successive battles at Philippi in October 42. Thereafter Octavian in the west had to besiege Perusia in the course of unrest during the winter of 41/40. Elimination of S. Pompeius—a formidable opponent—was his next pressing difficulty. Only when his fleet had been strengthened by Agrippa, did he eventually defeat Pompeius at Naulochus in 36. His campaigns in Illyricum between 35 and 33 were intended to safeguard north east Italy.

In the east Antony, who joined himself to Cleopatra, was faced by two crises. An Illyrian tribe, the Parthini, was invading Macedonia, while further east the Parthians were overrunning Syria and threatening Asia Minor. By the end of 39 Antony's lieutenants had beaten back all these incursions. But his own retaliatory campaign through Armenia into Parthia in 36 was a disaster. He failed to capture Phraaspa, capital of Media Atropatene, and could not shake off Parthian harassment. An invasion confined to Armenia in 34 was more successful; Roman control there lasted two years.

Deteriorating relations between Octavian and Antony led to war in 31. Antony advanced to Greece, where he was defeated in land and sea operations at Actium. Having fled back to Egypt, he was pursued there by Octavian the following year. He and Cleopatra committed suicide, leaving Octavian master of the Roman world.

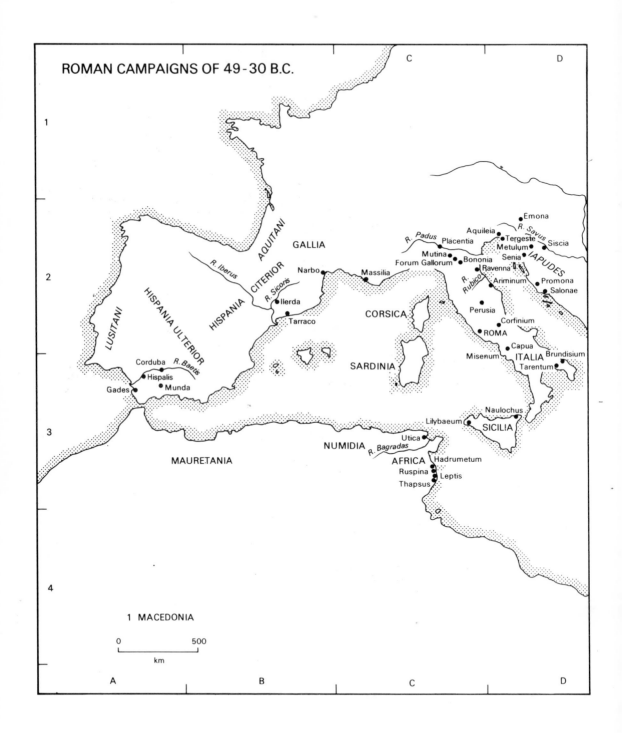

ROMAN CAMPAIGNS OF 49-30 B.C.

1

GALLIA

AQUITANI

HISPANIA CITERIOR

HISPANIA ULTERIOR

LUSITANI

R. Iberus

R. Sicoris

Narbo

Massilia

Ilerda

Tarraco

Corduba *R. Baetis*

Hispalis

Gades

Munda

2

CORSICA

SARDINIA

Emona

R. Savus

Aquileia
Placentia
Tergeste
Siscia
Metulum
Mutina
Senia
Forum Gallorum
Bononia
Senia
IAPUDES
Ravenna
R. Padus
Ariminum
Promona
R. Rubico
Salonae
Perusia
Corfinium
ROMA
Capua
Brundisium
Misenum
ITALIA
Tarentum

3

NUMIDIA

R. Bagradas

Utica

AFRICA
Hadrumetum
Ruspina
Leptis
Thapsus

MAURETANIA

Lilybaeum

SICILIA

Naulochus

4

1 MACEDONIA

0   500

km

A   B   C   D

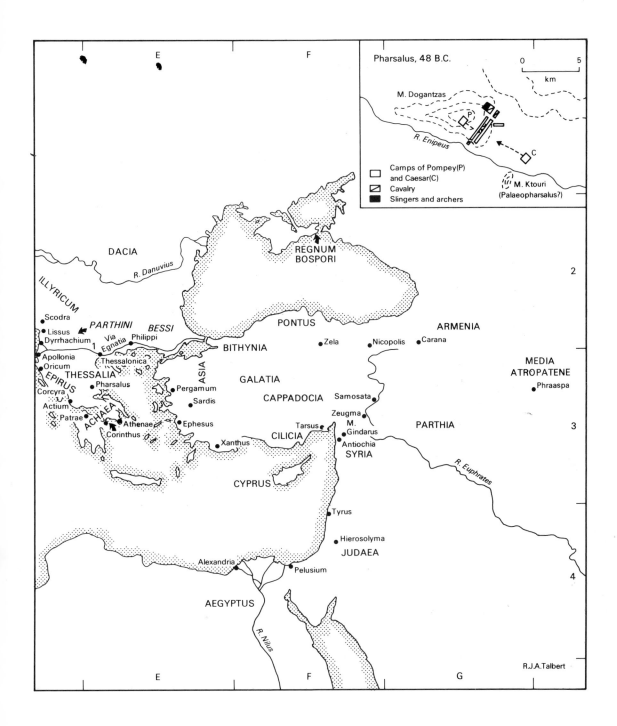

Pharsalus, 48 B.C.

M. Dogantzas

R. Enipeus

Camps of Pompey(P) and Caesar(C)

Cavalry

Slingers and archers

M. Ktouri (Palaeopharsalus?)

0   5
km

DACIA

R. Danuvius

REGNUM BOSPORI

ILLYRICUM

Scodra

PARTHINI   *BESSI*

Lissus

Dyrrhachium   Via Egnatia   Philippi

PONTUS

ARMENIA

Zela   Nicopolis   Carana

Apollonia

Oricum

BITHYNIA

EPIRUS   Thessalonica

THESSALIA

MEDIA ATROPATENE

GALATIA

Corcyra   Pharsalus

ASIA

CAPPADOCIA

Phraaspa

Actium   Pergamum

Samosata

Patrae   ACHAEA   Sardis

Zeugma

PARTHIA

Athenae   Ephesus

M.

Corinthus   Tarsus   Gindarus

R. Euphrates

Xanthus   CILICIA   Antiochia

SYRIA

CYPRUS

Tyrus

Hierosolyma

JUDAEA

Alexandria

Pelusium

AEGYPTUS

R. Nilus

R.J.A.Talbert

105

Pharsalus, 48 BC

The site of the battle is disputed. For all its detail our main account, that of Caesar (*Civil War* 3.82-99), remains topographically vague enough for it to be unclear how close to the town the armies met, or on which side of the R. Enipeus. This plan assumes a site north of the river, 12 km or so north west of the town. Its main aim, however, is to show the general development of the battle, which is not greatly in doubt.

Over several days Pompey's army, secure on high ground, was repeatedly challenged to battle by Caesar, who each time moved closer. As it happened, only at the point when Caesar had decided to abandon his attempt and move off, did Pompey unexpectedly respond. With his right flank protected by the river, he intended that on the left his superior cavalry, followed by slingers and archers, should attack Caesar's lines in the flank and rear, while his infantry (which also outnumbered those of Caesar) would resolutely stand their ground when the enemy advanced. Caesar's reactions were to ensure that when his front two lines (only) charged, they did not over-tax themselves; and to place eight cohorts obliquely behind his cavalry and right flank. These not only surprised and broke the charge of Pompey's cavalry, slingers and archers, but also then outflanked the enemy, who were put under intolerable pressure as Caesar now threw his third line into the battle. Pompey's army was scattered.

AUGUSTA PRAETORIA (AOSTA)

N

Capitolium and so-called forum

Amphitheatre

Baths

Theatre

Arch of Augustus, 370m. to east

0   400
m

T.W.Potter

Augusta Praetoria

Augusta Praetoria was founded in 25 BC as a military *colonia* designed to guard the Alpine passes of Great and Little St Bernard to the north and west respectively. The town was thus strongly protected. Its walls stood over 10 metres high and were heavily buttressed along the inner face, a highly unusual feature. In addition there were 20 square towers and four gates. These defences—still preserved in large part—enclosed a military-style rectangle, 724 × 572 metres, which was divided into 16 main building blocks and many other subdivisions. Much of this street plan is fossilised in the present-day layout. What is likely to have been the Capitolium has been identified in the northern part of the town, as have a covered theatre, or *odeon*, and an amphitheatre notable for its location inside the walls. Despite the traditional identification, the forum is most likely to have lain at the centre of the town. There are traces of public baths; however, few details of private housing have yet been uncovered. Some distance to the east of the town a bridge over the R. Buthier and the arch of Augustus are both still well preserved. Originally settled by 3,000 Praetorians, Augusta was never very large; but its continued strategic role is clearly highlighted by an unbroken sequence of occupation from antiquity to the present day.

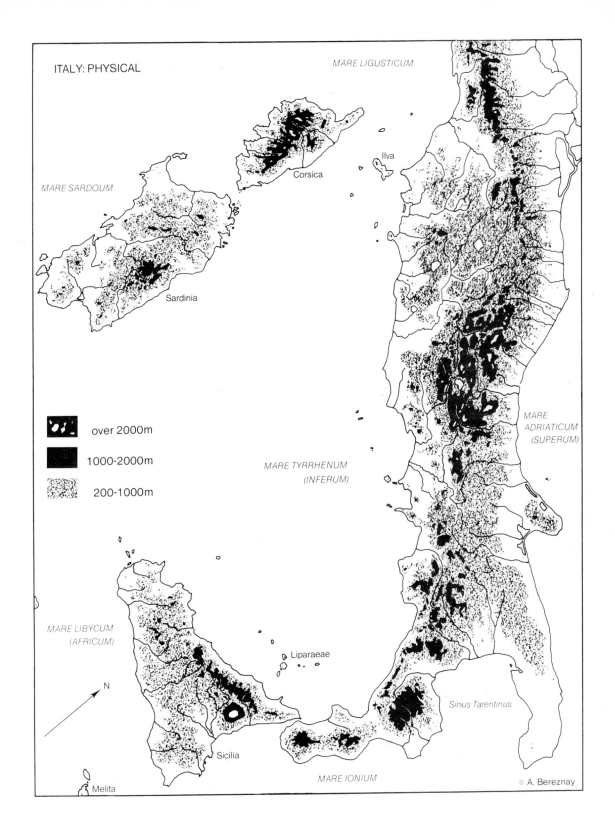

ITALY: PHYSICAL

MARE LIGUSTICUM

MARE SARDOUM

Ilva

Corsica

Sardinia

MARE ADRIATICUM
(SUPERUM)

over 2000m

1000-2000m

200-1000m

MARE TYRRHENUM
(INFERUM)

MARE LIBYCUM
(AFRICUM)

N

Liparaeae

Sinus Tarentinus

Sicilia

MARE IONIUM

Melita

© A. Bereznay

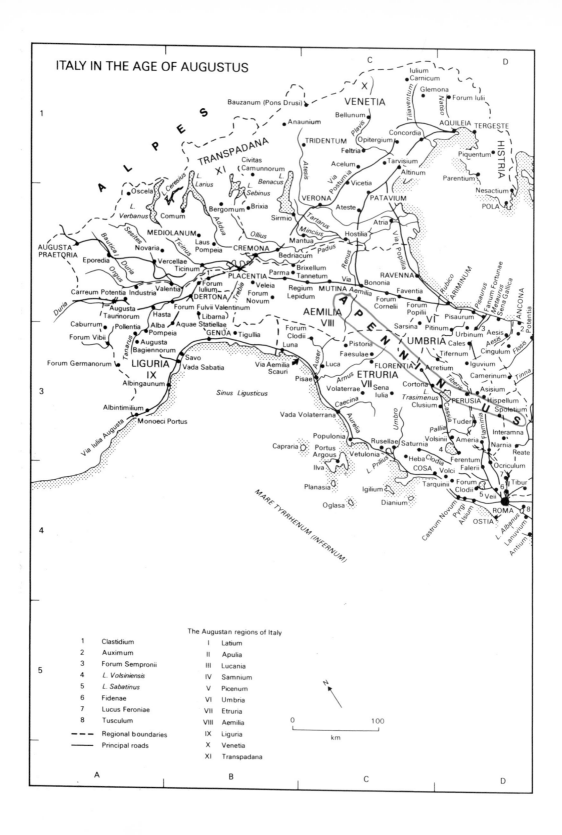

ITALY IN THE AGE OF AUGUSTUS

The Augustan regions of Italy

1	Clastidium	I	Latium
2	Auximum	II	Apulia
3	Forum Sempronii	III	Lucania
4	*L. Volsiniensis*	IV	Samnium
5	*L. Sabatinus*	V	Picenum
6	Fidenae	VI	Umbria
7	Lucus Feroniae	VII	Etruria
8	Tusculum	VIII	Aemilia
		IX	Liguria
--- Regional boundaries		X	Venetia
—— Principal roads		XI	Transpadana

0   100
km

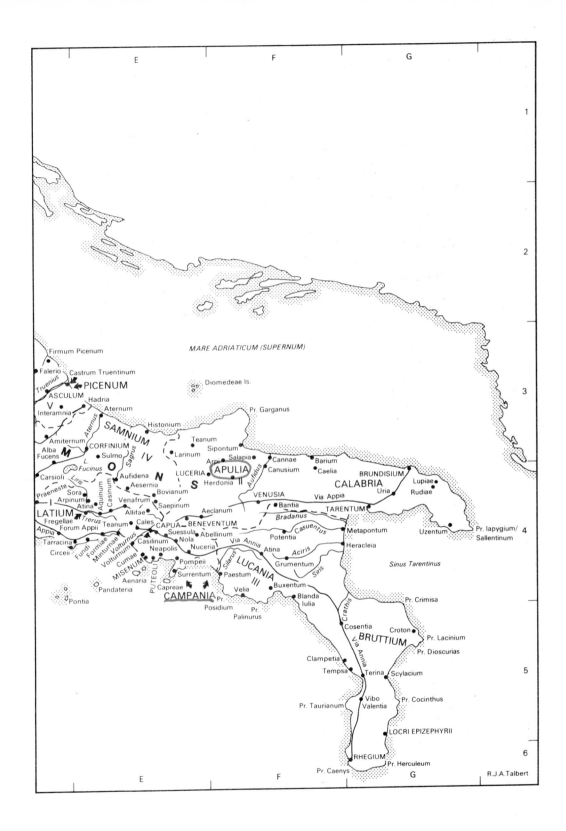

MARE ADRIATICUM (SUPERNUM)

Firmum Picenum
Falerio
Castrum Truentinum
Truentus
PICENUM
Diomedeae Is.
ASCULUM
Hadria
Interamnia
Aternum
Aternus
Pr. Garganus
SAMNIUM
Histonium
Teanum
Amiternum
CORFINIUM
Larinum
Sipontum
Alba
Fucens
Sulmo
Arpi
Salapia
Cannae
Barium
L. Fucinus
LUCERIA
APULIA
Canusium
Caelia
Carsioli
Aufidena
Herdonia
Aufidus
BRUNDISIUM
Praeneste
Aesernia
VENUSIA
Uria
Lupiae
Sora
Liris
Bovianum
CALABRIA
Rudiae
Arpinum
Atina
Venafrum
Saepinum
Bantia
Aquinum
Casinum
Allifae
Aeclanum
TARENTUM
LATIUM
Teanum
Cales
Bradanus
Pr. Iapygium/
Fregellae
CAPUA
BENEVENTUM
Sallentinum
Appia
Forum Appii
Suessula
Abellinum
Potentia
Casuentus
Metapontum
Uzentum
Tarracina
Fundi
Minturnae
Volturnus
Nola
Nuceria
Via Annia
Atina
Aciris
Heraclea
Circeii
Cumae
MISENUM
Neapolis
Siris
Siris
Pandateria
PUTEOLI
Pompeii
Surrentum
Silarus
Paestum
LUCANIA
Grumentum
Sinus Tarentinus
Aenaria
Capreae
CAMPANIA
Velia
Buxentum
Pontia
Pr. Posidium
Pr. Palinurus
Blanda
Iulia
Pr. Crimisa
Crathis
Cosentia
Croton
Pr. Lacinium
BRUTTIUM
Pr. Dioscurias
Clampetia
Via Annia
Tempsa
Terina
Scylacium
Vibo
Valentia
Pr. Cocinthus
Pr. Taurianum
LOCRI EPIZEPHYRII
RHEGIUM
Pr. Herculeum
Pr. Caenys

R.J.A.Talbert

109

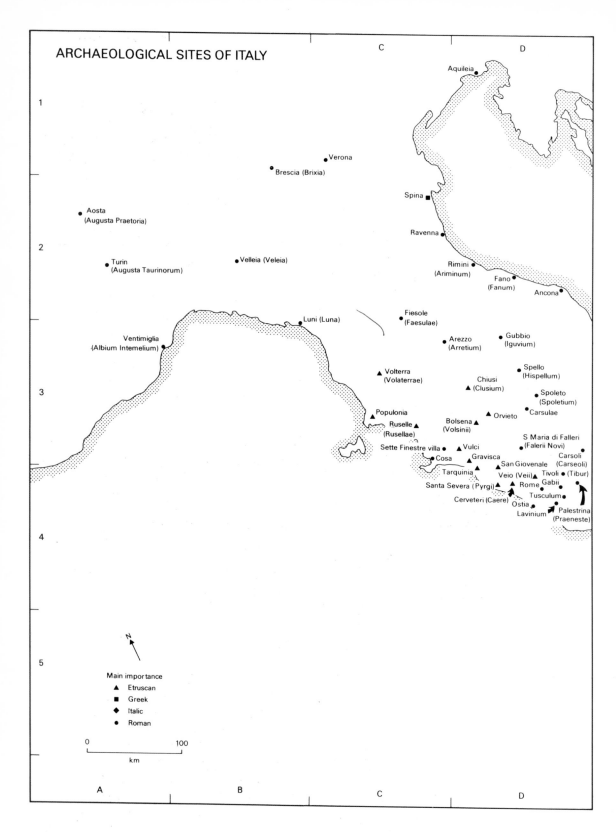

ARCHAEOLOGICAL SITES OF ITALY

Aquileia

Verona
Brescia (Brixia)

Spina

Ravenna

Aosta
(Augusta Praetoria)

Rimini
(Ariminum)

Fano
(Fanum)

Ancona

Turin
(Augusta Taurinorum)

Velleia (Veleia)

Luni (Luna)

Fiesole
(Faesulae)

Arezzo
(Arretium)

Gubbio
(Iguvium)

Ventimiglia
(Albium Intemelium)

Volterra
(Volaterrae)

Spello
(Hispellum)

Chiusi
(Clusium)

Spoleto
(Spoletium)

Populonia

Ruselle
(Rusellae)

Bolsena
(Volsinii)

Orvieto

Carsulae

S Maria di Falleri
(Falerii Novi)

Sette Finestre villa

Vulci

Gravisca

Cosa

San Giovenale

Carsoli
(Carseoli)

Tarquinia

Veio (Veii)

Tivoli (Tibur)

Santa Severa (Pyrgi)

Rome

Gabii

Cerveteri (Caere)

Ostia

Tusculum

Lavinium

Palestrina
(Praeneste)

N

Main importance

▲ Etruscan
■ Greek
◆ Italic
● Roman

0   100

km

110

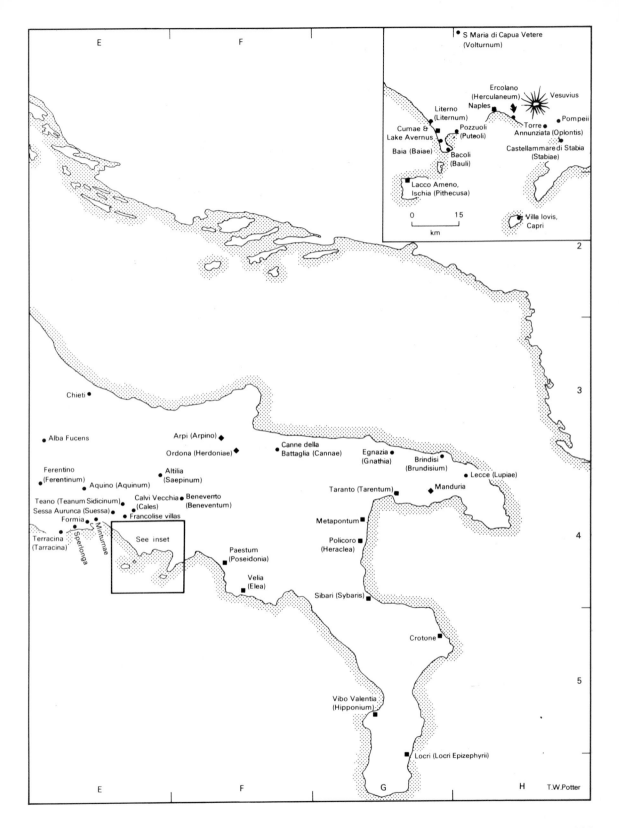

Inset labels:
S Maria di Capua Vetere (Volturnum)
Ercolano (Herculaneum)
Naples
Vesuvius
Pompeii
Literno (Liternum)
Pozzuoli (Puteoli)
Torre Annunziata (Oplontis)
Cumae & Lake Avernus
Baia (Baiae)
Bacoli (Bauli)
Castellammare di Stabia (Stabiae)
Lacco Ameno, Ischia (Pithecusa)
Villa Iovis, Capri

0   15
km

Main map labels:
E   F   H
2
3
Chieti
Alba Fucens
Arpi (Arpino)
Ordona (Herdoniae)
Canne della Battaglia (Cannae)
Egnazia (Gnathia)
Brindisi (Brundisium)
Lecce (Lupiae)
Ferentino (Ferentinum)
Altilia (Saepinum)
Aquino (Aquinum)
Taranto (Tarentum)
Manduria
Teano (Teanum Sidicinum)
Calvi Vecchia (Cales)
Benevento (Beneventum)
Sessa Aurunca (Suessa)
Formia
Francolise villas
Metapontum
Terracina (Tarracina)
Sperlonga
Minturnae
See inset
Paestum (Poseidonia)
Policoro (Heraclea)
4
Velia (Elea)
Sibari (Sybaris)
Crotone
5
Vibo Valentia (Hipponium)
Locri (Locri Epizephyrii)
E   F   G   H
T.W.Potter

111

Archaeological Sites of Italy

Italy is conspicuously rich in archaeological sites of almost every period. Moreover, many are quite astonishingly well preserved, in particular the immensely durable concrete structures of the later Republican and imperial periods. Even so, a great many more sites (notably villas and farms) remain to be discovered. This at least is clear from current programmes of systematic field survey, which aim to map all surface traces of sites, so as to record entire landscapes of antiquity. The technique has been particularly successful to the north of Rome, where over 1,000 sq km have been studied in this way.

Of course thousands of sites have also been examined through excavation, even if there is no site that can be said to have been completely uncovered. The map lists a selection of the more important, particularly (although not exclusively) those where there are still visible remains. Most are town sites with long histories, in many cases extending back well into the first millennium BC. Equally, a significant number remains in occupation down to the present day, underlining the care with which their locations were originally chosen. However, it is useful to draw attention to the most important period in a site's history, and for this reason four main groups have been distinguished.

The first includes the Etruscan cities and their cemeteries, most of which came into being early in the first millennium BC. Until very recently archaeological work has tended to concentrate upon the religious sanctuaries (e.g. Pyrgi, Gravisca) and the cemeteries—vivid indices of the wealth and widespread contacts of the Etruscans. Yet the unplanned growth of all but a few cities is nonetheless manifest from work at Veii, Rusellae and elsewhere. The second group comprises the Greek colonies of southern Italy, the oldest of which was at Pithecusa on the island of Ischia, founded *c.* 775 BC. Experiments in town planning are evident at many early sites such as Metapontum and Paestum: these were to provide Rome with a model to adapt when founding new settlements. Many of the sites conserve outstanding remains, although often, as at Sybaris or Paestum, there is a heavy overlay of Roman buildings. Thirdly, there are town sites of the Italic tribes, such as the Daunian city of Arpino (Arpi), or the Messapian centre of Manduria. Many of the more important of these settlements were to take on a significant role in the Roman urban network.

Finally, there are the Roman sites themselves. These fall into three main subdivisions. First, towns which developed out of older settlements, such as Pompeii and Herculaneum. Second, new foundations, many of which were colonies, like Cosa, Luni, or Aosta; Augustus records founding 28 colonies in Italy. Third, sites of the countryside, among them farms, sanctuaries and villas. The latter vary widely. They range from great mansions such as Tiberius' Villa Iovis on the island of Capri to elaborate, but nevertheless functional, complexes such as the Sette Finestre villa near Cosa. Most were in fact the centres of farming estates, and varied in size and magnificence according to the wealth of the owner. Increasingly, like the towns, they are being scientifically excavated, so that our knowledge of the layout, function and history of many sites should be transformed in the years ahead.

Ostia

The harbour town of Ostia occupied low-lying ground 25 km south west of Rome, close to the mouth of the R. Tiber. Its irregular plan displays a long history of growth and rebuilding. Ostia was originally a military *castrum*, just over two hectares in extent, located in the central part of the later town. The *decumanus maximus* ran through the *castrum*, the east gate of which can still be seen. Probably because of a greatly increased level of trade, the town was much expanded early in the first century BC to a size of some 63 hectares, and the existing walls were constructed. Certainly Ostia grew to be most prosperous, as its wealth of public monuments shows. There was a very long forum with temples at either end, while the magnificent Piazzale delle Corporazioni housed 61 offices—mostly with appropriate advertising in the mosaic floors—of various local and overseas traders. As the map shows, huge warehouses for

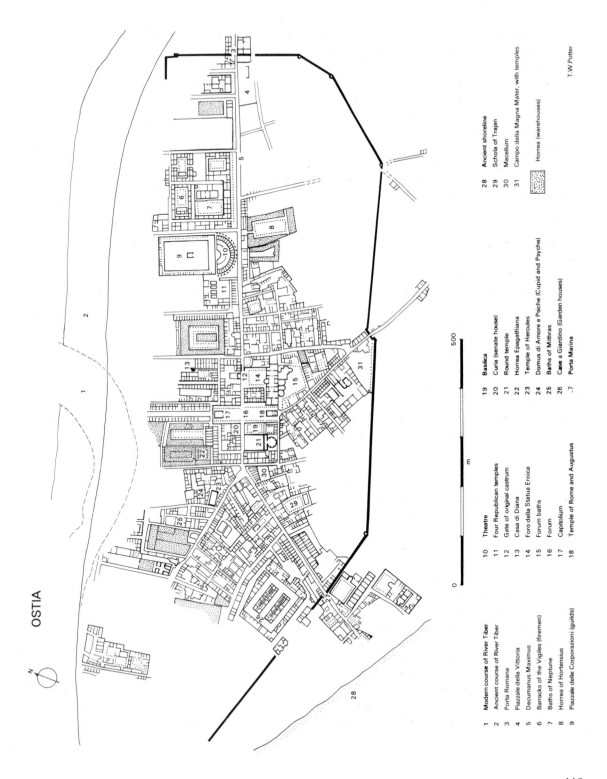

OSTIA

N

1	Modern course of River Tiber	10	Theatre
2	Ancient course of River Tiber	11	Four Republican temples
3	Porta Romana	12	Gate of original castrum
4	Piazzale della Vittoria	13	Casa di Diana
5	Decumanus Maximus	14	Foro della Statua Eroica
6	Barracks of the Vigiles (firemen)	15	Horrea Epagathiana
7	Baths of Neptune	16	Forum baths
8	Horrea of Hortensius	17	Capitolium
9	Piazzale delle Corporazioni (guilds)	18	Temple of Rome and Augustus

19	Basilica	28	Ancient shoreline
20	Curia (senate house)	29	Schola of Trajan
21	Round temple	30	Macellum
22	Horrea Epagathiana	31	Campo della Magna Mater, with temples
23	Temple of Hercules		Horrea (warehouses)
24	Domus di Amore e Psiche (Cupid and Psyche)		
25	Baths of Mithras		
26	Case a Giardino (Garden houses)		
27	Porta Marina		

T.W.Potter

0   m   500

113

the storage of grain, wine, oil and other goods became commonplace, and no less than 18 sets of baths have been identified—compared with three at Pompeii. The building work entailed considerable replanning of some quarters of the town, epitomised, for example, by the orderly layout of the streets to the north east. Ostia is perhaps best known for its *insulae*, or great apartment blocks, which probably rose to a total height of 60 Roman feet. The development of such housing—which must have been typical of Rome and no doubt of many other Italian towns—is only represented on a small scale at Pompeii and Herculaneum, since both were fossilised by the volcanic eruption of AD 79; this trend in domestic housing only became

well established later. Some more elaborate houses are known at Ostia, but they are very much the exception.

In AD 42 work was begun on the construction of a huge new harbour, four km to the north west. Silting created grave problems, however, and under Trajan a second, hexagonal harbour was built. This new commercial centre soon became the focus of warehouses, domestic buildings and even a so-called imperial palace. Eventually to be known as Portus, the port area gradually increased in importance, eclipsing the old city's commercial role. This was recognised in an edict of 314, when Ostia was stripped of its municipal rights and began slowly to be abandoned.

Second Battle of Cremona, AD 69

This crucial battle between the partisans of Vitellius and Vespasian in the Year of the Four Emperors was fought on the flat, rich plain about eight km east of Cremona during the night of 24/5 October 69. The account of Tacitus (*Histories* 3.15-25), together with the preservation of Roman centuriation, makes it possible to identify the site with some accuracy. The battle was a heroic feat of endurance for both sides. Though the Flavian troops had already been stretched—the cavalry by clashes with squadrons from the Vitellian garrison in Cremona, the infantry by a long march—there was a demand by late afternoon for an immediate assault, which the commander, Antonius Primus, only prevented with great difficulty. He did prepare for battle, however, on receiving news that the garrison had just been substantially swelled to 35,000 legionaries (against his own 25,000) by a force which had dashed 100 miles in five days, yet was equally eager to do battle at once. Antonius chose his ground astride the Via Postumia, and the Vitellians, led by F. Fabullus, rashly risked a night encounter. Throughout, the fighting was bitter, confused, indecisive. But once the moon rose (by 10 p.m.), the Flavians gained some advantage from its light, and by dawn a rumour, albeit groundless, that they were being reinforced gave the final impetus for a successful thrust towards Cremona.

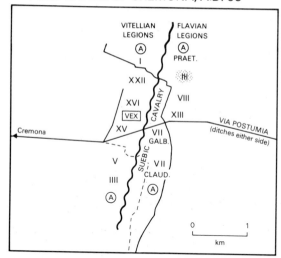

SECOND BATTLE OF CREMONA, A.D. 69

	Roads
- - -	Steep drainage ditch
	Plantation of trees
~	Approximate line of clash
PRAET.	Contingent of ex-Praetorian guardsmen

(A) Auxiliary units. Cavalry, too, were deployed to protect the flanks and rear of both sides

VEX. Vexillations, or detachments, from Legions II, IX, XX. Others from Legions Rapax and Italica were also interspersed along the Vitellian line

R.J.A.Talbert

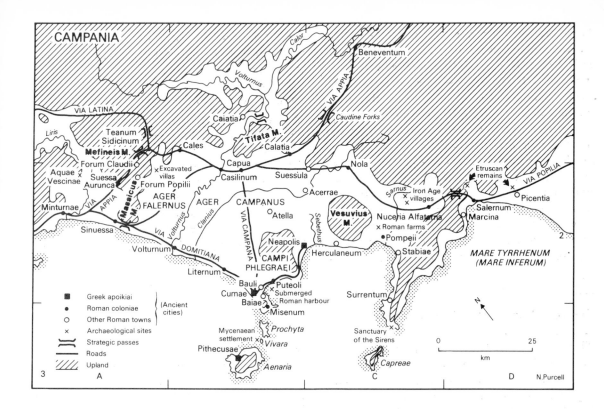

Campania

The distinctive physical geography of Campania is
immediately apparent from the map. The high
limestone ridges of the Appennines and their
outliers surround a series of low-lying plains.
While easily accessible from one another, these are
broken up by Mount Vesuvius and the volcanic
hills of the Campi Phlegraei ('Burning Fields'), as
well as by extensive areas of intractable marshland
along the rivers. For the rest, the land is extremely
fertile: thus it was not only the most highly prized,
but also some of the most intensively exploited
arable terrain of ancient Italy. Capua (near
modern Caserta) was one of the most important
settlements of the region throughout antiquity; its
central position is plain. Other towns which controlled access to the region also grew dramatically:
Teanum and Nuceria at mountain passes;
Sinuessa, Cumae, Puteoli and Pompeii as harbour
towns. Although the relations between coast and
interior were always close, the separation of the
harbours from the plains by hill or marsh assisted a
certain cultural divergence. Despite the predomi-
nance of Etruscan and local cultures inland, the
Greek colonies of the coast kept their distinctive
character; even widespread penetration by Oscan
speakers at the end of the fifth century did not end
this situation. Most notably Puteoli and Neapolis,
assisted by the tenacious links of the Campanian
ports with the eastern Mediterranean, retained
many Hellenic characteristics to the end of the
Roman empire. This Hellenism, added to the
advantages of wealth, populousness and great
natural beauty, attracted the wealthy of Rome to
such an extent that the Bay of Naples, and Baiae in
particular, became a notorious playground of the
elite. Eventually, as tectonic activity drowned the
pleasure palaces and the harbour works, and as the
draining of the Sebethus and Clanius marshes
improved communications with the interior,
Neapolis succeeded Puteoli as the chief city of the
area. Modern Naples enjoys the same primacy
today.

115

POMPEII

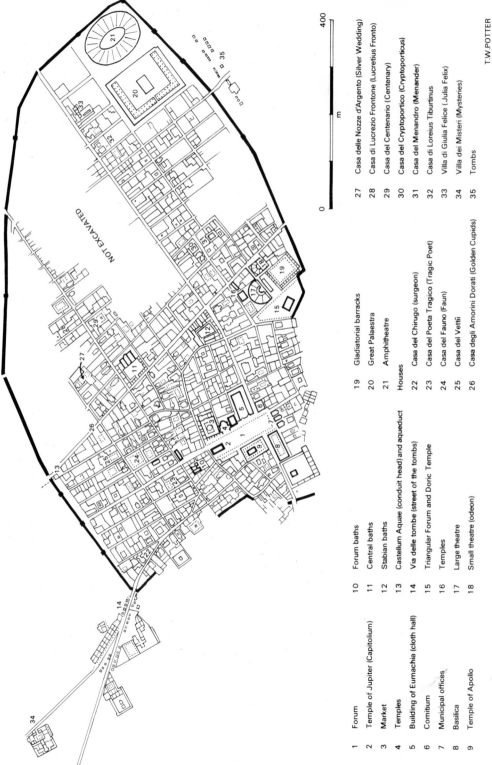

NOT EXCAVATED

T.W. POTTER

1	Forum
2	Temple of Jupiter (Capitolium)
3	Market
4	Temples
5	Building of Eumachia (cloth hall)
6	Comitium
7	Municipal offices
8	Basilica
9	Temple of Apollo

10	Forum baths
11	Central baths
12	Stabian baths
13	Castellum Aquae (conduit head) and aqueduct
14	Via delle tombe (street of the tombs)
15	Triangular Forum and Doric Temple
16	Temples
17	Large theatre
18	Small theatre (odeon)

19	Gladiatorial barracks
20	Great Palaestra
21	Amphitheatre
	Houses
22	Casa del Chirugo (surgeon)
23	Casa del Poeta Tragico (Tragic Poet)
24	Casa del Fauno (Faun)
25	Casa del Vettii
26	Casa degli Amorini Dorati (Golden Cupids)

27	Casa delle Nozze d'Argento (Silver Wedding)
28	Casa di Lucrezio Frontone (Lucretius Fronto)
29	Casa del Centenario (Centenary)
30	Casa del Cryptoportico (Cryptoporticus)
31	Casa del Menandro (Menander)
32	Casa di Loreius Tiburtinus
33	Villa di Giulia Felice (Julia Felix)
34	Villa dei Misteri (Mysteries)
35	Tombs

Pompeii

Pompeii was the leading city and port of the southern part of the bay of Naples, measuring some 1,200 × 720 metres within its walls. Roughly two-thirds of the site has been liberated from the thick mantle of volcanic deposits which enveloped it in August AD 79. Like any city, Pompeii contains buildings of many different centuries. The oldest is a Greek Doric temple of the sixth century BC, part of an early nucleus underlying the forum area; but most structures belong to the second century BC and later.

There are three main areas of public buildings. First, the unusually long forum—with a Corinthian temple, the Capitolium, at one end. Around were more temples, a cloth hall, the judicial basilica, a market, and three other halls (municipal offices?). Then to the east lay the triangular forum with its Doric temple; nearby were the Greek theatre and a small covered theatre, as well as a temple of Isis. Finally, at the town's eastern edge, were the amphitheatre of c. 80 BC and the Great Palaestra, a large enclosure surrounding a swimming pool. There were three sets of public baths, of which the central one was unfinished in 79. All were supplied by an aqueduct, from which water passed through lead pipes. The aqueduct also fed private baths and the innumerable fountains, whose overflow was used to wash down the streets and sewers. Houses varied considerably in scale, from one-room shops with a room above, to palatial, elaborately decorated residences. The layout of most of the latter is that described by the architect Vitruvius, with a roofed *atrium* containing a central opening to collect rainwater in a cistern below; and a peristyle, a garden court, surrounded by a colonnade.

Pompeii was a busy city which became prosperous through trade and agriculture, though it also developed industries like the production of lava millstones, cloth and fish sauce. By 79, with a population of some 20,000, it was expanding considerably, particularly westwards, where sections of the old town walls became obliterated.

Herculaneum

Partly because Herculaneum is buried beneath no less than 15 metres of volcanic mud, only a relatively small part of the city has been excavated. Nonetheless it would seem to have been quite modest in size, perhaps measuring 320 × 370 metres. The population may have numbered about 5,000. The preservation of organic materials like wood is excellent, and many of the buildings have yielded an extraordinary quantity of detailed information. The *decumani* (east-west streets) and the *cardines* (north-south streets) divide the city into blocks or *insulae*. To the north was a particularly wide *decumanus*, closed off to vehicular traffic, which may have served as the forum. The basilica is thought to lie on the north side of the *decumanus maximus*, while to the east was a palaestra with a large pool at the centre of the peristyle court. A theatre is also known from the old excavations in the north west area, and there were public baths nearby.

Herculaneum is at least as old as the sixth century, but the visible remains of the houses belong mainly to the latter centuries of the Republic. Many are laid out around an *atrium*, in the Italic style, but there is considerable variation in plan. Some have porticoes in front, while a great many possessed a second or even a third storey. Attached to the houses were shops selling wine, grain, metal-work, glassware and other commodities; one even conserves its painted sign. To the south, at the extremity of the early city, were some much grander houses, with peristyles, gardens and other rooms, giving a panoramic view over the sea. They belong mainly to the Augustan period and later. Beyond was an extensive complex of baths and various religious buildings. These splendid structures, with their fine statues and paintings, underline the affluence and high rank of many families who owned property in Herculaneum.

HERCULANEUM

N

1 Basilica

2 Decumanus maximus (forum)

4 Hall

Loggia

5 Palaestra

Piscina

3

15

16

17

11

6

18

12

13

10

21

19 20 22

14

9

7

8

0 200

m

T.W.Potter

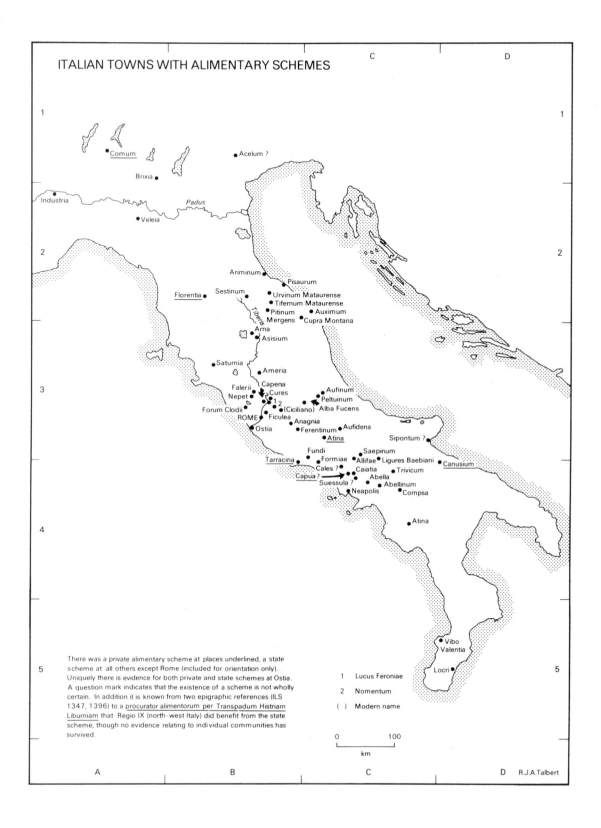

ITALIAN TOWNS WITH ALIMENTARY SCHEMES

Comum

Acelum ?

Brixia

Industria

Padus

Veleia

Ariminum

Pisaurum

Florentia

Sestinum

Urvinum Mataurense

Tifernum Mataurense

Pitinum

Auximum

Mergens

Cupra Montana

Tiberis

Arna

Asisium

Saturnia

Ameria

Capena

Falerii

Cures

Aufinum

Nepet

Peltuinum

Forum Clodii

(Ciciliano)

Alba Fucens

1 2

ROME

Ficulea

Anagnia

Ostia

Ferentinum

Aufidena

Atina

Sipontum ?

Fundi

Saepinum

Tarracina

Formiae

Allifae

Ligures Baebiani

Cales ?

Caiatia

Trivicum

Canusium

Capua ?

Abella

Suessula ?

Abellinum

Neapolis

Compsa

Atina

Vibo
Valentia

Locri

There was a private alimentary scheme at places underlined, a state
scheme at all others except Rome (included for orientation only).
Uniquely there is evidence for both private and state schemes at Ostia.
A question mark indicates that the existence of a scheme is not wholly
certain. In addition it is known from two epigraphic references (ILS
1347, 1396) to a procurator alimentorum per Transpadum Histriam
Liburniam that Regio IX (north-west Italy) did benefit from the state
scheme, though no evidence relating to individual communities has
survived.

1   Lucus Feroniae

2   Nomentum

( )   Modern name

0   100

km

A   B   C   D   R.J.A.Talbert

119

Italian Towns with Alimentary Schemes

Alimentary schemes (*alimenta*) for the support of children are known from the mid-first century AD onwards. Private benefactors took the initiative in the first instance, but Nerva and Trajan came to sponsor a major state programme throughout Italy, best documented in substantial records from Veleia and Ligures Baebiani. The state offered capital, though in all other respects its schemes were locally based in each participating community, and designed to operate with the minimum of future adjustment. The larger local landowners accepted from the state perpetual loans amounting to approximately 8 per cent of the value of their property; the interest paid at the low rate of 5 per cent furnished the modest monthly support grants. The method by which the children to benefit from the schemes were chosen is unknown. They are certainly unlikely to have been orphans, yet the assumption that they would always be from the poorest families is unwarranted. While the state programme was definitely not initiated in order to provide smaller landowners with working capital (as has been claimed), its real aims remain obscure: arguably these were a mixture of philanthropy and concern for a supposed population decline which might affect legionary recruitment. State *alimenta* were perhaps extended a little by later second-century emperors and continued in existence into the third century. At best their usefulness was only ever limited.

Evidence for *alimenta* is almost exclusively epigraphic. While the spread of the 50 or so communities from which relevant indications have emerged (references to a local *quaestor alimentorum* and the like) may reflect little beyond the random survival of this material, there must still be a suspicion that the state scheme was hardly extended to the remoter or poorer areas of the peninsula. Evidence for private schemes is slight, although the arrangements for one set up by Pliny at Comum are described in his *Letters* (7.18).

Key to P. 121: Temples 1. Divus Traianus. 2. Mars Ultor. 3. Venus Genitrix. 4. Minerva. 5. Vediovis. 6. Concordia. 7. Divus Vespasianus. 8. Saturnus. 9. Ianus? 10. Castores. 11. Divus Iulius. 12. Divus Antoninus. 13. Vesta. 14. Iuturna. 15. Penates (the form indicated is post-Caracallan). 16. Iuturna *or* Iuno Curritis. 17. Fortuna Huiusce Diei. 18. Feronia. 19. Lares Permarini. 20. Hercules Musarum. 21. Iuppiter Stator. 22. Iuno Regina. 23. Apollo Sosianus. 24. Bellona. 25. Iuppiter Tonans. 26. Fortuna Primigenia. 27. Iuppiter Victor. 28. Apollo Palatinus. 29. Ianus. 30. Spes. 31. Iuno Sospita. 32. Fortuna. 33. Mater Matuta. Other temples are indicated by the name of the deity worshipped there. *Other monuments* 34. Porticus Vipsania *or* Minucia? 35. Markets of Trajan. 36. Unidentified porticus. 37. Libraries and column of Trajan. 38. Tabularium. 39. Curia. 40. Regia. 41. Porticus Minucia? Templum Nympharum? 42. Ara Gentis Iuliae? 43. Unidentified porticus. 44. Market-building of Forum Holitorium. 45. Houses of Augustus and his family. 46. Palatine libraries. 47. Site of the later basilica of Maxentius.

Rome in the Age of the Severi

The orientation of the map is based on that of the Marble Plan of the city which was set up in the early third century AD and survives in fragments. The Aurelianic Walls of 271–5 are indicated faintly as a guide to the later topography. The map is intended to show not so much architectural detail, but rather the overall layout of the imperial city and its main topographical centres and regions, as well as the principal morphological zones, in so far as they can be reconstructed.

The shape of the city was still defined by the Republican wall-circuit, although this will have been ruinous and built over in places. Its gates were great topographical landmarks. The monumental centre is left *unshaded*. Its enormous extent is at once apparent. The monuments here may be seen in detail in 'The Centre of Rome in the Age of Caracalla' (area within dotted rectangle). In *heavy shading* is the area of the densest housing. Here

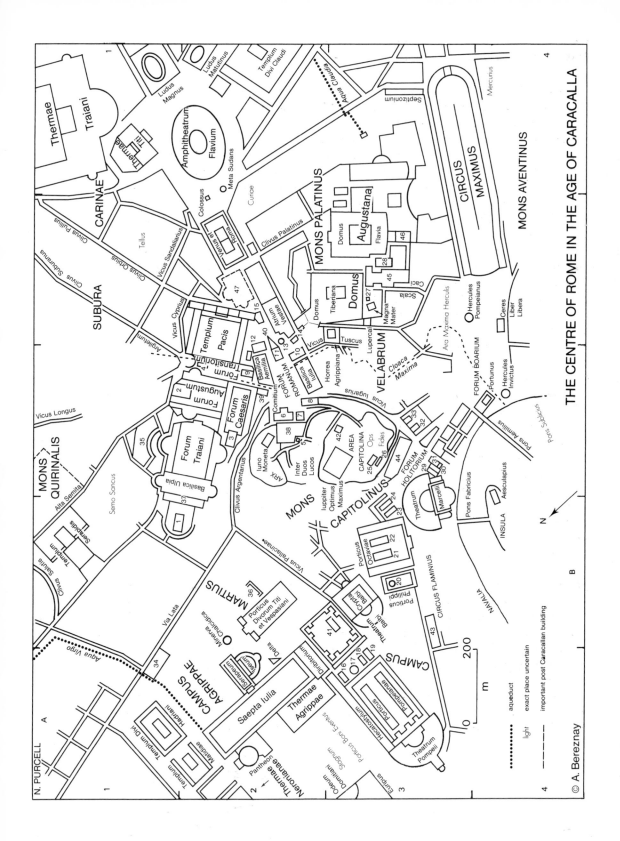

THE CENTRE OF ROME IN THE AGE OF CARACALLA

N. PURCELL

© A. Bereznay

aqueduct

light

exact place uncertain

important post Caracallan building

MONS QUIRINALIS

MONS PALATINUS

MONS AVENTINUS

MONS CAPITOLINUS

CAMPUS MARTIUS

CAMPUS AGRIPPAE

SUBURA

CARINAE

VELABRUM

FORUM ROMANUM

FORUM BOARIUM

FORUM HOLITORIUM

CIRCUS MAXIMUS

CIRCUS FLAMINIUS

Thermae Traiani

Thermae Titi

Amphitheatrum Flavium

Ludus Magnus

Ludus Matutinus

Templum Divi Claudi

Aqua Claudia

Septizonium

Mercurius

Meta Sudans

Colossus

Curiae

Roma

Venerisvet

Clivus Palatinus

Domus Augustana

Flavia

Domus Tiberiana

Magna Mater

Scala Caci

Ara Maxima Herculis

Hercules Pompeianus

Ceres Liber Libera

Hercules Invictus

Portunus

Templum Pacis

Forum Transitorium

Atrium Vestae

Basilica Aemilia

Basilica Iulia

Comitium

Horrea Agrippiana

Cloaca Maxima

Lupercal

Tuscus

Vicus

Vicus Iugarius

Forum Augustum

Forum Caesaris

Forum Traiani

Basilica Ulpia

Clivus Argentarius

Iuno Moneta

Arx

Inter Duos Lucos

AREA CAPITOLINA

Iuppiter Optimus Maximus

Ops

Fides

Pons Aemilius

Pons Sublicius

Pons Fabricius

Aesculapius

INSULA

Theatrum Marcelli

Porticus Octaviae

Porticus Philippi

Minerva Chalcidica

Porticus Divorum Titi et Vespasiani

Iseum

Serapeum

Delta

Saepta Iulia

Thermae Agrippae

Crypta Balbi

Theatrum Balbi

Hecatostylum

Porticus Pompeianae

Theatrum Pompeii

Odeum

Stadium Domitiani

Porticus Boni Eventus

Pantheon

Thermae Neronianae

Templum Divi Hadriani

Matidiae

Via Lata

Aqua Virgo

Vicus Longus

Alta Semita

Semo Sancus

Serapidis

Templum Salutis

Clivus Salutis

Vicus Pullius

Clivus Suburanus

Clivus Pullius

Tellus

Vicus Sandalianus

Vicus Orbius

Vicus Cyprius

Argiletum

Vicus Pallacinae

Dinotholum

N

m   0   200

A

B

1

2

3

4

lived the great mass of Rome's population—several hundred thousand people—for the most part in tall tenement buildings (*insulae*). The *hatched* area is the urban periphery. It, too, was quite densely populated, and was considered by Romans to be part of the built-up area or *continentia aedificia*. Here the suburban mansions (*horti*) of the emperor and the very wealthy jostled with aqueducts, tombs, market gardens and some *insulae*. *Stippled* are the commercial zones beside the river.

Certain prominent sacred buildings are indicated by a small circle. In addition a star indicates some important aspect of the city's layout:

A The Lateran. Luxury villas here were confiscated under Nero and destroyed to make room for the barracks of the imperial *equites singulares* or mounted bodyguard; subsequently the site of the cathedral of Rome under Constantine.

B Campus Esquilinus, with grove of Libitina, goddess of funerals. Place for public executions and paupers' cemetery, partly improved (by Maecenas in particular) to form lavish suburban estates.

C Camp (marked) and parade ground of the Praetorian Guard.

D Area later occupied by the Baths of Diocletian.

E Horti Sallustiani, enormous suburban palace which soon became one of the most important imperial properties.

F Horti Luculliani, most lavish of all the suburban villas, and also an imperial estate.

G Tombs and villas on the Via Flaminia, including the tomb of Nero.

H Mausoleum of Augustus (circle marked), Ara Pacis Augustae, giant sundial of Augustus and the park which linked them.

I Funerary monuments of the Antonine emperors.

J Ad Ciconias Nixas, the upstream river-harbour of the city, and the principal wine wharves.

K Mausoleum of Hadrian (marked) and the wealthy suburb of the Ager Vaticanus. Racetrack of Caligula and Nero, naval arena of Augustus, and paupers' cemetery with strong religious associations for Christians and followers of Phrygian cults.

L Trigarium, practice horse-race track, with the stables of the circus factions nearby. This area was still suburban in the late Republic but was built up by the Severan period; it later became the centre of medieval Rome.

M Main river harbour of Rome, which spread downstream from the Forum Boarium from the second century BC onwards.

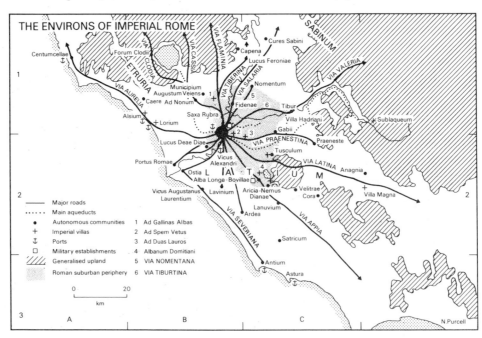

THE ENVIRONS OF IMPERIAL ROME

Major roads
Main aqueducts
• Autonomous communities
+ Imperial villas
⚓ Ports
□ Military establishments
▨ Generalised upland
░ Roman suburban periphery

1 Ad Gallinas Albas
2 Ad Spem Vetus
3 Ad Duas Lauros
4 Albanum Domitiani
5 VIA NOMENTANA
6 VIA TIBURTINA

0   20
km

N. Purcell

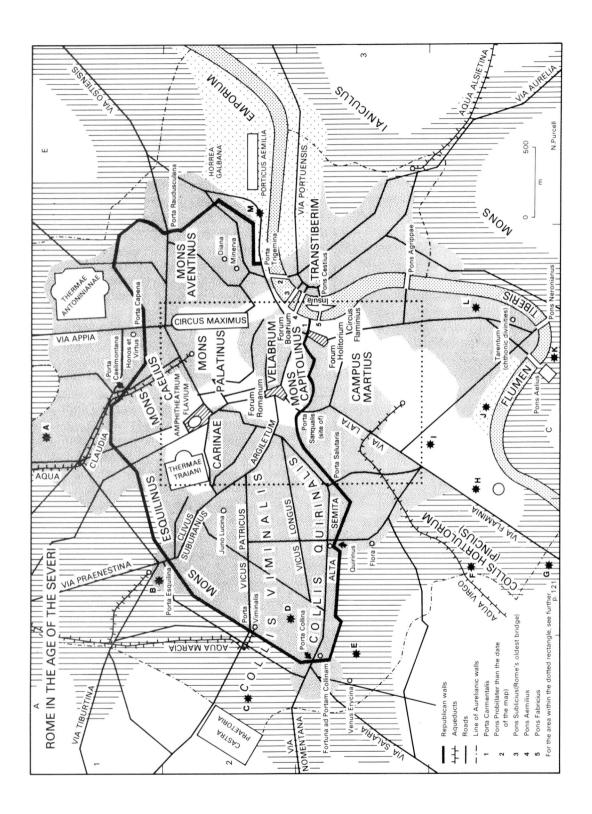

ROME IN THE AGE OF THE SEVERI

VIA OSTIENSIS

EMPORIUM

HORREA GALBANA

PORTICUS AEMILIA

VIA PORTUENSIS

IANICULUS

AQUA ALSIETINA

VIA AURELIA

SNOW

N.Purcell

500

m

0

THERMAE ANTONINIANAE

Porta Raudusculana

MONS AVENTINUS

Diana
Minerva

Porta Trigemina

TRANSTIBERIM

Pons Cestius

Pons Agrippae

Pons Neronianus

TIBERIS

Pons Aelius

FLUMEN

K

VIA APPIA

Porta Capena

Honos et Virtus

Porta Caelimontana

CIRCUS MAXIMUS

MONS PALATINUS

VELABRUM

Forum Boarium

MONS CAPITOLINUS

Insula

Circus Flaminius

Forum Holitorium

CAMPUS MARTIUS

Tarentum (chthonic divinities)

L

J

I

AQUA

CLAUDIA

MONS CAELIUS

AMPHITHEATRUM FLAVIUM

CARINAE

Forum Romanum

ARGILETUM

Porta Sanqualis (site of)

Porta Salutaris

VIA LATA

H

A

THERMAE TRAIANI

ESQUILINUS

CLIVUS SUBURANUS

Juno Lucina

VICUS PATRICIUS

VICUS LONGUS

COLLIS QUIRINALIS

ALTA SEMITA

Quirinus

Flora

COLLIS (PINCIUS) HORTULORUM

VIA FLAMINIA

AQUA VIRGO

F

G

For the area within the dotted rectangle, see further, p. 121

VIA PRAENESTINA

SNOW

B

Porta Esquilina

COLLIS VIMINALIS

Porta Viminalis

Porta Collina

D

Venus Erycina

E

VIA TIBURTINA

AQUA MARCIA

VIA NOMENTANA

VIA SALARIA

Fortuna ad Portam Collinam

CASTRA PRAETORIA

1

2

Republican walls
Aqueducts
Roads
Line of Aurelianic walls

1   Porta Carmentalis
2   Pons Probi later than the date of the map)
3   Pons Sublicius(Rome's oldest bridge)
4   Pons Aemilius
5   Pons Fabricius

For the area within the dotted rectangle, see further

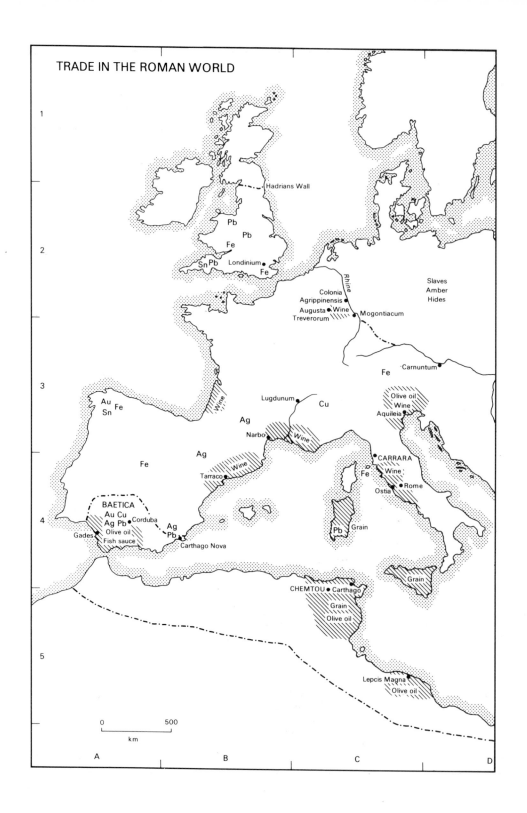

TRADE IN THE ROMAN WORLD

1

Hadrians Wall

Pb
Pb
Fe

Sn Pb Londinium
Fe

Colonia
Agrippinensis
Augusta Wine
Treverorum Mogontiacum

Rhine

Slaves
Amber
Hides

Fe Carnuntum

3

Au Fe
Sn

Fe

Wine

Lugdunum Cu

Olive oil
Wine
Aquileia

Ag

Narbo Wine

CARRARA
Wine

Ag

Wine

Tarraco

Fe

Rome

Ostia

BAETICA
Au Cu
Ag Pb Corduba
Olive oil
Gades Fish sauce

Pb Grain

4

Ag
Pb
Carthago Nova

Grain

CHEMTOU Carthago
Grain
Olive oil

5

Lepcis Magna
Olive oil

0   500
km

A   B   C   D

124

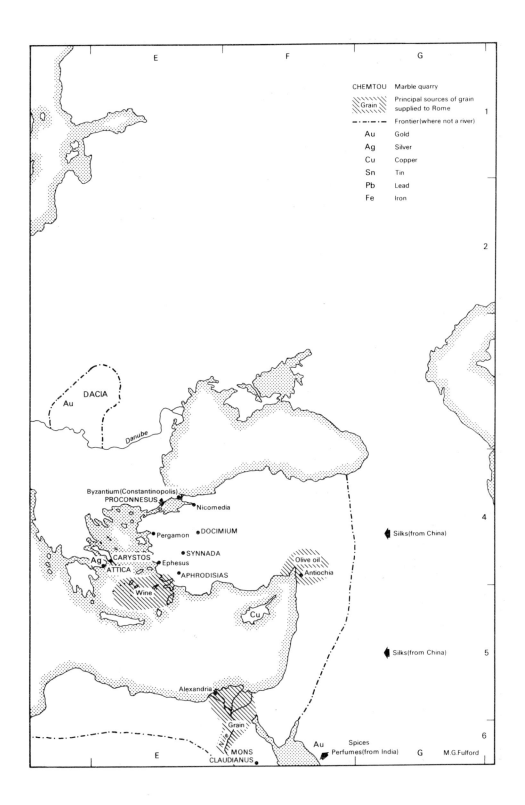

CHEMTOU — Marble quarry

Grain — Principal sources of grain supplied to Rome

—·—·— Frontier (where not a river)

Au — Gold
Ag — Silver
Cu — Copper
Sn — Tin
Pb — Lead
Fe — Iron

DACIA
Au

Danube

Byzantium (Constantinopolis)
PROCONNESUS
Nicomedia
DOCIMIUM
Pergamon
SYNNADA
CARYSTOS
Ephesus
ATTICA
APHRODISIAS
Ag
Wine
Cu
Olive oil
Antiochia
Silks (from China)
Silks (from China)
Alexandria
Grain
Nile
Au
Spices
Perfumes (from India)
MONS
CLAUDIANUS
M.G. Fulford

125

Trade in the Roman World

In the Roman world trade was a complex affair. Trade for profit, carried out by entrepreneurs, was limited. Institutions such as the imperial government (and later the church) were responsible for the larger share of trade, and this was promoted for non-commercial reasons. So, too, was the movement of goods between estates of the same landowners. Trade was lubricated by a uniform coinage, but it remained incidental to the latter's main function, which was to discharge government debts to the army and civil service. Not everyone had access to coinage, so that barter and exchange continued among some groups, as it did also between the Roman world and barbarian societies beyond.

Roman trade resembled that of the classical Greek world in so far as it was primarily concerned with the movement of raw materials and foodstuffs, rather than of manufactured goods. A completely self-sufficient community would have been rare indeed. Yet an important distinction lies in the extent of state involvement, as seen early in the supply of corn to Rome. During the Republic, imports from Sardinia and Sicily proved sufficient, but thereafter the city's growing population led to dependence on regular shipments from Africa and Egypt.

The extraction of minerals—gold, silver, copper, tin, lead—was an imperial monopoly. Imperial involvement in the quarrying and supply of marble for building is also clear. During the late Republic and early Empire, quarries in Africa, Asia Minor, Egypt and Greece, as well as in Italy itself, were important sources of fine marble for the city of Rome. By the second century the use of these exotic materials had spread to other Mediterranean cities. Thus at Lepcis Magna marble and granite from Attica, Carystos, Proconnesus and Egypt were employed in both public and private building. As with corn, the supply of these commodities was evidently left to private merchants (*negotiatores*) and shippers (*navicularii*), who were then able to use surplus carrying capacity to further their own interests. The direction of these activities lay in the hands of the state.

Negotiatores were also involved in supplying armies stationed on the frontiers of the empire from Augustus' time. Although frontier provinces themselves were probably forced to provide more than their fair share, much revenue from elsewhere, too, was clearly spent on soldiers, arms and defences. The distribution of artefacts and inscriptions along the river systems of Gaul indicates the volume of trade drawn out of the Mediterranean world to serve the frontiers. However, not all long-distance trade in this direction was determined by the army. Well before barbarian societies were incorporated within the empire, merchants had found in them a profitable market for wine and manufactured goods, exchanged for slaves and raw materials.

Long-distance trade thrived where transport costs were low. Diocletian's price edict of AD 301 shows how much cheaper it was to send goods by sea than by land. River transport, too, was relatively cheap, although costs rose the more that cargoes had to be handled. Predictably it was cities on the Mediterranean, or on major river routes, which prospered at the expense of land-locked towns.

More locally, Strabo and Pliny the Elder outline the character of provincial economies and their particular strengths—whether in minerals, or in foodstuffs such as wine, cereals, or olive oil. Literary sources also illustrate the social context in which commercial trade took place. Notably the aristocracy, while profiting by the sale of goods from its estates, distanced itself from direct involvement in commerce and manufacturing. Archaeology aids definition of the direction, scale and complexity of Roman trade both locally and empire-wide. Paradoxically the most abundant evidence is that from manufactured goods such as cheap pottery and trinkets: this can be used as a 'proxy' for the trade in perishables. Only in the case of pottery jars (*amphorae*) which carried wine, olive oil, fish sauce, dried fruit and the like, do we gain direct insight into the trade of foodstuffs. Italy emerges as the main supplier of wine in the later Republic, Baetica of olive oil in the early Empire (later overtaken by Africa). Evidence from shipwrecks is instructive: these reveal that cargoes were mainly devoted to the carriage of basic commodities, leaving little space for the less valuable manufactured goods. At times the extent of trade networks was great. Fragments of Italian amphorae and fine tableware, for example, show how in Augustus' day communities as far apart as Britain and India—both beyond the frontiers of the empire—were enjoying the same wines as were drunk in Rome.

The Roman Empire in AD 60

During the 120 years between 60 BC (see p. 102) and AD 60 Rome's empire was impressively extended and consolidated. Though it was Julius Caesar who conquered Gaul in the 50s BC and later enlarged Africa, the expansion was above all the achievement of Augustus. During his Principate Egypt was annexed (30 BC), while Spain, Gaul and the Alps were all pacified and organised (by 13 BC). Persistent efforts to subdue Germany and push Roman control as far as the R. Elbe (Albis) failed, however; the R. Rhine was therefore made the frontier in this area, and heavily garrisoned. Arguably Augustus' greatest contribution to the consolidation of the empire was to link its western and eastern sections by subduing all the territory up to the R. Danube along its whole course; this frontier, too, was strongly garrisoned. At Augustus' death in AD 14 much of the empire was indeed, as Tacitus says (*Ann.* 1.9), 'bordered by the ocean or by long rivers'. In the east the R. Euphrates formed part of the frontier, yet this was less secure and less sharply defined than in the west, with significant areas still left in the hands of friendly 'client kings' (though Galatia had been annexed in 25 BC), and with no substantial garrison. For a variety of reasons—political and financial, as well as military—Augustus had no wish to station many legions in the east, and feared no pressing danger from there. For all its size the neighbouring Parthian empire was normally weak and divided, while most of its monarchs respected Roman concern that kings of Armenia (the mountainous area with which both empires shared a frontier) should swear allegiance to the emperor.

Although Tiberius did incorporate the former 'client kingdom' of Cappadocia within the empire in AD 17, in general he followed Augustus' advice against expansion. Claudius, by contrast, proved more ambitious. During the 40s he incorporated further 'client kingdoms'—in Mauretania, Thrace, Lycia and Judaea—while embarking upon the conquest of Britain. By 60 Roman forces there were facing a native rebellion. At the same time the eastern legions needed reinforcement to combat an unusually strong and aggressive Parthian monarch, Vologeses I, who was refusing to recognise even Rome's nominal claim to Armenia.

From 27 BC governors were appointed by two different methods. For certain provinces senatorial proconsuls chosen by lot continued to be sent out for one-year terms, as in the Republic. Such senators were all ex-praetors, except those sent to Africa and Asia, who were senior ex-consuls. By AD 14 only one legion remained under proconsular command (in Africa), and that, too, was removed in 39. In all other provinces the governor was the emperor's legate, appointed by him and holding office at his pleasure, though a term of around three years might be expected. Such imperial governors were drawn not only from among ex-consuls (for heavily garrisoned provinces especially) and ex-praetors, but also from among *equites* in the emperor's service (for Egypt and minor provinces).

THE ROMAN EMPIRE IN A.D. 60

1

2

□ LINDUM
VIROCONIUM
BRITANNIA
(4 legions)
• LONDINIUM

BELGICA
□ VETERA (2)
2
□ NOVAESIUM
□ BONNA
□ MOGUNTIACUM
• DUROCORTORUM
□ VINDONISSA
1
LUGDUNENSIS
ARGENTORATE □

AGRI
DECUMATES

Albis

Rhenus

Danuvius

AQUITANIA

• BURDIGALA
LUGDUNUM •

• AUGUSTA
VINDELICUM
RAETIA
VIRUNUM •

NORICUM
CARNUNTUM
□

PANNONIA

3

NARBONENSIS

ALPES
COTTIAE
ALPES
MARITIMAE

• POETOVIO

DALMATIA

• NARBO

ITALIA

□ BURNUM

TARRACONENSIS
(with Lusitania 3 legions)
TARRACO •

SALONAE •

LUSITANIA

SARDINIA
ET
CORSICA

• ROMA

4

• EMERITA AUGUSTA

BAETICA
• CORDUBA

• CARALES

SICILIA

• TINGIS

• CAESAREA (IOL)

• CARTHAGO

• SYRACUSE

MAURETANIA
TINGITANA

THEVESTE □
MAURETANIA CAESARIENSIS

AFRICA

5

NUMIDIA

1 GERMANIA SUPERIOR
(military area)

2 GERMANIA INFERIOR
(military area)

0   500
km

A   B   C   D

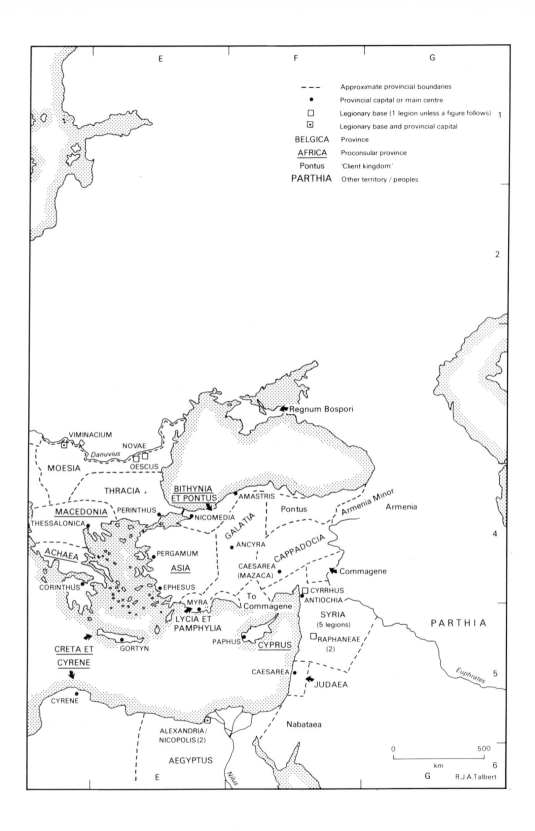

Approximate provincial boundaries
Provincial capital or main centre
□ Legionary base (1 legion unless a figure follows)
▣ Legionary base and provincial capital
BELGICA Province
<u>AFRICA</u> Proconsular province
Pontus 'Client kingdom'
PARTHIA Other territory / peoples

Regnum Bospori

VIMINACIUM
NOVAE
Danuvius
OESCUS
MOESIA
THRACIA
**BITHYNIA
ET PONTUS**
AMASTRIS
Pontus
Armenia Minor
Armenia
PERINTHUS
NICOMEDIA
GALATIA
MACEDONIA
THESSALONICA
ANCYRA
CAPPADOCIA
<u>ACHAEA</u>
PERGAMUM
Commagene
ASIA
CAESAREA
(MAZACA)
CORINTHUS
CYRRHUS
EPHESUS
ANTIOCHIA
MYRA
To
Commagene
PARTHIA
**LYCIA ET
PAMPHILIA**
SYRIA
(5 legions)
PAPHUS
<u>CYPRUS</u>
RAPHANEAE
(2)
<u>CRETA ET
CYRENE</u>
GORTYN
Euphrates
CAESAREA
CYRENE
JUDAEA
Nabataea
ALEXANDRIA/
NICOPOLIS (2)
0   500
AEGYPTUS
km
Nilus
R.J.A.Talbert

E   F   G

1

2

4

5

6

ROMAN BRITAIN

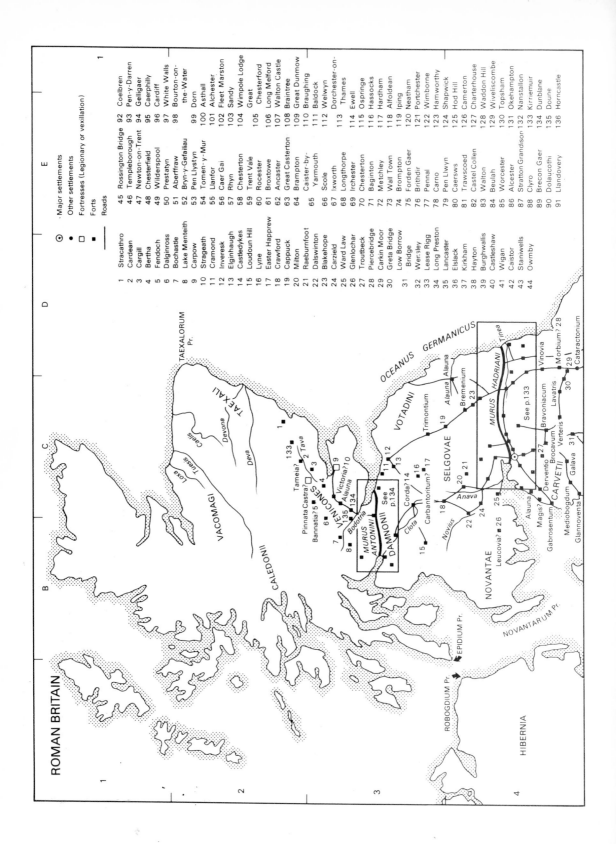

Legend:

⊙ Major settlements
● Other settlements
□ Fortresses (Legionary or vexillation)
■ Forts
▬ Roads

No.	Name	No.	Name
1	Stracathro	45	Rossington Bridge
2	Cardean	46	Templeborough
3	Cargill	47	Newton-on-Trent
4	Bertha	48	Chesterfield
5	Fendoch	49	Wilderspool
6	Dalginross	50	Prestatyn
7	Bochastle	51	Bryn-y-Gefaliau
8	Lake Menteith	52	Aberffraw
9	Carpow	53	Pen Llystyn
10	Strageath	54	Tomen-y-Mur
11	Cramond	55	Llanfor
12	Inveresk	56	Caer Gai
13	Elginhaugh	57	Rhyn
14	Castledykes	58	Chesterton
15	Loudoun Hill	59	Trent Vale
16	Lyne	60	Rocester
17	Easter Happrew	61	Broxtowe
18	Crawford	62	Ancaster
19	Cappuck	63	Great Casterton
20	Milton	64	Brampton
21	Raeburnfoot	65	Caister-by-Yarmouth
22	Dalswinton	66	Scole
23	Blakehope	67	Ixworth
24	Carzield	68	Longthorpe
25	Ward Law	69	Irchester
26	Glenlochar	70	Chesterton
27	Troutbeck	71	Baginton
28	Piercebridge	72	Metchley
29	Carkin Moor	73	Wall Town
30	Greta Bridge	74	Brompton
31	Low Borrow Bridge	75	Forden Gaer
32	Wersley	76	Brithdir
33	Lease Rigg	77	Pennal
34	Long Preston	78	Carno
35	Lancaster	79	Pen Llwyn
36	Elslack	80	Caersws
37	Kirkham	81	Trawscoed
38	Hayton	82	Castel Collen
39	Burghwallis	83	Walton
40	Castleshaw	84	Beulah
41	Wigan	85	Worcester
42	Caistor	86	Alcester
43	Staniwells	87	Stratton Grandson
44	Owmby	88	Clyro
89	Brecon Gaer	113	Dorchester-on-Thames
90	Dolaucothi	114	Ewell
91	Llandovery	115	Ospringe
92	Coelbren	116	Hassocks
93	Pen-y-Darren	117	Hardham
94	Gelligaer	118	Alfoldean
95	Caerphilly	119	Iping
96	Cardiff	120	Neatham
97	White Walls	121	Portchester
98	Bourton-on-the-Water	122	Wimborne
99	Dorn	123	Hamworthy
100	Asthall	124	Shapwick
101	Alchester	125	Hod Hill
102	Fleet Marston	126	Camerton
103	Sandy	127	Charterhouse
104	Wimpole Lodge	128	Waddon Hill
105	Great Chesterford	129	Wiveliscombe
106	Long Melford	130	Topsham
107	Walton Castle	131	Okehampton
108	Braintree	132	Nanstallon
109	Great Dunmow	133	Kirriemuir
110	Braughing	134	Dunblane
111	Baldock	135	Doune
112	Welwyn	136	Horncastle

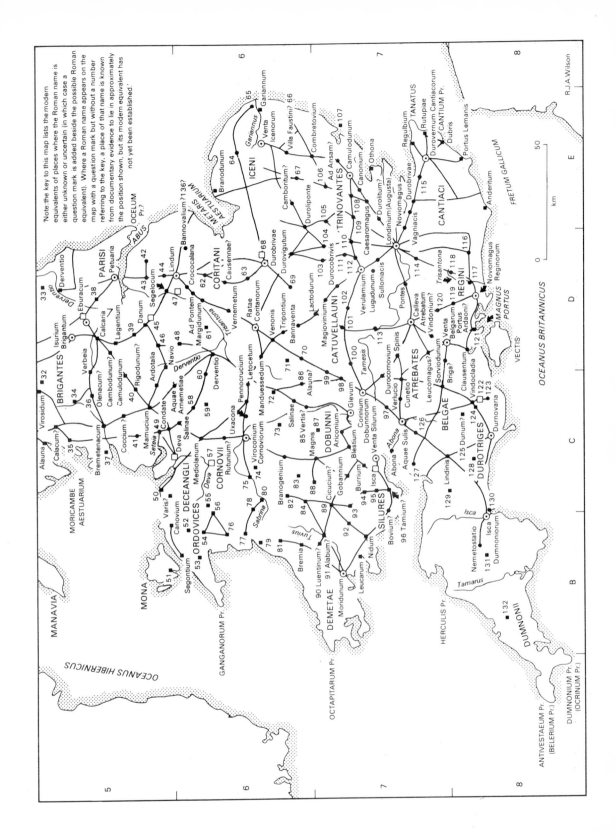

Note: the key to this map lists the modern equivalents of places where the Roman name is either unknown or uncertain (in which case a question mark is added beside the possible Roman equivalent). Where a Roman name appears on the map with a question mark but without a number referring to the key, a place of that name is known from documentary evidence to lie in approximately the position shown, but its modern equivalent has not yet been established.'

R.J.A. Wilson

131

Roman Britain

Intensive research and excavation have made Britain the best studied of all the provinces of the Roman empire. It was annexed in AD 43 on completion of the initial phase of invasion by A. Plautius; formally it ceased to be a province 367 years later, when the emperor Honorius withdrew the remaining garrisons. The map inevitably presents only a partial picture, and one that must amalgamate the developments of more than one century. There is no hint here, for example, that the majority of both major and minor civilian settlements in lowland Britain began as forts or fortresses during the conquest phase. The only military sites shown south east of the line joining the R. Severn (Sabrina) and the R. Trent (Trisantona), are either ones of the first century which were not overlain by later towns; or—in the case of the coastal forts from the Wash to the Isle of Wight—they are those which belong to the less secure period from the late third century onwards, when pirate raids in the North Sea and the Straits of Dover were becoming an increasing menace to the peace and security of the civilian heartlands.

As a spur to romanisation three *coloniae* of retired Roman legionaries were settled at Camulodunum, Glevum and Lindum in the first century; later, honorary colonial status was given to the civilian settlement at Eburacum, and almost certainly to Londinium too. But most of the rest of the 'major settlements' were organised as *civitates*, newly planted, self-governing capitals controlling tribal areas, each roughly representing (with some Roman manipulation) the same region occupied by each tribe before the Roman invasion. It is vivid testimony to the genius of Roman planning that many of these settlements are still thriving communities today, and that long stretches of the Roman road system which linked them are still in use. The flourishing state of Romano-British agriculture is witnessed by the thousand or so villas and farms located to date. The mosaics, painted plaster and lavish bath suites of the richer establishments (in country and town) testify to the high standard of material comfort achieved by the wealthier propertied classes, as well as to their thorough romanisation.

To protect the civilian zone, however, a permanent buffer of garrison forts was required in Wales and the north of England, controlled from three permanent legionary fortresses at Isca, Deva and Eburacum. All but one of the other fortresses shown, whether legionary (16–20 hectares) or vexillation (8–12 hectares) size, belong to the first century when the military situation was still fluid; Carpow alone is third century. Not all the forts shown were occupied simultaneously. It is impossible to show essential back-up features in the framework of military occupation, such as fortlets and signal stations. Omitted, too, are the marching camps representing the army on manoeuvres or campaign: it is from these, for example, that Roman armies are known to have reached the mouth of the R. Spey (Tuesis) under Agricola in 84, and again later, probably in the third century. For most of Roman Britain's history, however, it was Hadrian's Wall which formed the northern frontier.

Hadrian's Wall and the Antonine Wall

Agricola was the first to appreciate the strategic importance of the Tyne-Solway line: during his governorship (78–84/5) he built a road ('The Stanegate') from Luguvalium to Red House and several of the forts along it. After the withdrawal from southern Scotland *c.* 105 the Stanegate served as the frontier; it was probably now that its line was extended westwards and eastwards, and fresh forts built along it. Hadrian, however, effected a bolder solution to the frontier problem with the erection of a continuous 118 km barrier from coast to coast a few miles north of the Stanegate—in stone three metres thick from Pons Aelius to the R. Irthing, and in turf from the Irthing to the Solway. At intervals of one Roman mile fortlets ('milecastles') were built along it, with two signalling towers (turrets) spaced out between each—milecastles of stone in the eastern sector, of turf and timber in the western sector, but turrets of stone throughout. An impressive V-ditch was dug outside the entire frontier line, except where the crags rendered it superfluous. The main fighting garrisons were to remain in the Stanegate forts.

Drastic modifications were made *c.* 124. Forts were now placed on the Wall itself, originally 12 in number, later 16, demolishing turrets or milecastles already built, if they were in the way. To speed up the work, the stone Wall was narrowed to 2.5 metres, and extended eastwards to Segedunum to provide better cover for the Tyne. Most idiosyncratic of all, a continuous flat-bottomed ditch, with accompanying earth mounds both north and south of it ('The Vallum'), ran behind the Wall to provide a clear delineation of the military zone: now the only crossing points were at control gates opposite each fort. This oddity of Roman planning came to be ignored soon after it was built, and was partly filled in. But its construction, and the decision to move the main garrisons onto the Wall itself, both presumably reflect the hostility with which the whole idea of a frontier barrier was greeted locally.

Another integral part of Hadrian's frontier was the system of stone watch towers and timber fortlets which continued down the Solway coast, probably as far as St Bees Head, south of Gabrosentum (see above, 'Roman Britain'); recent work between Bibra and Maia suggests that the original scheme here may have been a continuous timber palisade of uncertain length and height, similar to that known on the contemporary frontier in Germany. Also essential to defence of the frontier were the outpost forts to the north—Blatobulgium, Castra Exploratorum and Fanum Cocidi, later to be joined by Habitancum and others.

HADRIAN'S WALL

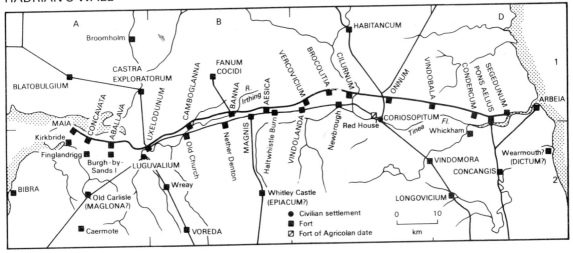

The Hadrianic frontier was essentially complete *c*. 128. Yet a bare ten years later Antoninus Pius ordered a fresh advance and the building of another Wall—entirely of turf, a mere 59 km long—between Forth and Clyde. The planners of the Antonine frontier also had their afterthoughts. A tentative early scheme to build in stone (as seen at Balmuildy fort) was scrapped in favour of a turf Wall and ditch. At first the plan seems to have envisaged widely placed turf-and-timber forts, with fortlets like the milecastles of Hadrian's turf Wall in between: nine such fortlets are now known, though it is too early to say if a complete series was built. Clearly some at least were dismantled and superseded by adjacent forts, even before the Wall had been finished. Thus the Antonine frontier as finally completed *c*. 142 had 19 forts in all—more than Hadrian's Wall, which was twice as long. There was no Vallum, and apart from six platforms, perhaps used as beacon stances in signalling, no structure resembling a turret. The western flanks were protected by a fort at Bishopton and a couple of fortlets further west; to the east of the Wall were garrisons at Cramond and Inveresk, while Alauna, Victoria (Strageath) and Bertha served as outpost forts to the north.

The Antonine Wall had an active service life of less than 20 years. Temporarily abandoned *c*. 155/8 and re-occupied after an interval of only a year or two, it was finally given up *c*. 163/4. Hadrian's Wall—its western sector now rebuilt in stone—henceforth served as the definitive frontier.

ANTONINE WALL

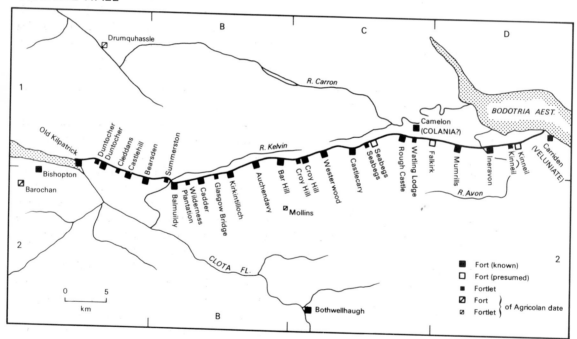

R.J.A.Wilson

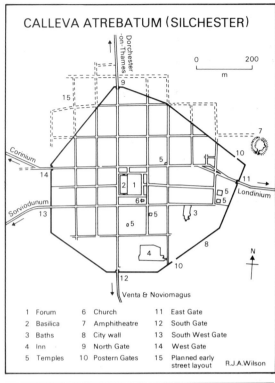

CALLEVA ATREBATUM (SILCHESTER)

Dorchester-on-Thames

0 — 200 m

Corinium

Sorviodunum

Londinium

Venta & Noviomagus

N

1	Forum	6	Church	11	East Gate
2	Basilica	7	Amphitheatre	12	South Gate
3	Baths	8	City wall	13	South West Gate
4	Inn	9	North Gate	14	West Gate
5	Temples	10	Postern Gates	15	Planned early street layout

R.J.A.Wilson

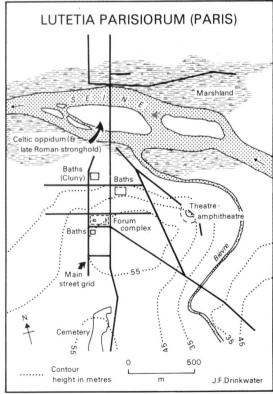

LUTETIA PARISIORUM (PARIS)

S E I N E

Marshland

Celtic oppidum (& late Roman stronghold)

Baths (Cluny)

Baths

Theatre-amphitheatre

Forum complex

Baths

Bièvre

Main street grid

55

N

Cemetery

55

45 35 35 45

0 — 500 m

Contour height in metres

J.F.Drinkwater

Silchester (Calleva Atrebatum)

Situated in Hampshire 13 km south of the R. Thames, Silchester has been almost deserted since Roman times, so that excavations in 1890–1909 revealed the most detailed example of a Romano-British town. As the capital of the Atrebates, Silchester predates the invasion in AD 43, but the Roman town developed slowly. The baths (c. 55/65) were its earliest amenity, oriented differently to the over-ambitious street grid of the late first century. The forum/basilica complex and amphitheatre were both started at the same time as the street grid; the former took some 30 years to complete. In the late second century a defensive bank of gravel with stone gateways enclosed 40 hectares—average area for a Romano-British town of medium size—and this was fronted by a stone wall after 250. Though full evidence is lacking, decline clearly followed, with the basilica being put to industrial use for metal-working. A tiny church was erected about 350.

Lutetia Parisiorum

Lutetia Parisiorum (Paris) was a typical northern Gallic *civitas*-capital, with a population of about 7,500. It succeeded a Celtic *oppidum* located on the Île de la Cité—an easily defended site which controlled an important route across the R. Seine. However continuity of settlement was only assured when the Romans built a road which crossed the river at the same point. The main part of the Romano-Gallic city lay on the left bank. Its layout reflects the Gauls' ready acceptance of Greco-Roman ideas of urbanisation. There was regular street planning, and lavish provision of public buildings for administration, entertainment and relaxation. To be noted are the central forum complex—which included an open area with surrounding portico, a great hall and temple—and the bath buildings. The city was unwalled, a tribute to secure conditions during the Principate. In true Roman fashion its cemeteries were placed beyond its sacred boundary. The later Roman and medieval cities retreated again to the island in the Seine.

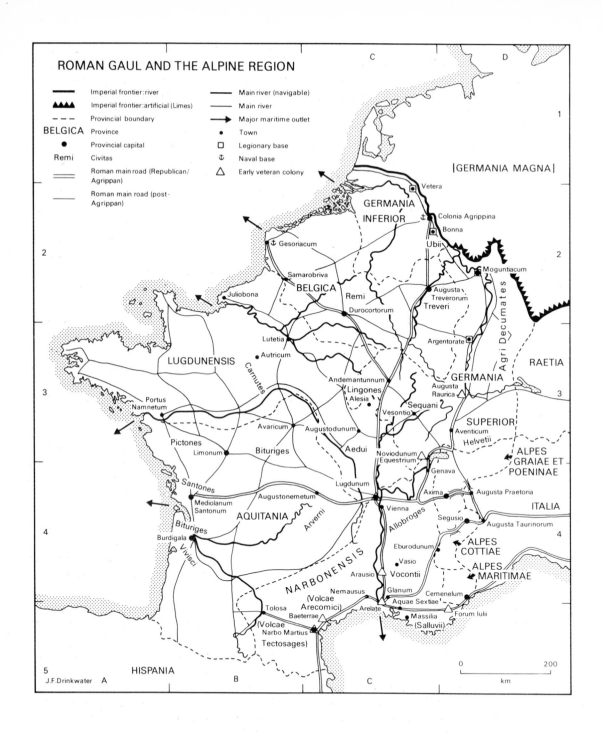

ROMAN GAUL AND THE ALPINE REGION

Imperial frontier: river
Imperial frontier: artificial (Limes)
Provincial boundary
BELGICA Province
● Provincial capital
Remi Civitas
Roman main road (Republican/ Agrippan)
Roman main road (post- Agrippan)

Main river (navigable)
Main river
Major maritime outlet
● Town
□ Legionary base
⚓ Naval base
△ Early veteran colony

|GERMANIA MAGNA|

Vetera
GERMANIA INFERIOR
Colonia Agrippina
Bonna
Ubii
Moguntiacum
Gesoriacum
Samarobriva
BELGICA
Remi
Durocortorum
Augusta Treverorum
Treveri
Agri Decumates
Juliobona
Lutetia
Autricum
LUGDUNENSIS
Carnutes
Argentorate
Andemantunnum
Lingones
Alesia
GERMANIA
Augusta Raurica
RAETIA
Vesontio
Sequani
SUPERIOR
Portus Namnetum
Avaricum
Augustodunum
Aventicum
Helvetii
ALPES GRAIAE ET POENINAE
Pictones
Limonum
Bituriges
Aedui
Noviodunum Equestrium
Genava
Axima
Augusta Praetoria
Santones
Mediolanum Santonum
AQUITANIA
Lugdunum
Augustonemetum
Arverni
Vienna
Allobroges
Segusio
ITALIA
Augusta Taurinorum
Bituriges
Burdigala
Vivisci
Eburodunum
Vasio
Voconti
ALPES COTTIAE
ALPES MARITIMAE
NARBONENSIS
Arausio
Nemausus (Volcae Arecomici)
Glanum
Cemenelum
Aquae Sextiae
Forum Iulii
Tolosa
Baeterrae
Arelate
Massilia (Salluvii)
(Volcae Narbo Martius Tectosages)

HISPANIA

J.F.Drinkwater

0   200
km

136

Roman Gaul and the Alpine Region

Rome effectively acquired southern Gaul late in the second century BC, by her intervention to help Massilia against the Salluvii. Subsequent war with the Allobroges extended Roman territory to Lake Geneva. Aquae Sextiae was established as a garrison town, and a colony was founded at Narbo Martius. The area became known as 'Provincia'—'The Province'. Incessant feuding among the remaining Gallic nations (*civitates*) blinded them to the threat posed by Romans in the south and Germanic peoples from the north. Rome herself, however, was increasingly aware of the German menace. Thus between 58 and 51 BC Julius Caesar could use it to justify his interference in the affairs of the Helvetii, Aedui, Arverni and Sequani, and indeed his conquest of the whole of Gaul.

The Republic had prized 'The Province' only as a safe route to Spain. Caesar, once dictator, went further, and established full veteran colonies at Narbo, Arelate, Forum Iulii and Baeterrae. Augustus followed the same pattern. He founded more full colonies in Narbonensis, as 'The Province' was now renamed—for example at Arausio; he also promoted Nemausus and many other indigenous settlements to colonial status. Thus began the intensive romanisation of Narbonensis, and the displacement of *civitates* by Greco-Roman style city-states—as among the Volcae Arecomici, to cite one instance.

In the new territories, however, Caesar was responsible for only three colonies—Noviodunum, Raurica, Lugdunum—to prevent German invasion from the Rhine. Augustus created no new colonies in the north. He slightly remodelled the *civitates*, giving them single centres of administration (the '*civitas*-capitals', e.g. Augustodunum), but otherwise left them alone. His major innovation was to establish three new provinces: Lugdunensis (capital: Lugdunum), Aquitania (capital: first Mediolanum, then Limonum, and finally Burdigala), and Belgica (capital: first Durocortorum, then probably Augusta Treverorum). The 'Three Gauls' developed a Gallo-Roman rather than a Roman culture. Augustus also set in train the subjugation of the western Alps, which considerably eased overland communications between Gaul and Italy, and resulted ultimately in the provinces of Alpes Graiae et Poeninae (capital: Axima), Alpes Cottiae (capital: Segusio), and Alpes Maritimae (capital: Cemenelum).

Following the failure of Augustus' province of Germania Magna, and the return of the imperial frontier to the Rhine, martial law zones of Germania Inferior and Germania Superior were carved out of Belgica and Lugdunensis. In the late first century, under Domitian, these were constituted as formal provinces, with capitals at Colonia Agrippina and Moguntiacum respectively. Germania Superior included the only permanent Roman acquisition across the Rhine, the 'Agri Decumates', annexed by Vespasian and his son Domitian to shorten the northern frontier. During the second century its impressive overland boundary, the *Limes*, was progressively strengthened (see p. 140). Legions came to be stationed at Vetera, Bonna, Moguntiacum and Argentorate. Taken together with associated auxiliaries, and the naval personnel at Gesoriacum and Colonia Agrippina, they amounted to a considerable garrison.

The army's presence was of great importance for Gaul. Military needs prompted the improvement of road and river communications, while the troops' spending power greatly stimulated the Gallic economy. Increased wealth was reflected in urbanisation, not only in colonies and *civitas*-capitals, but also in agglomerations which grew up around the military bases and along the main routes. The greatest city was Lugdunum, whose suburb of Condate housed the great Altar of Roma and Augustus, the main focus of Gallic emperor-worship. Prosperity, and perhaps a growing population, are also seen in the widespread appearance of substantial romanised farmhouses and villas, as revealed by aerial photography around Samarobriva, for example.

Gaul suffered particularly badly in the mid-third century, when external attack and internal discord brought anarchy to the empire. The frontier collapsed, the Agri Decumates were lost, and many towns and villas were destroyed. Order was restored by the fourth-century emperors, but the great age of imperial peace had passed.

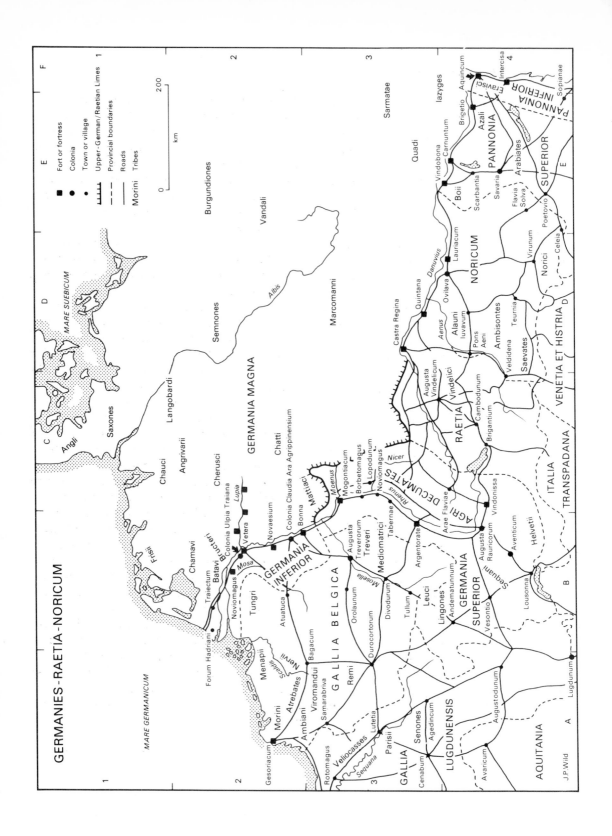

GERMANIES-RAETIA-NORICUM

Germanies-Raetia-Noricum

For much of the Roman period the rivers Rhine and Danube marked the limit of Roman expansion northwards in western and central Europe. At the end of the first century BC the Celtic speaking peoples of the region (who lived both north and south of the rivers) were at differing levels of political, social and economic development; but they did provide a common bond between Rome's frontier provinces.

In the west Julius Caesar reached the Rhine in 55 BC. In 15 BC, however, Augustus initiated a series of campaigns to annex the lands between the Rhine and the Elbe (Albis). He built fortresses on the west bank of the Rhine (including Noviomagus, Vetera, Novaesium and Mogontiacum), and bases in the Lippe valley further east. This forward policy was reversed after a major disaster in AD 9, following which the Rhine was adopted as the frontier. The rump of Augustan Germania—two narrow military zones on the west bank—became by AD 90 the provinces of Germania Inferior and Superior.

After Augustus' subjugation of the Alpine tribes in 15 BC, the Vindelici and the kingdom of Noricum were overrun up to the Danube, though the two provinces of Raetia and Noricum were not formally created until Claudius' reign. Lying between the fortresses of Upper Germany and Pannonia, neither was garrisoned by legionary troops until the later second century.

Claudius reinforced both river frontiers with new forts. However the political upheavals of 69–70 caused widespread destruction, so that shortly afterwards Vespasian thoroughly overhauled the defensive systems. On the Danube he rebuilt the Claudian forts; east of the Upper Rhine he linked Mogontiacum and Augusta Vindelicum by new roads, and fortified the Upper Neckar (Nicer). After the Chattan War of 83–5 his son Domitian constructed the first *limes* in the Wetterau north east of Mogontiacum—a patrol road with towers and fortlets at intervals. At the same time he built a line of new forts north of the Danube. Around 90, following further Chattan incursions, he joined the Wetterau forts with Vespasian's strongpoints on the Upper Neckar by a *limes* through the Odenwald. Further improvements were made under Trajan and Hadrian; later, around 150, the garrisons of the Odenwald-Neckar *limes* were moved 20–25 km eastwards.

Under threat of attack by the Marcomanni, in 179 Raetia was given the protection of a new legionary base at Regensburg (Castra Regina); soon afterwards Lauriacum took on the same role in Noricum. Germanic raids across the whole length of the Rhine and Danube frontier progressively threatened the security of provincial life, especially after 233. The Agri Decumates behind the Upper German-Raetian *limes* were gradually evacuated, and by 259–60 the Upper Rhine and Danube once more became the front line. Then from the late third century new strongpoints were built along both the rivers and some main routes in the hinterland. Thus Rome had moved effectively from the offensive to the defensive.

It is clear that the army was the agent of rapid romanisation in the frontier provinces: there is ample archaeological evidence for urbanisation and the intensive exploitation of natural resources. Colonies such as Colonia Claudia Ara Agrippinensium and Augusta Rauricorum were founded, and many lesser towns sprang up. Most forts, too, had dependent civil settlements, sometimes of considerable importance. Villa estates in the countryside supported a prosperous upper class, and marginal land was farmed by a numerous peasantry. The barbarian invasions of the third century did not put an end to progress; but they coincided with notable changes in the Roman social and economic system, so that their effect was far reaching.

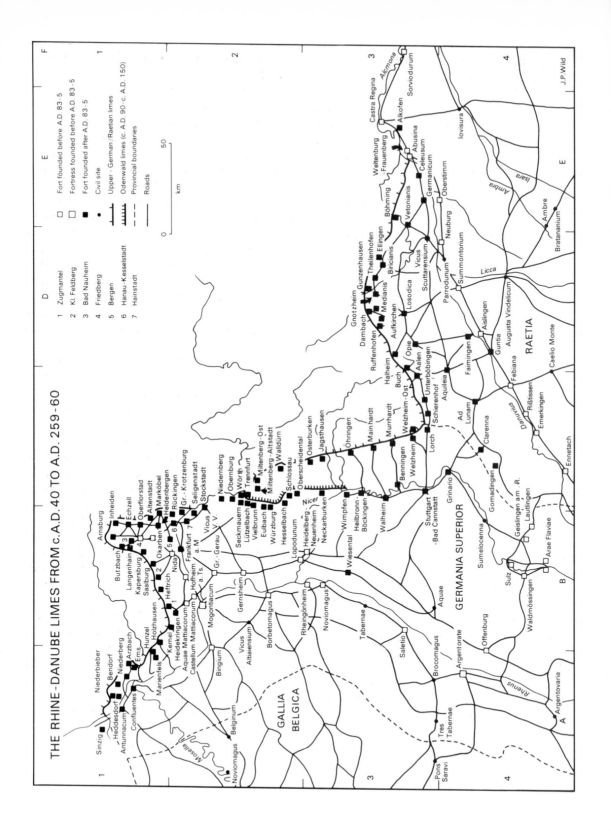

THE RHINE-DANUBE LIMES FROM c. A.D. 40 TO A.D. 259-60

□	Fort founded before A.D. 83-5	D	1 Zugmantel
▢	Fortress founded before A.D. 83-5		2 Kl. Feldberg
■	Fort founded after A.D. 83-5		3 Bad Nauheim
•	Civil site		4 Friedberg
⊞	Upper-German/Raetian limes		5 Bergen
┅	Odenwald limes (c. A.D. 90 - c. A.D. 150)		6 Hanau-Kesselstadt
╌	Provincial boundaries		7 Hainstadt
—	Roads		

km
0 ___ 50

J.P.Wild

140

The Rhine-Danube Limes from *c.* AD 40 to AD 259–60

The triangle of land between the upper courses of the Rhine and Danube formed a re-entrant into Roman territory and a potential weak spot in the northern defences. It was directly controlled by Rome only between the late first and the mid-third centuries AD. After Augustus' failure to create a Greater German province up to the Elbe, the Rhine and Danube were accepted as the frontier. Fortresses at Mogontiacum, Argentorate and Vindonissa were supported by auxiliary forts in the Rhine Valley and south of the Danube. Claudius moved troops up to the two river lines and strengthened both. After the disturbances of 69–70 Vespasian reorganised the region's defences. He drove a road east of the Rhine from Mogontiacum to Augusta Vindelicum and established forts on the Upper Neckar (Nicer). In 85, after his first Chattan War, Domitian protected the Wetterau north east of Mogontiacum by a *limes*—that is, a patrol road with wooden look-out towers and fortlets at intervals; he also built a series of forts north of the Danube. To link the Wetterau system with the Upper Neckar, around 90 he constructed a *limes* through the Odenwald, secured by fortlets. Hadrian added a wooden palisade in front of the road.

Around 150 the garrisons of the Odenwald-Neckar *limes* were moved to a new line 20–25 km further east, and the work of replacing wooden forts and towers in stone was completed. In the early third century the Upper German *limes* was reinforced by a rampart and ditch set behind the wooden palisade; but in the Raetian sector the palisade was replaced by a stone wall and interval towers.

Alamannic invasions in the second quarter of the third century led to Roman retrenchment. By 259–60 the *limes* had been abandoned, the towns and villas of the Agri Decumates had been evacuated, and the Rhine and Danube resumed their defensive role.

The Danubian Provinces/Balkan Area *c.* AD 200

Until the end of the first century BC Rome's interests in the Balkans were confined to the Istrian peninsula and the occupation of Macedonia. However Roman control came to be extended to the R. Danube as a result of Augustus' campaigns down the R. Save (Savus) valley, together with the conquest of the interior of Dalmatia and the route to the Danube down the valley of the R. Morava (Margus). By Tiberius' time three provinces of Dalmatia, Pannonia and Moesia had been created. Of these Moesia was to be divided later by Domitian, Pannonia by Trajan. When Dacia was annexed at the beginning of the second century, it was sometimes governed as a single province, at other times as two, or even three.

Towns—both Macedonian foundations and Greek colonies—only existed on the periphery of the new conquests, on the Aegean coast of Thrace and on the Black Sea. New towns were founded under Augustus and Tiberius, notably in Liburnia and northern Macedonia: these were both *coloniae*, settlements of Roman veterans, and *municipia*, native settlements granted urban autonomy. All provided civilian administration for newly conquered territory. In addition the colonies—such as Emona on the road from Italy to Pannonia—guaranteed a military reserve at strategic centres vacated by the legions after the initial phase of conquest. By the mid-first century AD the Dalmatian coast from Liburnia to Macedonia possessed numerous new towns.

In the interior the pace of urbanism was much slower. Native tribal administration was maintained in central Pannonia and Moesia, regularly supervised by centurions detached from the legions. The first urban foundation on the middle Danube—the Claudian colony at Savaria—commanded the Amber road, the route north from Italy to the legionary fortress at Carnuntum; its citizens included both legionary veterans and

Italian traders, anxious to seek out the important military markets on the Danube. Later in the first century Sirmium and Siscia (the latter founded with discharged sailors from the fleet) were established to strengthen the economic development of the Save valley: it formed the second most important route in Pannonia, leading south east to the Danube at Singidunum (Belgrade). Sufficiently romanised native communities were also granted urban status under the Flavians, among them Neviodunum, Andautonia and Scarbantia. In Moesia tribal administration was maintained; romanisation proved more difficult. The only colony here was the Domitianic foundation of Scupi. It was a mixed community of Syrian, Gallic and Macedonian veterans drawn from all four Moesian legions.

The greatest impetus to urban development came from the conquest and eventual annexation of Dacia in 106. Three new colonies were founded—at Oescus in Moesia Inferior, at Ratiaria in Moesia Superior, and at Poetovio in Pannonia. Hadrian granted civic status to native settlements in the interior of Pannonia, such as Cibalae and Bassiana. On the Danubian *limes* substantial civilian settlements (*canabae*) had been formed close to the legionary fortresses by a mixture of legionary and auxiliary veterans, native traders and foreign immigrants. Hadrian raised several such settlements to municipal status, notably Viminacium, Carnuntum and Aquincum.

In the eastern Balkans the task was less easy. Thrace, annexed by Claudius, had few urban centres away from the coast. Though Vespasian did found a colony at Deultum, the real task of creating towns in Thrace was left to Trajan. While Serdica, Pautalia and Augusta Traiana could claim native origins, his foundations at Nicopolis ad Nestum, Nicopolis ad Istrum and Marcianopolis (the latter two north of the Haemus range) were all new creations. This attempt to spread urbanisation was not fully successful, however. Hadrian founded only one more town in Thrace—Hadrianopolis. So the province remained largely administered by villages: remote from the towns, these controlled extensive territories exploited through *emporia*, subsidiary market centres.

The conquest of Dacia, too, was not followed by the creation of towns on the scale of the Augustan programme in Dalmatia or the Flavian one in Pannonia. The establishment of Sarmizegethusa as a colony only three years after the conquest was a political decision: it demonstrated Rome's power, not her intention to romanise the Dacian population. Hadrian added only two new towns, Drobeta and Romula, both south of the Dacian heartlands of Transcarpathia.

The second century witnessed the most prosperous period in the development of the Danubian provinces. Towns of the interior were provided with temples, *fora* and lavishly decorated public buildings. By contrast country farms were generally small, lacking the luxury of Gallic or African villas. Mining, though an imperial monopoly, encouraged the growth of settlements in Moesia Superior and western Dacia: these gained municipal rights by the third century. Ampelum, the centre of gold mining in Dacia, attracted skilled miners from Dalmatia. Moesia Superior was exploited for its lead and silver, western Thrace for gold, northern Dalmatia for iron.

Military centres which had attracted substantial civilian settlements in Dacia (like Potaissa, Napoca, Porolissum) and in Moesia Inferior (Troesmis, Durostorum) received civic rights, as did the native settlements of Naissus, Margum and Horreum Margi in the Morava valley of Moesia Superior. The development of towns also reflects the general economic development of the provinces, the romanisation of their native populations, and their general attractiveness to immigrants from both east and west. From the early third century, the award of the title *colonia* to existing settlements becomes increasingly common: Potaissa in Dacia and Aquincum in Pannonia were so honoured. However, by the second decade of the third century the barbarian invasions had commenced, bringing devastation to the Balkan provinces, and ending nearly two centuries of economic and urban development which had reached its peak by *c.* 200.

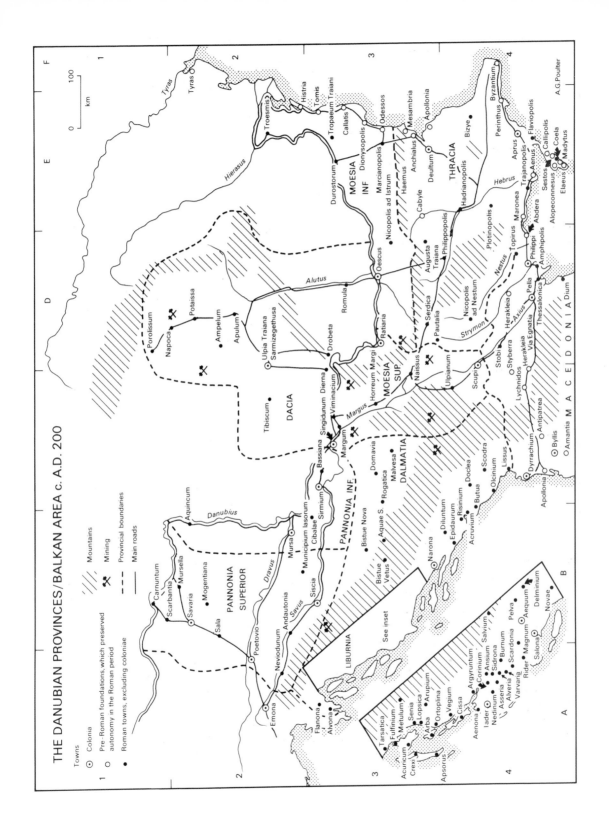

THE DANUBIAN PROVINCES/BALKAN AREA c. A.D. 200

Towns

⊙ Colonia

1 Pre-Roman foundations, which preserved
○ autonomy in the Roman period

● Roman towns, excluding coloniae

///// Mountains

✕ Mining

– – – Provincial boundaries

—— Main roads

A.G.Poulter

143

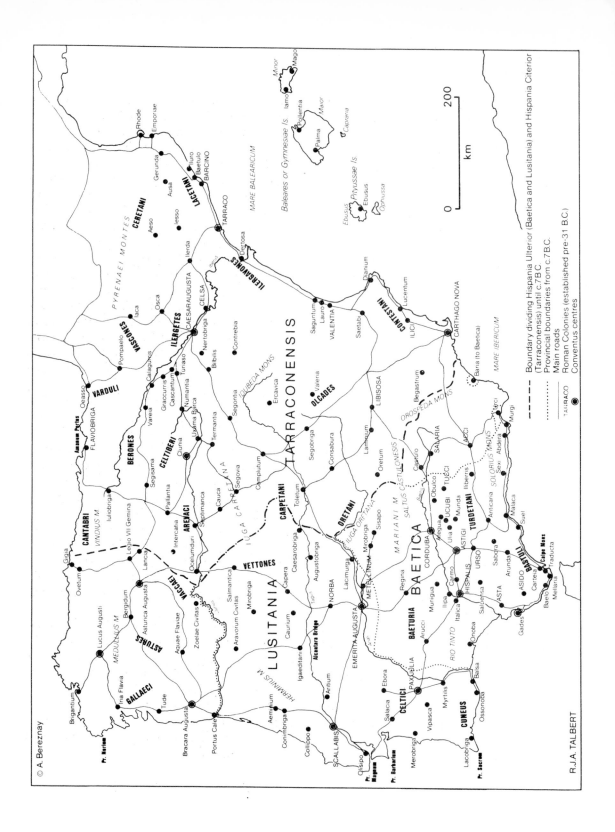

© A. Bereznay

Boundary dividing Hispania Ulterior (Baetica and Lusitania) and Hispania Citerior (Tarraconensis) until c.7BC.

.... **Provincial boundaries from c.7BC.**

Main roads

Roman Colonies (established pre-31 B.C.)

Conventus centres

TARRACO

R.J.A. TALBERT

Iberian Peninsula

The large Iberian peninsula, separated from the rest of Europe by the Pyrenees, has always displayed extremes of landscape and climate. Serious Roman interest dates from the Second Punic War. By its end Rome had dislodged the Carthaginians there to occupy the most productive areas in the peninsula, the valley of the lower R. Ebro, the east coast, and the valley of the R. Baetis. Two provinces, Citerior and Ulterior, were marked out in 197. In the following decades the need to protect and stabilise conquered territory combined with greed for Spain's rich variety of resources to encourage continuing Roman expansion. Long and bitter conflict with native tribes culminated in a major struggle with an alliance led by the Lusitanian Viriathus, and the capture of Numantia in 133. With Rome now in possession of perhaps two-thirds of the peninsula, there was little further conquest for the next century, although the provinces were unsettled by Roman civil wars there against Sertorius in the 70s and Pompeians in the 40s. Final conquest of the entire peninsula (especially the rugged north west) was achieved by Augustus in the 20s BC. As a result three provinces were created from his reign, Tarraconensis and Lusitania each governed by an imperial legate, Baetica by a proconsul. Thereafter the peninsula for long enjoyed a fair measure of internal stability, with only one recorded mention of fighting against the Astures in Nero's reign (*ILS* 2648). The three legions placed there by Augustus were reduced by Vespasian to one—Legio VII Gemina, stationed at the place named after itself.

The fullest surviving descriptions of the peninsula under Roman rule are those of Strabo dating to Augustus' reign, and of Pliny the Elder in the Flavian period. They indicate the impressive number of new colonies founded by Julius Caesar and Augustus and of existing towns granted either colonial or some lesser Roman status. Emerita Augusta, established in 25 BC for legionary veterans, is one outstanding example of the former

group, while among the latter the ancient Phoenician foundation of Gades, given Roman municipal status by Caesar, prospered sufficiently to boast as many as 500 men of equestrian census. Much survives on bronze of the municipal charters of Salpensa and Malaca, drawn up in Domitian's reign. Although his father Vespasian had bestowed 'Latin' rights upon every community in the Spanish provinces, it should not be overlooked that there still remained a stark contrast between the south—rich, urban, romanised—and the rest of the peninsula, where cities were relatively few, and tribal organisation persisted along with native customs and languages. All the same, while many Spaniards may indeed have been 'obscure people with barbaric names', as Pliny put it, the number of educated men from the peninsula who rose to make their mark at Rome (especially as senators and writers) was remarkable.

The sources of Spain's wealth were diverse. The peninsula was rich in herds and crops, especially corn, vines, olives, flax. Fish were caught on a large scale, both for pickling and for the manufacture of *garum*, the salty fish sauce which added zest to every Roman meal. Most valuable of all, however, were Spain's minerals—gold, silver, lead, tin, iron and copper: the last was mined over extensive areas, principally at Rio Tinto and Vipasca, from which regulations of the early second century AD survive. Most mines came to be owned by the state. Export of all Spanish products was facilitated by navigable rivers and a well-developed system of main roads.

Rome's Spanish provinces arguably reached the peak of their prosperity in the second century AD. Beyond that date, for some reason, the number of Spaniards to achieve prominence at Rome declines. The peninsula itself was harmed successively by Moorish invasions, widespread banditry, and the effects of the empire-wide civil wars of the 190s. It suffered again from Frankish invasions during the third century.

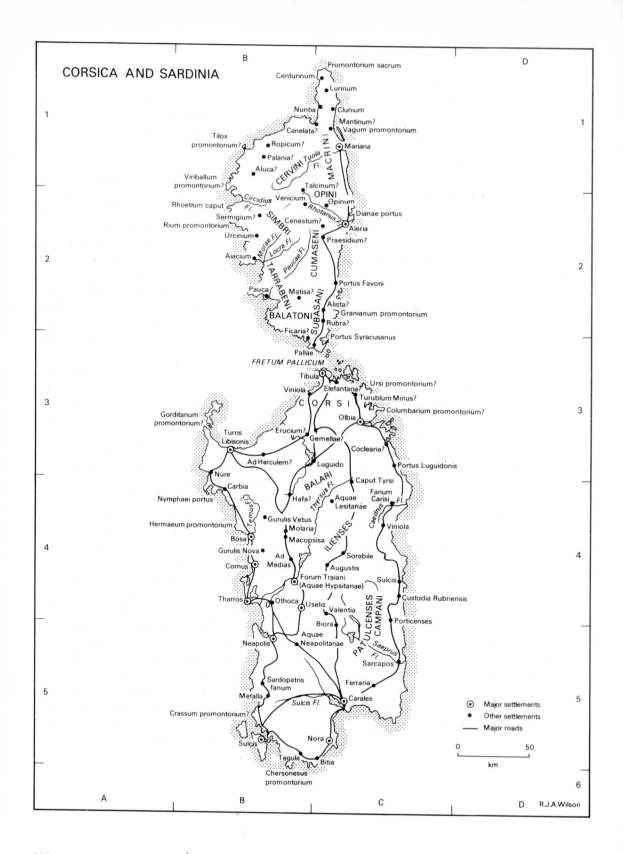

CORSICA AND SARDINIA

Promontorium sacrum
Centurinum
Lurinum
Nuntia
Clunium
Canelata?
Mantinum?
Vagum promontorium
Tilox promontorium?
Ropicum?
Mariana
Palania
CERVINI *Tuola Fl.* MACRIN
Aluca?
Viriballum promontorium?
Talcinum?
OPINI
Venicium
Opinum
Rhoetum caput
Circidius Fl.
Cenestum?
Rhotanus Fl.
Dianae portus
Sermigium?
SIMBRI
Aleria
Rium promontorium
Praesidium?
Urcinium
Morae Fl.
CUMASENI
Aiacium
Locra Fl.
Paucae Fl.
TARRABENI
Portus Favoni
Pauca
Matisa?
SUBASANI
BALATONI
Alista?
Granianum promontorium
Rubra?
Ficaria?
Portus Syracusanus
Pallae

FRETUM PALLICUM

Tibula
Ursi promontorium?
Viniola
Elefantaria?
Turublum Minus?
C O R S I
Columbarium promontorium?
Gorditanum promontorium?
Olbia
Turris Libisonis
Erucium?
Gemellae?
Coclearia?
Ad Herculem?
Luguido
Portus Luguidonis
Nure
BALARI
Caput Tyrsi
Carbia
Hafa?
Thyrsus Fl.
Fanum Carisi
Nymphaei portus
Aquae Lesitanae
Fl.
Hermaeum promontorium
Gurulis Vetus
Molaria
Viniola
Bosa
Macopsisa
ILIENSES
Caedrus
Gurulis Nova
Ad Medias
Sorabile
Cornus
Augustis
Forum Traiani
Sulcis
(Aquae Hypsitanae)
Custodia Rubriensis
Tharros
Othoca
Uselis
Valentia
Biora
Porticenses
PATULCENSES CAMPANI
Aquae
Neapolis
Neapolitanae
Saeprus Fl.
Sardopatris fanum
Sarcapos
Ferraria
Metalla
Sulcis Fl.
Carales
Crassum promontorium?
Nora
Sulcis
Tegula
Bitia
Chersonesus promontorium

Major settlements
Other settlements
Major roads

0   50
km

R.J.A.Wilson

Corsica and Sardinia

These two wild and rugged islands had rather different cultural backgrounds until their absorption by Rome in the third century BC. In Sardinia the best anchorages along the western and southern coasts had been colonised by Phoenicians in the eighth and seventh centuries. These settlements, bolstered by trade and each controlling a fertile agricultural hinterland, flourished under Carthaginian control, despite somewhat hostile relations with the Nuraghic peoples of the interior: the Carthaginian sphere of influence never extended far inland. In Corsica Phocaeans made an ill-fated attempt to found a Greek colony at Alalia (Aleria) around 565, but the island passed under Etruscan influence less than 30 years later, and the Etruscans are said to have founded Nicaea, perhaps on the site of Mariana, about the same time. Later at least part of Corsica, too, came under Carthaginian control, and it was from this that Rome wrested both islands in 238. But further campaigns were necessary before Roman power was consolidated: not until 227 was the new province of Sardinia-Corsica formally organised. The mountainous interiors, however, remained untamed. Continued forays by Roman armies in both islands were necessary to quell native revolts until the end of the second century BC; even after that, brigandage in Sardinia at least was not finally stamped out until the early empire.

With both islands so unsettled, it is hardly surprising that the progress of romanisation was slow. In Corsica a *colonia* was founded by Marius at Mariana and another at Aleria by Sulla, but no other cities merit a reference in the Corsican section of Pliny's detailed and wide ranging survey of Roman provinces, and only a single road—the east coast one—is listed in the Antonine Itinerary. The rest of the Corsican settlements shown on the map derive from Ptolemy's Geography: doubts remain about the precise location of some, and in the absence of archaeological investigation it is impossible to determine the degree of romani-

sation of the others. From the garrison at Praesidium Rome kept a watchful eye on the interior, while there was an important detachment of the Misenum fleet stationed in the sheltered lagoon of Portus Dianae.

Sardinia in time became more developed. Early in Augustus' reign only Turris Libisonis was a *colonia*, and Carales the sole city with municipal rights. However, Uselis soon joined Turris as a *colonia*, and Nora and Sulcis at least became *municipia*; Cornus, too, gained municipal or colonial rank. But the interior remained unsettled. This may be seen first from the presence of auxiliary garrisons there—most probably at Sorabile, Luguido, Augustis and Valentia (though certainty is impossible). The constant switching of the island's status is another sign of instability. Having been split from Corsica and organised as a separate province some time early in the empire, Sardinia shifted between being a senatorial province and coming under direct imperial control half-a-dozen times from Augustus' day to the late second century.

Corsica's main contribution to the Roman economy was its timber. Sardinian grain was not insignificant, and the lead and silver mines of the Metalla district, as well as iron and copper sources elsewhere in the island, also produced useful yields. In addition granite was extracted from quarries on both sides of the Fretum Pallicum—mostly for local needs. Certainly by the time of the middle Empire places such as Turris Libisonis (probably the capital), Carales, Nora and Olbia had equipped themselves with at least some public buildings in brick-faced concrete of the type to be expected in any medium-sized town in the Italian peninsula. But Punic influence in the coastal cities died hard: even in the late second century AD Bitia erected an inscription in neo-Punic which indicates that the town's constitution continued to be modelled along Carthaginian lines, with *suffetes* as chief magistrates.

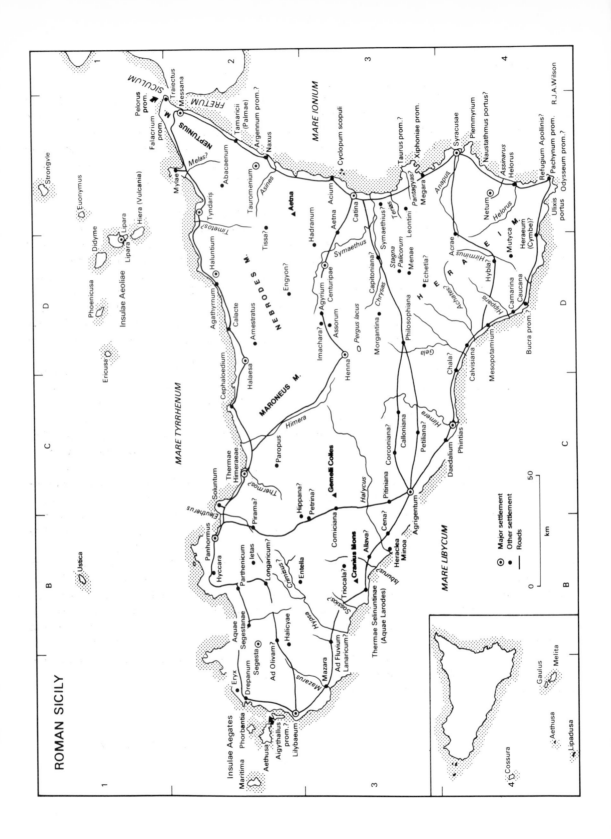

ROMAN SICILY

MARE TYRRHENUM

MARE IONIUM

MARE LIBYCUM

Strongyle

Euonymus

Insulae Aeoliae
Phoenicusa
Didyme
Lipara
Ericusa
Hiera (Vulcania)

Pelorus prom.
FRETUM SICULUM
Traiectus
Messana
Falacrium prom.
M NEPTUNIUS
Argennum prom.?
Tamaricii (Palmae)
Naxus
Abacaenum
Myiae
Melas?
Asines
Cyclopum scopuli
Taurus prom.?
Xiphoniae prom.
Tyndaris
Timetos?
▲ Aetna
Acium
Argennum prom.?
Tauromenium
Aetna
Catina
Syracusae
Plemmyrium
Haluntium
Hadranum
Naustathmus portus?
Agathyrnum
Tissa?
Symaethus
Symaethus?
Leontini
Megara
Netum
Assinarus
Helorus
Refugium Apollinis?
Pachynum prom.
Odysseum prom.?
Calacte
Engyon?
Centuripae
Menae
Acrae
Ulixis portus
Cephaloedium
Amestratus
Agyrium
Assorum
Palicorum
Echetla?
Hybla?
Mutyca
Heraeum (Cymbe)?
Halaesa
NEBRODES M.
Imachara?
Capitoniana?
Chryses
Morgantina
Philosophiana
Camarina
Caucana
Thermae
MARONEUS M.
Henna
Pergus lacus
Gela
Chala?
Calvisiana
Mesopotamium
Bucra prom.
Himera
Paropus
Calloniana
Petiliana?
Phintias
Daedalium
Himeraeae
Soluntum
Thermos?
Corconiana?
Pirama?
Hippana?
Petrina?
Pitiniana
Calloniana?
Panhormus
Eleutherus
Comiciana
Cena?
Agrigentum
Hyccara
Parthenicum
Ietas
Longaricum?
Entella
Allava?
▲ Cranius Mons
Heraclea Minoa
Aquae Segestanae
Segesta
Halicyae
Crimisus?
▲ Gemelli Colles
Halycus
▲ Cranius Mons
Eryx
Drepanum
Phorbantia
Ad Olivam?
Hypsas
Trocala?
Sossios?
Thermae Selinuntinae (Aquae Larodes)
Mazara
Ad Fluvium
Lanaricum?
Insulae Aegates
Maritima
Aegythallus prom.?
Lilybaeum
Mazarus

Legend:
⊙ Major settlement
• Other settlement
— Roads

km
0   50

Cossura

Aethusa
Gaulus
Melita
Lipadusa

R.J.A.Wilson

Roman Sicily

Sicily became the first of Rome's provinces at the end of the First Punic War (241 BC), and remained one until the island passed under Byzantine control in AD 535. The map inevitably represents a conflation of more than one period in that long span of nearly 800 years. It is drawn from two main sources.

The first is Pliny's list of Sicilian communities based on an Augustan document which, with one or two supplements from Cicero's *Verrines*, provides a list of the most important Sicilian cities in the late Republic. A comparison with the map of Greek Sicily (p. 38) will show that some of the famous old Greek cities, such as Gela, Himera and Selinus, were already dead (these three, in fact, by 241), and that some of the hill towns of the interior had also disappeared. In some cases the latter had been peacefully abandoned in the course of the late third century, when the arrival of the *pax Romana* made defensive capability no longer the most important factor in the choice of urban site. Right into the Empire the other hill towns were gradually deserted in favour of a pattern of more dispersed settlement on farms, and in villages and new market centres. The latter sprang up in the valleys and along the new trunk roads which the Romans built. Archaeology has demonstrated clearly that some of the places mentioned by Cicero and Pliny, such as Megara Hyblaea, Camarina, Morgantina, Heraclea Minoa and Ietas, either vanished altogether in the period between 50 BC and AD 50, or else dwindled to the size of hamlets; others, notably Helorus and Soluntum, and possibly Segesta and Entella, did not much outlast the second century AD.

The second main source for Sicilian place names in the Roman period is the Antonine Itinerary, in origin a third century AD document, which along with other similar late-Roman and post-Roman handbooks, lists places along the major trunk routes. In particular it provides the names of several of the new market centres referred to above, although many of these remain to be securely identified on the ground.

During both Republic and Empire, Sicily's economic importance lay almost exclusively in her role as a major corn producing province. In addition Sicilian wines were known on the tables of Rome, whilst horses, timber and sulphur were among other local assets with an export market. During the Republic the Sicilian communities were left largely to their own devices, provided they paid their tithes and other taxes. They retained a good measure of local autonomy, as well as their Greek-style constitutions and magistrates: culturally, Sicily under the Republic remained part of the Greek Hellenistic world. Romans showed an increasing interest in property speculation and other business affairs, but the numbers resident in Sicily stayed small until the first century BC. The Roman influx became more significant when six *coloniae* were created by Augustus, some of which erected buildings in the style of the concrete architecture of mainland Italy. However in other parts of Sicily building traditions remained conservative down to the late Empire. Latin was the official language of government, at least in the *coloniae* and *municipia*, though even they occasionally erected official inscriptions in Greek. This undoubtedly remained the language of normal everyday communication. Despite its geographical proximity to Italy and more than seven centuries as a Roman province, Sicily retained a distinctly Greek flavour down into Byzantine times.

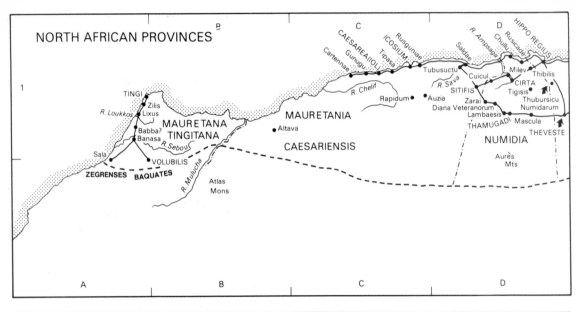

NORTH AFRICAN PROVINCES

CAESAREA(IOL)
ICOSIUM
Rusguniae
CAESAREA(IOL)
Tipasa
HIPPO REGIUS
R. Ampsaga
Rusicade
Chullu
Saldae
Tubusuctu
Cartennae
Gunugu
R. Sava
Milev
Thibilis
Cuicul
CIRTA
SITIFIS
Tigisis
Thubursicu
Rapidum
Auzia
Zarai
Numidarum
Diana Veteranorum
Lambaesis
THAMUGADI
Mascula
THAMUGADI
THEVESTE
NUMIDIA

TINGI
Zilis
Lixus
R. Loukkos
Babba?
Banasa
R. Sebou
MAURETANA
TINGITANA
MAURETANIA
CAESARIENSIS
Sala
R. Chelif
Altava
VOLUBILIS
ZEGRENSES   BAQUATES
R. Mulucha
Aurès
Mts
Atlas
Mons

A   B   C   D

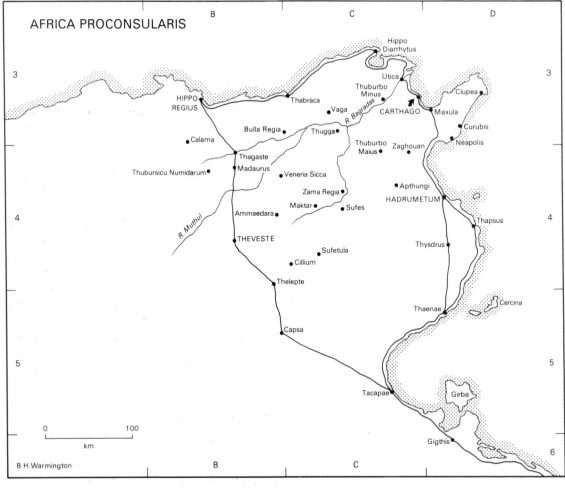

AFRICA PROCONSULARIS

Hippo
Diarrhytus
Utica
Thuburbo
Minus
Clupea
HIPPO
REGIUS
Thabraca
CARTHAGO
Maxula
Vaga
R. Bagradas
Curubis
Calama
Bulla Regia
Thugga
Neapolis
Thuburbo
Maius
Zaghouan
Thagaste
Thubursicu Numidarum
Madaurus
Veneria Sicca
Apthungi
Zama Regia
HADRUMETUM
Maktar
Ammaedara
Sufes
R. Muthul
THEVESTE
Thysdrus
Sufetula
Thapsus
Cillium
Thelepte
Thaenae
Cercina
Capsa
Girba
Tacapae
Gigthis

0   100
km

B.H.Warmington

B   C   D

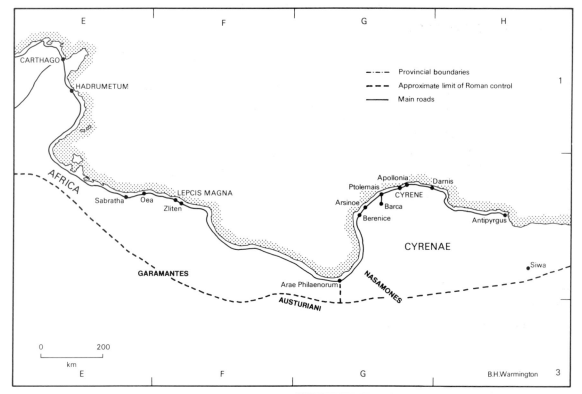

B.H.Warmington

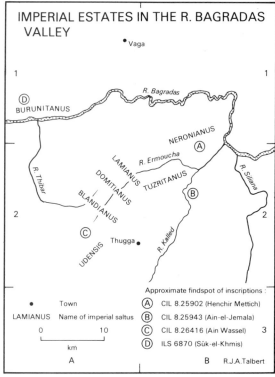

IMPERIAL ESTATES IN THE R. BAGRADAS VALLEY

Vaga

R. Bagradas

BURUNITANUS

NERONIANUS

Ⓐ

LAMIANUS

R. Ermoucha

TUZRITANUS

DOMITIANUS

R. Thibar

BLANDIANUS

Ⓑ

R. Kalled

R. Siliana

UDENSIS

Ⓒ

Thugga

Approximate findspot of inscriptions :

• Town

LAMIANUS Name of imperial saltus

Ⓐ CIL 8.25902 (Henchir Mettich)

Ⓑ CIL 8.25943 (Ain-el-Jemala)

0   10

Ⓒ CIL 8.26416 (Ain Wassel)

km

Ⓓ ILS 6870 (Sûk-el-Khmis)

A

B   R.J.A.Talbert

Imperial Estates in the R. Bagradas Valley

Emperors acquired extensive landholdings throughout the provinces by such means as inheritance, gift and confiscation. Four key inscriptions found in the R. Bagradas valley between 1879 and 1906 illuminate the character of imperial estates (*saltus*) there, though how far generalisation from them is valid remains doubtful. Of special interest is administration by procurators directly responsible to the emperor, acting in liaison with a *conductor* for each estate. Though technically himself a tenant, with official connivance the latter could oppress his fellows, as inscription D of Commodus' time shows. The others all preserve regulations encouraging tenants' cultivation of marginal land (*subseciva*). The map shows their approximate findspots and the presumed location of the estates named. The *fundus villae Magne Variane id est mappalia Siga*, to which inscription A (of Trajanic date) relates, is thought to have formed part of the *saltus Neronianus*. The *saltus Tuzritanus* and *saltus Thusdritanus*, to which the otherwise similar texts of inscriptions B (Hadrianic date) and C (Severan date) respectively relate, are likely to be identical.

151

North African Provinces

Rome's first province in Africa was acquired after the destruction of Carthage in 146 BC. It consisted of a relatively small area of northern Tunisia, and was governed from Utica. In 46 BC Julius Caesar added a new province created from the kingdom of Numidia; the two were combined by Augustus about 27 BC. Africa in this form remained a senatorial province governed from Carthage, which had been refounded as a *colonia* by Augustus. In AD 39 command of the province's single legion was transferred by Gaius from the proconsul to a *legatus Augusti* of praetorian rank. For all practical purposes he took charge of Numidia—which was not officially designated as a separate province till 196—as well as the military zone on the desert fringes as far east as the border with Cyrenaica. In 42/3 the client kingdom of Mauretania was annexed and split into two provinces, Mauretania Caesariensis and Mauretania Tingitana, separated by mountains; both were governed by equestrian procurators. Later, under Diocletian, the proconsular province was divided into three provinces, and Mauretania Caesariensis into two. No serious external or internal threats were felt to exist: the African garrison amounted to just one legion with numerous auxiliaries, in all about 28,000 men.

In the Punic period urban life had developed on a number of coastal sites, which came to survive the destruction of Carthage. Further impetus to development was given by considerable immigration from Italy under Caesar and Augustus. Several *coloniae* were founded, and there was much private settlement. The restriction of nomadic and pastoral movements opened wide areas to intensive agriculture, particularly cereals in northern Tunisia and later, after 100, olives in the southern areas. This was the basis of a population increase which in turn led to further urbanisation in favoured areas, among them parts of Numidia in the region of Cirta. The army also played a role in urbanisation from its successive bases at Ammaedara, Theveste and Lambaesis.

Tribal structures broke down rapidly in some areas (though not in the mountains), so that some 400 or 500 indigenous communities, mostly no more than villages, came to be recognised by the government as having local administrative responsibilities. With increased wealth, a substantial number developed into proper towns, acquiring Roman citizenship during the second century. Some, like Lepcis Magna and Hadrumetum, were old Phoenician settlements; others like Thugga, Thubursicu Numidarum, Thuburbo Maius and Maktar were of Libyan origin. By the end of the second century the density of urban life in northern Tunisia rivalled that of Italy. The population of the majority of these communities probably did not exceed 10,000; but Cirta and Hadrumetum had perhaps 30,000, and Carthage, which became the largest city in the western Mediterranean after Rome, perhaps 250,000.

Throughout north Africa there were extensive imperial estates; much land, too, was held by absentee owners. But many provincials also prospered, and they are found in increasing numbers in the highest ranks of the imperial administration. Septimius Severus, an African from Lepcis Magna, even rose to be emperor at the end of the second century. A further notable feature of the north African provinces is the speed with which Christianity spread there—faster than in any other Latin speaking region. Many of the most important early Christian writers in Latin—among them Tertullian, Cyprian, Lactantius, Augustine—were Africans.

In contrast to the advancement of Latin culture further west, Cyrenaica retained the Hellenic character which stemmed from the original settlement by Greeks in the seventh century BC. During the Roman period immigration from Italy was slight. Following its annexation in 74 BC Cyrenaica formed a proconsular province jointly with Crete—a connection not broken until some time in the third century AD. Diocletian next divided Cyrenaica into Libya Superior and Libya Inferior. The traditional Greek way of life continued in the coastal cities, the term Pentapolis being applied to Apollonia, Cyrene (see p. 40), Ptolemais, Arsinoe and Berenice. Serious damage was caused in a revolt by Jewish inhabitants in 115, but the province suffered no major military problem till the fourth century when pressure exerted on the cultivated areas by desert tribes became intense.

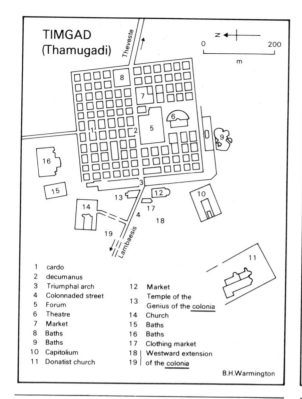

TIMGAD (Thamugadi)

Theveste

z

0 — 200
m

Lambaesis

1 cardo
2 decumanus
3 Triumphal arch
4 Colonnaded street
5 Forum
6 Theatre
7 Market
8 Baths
9 Baths
10 Capitolium
11 Donatist church
12 Market
13 Temple of the Genius of the colonia
14 Church
15 Baths
16 Baths
17 Clothing market
18 Westward extension
19 of the colonia

B.H.Warmington

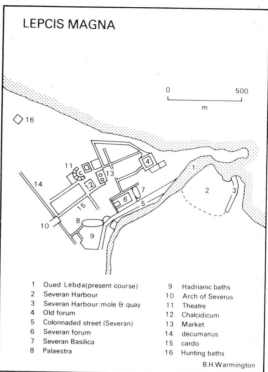

LEPCIS MAGNA

0 — 500
m

1 Oued Lebda(present course)
2 Severan Harbour
3 Severan Harbour:mole & quay
4 Old forum
5 Colonnaded street (Severan)
6 Severan forum
7 Severan Basilica
8 Palaestra
9 Hadrianic baths
10 Arch of Severus
11 Theatre
12 Chalcidicum
13 Market
14 decumanus
15 cardo
16 Hunting baths

B.H.Warmington

Timgad

Thamugadi (modern Timgad) has impressive remains which, unencumbered by post-Roman building, reveal the most complete aspect of a Roman colonial city to have survived. Founded in AD 100 as Colonia Marciana Traiana Thamugadi 38 km east of Lambaesis (the base of Legio III Augusta which provided the first settlers) on the road to Theveste, the city was planned like a military camp, being almost square. The perimeter wall was 355 metres per side and contained 111 roughly equal blocks, some occupied by public buildings. As a result of a rapid increase in population, the wall was dismantled within a generation and relatively unplanned expansion occurred, particularly to the west and north. The Capitolium itself was built *c.* 160 outside the original perimeter. The city's public buildings (among them 15 sets of baths) and impressive works of art testify to its wealth, derived from the agricultural resources of the region. Thamugadi became a stronghold of the Donatists, a Christian schismatic movement of the fourth century.

Lepcis Magna

Lepcis, or less correctly Leptis, Magna (modern Lebda) lies on the coast road 120 km east of Tripoli. A small harbour there on the Oued Lebda had been settled by Phoenicians around 600 BC. In Augustus' time its mixed Phoenician and Libyan inhabitants lavishly transformed it into a city on the Roman model. Some Phoenician institutions were still retained until Trajan gave the community the status of a *colonia*. The initial rebuilding was in the area of the 'old forum'. Further notable expansion took place under Hadrian, but the climax was reached around 200 when the emperor Septimius Severus and his praetorian prefect Fulvius Plautianus—both natives of Lepcis—added yet more magnificent buildings, including a new forum and harbour. Much remains superbly preserved. While the city may have profited from trans-Saharan trade in exotic goods, its wealth must have derived mainly from cultivation of the land between desert and sea. Stagnation set in after Severus' time, and the city's hinterland suffered increasingly from pressure by nomads.

153

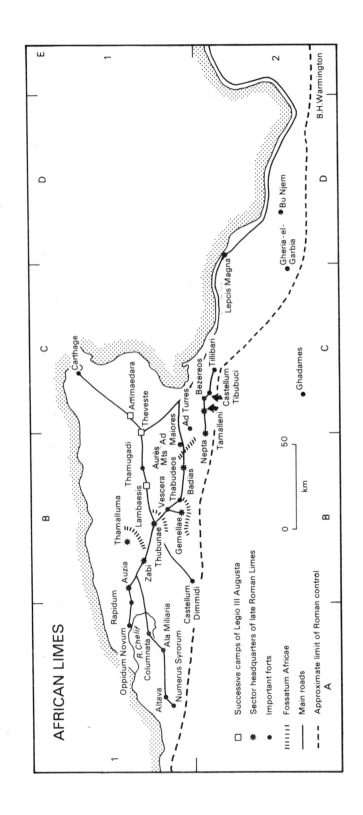

AFRICAN LIMES

□ Successive camps of Legio III Augusta

✳ Sector headquarters of late Roman Limes

● Important forts

︱︱︱︱︱ Fossatum Africae

——— Main roads

– – – Approximate limit of Roman control

0   50

km

B.H.Warmington

Carthage

Ammaedara

Theveste

Thamugadi

Lambaesis

Thamalluma

Auzia

Rapidum

Oppidum Novum

R. Chelif

Columnata

Altava

Ala Miliaria

Numerus Syrorum

Castellum Dimmidi

Zabi

Thubunae

Gemellae

Vescera

Thabudeos

Aurès Mts

Ad Maiores

Ad Turres

Badias

Nepta

Tamalleni

Bezereos

Castellum

Tibubuci

Tillibari

Lepcis Magna

Gheria-el-Garbia

Bu Njem

Ghadames

154

African Limes

Rome's African frontier system did not rest upon natural boundaries or defend the empire from a powerful rival. Rather, it delimited flexibly the area north of the Sahara in which an economic and political system of Mediterranean type could flourish. No serious military threat existed, and hence Africa needed fewer troops (about 28,000) than equivalent areas, and the frontier was capable of further extension to the west. The key areas were southern Algeria and Tunisia. The only legion, *III Augusta*, moved from Ammaedara to Theveste under Vespasian, and then to Lambaesis, its final base, under Trajan. During this period the Aurès mountains were penetrated and encircled; the land to the south, from Gemellae eastwards to Tamalleni, was dominated by a series of forts and roads. Probably under Hadrian the *fossatum Africae*—discontinuous stretches of ditch and wall—was built in various places to channel and control natives' movement. The furthest extension of the *limes* as far as Castellum Dimmidi came under Severus, but this addition was evacuated by Gordian III around 240. Irrigation and settlement went hand in hand with the advance of military control, the effective limit being climatic and economic.

In Mauretania Caesariensis auxiliary forts were at first concentrated on the line Auzia-Rapidum and the Chelif valley, until Severus developed a more southerly system. There was no permanent land connection between the Mauretanian provinces. In Tingitana the auxiliary units were relatively numerous and stationed inside the province. Inscriptions imply diplomatic arrangements with a neighbouring tribe outside the empire, the Baquates, between 140 and 280.

Immediately east of Tunisia, Tripolitania had no troops till the late second century when outposts were stationed as far south as Ghadames. From the third century fortified farmhouses here and in Cyrenaica testify to the need for self-protection against increasing nomadic threats, due perhaps to more widespread use of the camel. In the fourth century the entire *limes* (excluding Tingitana) was divided into sectors under *praepositi limitis*.

Greek and Roman Crete

Some time after the collapse of the Minoan civilisation (see pp. 4–5), Dorian Greeks settled in Crete beside the survivors of the earlier population, to form that mixture of Cretan peoples—'Achaeans, Eteocretans, Kydonians, Dorians and Pelasgians'—described in *Odyssey* 19. 175–7. In the tenth and ninth centuries conditions seem to have been harsh, and there was continued occupation of some of the inaccessible hilltop sites like Vrokastro and Kavousi that had first been occupied by Minoan refugees. By the eighth century, however, several new Dorian cities had been founded, so that in the seventh century Crete was a prosperous island of independent cities, in which the arts flourished sufficiently to influence developments throughout the Greek world. These communities of archaic Crete were also the first in Greece to introduce written codes of law.

Such prosperity seems to have come to an abrupt end in the sixth century. From that time on Crete never again occupied a comparably dominant position in either the historical or the archaeological record. From the fifth century until the Roman conquest in 67 BC the island suffered from frequent inter-city wars, in which the larger communities of Kydonia, Knossos, Gortyn and Hierapytna fought to increase their power over the weaker ones. During this period settlement was concentrated in walled cities occupying strong positions on hill tops.

The Roman conquest was carried out by Q. Caecilius Metellus in 69–7 BC, following accusations that the Cretans were guilty of piracy and were helping Mithradates in his fight against Rome. After the annexation Gortyn became the provincial capital, and Crete was combined with Cyrene to form a single province—an arrangement which continued into the third century AD. In the peaceful conditions under the Principate, settlements in low lying and coastal areas became more common. A certain prosperity is indicated by the building of a number of country villas in the second and third centuries.

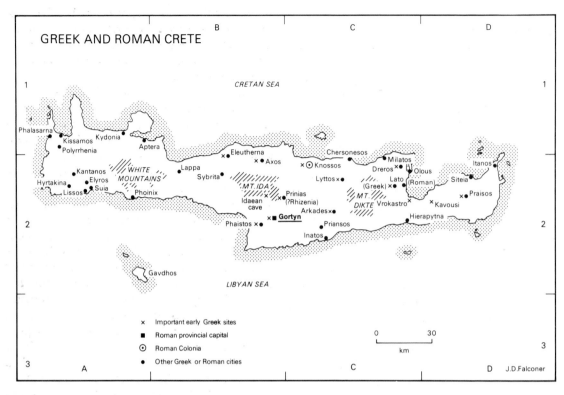

GREEK AND ROMAN CRETE

CRETAN SEA

Phalasarna
Kissamos Kydonia
Polyrrhenia Aptera
Kantanos Lappa
Hyrtakina Elyros Sybrita
Lissos Suia Phoinix
WHITE MOUNTAINS
Eleutherna Axos
MT.IDA Prinias (?Rhizenia)
Idaean cave
Arkades
Phaistos **Gortyn**
Inatos
Priansos
Chersonesos
Knossos
Lyttos
Dreros Milatos
Lato (Greek) Olous (Roman)
Vrokastro
MT. DIKTE
Hierapytna
Itanos
Siteia
Praisos
Kavousi

LIBYAN SEA

Gavdhos

× Important early Greek sites
■ Roman provincial capital
⊙ Roman Colonia
● Other Greek or Roman cities

0 ——— 30
km

J.D.Falconer

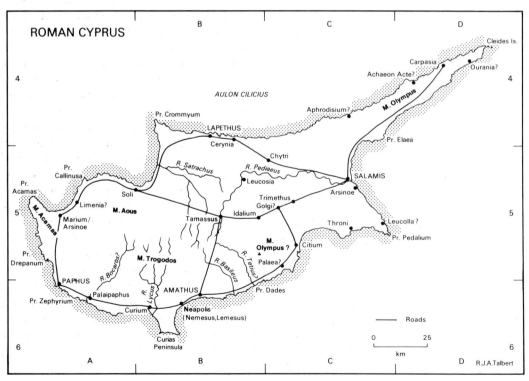

ROMAN CYPRUS

Cleides Is.
Carpasia
Achaeon Acte? Ourania?
AULON CILICIUS
Aphrodisium? **M. Olympus**
Pr. Crommyum
LAPETHUS
Cerynia Pr. Elaea
Chytri
Pr. Callinusa *R. Satrachus* *R. Pediaeus*
Pr. Acamas Leucosia SALAMIS
Limenia? Soli Arsinoe
M. Acamas **M. Aous** Trimethus Golgi?
Marium/Arsinoe Tamassus Idalium Throni Leucolla?
Pr. Drepanum **M. Olympus ?** Pr. Pedalium
R. Bocarus? Citium
M. Trogodos *R. Basileus* *R. Tertius?* Palaea
PAPHUS Palaea
R. Lycus AMATHUS Pr. Dades
Palaipaphus
Pr. Zephyrium Curium
Neapolis (Nemesus,Lemesus)
Curias Peninsula

——— Roads

0 ——— 25
km

R.J.A.Talbert

156

Roman Cyprus

Roman annexation of the Greek island of Cyprus in 58 BC followed two-and-a-half centuries of Ptolemaic rule. The island was first administered with Cilicia; Julius Caesar and Antony returned it to Egyptian rule. But Octavian claimed it permanently for Rome after his victory at Actium, and from 22 BC onwards it constituted a separate senatorial province divided into four districts centred around Paphus, Salamis, Amathus and Lapethus. Paphus, famous for its temple of Aphrodite, was developed as the administrative capital of the island and seat of the provincial *koinon* or council. Salamis, however, with its harbour and fertile hinterland was the largest and most cosmopolitan city, and the main commercial centre. It exported the island's principal products—copper, timber, corn—and was well situated to exploit trading opportunities with Syria, Judaea and Egypt. Copper mining, under state control, was concentrated on the coastal strip between Marium and Soli and in the rugged interior at Tamassus. The island did suffer occasional earthquake damage, and it was also greatly disturbed by its sizeable Jewish population at the time of the Jewish risings throughout the east late in Trajan's reign. Yet archaeological findings taken together with meagre literary and epigraphic evidence do confirm the general impression that under Roman rule Cyprus was a quiet, comparatively prosperous backwater.

Bithynia and Asia *c.* AD 100

Competition for status and its rewards was a prominent feature of Greek society, in public as in private life. The map illustrates the local government structure of two provinces and shows the major status categories competed for by cities.

In the case of Asia the cities are relatively well known from copious inscriptions of the late Hellenistic and early imperial periods. For Bithynia in the time of Trajan unique literary evidence is available: Pliny's official correspondence with the emperor while governor *c.* 109–11 is complemented by the political speeches of Dio Chrysostom concerning both the troubled internal affairs of his native Prusa in the years preceding Pliny's appointment, and the rivalries between Bithynian cities over points of honour.

In material terms the most valuable positions a city could hold were those of 'temple warden' (*neokoros*) and assize centre (*dioikesis/conventus*). The former title was officially held by cities which possessed a provincial temple of the imperial cult. In this capacity they hosted games which accompanied the cult and attracted crowds of visitors. Meetings of the *koinon*, the provincial congress responsible for the cult, were also held there. Assize centres were regularly visited by provincial governors to conduct judicial business. Litigants who required a hearing before a Roman tribunal had to travel to such a centre, and were naturally a source of prosperity to the community concerned. Paradoxically, however, some of the bitterest disputes involved not these positions, but the prestigious, though largely empty titles of *metropolis* and *prote* ('first city'). Dio deals with just such a wrangle between Nicomedea and Nicaea in his *Oration* 38. In the imperial period *metropolis*, which had originally signified the mother city of a Greek colony, came to be a title for the chief city of a province or region.

A few cities of the Greek east were absorbed by settlements of Roman veterans in the great demobilisations of Augustus' time, and thereby acquired the status of a Roman *colonia*, free from tribute and generally from interference by proconsuls. A number enjoyed the status of 'free city', which covered a range of different relationships with Rome, from nominal independence guaranteed by treaty or decree to more limited local autonomy dependent upon the emperor's goodwill. Finally there were areas where Greek institutions had not yet penetrated, and the people were still organised in tribal communities. However, there are several places marked which owed to imperial policy their development from tribal market centre to hellenised city. Such transformation was usually commemorated—at least temporarily—by the adoption of a dynastic name (like Flaviopolis, Trajanopolis).

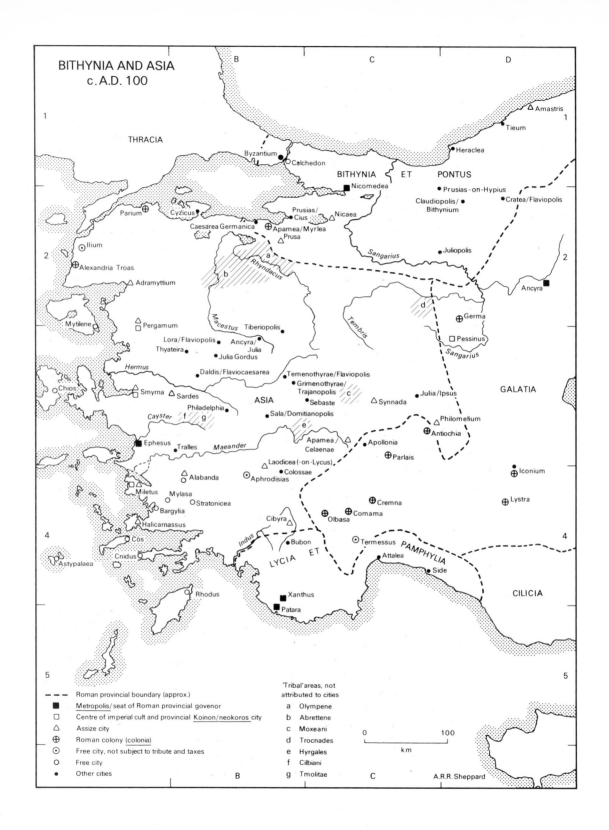

BITHYNIA AND ASIA
c. A.D. 100

THRACIA

Byzantium
Calchedon

BITHYNIA ET PONTUS

Amastris
Tieum
Heraclea

Nicomedea

Prusias - on - Hypius
Claudiopolis/ Bithynium
Cratea/Flaviopolis

Parium
Cyzicus
Prusias/Cius
Nicaea

Caesarea Germanica
Apamea/Myrlea
Prusa

Sangarius

Juliopolis

Ilium

Alexandria Troas

a

Rhyndacus

b

Adramyttium

Tembris

d

Germa

Sangarius

Ancyra

Mytilene

Pergamum

Macestus
Tiberiopolis

Pessinus

Lora/Flaviopolis
Ancyra/Julia
Thyateira
Julia Gordus

GALATIA

Hermus

Daldis/Flaviocaesarea

Chios

Smyrna
Sardes

ASIA

Temenothyrae/Flaviopolis
Grimenothyrae/Trajanopolis
c
Sebaste

Julia/Ipsus

Philadelphia

f g

Sala/Domitianopolis

e

Synnada

Philomelium

Antiochia

Cayster

Ephesus
Tralles

Maeander

Apamea/Celaenae

Apollonia

Parlais

Iconium

Laodicea (-on-Lycus)
Colossae

Alabanda
Aphrodisias

Lystra

Miletus

Mylasa
Stratonicea

Cremna

Bargylia
Halicarnassus

Cibyra
Olbasa

Comama

Termessus

PAMPHYLIA

Cos

Cnidus

Bubon

LYCIA ET

Attalea
Side

CILICIA

Astypalaea

Indus

Rhodus

Xanthus
Patara

'Tribal' areas, not
attributed to cities

- - - Roman provincial boundary (approx.)

■ Metropolis/seat of Roman provincial govenor

□ Centre of imperial cult and provincial Koinon/neokoros city

△ Assize city

⊕ Roman colony (colonia)

⊙ Free city, not subject to tribute and taxes

○ Free city

• Other cities

a Olympene
b Abrettene
c Moxeani
d Trocnades
e Hyrgales
f Cilbiani
g Tmolitae

0   100
km

A.R.R. Sheppard

Roman Asia Minor

The geographical centre of Asia Minor—in ancient terms Phrygia, Galatia, Lycaonia and western Cappadocia—consists of a rolling plateau at an average altitude of 1,100 metres, drained by the Sangarius and Halys rivers and by lakes of varying salinity; rainfall is low, and winters severe. This plateau is bounded to the north by the Paphlagonian mountains; their wooded northern slopes drop to a narrow coastal plain. Southwards the Taurus range begins in Lycia, runs roughly parallel to the coast and finally, east of the Cilician Gates, merges into the mountain mass 300 km wide which separates the Pontic coast from the Cilician and north Syrian plains. Westwards the plateau and the Pisidian mountains are broken by large river valleys, notably those of the Maeander, Hermus and Sangarius: these made Lydia, Mysia and Bithynia the richest parts of Asia Minor.

Serious Roman interest began here with the war against Antiochus III. Victory in 190 BC left Rome as arbiter of the peninsula. The Seleucids were generally confined to Cilicia, while native kings were retained in control of Cappadocia and the northern seaboard. Of Rome's allies, Rhodes was given territory in Caria and Lycia, and the small but well organised kingdom of Pergamum was encouraged to expand inland to fill the vacuum left by Antiochus' withdrawal.

In 133 Attalus III of Pergamum bequeathed his kingdom to Rome, and its richer and more accessible parts became the province of Asia. In 74 a similar bequest by Nicomedes III led to the formation of the province of Bithynia. On the south coast the province of 'Cilicia', which originally consisted mainly of Pamphylia, had been set up to curb pirates. But until Pompey's campaign against them in 67 and his subsequent rearrangement of the east, there was no continuous and effective Roman presence here, so that Cilicia in the strict sense remained nominally Seleucid property. After the defeat of Mithradates of Pontus by Pompey, most of his kingdom was added to Bithynia.

Next, in 25, Amyntas of Galatia bequeathed his kingdom—including much newly captured territory that was ethnically Pisidian, Phrygian, Lycaonian and Isaurian—to form the basis of a new imperial province of Galatia. Cappadocia was taken over early in Tiberius' reign. Initially it was controlled by a procurator, though later it was attached to Galatia, and finally became a separate imperial province under Trajan. Lycia and Pamphylia, after 250 years of experiments with different forms of government, were definitively annexed only under Vespasian. He also reinstated the province of Cilicia, which for more than a century had formed part of Syria. Thereafter, except for minor adjustments, this pattern of provinces remained intact until Diocletian's reorganisation.

Within the province of Asia certain cities were designated as district (*conventus*) centres where the governor on circuit would hold assizes. No doubt this system applied further east too, but there is little evidence for its organisation. In more developed areas cities on the Greek pattern were usually the main unit of local government, and new cities continued to be created into the Byzantine period. Elsewhere the tribe was the unit of government rather than the city; there were also large imperial estates that never acquired city status. Roman colonies were rare, apart from a group founded by Augustus to hem in the turbulent Pisidians.

The Roman road system began as a regularisation of existing routes, though at any rate the Via Sebaste, linking Augustus' Pisidian colonies, as well as stretches near the Euphrates frontier, were built specifically for military purposes. The Peutinger Table and the Antonine and Jerusalem Itineraries show the network as it existed in the fourth century AD. Milestones are common, even if their value may be reduced by the tendency of engravers to omit distances, and by the old Turkish habit of transporting such stones for reuse as grave markers. Though recent work has brought significant advances in understanding, the road pattern shown remains far from definitive, especially in Cappadocia.

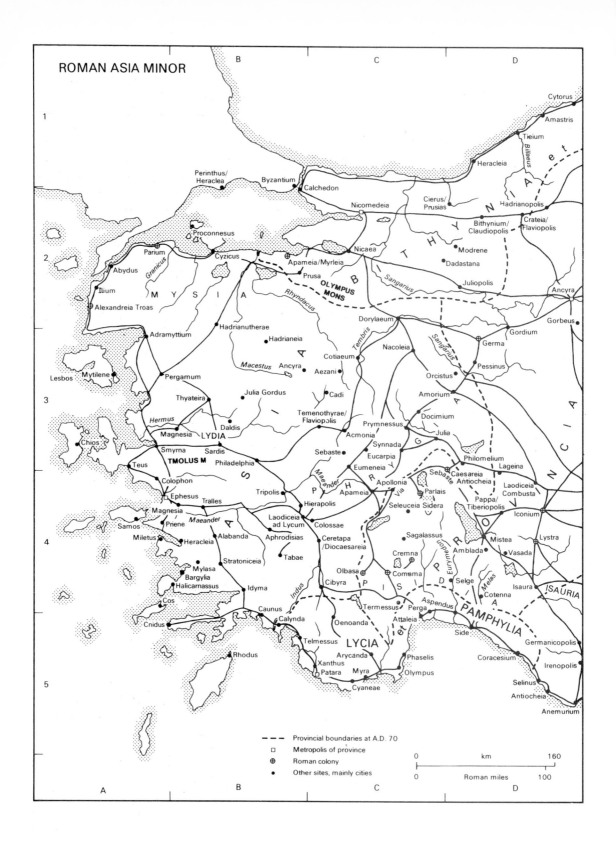

ROMAN ASIA MINOR

Provincial boundaries at A.D. 70
Metropolis of province
Roman colony
Other sites, mainly cities

km   160

Roman miles   100

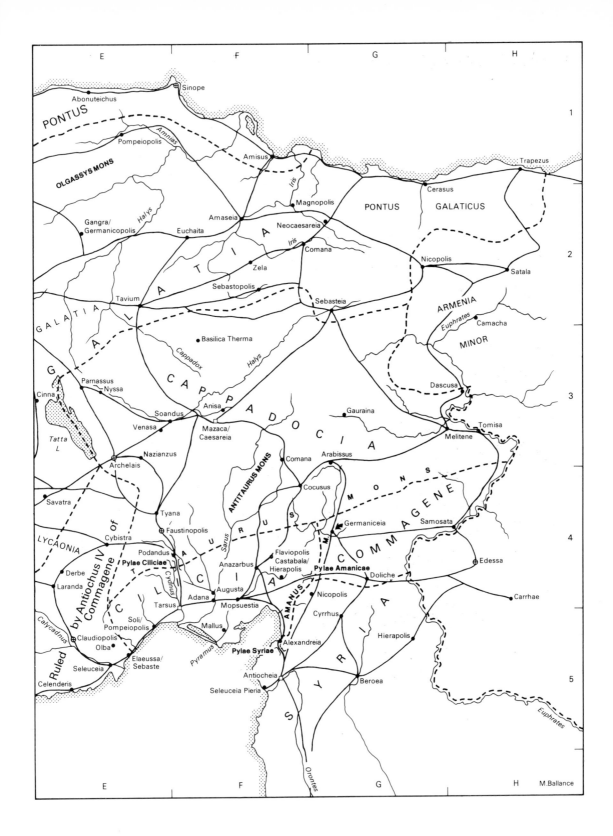

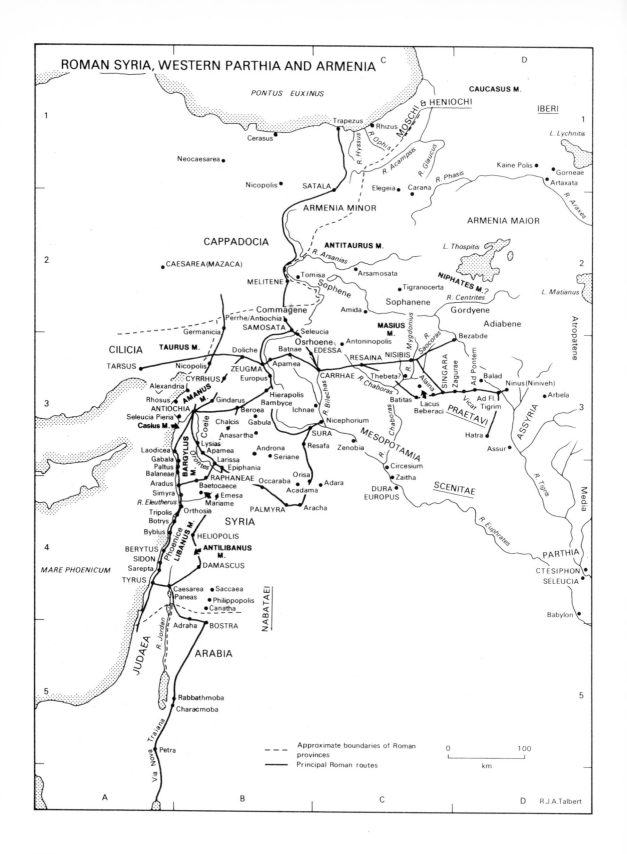

ROMAN SYRIA, WESTERN PARTHIA AND ARMENIA

PONTUS EUXINUS

MOSCHI & HENIOCHI
CAUCASUS M.
IBERI

Trapezus
Rhizus
R. Hyssus
R. Ophis
R. Acampsis
R. Glaucus
L. Lychnitis

Cerasus

Kaine Polis
Gorneae
Artaxata

Neocaesarea

Nicopolis
SATALA
Elegeia
Carana
R. Phasis

ARMENIA MINOR

R. Araxes

CAPPADOCIA

ANTITAURUS M.
R. Arsanias

ARMENIA MAIOR

L. Thospitis

CAESAREA (MAZACA)
Arsamosata
Tigranocerta
NIPHATES M.?
L. Matianus

MELITENE
Tomisa
Sophene
Sophanene

Commagene
Amida
Gordyene
Adiabene

Perrhe/Antiochia
MASIUS M.
Atropatene

Germanicia
SAMOSATA
Seleucia
Antoninopolis
Bezabde

CILICIA
TAURUS M.
Osrhoene
R. Mygdonius
R. Saocoras

Doliche
Batnae
EDESSA
NISIBIS
Ninus (Niniveh)

TARSUS
Nicopolis
Apamea
RESAINA
Singara
Ad Pontem
Balad

CYRRHUS
ZEUGMA
CARRHAE
R. Chaboras
Thebeta?
Alaina
Zagurae
Ad Fl.
Tigrim
Arbela

Alexandria
Europus
Batitas
Lacus
Beberaci
PRAETAVI
Hatra
Assur
ASSYRIA

Rhosus
AMANUS M.
Gindarus
Hierapolis
Bambyce
Ichnae
R. Bilechas
Nicephorium
MESOPOTAMIA

ANTIOCHIA
Beroea
Gabula
SURA
Resafa
Zenobia

Seleucia Pieria
Casius M.
Chalcis
Anasartha
Androna
Seriane
Circesium
Zaitha

Laodicea
Apamea
Orisa
Adara
DURA
EUROPUS
SCENITAE

Gabala
Paltus
Balaneae
Larissa
Epiphania
Occaraba
Acadama
Aracha

Aradus
Simyra
RAPHANEAE
Baetocaece
PALMYRA

R. Eleutherus
Mariame
Emesa

Tripolis
Botrys
Byblus
Orthosia
SYRIA

BERYTUS
SIDON
Sarepta
TYRUS
HELIOPOLIS
ANTILIBANUS M.
DAMASCUS
PARTHIA
CTESIPHON
SELEUCIA

MARE PHOENICUM
Caesarea
Saccaea
Paneas
Philippopolis
Canatha
NABATAEI
Babylon

JUDAEA
R. Jordan
Adraha
BOSTRA
ARABIA

Rabbathmoba
Characmoba

Via Nova Traiana
Petra

--- Approximate boundaries of Roman provinces
— Principal Roman routes

0   100
km

162

R.J.A.Talbert

Roman Syria, Western Parthia and Armenia

In ancient times Syria was the name given to the fertile strip along the entire eastern shore of the Mediterranean, from the Taurus Mountains to Egypt. It was held by Seleucids prior to annexation for Rome by Pompey in 63 BC. Thereafter its south west region was always separately administered—from AD 70 as the regular province of Judaea. The south east region, beyond the R. Jordan, was not directly controlled by Rome until AD 106 when the rule of its Nabataean kings came to an end, and it was then made the province of Arabia, governed from Bostra. In Roman parlance, therefore, the name 'Syria', came to be associated with the more fragmented northern region, to which Commagene was added from AD 72. Behind the narrow coastal plain here lie two parallel chains of mountains, broken at several points, and separated by valleys along which the R. Orontes flows northwards, the R. Jordan southwards. Beyond the mountains there come vast tracts of desert, which give Syria no defined frontier to the east; to the north the R. Euphrates marked the border. The prosperity of the cultivable regions derived from vines, olives, fruit and vegetables; the weaving of linen and wool were important, too, together with dyeing. The province also gained wealth from importing silk and other eastern luxury goods by caravan across the desert. Despite the unusually high duty of 25 per cent imposed on eastern imports by Rome, the trade continued to flourish. It encouraged the growth of communities on the edge of the desert (especially Damascus), and at oases (especially Palmyra), as well as seaports on the Mediterranean coast. Apart from these exceptions, however, Syria was hardly urbanised; its territory remained rural, with the village as the centre of local life. The great majority of the population continued to speak Syriac, and were little influenced by Greco-Roman culture.

As one of Rome's most splendid possessions Syria was governed by a senior consular in command of a substantial garrison, much of it recruited locally. The capital, Antioch, ranked among the greatest cities of the empire. At the end of the second century Septimius Severus divided the province into two—Coele to the north, governed from Antioch; Phoenice to the south, governed from Tyrus. Further division followed in the late third century.

East of Syria lay another part of the Seleucid inheritance, the Parthian empire. The attractive area closest to the Roman province, the north west of the Mesopotamian plain, was ruled by Parthian vassals, the princes of Osrhoene, from their capital at Edessa. The Parthian capital itself, Ctesiphon on the R. Tigris, lay far to the south, and its realm stretched on into the infinite distance, beyond the Caspian Sea. Although Parthian power was potentially a grave threat to the Roman empire, the state was for long in practice so weak and divided that Rome—her resources already strained elsewhere—seldom sought any permanent commitment beyond the R. Euphrates. Only from the late second century was northern Mesopotamia kept under regular occupation. Thereby Rome was at last enabled to station troops within striking distance of Ctesiphon, while at the same time acquiring a base for domination of Armenia.

The strategic situation of this mountainous, undeveloped land had always made the allegiance of its rulers a matter of concern to both Parthia (which enjoyed close ties of race and culture with its people) and Rome. But despite certain more or less successful forays, Rome failed to hold any of the country until Diocletian's time (when an area on the upper Tigris was gained), and would usually exert influence there only by diplomacy. In any event, before the mid-third century, with the displacement of her Arsacid kings by Sassanids, Parthia's conflict with Rome had entered a new phase. She became unprecedentedly aggressive. Armenia, Mesopotamia and Syria were all overrun, and the emperor Valerian captured by Sapor I in 260. Rome's position was restored only with great difficulty.

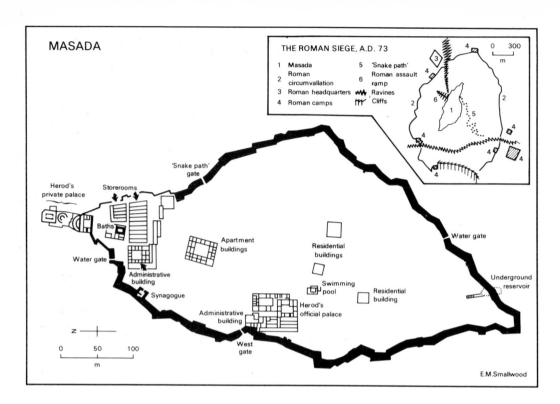

MASADA

THE ROMAN SIEGE, A.D. 73

1 Masada
2 Roman circumvallation
3 Roman headquarters
4 Roman camps
5 'Snake path'
6 Roman assault ramp
〰 Ravines
𝝠 Cliffs

0   300
m

Herod's private palace
Storerooms
'Snake path' gate
Baths
Water gate
Administrative building
Synagogue
Apartment buildings
Administrative building
West gate
Residential buildings
Swimming pool
Herod's official palace
Residential building
Water gate
Underground reservoir

z

0   50   100
m

E.M.Smallwood

JERUSALEM

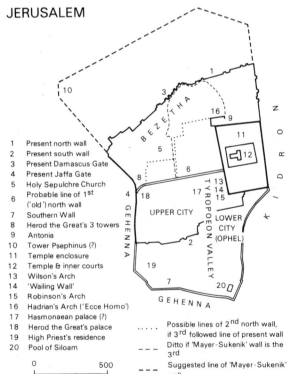

1   Present north wall
2   Present south wall
3   Present Damascus Gate
4   Present Jaffa Gate
5   Holy Sepulchre Church
6   Probable line of 1st ('old') north wall
7   Southern Wall
8   Herod the Great's 3 towers
9   Antonia
10 Tower Psephinus (?)
11 Temple enclosure
12 Temple & inner courts
13 Wilson's Arch
14 'Wailing Wall'
15 Robinson's Arch
16 Hadrian's Arch ('Ecce Homo')
17 Hasmonaean palace (?)
18 Herod the Great's palace
19 High Priest's residence
20 Pool of Siloam

BEZETHA
UPPER CITY
LOWER CITY (OPHEL)
TYROPOEON VALLEY
GEHENNA
KIDRON

0   500
m

..... Possible lines of 2nd north wall, if 3rd followed line of present wall
‒ ‒ ‒ Ditto if 'Mayer-Sukenik' wall is the 3rd
‒ ‒ ‒ Suggested line of 'Mayer-Sukenik' wall

E.M.Smallwood

Jerusalem

Jerusalem had the protection of the deep, steep-sided valleys of Kidron and Gehenna to the east, south and west: these acted as vast natural fosses in front of the city walls and of the east wall of the Temple enclosure, which was itself part of the fortifications. On the north there was only man-made protection. The first north wall was Hasmonaean. The second was possibly built in the latter part of the first century BC by Herod the Great, who strengthened the north west angle with three massive towers. The line of this wall is conjectural, but it is known to have run from near Herod's towers to Antonia, his new fortress built for the protection of the Temple on more or less the same site as two earlier ones. These two walls were not demolished when Agrippa I planned a new north wall (not actually completed until early in the war of AD 66–70) to enclose the growing suburb of Bezetha. Some scholars hold that this new wall followed roughly the line of the present sixteenth-century wall, but evidence is accumulating for the more northerly line of the wall, named 'Mayer-Sukenik' after the archaeologists who found the first traces of it.

Robinson's Arch at the southern end of the western wall of the Temple enclosure supported a broad stairway leading down to the Tyropoeon or Cheesemakers' Valley. Wilson's Arch is the first arch of a viaduct leading across the valley to the Upper City. Josephus describes the city, its fortifications, and the Temple in his *Jewish War* 5.136–247.

Masada

Masada is a rock plateau rising 366 metres from the narrow plain between the Dead Sea and the Judaean mountains, with access only by the dangerous 'Snake Path'. Herod the Great strengthened the earlier Hasmonaean fortress by building a casemate wall round the cliff edge except at the northern tip, where the precipices are almost vertical. There, on three descending rock terraces, he had a small private palace. Large, well-stocked storerooms and numerous reservoirs, mostly in the cliffs, fed by an aqueduct from a wadi on the west and by occasional rain, enabled the fortress to stand a long siege. During the war of AD 66–70 the Sicarii took possession of Masada, converting the casemates into dwellings. In 73 the Romans invested the fortress with a circumvallation (except where the terrain made penetration impossible) and eight camps. They then used a projecting rock bastion on the west as an assault ramp, raising it with stone and timber to the level of the wall, which they breached with battering rams. From 73 the Romans maintained a permanent garrison in the besiegers' headquarters camp. A description of Masada and an account of the siege are given by Josephus, *Jewish War* 7.275–406.

Palestine

When the Jews under the Hasmonaean dynasty achieved political independence from Seleucid Syria in the mid-second century BC, their territory consisted of Judaea only, cut off from the sea by the line of Greco-Syrian (formerly Phoenician) cities along the coast. A period of rapid territorial expansion followed. By the death of Jannaeus in 76 BC Jewish dominions comprised Galilee (which had a considerable Jewish population before annexation), Samaritis (where a schismatic form of Judaism was practised), Idumaea (which was forced to accept Judaism), Peraea, the coastal cities, and some other Greco-Syrian cities in northern Transjordan. The boundaries between these and the other various districts comprising Palestine are not known for certain, and consequently are left unmarked on the map.

In 63 when Pompey turned Palestine under its last Hasmonaean king into a client kingdom, the Jews' cities in northern Transjordan were removed from their control and linked with others as the semi-autonomous Decapolis. The Idumaean Herod the Great, who was put on the throne by Rome in 40 BC, had Ulatha, Paneas and extensive territory to the north east added to his kingdom in the course of his reign. When he died in 4 BC, his kingdom was divided between three of his sons: Philip ruled the north eastern territories till his death in AD 34; Antipas ruled Galilee, Samaritis and Peraea until 40; Judaea and Idumaea were ruled by Archelaus until 6, when his oppression provoked his subjects to ask for annexation by Rome. In consequence the province of Judaea was established.

Next, in 37 Herod Agrippa, a grandson of Herod the Great, was appointed king of Philip's former territory, while in 40 Antipas was deposed and his realm, too, was put under Agrippa. Then in 41 the Roman province of Judaea was added to Agrippa's kingdom. Finally on his death in 44 Roman Judaea was reconstituted and enlarged to include all the former territories of both Agrippa and Antipas. This arrangement remained permanent. Neither the first Jewish revolt in 66–70, nor the second in 132–5, resulted in territorial alterations to the province. However in 135 it was renamed Syria Palaestina, and Jerusalem was refounded as the Greek city of Aelia Capitolina, from which Jews were excluded. Praetorian legates superseded equestrian procurators as governors from 70.

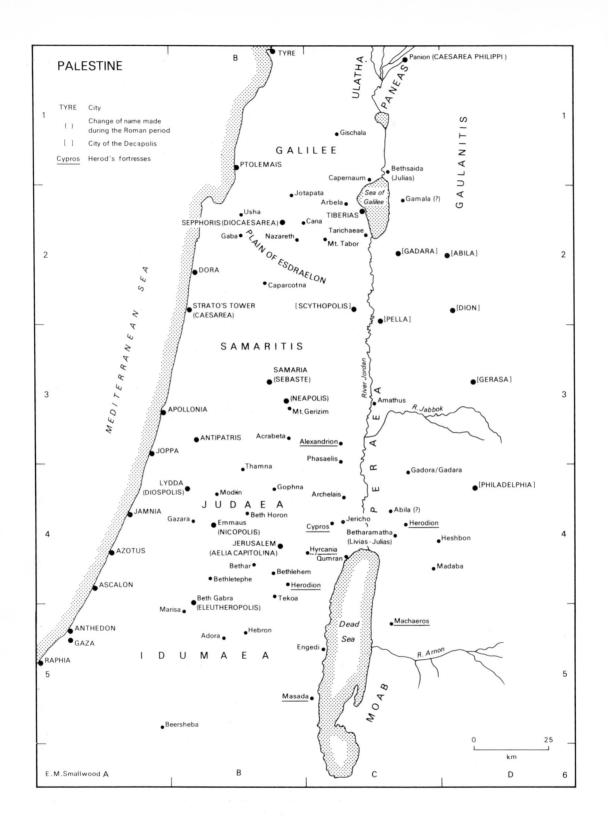

PALESTINE

TYRE   City
(   )   Change of name made
            during the Roman period
[   ]   City of the Decapolis
Cypros   Herod's fortresses

TYRE

B

Panion (CAESAREA PHILIPPI)

ULATHA

PANEAS

GAULANITIS

GALILEE

Gischala

PTOLEMAIS

Capernaum   Bethsaida
                 (Julias)

Jotapata   Sea of
Arbela   Galilee   Gamala (?)
Usha   TIBERIAS
SEPPHORIS (DIOCAESAREA)   Cana
Gaba   Nazareth   Tarichaeae
              Mt. Tabor   [GADARA]   [ABILA]

DORA
                 Caparcotna

STRATO'S TOWER
(CAESAREA)   [SCYTHOPOLIS]
                                    [PELLA]   [DION]

SAMARITIS

SAMARIA
(SEBASTE)   [GERASA]

(NEAPOLIS)
Mt. Gerizim   Amathus   R. Jabbok

APOLLONIA

ANTIPATRIS   Acrabeta   Alexandrion
                      Phasaelis
JOPPA
              Thamna   Gadora/Gadara

LYDDA
(DIOSPOLIS)   Modiin   Gophna   [PHILADELPHIA]
              JUDAEA   Archelais
JAMNIA   Gazara   Beth Horon   Abila (?)
          Emmaus   Jericho   Herodion
          (NICOPOLIS)   Cypros   Heshbon
          JERUSALEM   Betharamatha
          (AELIA CAPITOLINA)   Hyrcania   (Livias - Julias)
AZOTUS   Bethar   Qumran   Madaba
          Bethlehem
          Bethletephe   Herodion
ASCALON   Tekoa
          Beth Gabra
Marisa   (ELEUTHEROPOLIS)   Machaeros
ANTHEDON   Adora   Hebron   Dead
GAZA   Sea
                 Engedi   R. Arnon
RAPHIA   I D U M A E A
                                    MOAB

Masada

Beersheba

MEDITERRANEAN SEA

River Jordan

PERAEA

Dead Sea

0   25
        km

E.M.Smallwood A   B   C   D

166

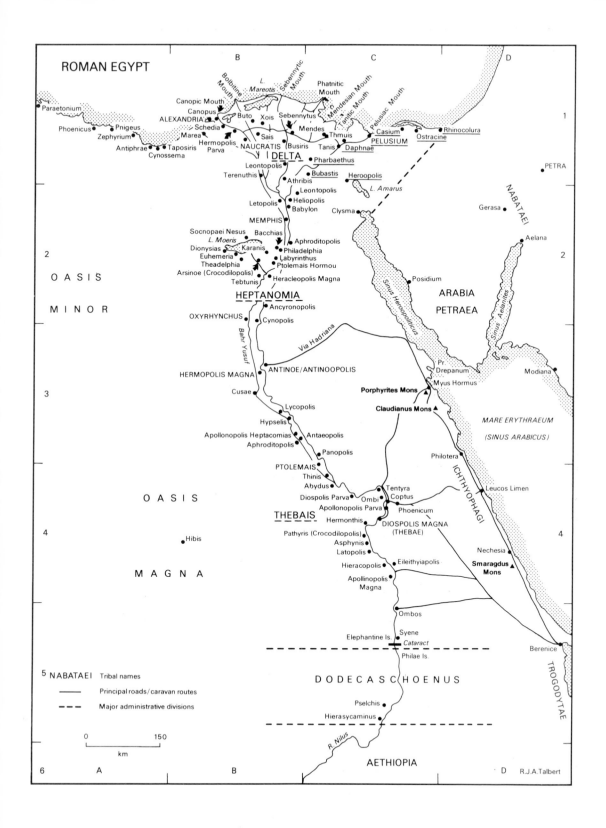

ROMAN EGYPT

B **C** **D**

Paraetonium

Phoenicus Pnigeus *L. Mareotis* Bolbitine Mouth Sebennytic Mouth Phatnitic Mouth Mendesian Mouth Tanitic Mouth Pelusiac Mouth

Zephyrium Canopic Mouth Canopus

Antiphrae Taposiris Marea ALEXANDRIA Schedia Buto Xois Sebennytus PETRA

Cynossema Hermopolis Parva NAUCRATIS Sais Mendes Thmuis Casium Rhinocolura

Busiris Tanis **Daphnae** **PELUSIUM** Ostracine

1 **DELTA** Pharbaethus

Leontopolis **Bubastis** Heroopolis

Terenuthis Athribis Leontopolis *L. Amarus* NABATAEI

Letopolis Heliopolis Gerasa

Babylon Clysma Aelana

MEMPHIS

Socnopaei Nesus Bacchias Aphroditopolis Posidium ARABIA

L. Moeris Dionysias Karanis Philadelphia PETRAEA

Euhemeria Labyrinthus

2 Theadelphia Ptolemais Hormou

Arsinoe (Crocodilopolis) Heracleopolis Magna

Tebtunis

HEPTANOMIA

OASIS Ancyronopolis

OXYRHYNCHUS Cynopolis

MINOR *Bahr Yusuf* Via Hadriana Pr. Drepanum Modiana

HERMOPOLIS MAGNA ANTINOE/ANTINOOPOLIS Myus Hormus

3 Cusae **Porphyrites Mons** *MARE ERYTHRAEUM*

Lycopolis **Claudianus Mons** *(SINUS ARABICUS)*

Hypselis

Apollonopolis Heptacomias Antaeopolis Philotera

Aphroditopolis

Panopolis Leucos Limen

PTOLEMAIS

OASIS Thinis

Abydus Tentyra

Diospolis Parva Ombi Coptus

Apollonopolis Parva Phoenicum

THEBAIS Hermonthis DIOSPOLIS MAGNA

4 Pathyris (Crocodilopolis) (THEBAE) Nechesia

MAGNA Asphynis

Latopolis **Smaragdus Mons**

Hibis Hieracopolis Eileithyiapolis

Apollinopolis Magna

Ombos

Elephantine Is. Syene Berenice

Cataract

Philae Is.

5 NABATAEI Tribal names DODECASCHOENUS

Principal roads/caravan routes

Major administrative divisions Pselchis

Hierasycaminus

0   150

km *R. Nilus*

6 **A** **B** AETHIOPIA **D** R.J.A.Talbert

167

Roman Egypt

Egypt was annexed by Octavian in 30 BC and as a Roman province was closely controlled by the emperor through equestrian officials; senators were never appointed to posts there. The framework of the existing Ptolemaic organisation was retained, thus making for a tighter degree of supervision than Rome exercised over any other province. Uniquely detailed insight into the life of Roman Egypt is afforded by papyrus records preserved in the dry climate. Two legions (reduced to one from the early second century) and a fleet were based at Alexandria, though soldiers from the former were deployed throughout the country, and ships from the latter policed the R. Nile. For administrative and fiscal purposes the province was divided into three large districts—Delta, Heptanomia, and Thebaid; to the last of these was also joined the frontier zone of the Dodecaschoenus beyond the natural barrier of the First Cataract. Each district was headed by an *epistrategus*, and subdivided into a dozen or more *nomes*, the responsibility of a *strategus* and his assistant the Royal Scribe. The principal community of each nome ranked as a *metropolis*, enjoying some privileges and limited civic services provided by annually elected magistrates from the superior 'gymnasium' class, but otherwise controlled by the *strategus*; town councils were not instituted until the early third century. The other communities of each nome, the villages, were wholly under the supervision of the *strategus*. The limited number of Greek cities lay outside the nome structure and in every respect formed the most privileged communities of the province—the capital Alexandria, with its mixed Greek and Jewish population and the only good harbour on the coast of the Delta, ranking as the most privileged of all; Naucratis; Ptolemais; and the Hadrianic foundation of Antinoe/Antinoopolis.

Like the lands adjoining it, Egypt was almost all desert. The only fertile areas were the marshy lands of the Delta (where papyrus was principally grown), the country around Lake Moeris (the modern Fayum), and a narrow strip either side of the Nile. In consequence the river was the focus of the whole province and its annual inundation vital to general prosperity: the level was predicted at Elephantine Island from a 'Nilometer', or gauge, which survives. The flooding—at its greatest extent during October—both refertilised the land and watered crops. Regular maintenance of dykes, embankments and canals was so vital to the country's economy that five days' labour at this work was required annually from every native male.

Rome valued and exploited Egypt above all for its agricultural produce—chiefly cereals in sufficient quantities to fill whole convoys of vessels, but in addition vegetables, olives, vines and flax. Animals were raised, and there was also some quarrying and mining (notably for gold in the south east of the province). Highly lucrative, too, was the province's trade with Arabia and India through its Red Sea ports. Luxury goods landed there (and attracting a special duty of 25 per cent of their value) were transported by caravan to the Nile, and then shipped to Alexandria for re-export elsewhere in the empire. The manufacture of perfumes, ointments and medicines was well developed in consequence. In the long term, however, Roman rule of Egypt during the Principate was damaging both to the condition of the country and to the welfare of its people. The land was drained of resources. The vast majority of its inhabitants, the native Egyptians, was kept firmly at the bottom of a rigid class system, exploited, over-taxed and in complete subjection.

The Roman Empire in AD 211

The attempts made towards further extension of the empire during the century-and-a-half between 60 and 211 were just as impressive as those of the Julio-Claudian period. But by no means all the territory gained could be held. Following the deaths of the client kings of Pontus (64) and Commagene (72), the Flavian emperors took the opportunity to extend and consolidate the eastern provinces; the legions on this frontier were also increased in number and redeployed. In Germany the former two military areas were formally established as Upper and Lower provinces, and the 'Agri Decumates', territory forming a dangerous re-entrant angle between the Rhine and Danube, was annexed. The frontier line was thus shortened considerably, and the garrison reduced. In Britain the conquest of England and Wales was completed, and during the 80s forces under Agricola even penetrated deep into Scotland; but this initiative was not followed up. At the same time the Danube frontier came under intense pressure from tribes north of the river. For security the single provinces of Pannonia and Moesia were each divided, and an earth wall raised across the Dobrudja plain. The situation was stabilised only after two campaigns by Trajan (101–2 and 105–6), which resulted in the annexation of Dacia as a protection for the lower Danube area. In the east the improved Flavian frontier was rounded off with the annexation of Nabatea as the new province of Arabia in 105–6. About five years later Trajan made Parthian interference in Armenia his pretext for attempting to gain full control of the country, which Nero's legate, Corbulo, had over-run previously about 60 (with the purpose of handing it over to a client king). In 113/14 Trajan enjoyed similar success, but was then rashly encouraged to proceed further, sweeping as far south as the Persian Gulf, which he reached by the end of 115. Yet these new territories were too vast to hold: rebellion here, and unrest elsewhere in the empire, prompted their immediate abandonment by Hadrian on his accession in 117. In deliberate contrast to Trajan he pursued a strict policy of everywhere consolidating the empire and its frontiers, even to the extent of building a massive 118 km wall from Tyne to Solway to mark the northern limit of Britannia. His successor, Antoninus Pius, permitted a modest advance to the shorter Forth-Clyde line, where a turf wall was built and held for a brief period. Elsewhere general peace and stability continued into the 160s. They were then shattered first in the east, where Parthia once again seized Armenia. It was recovered only after a long struggle, and for its protection part of Upper Mesopotamia was now kept under Roman control. Next, M. Aurelius' struggle to repulse German tribes which swept across the upper and lower Danube deep into the empire, led him from 170 to attempt the subjugation of central and south eastern Europe north of the river, the territory of the Marcomanni, Quadi and Iazyges. His efforts might have been successful if a bid for the Principate by Avidius Cassius in 175 had not forced him to rush to the east. He returned to the Danube frontier in 177 to spend the last three years of his reign fighting the tribes north of the river, and again came close to subjugating them. But his son and successor, Commodus, preferred to abandon the campaign and make peace.

Septimius Severus, who emerged as victor in the civil wars of the 190s, attacked Parthia in retaliation for its support of his first rival, Pescennius Niger, and extended Roman control of Mesopotamia, which he made into a new province. In north Africa the security of the desert frontier was improved. Efforts to add Scotland to the Roman province of Britain were unsuccessful, however, and were not continued after his death at Eburacum (York) in 211. Since the substantial concentrations of legions in Syria and Britain had formed the support of his two main rivals, Severus split each of these provinces into separate commands, so that in future no governor should have control of more than a pair of legions. By raising three new ones he brought the total number of legions above thirty for the first time since the beginning of the Principate. He also broke with precedent by stationing one in Italy, at Albanum just south east of Rome, for deployment as a reserve or 'field army', with no responsibility for any particular area.

THE ROMAN EMPIRE IN A.D. 211

BRITANNIA
INFERIOR
□ EBURACUM
DEVA □

ISCA SILURUM □ BRITANNIA
SUPERIOR
● LONDINIUM

BELGICA
2
□ VETERA
□ BONNA
⊡ MOGUNTIACUM

LUGDUNENSIS
● DUROCORTORUM

1

MARCOMANNI

QUADI

ARGENTORATE □

CASTRA REGINA ⊡
LAURIACUM ⊡
VINDOBONA
CARNUNTUM
BRIGETIO
AQUINCUM

AQUITANIA

RAETIA
NORICUM

4

5

● BURDIGALA   LUGDUNUM ●

3

ALPES
COTTIAE
ALPES
MARITIMAE

DALMATIA

● SALONAE

□ LEGIO
VII GEMINA

NARBONENSIS

● NARBO

ITALIA
● ROMA
□ ALBANUM

LUSITANIA

TARRACONENSIS

SARDINIA
ET
CORSICA

EMERITA
AUGUSTA ●

● TARRACO

● CORDUBA

BAETICA

● CARALES

SICILIA

TINGIS

● SYRACUSE

● CAESAREA (IOL)

● CARTHAGO

MAURETANIA
TINGITANA

AFRICA

MAURETANIA CAESARIENSIS

□ LAMBAESIS

NUMIDIA

1 GERMANIA SUPERIOR
2 GERMANIA INFERIOR
3 ALPES ATRECTIANAE
ET POENINAE
4 PANNONIA SUPERIOR
5 PANNONIA INFERIOR

0   500
km

A   B   C   D

Albis
Rhenus
Danuvius

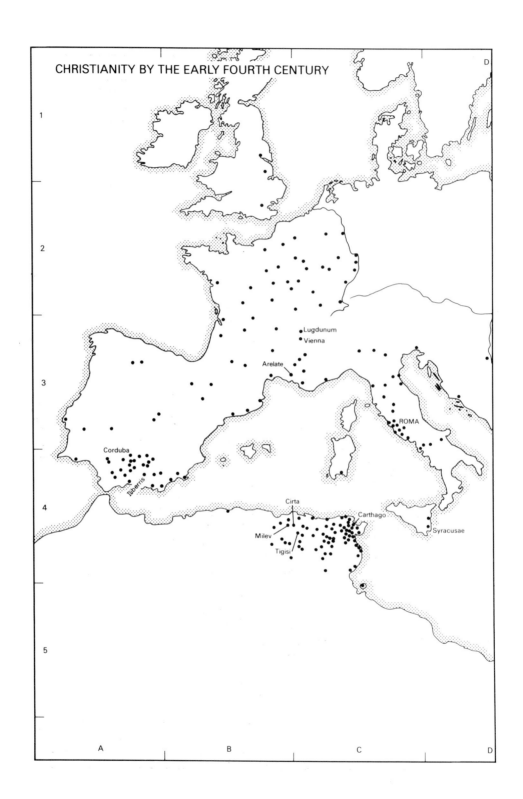

CHRISTIANITY BY THE EARLY FOURTH CENTURY

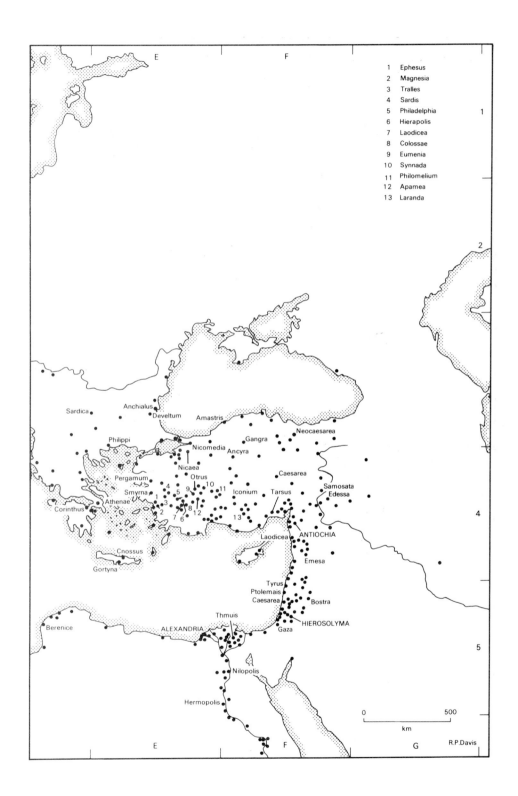

1	Ephesus
2	Magnesia
3	Tralles
4	Sardis
5	Philadelphia
6	Hierapolis
7	Laodicea
8	Colossae
9	Eumenia
10	Synnada
11	Philomelium
12	Apamea
13	Laranda

Sardica

Anchialus
Develtum
Amastris

Neocaesarea

Philippi

Gangra

Nicomedia
Ancyra

Pergamum

Nicaea
Otrus

Caesarea

Smyrna

10
9
4
5
11

Samosata
Edessa

Athenae

1
3
8
12
Iconium
Tarsus

Corinthus

2
7 6
13

Cnossus

Laodicea
ANTIOCHIA

Gortyna

Emesa

Tyrus
Ptolemais
Caesarea

Bostra

Berenice

Thmuis

ALEXANDRIA

HIEROSOLYMA
Gaza

Nilopolis

Hermopolis

0   500
km

R.P.Davis

Christianity by the Early Fourth Century

As with other forms of religion, it is impossible to map the Christian beliefs of individuals: the best which may be done is to chart the spread of organised churches, that is to say, of groups of Christians sufficiently numerous and stable to have regular meeting places for worship. In practice this means plotting on a map those places which are known, or may on reasonable evidence be assumed, to have had a bishop by the period in question. In this instance the latter may be defined as the time of the emergence of Christianity to full toleration and active imperial support during the reign of Constantine: he controlled Gaul and Britain from 306, Italy and Africa from 312, and the whole empire from 324 until his death in 337. At this stage Christians were possibly somewhere around 10 per cent of the population.

This procedure has its drawbacks. First, there is little doubt that individual Christians could be found in almost every town in the empire at a fairly early date: indeed, writing in about 200, Tertullian was able to claim that Christians were to be found even in parts of Britain inaccessible to the Romans. But any attempt to map the presence of individuals from scanty literary or archaeological evidence would be so random as to prove meaningless. Not even the record of a martyrdom at a given city is necessarily proof of an organised Christian community there.

Second, the evidence for the existence of bishoprics is itself far from complete. Most useful here are the lists of bishops who attended, or accepted the decisions of, church councils—held at Carthage in 256, Elvira (Iliberris) about 306, Rome in 313, Arles (Arelate) in 314, Nicaea in 325 and Sardica in 343—though with all these lists it should be noted that difficulties of topographical identification often arise. The Council of Nicaea seems to have been attended by the majority of eastern bishops, so that our picture of bishoprics for the eastern provinces may be taken as relatively complete. But some of the other councils were more localised: thus it is from the signatures of the councils of Carthage and Elvira that the clusters of bishoprics in Africa and southern Spain emerge. Recent studies of Sardica mean that information on Gaul is relatively good; yet evidence for the Danubian provinces remains thin. It is certain, too, that there were many more bishoprics in Italy than can be located: 60 Italian bishops apparently attended a council held at Rome in 251, though no list survives. Records of councils may be supplemented to some degree from literary sources, in particular Eusebius' *History of the Church*. As far as possible all the place names given by Eusebius have been marked on the map, along with other cities where councils were held, or which assume significance in early Christian history for different reasons.

Important facts emerge from the picture which results. Little progress had been made in evangelising the non-Roman world. In the early fourth century Christianity was still more widespread in the eastern provinces than in those of the west (apart from Africa). And it was predominantly an urban religion: hence the new meaning which the word *paganus*, a villager, was to acquire. Bishoprics were urban; their territory generally corresponded to the civil territory of the city. A hundred years later virtually all the cities of the empire had gained bishoprics, but the process was far from complete at the date of this map.

Some forms of higher jurisdiction had already begun to develop by the fourth century: the bishop of a provincial capital was coming to outrank his fellow provincial bishops, and to be known as the metropolitan (or 'archbishop') of his province. Equally, the Council of Nicaea recognised that the bishops of Rome and Alexandria had statuses not confined to the current civil provinces where their cities lay.

The Dioceses and Provinces of the Roman Empire in AD 314

By the death of Septimius Severus in 211 there were about 46 provinces (reckoning Italy as one). Subdivision continued through the third century. Thus Crete seems to have been hived off from Cyrene before the middle of the century, while a province of Phrygia et Caria was carved out of Asia in the 250s; in Gaul the province of Novem Populi may date from the same period. With the loss of the trans-Danubian territories, Aurelian (270–5) gave their name of Dacia to a new province created out of parts of Moesia Inferior and Superior and Thrace. He also began the reorganisation of Italy, while in his reign or shortly afterwards Bithynia was divided from Pontus. Other divisions, too, may have been made before 284.

This process was significantly encouraged by Diocletian (284–305) as part of his wide-ranging reforms: civil administration could thus be tightened up. Following some further divisions a peak was reached around 314 with approximately 101 provinces—including the divisions of Italy, whose special status had been ended by Diocletian. A record of the provinces at that date survives in a somewhat corrupt form in a manuscript preserved at Verona. The map is based on this 'Verona List', with the minimum necessary corrections. It should be appreciated that precise provincial boundaries are often uncertain (particularly so in Britain), and that the identification of provincial capitals is not equally secure in every case.

To provide greater supervision over the increased number of governors, Diocletian had further grouped the provinces into 12 'dioceses'. In the 320s Constantine divided the diocese of Moesia into two, styled Thracia and Macedonia, the latter consisting of the provinces from Epirus Nova and Macedonia southward. But there is evidence that Constantine considered the process of provincial division to have gone too far. Before the end of 314 the two Numidian provinces (created in 305) had been reunited, and it seems that subsequently some of the separate provinces in Dacia, Macedonia and Thracia (perhaps also in Pannonia, Hispaniae, Britanniae and other dioceses) were

suppressed. However, most of the suppressed provinces were reinstated later in the century, not always with the same names.

Under Diocletian's arrangements, each province was governed by an equestrian *praeses*, although the proconsulships of Africa and Asia were still senatorial posts, and the governors of the Italian districts, Sicilia, and Achaia, called *correctores*, could also be senators.

Each diocese was ruled by an equestrian *vicarius* (deputy of the equestrian praetorian prefects), except that the Italian diocese from the Apennines southward, along with the islands, was effectively not controlled by the *vicarius* of Italia, but by a *vicarius* at Rome. In addition to its vicar, each diocese had one or more *rationales* and *magistri* responsible for those aspects of financial affairs outside the control of the praetorian prefects and their vicars.

Senators now played little part in administration. From the time of Gallienus (254–68) they were finally excluded from the command of legions, and were probably no longer appointed as governors of garrisoned provinces, where the armies were placed under *duces*. Perhaps because he found that provinces were now inconveniently small for governors to deploy their forces adequately, Diocletian arranged for the *duces* to control rather larger areas. In effect he thus began the total divorce of civil and military commands; however, the process remained incomplete at his abdication, with some provincial governors (though never senators) still retaining military command. Yet Constantine did complete the change. Under him, not merely provincial *praesides* and diocesan *vicarii*, but even the praetorian prefects, lost all direct military responsibilities. He also laid much stress on the development of the hitherto small 'field armies'—the *comitatenses*, as opposed to the *limitanei* or frontier forces—placing these under the control of *magistri equitum* and *peditum*. Consequently a map of the civil provinces can give no idea of the complications of contemporary military arrangements.

THE DIOCESES AND PROVINCES OF THE ROMAN EMPIRE IN A.D. 314

BRITANNIA II

Eburacum

12 | 11 Lindum

BRITANNIAE

Corinium

Londinium 10

GERMANIA II

Colonia Agrippinensis

BELGICA II

Rotomagus Remi Treveri GERMANIA I

LUGDUNENSIS Augusta
II **GALLIAE** BELGICA Mogontiacum Vindelicorum
NORICUM
AQUITANICA II RIPENSE

Bituriges 7 8 Ovilava
Octodurum 18
Lugdunum Vesontio RAETIA 17
Burdigala 9 Virunum Savaria
VIENNENSIS Vienna Octodurum Sopianae
1 4 VENETIA ET HISTRIA 19 Siscia 20
Elusa 6 Segusio Aquileia Sirmium 21
Nemausus 5 13 Mediolanum 14
3 Aquae 15 **PANNONIAE**
Sextiae Eburodunum TUSCIA ET DALMATIA
Tarraco UMBRIA Salona

GALLAECIA

Bracara
Augusta

TARRACONENSIS

CORSICA

LUSITANIA **HISPANIAE** Aleria CAMPANIA

Emerita CARTHAGINIENSIS **ITALIA** 16
Augusta LUCANIA

Corduba SARDINIA
BAETICA Carthago
Nova Carales SICILIA

Tingis NUMIDIA
CIRTENSIS Syracusae
MAURETANIA Caesarea AFRICA
TINGITANA Sitifis PROCONSULARIS
Cirta (Constantina) Carthago
MAURETANIA
CAESARIENSIS Lambaesis Hadrumetum
MAURETANIA NUMIDIA BYZACENA
SITIFENSIS MILITANA

AFRICA

Lepcis

TRIPOLITANA

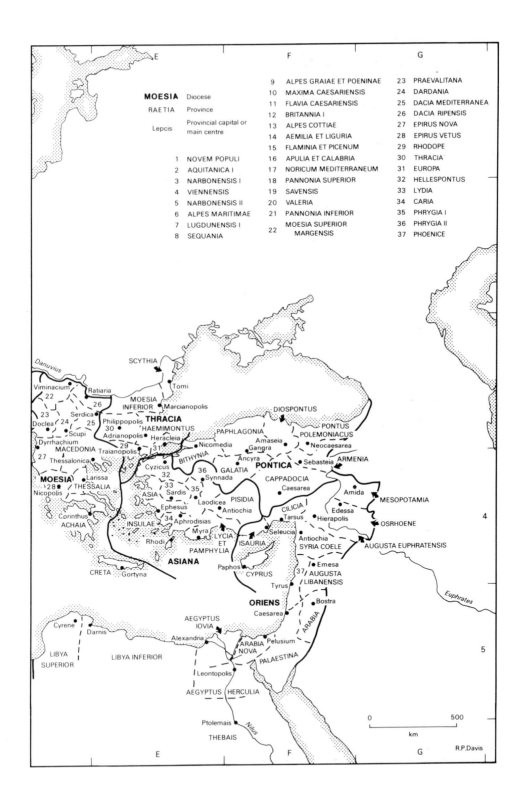

MOESIA   Diocese

RAETIA   Province

Lepcis   Provincial capital or main centre

9   ALPES GRAIAE ET POENINAE
10   MAXIMA CAESARIENSIS
11   FLAVIA CAESARIENSIS
12   BRITANNIA I
13   ALPES COTTIAE
14   AEMILIA ET LIGURIA
15   FLAMINIA ET PICENUM
16   APULIA ET CALABRIA
17   NORICUM MEDITERRANEUM
18   PANNONIA SUPERIOR
19   SAVENSIS
20   VALERIA
21   PANNONIA INFERIOR
22   MOESIA SUPERIOR MARGENSIS

1   NOVEM POPULI
2   AQUITANICA I
3   NARBONENSIS I
4   VIENNENSIS
5   NARBONENSIS II
6   ALPES MARITIMAE
7   LUGDUNENSIS I
8   SEQUANIA

23   PRAEVALITANA
24   DARDANIA
25   DACIA MEDITERRANEA
26   DACIA RIPENSIS
27   EPIRUS NOVA
28   EPIRUS VETUS
29   RHODOPE
30   THRACIA
31   EUROPA
32   HELLESPONTUS
33   LYDIA
34   CARIA
35   PHRYGIA I
36   PHRYGIA II
37   PHOENICE

R.P.Davis

REIGNS OF ROMAN EMPERORS IN BRIEF

Augustus		died AD 14
Tiberius		14–37
Gaius (Caligula)	Julio-Claudians	37–41
Claudius		41–54
Nero		54–68
Galba		68–9
Otho		69
Vitellius		69
Vespasian		69–79
Titus	Flavians	79–81
Domitian		81–96
Nerva		96–8
Trajan		98–117
Hadrian		117–38
Antoninus		138–61
Marcus Aurelius	Antonines	161–80
Lucius Verus		161–9
Commodus		177–92
Pertinax		193
Didius Julianus		193
Septimius Severus		193–211
Caracalla		198–217
Macrinus	Severans	217–18
Elagabalus		218–22
Severus Alexander		222–35
Maximinus		235–8
Gordian I and II		238
Balbinus and Pupienus		238
Gordian III		238–44
Philip		244–9
Decius		249–51
Gallus		251–3
Valerian		253–60
Gallienus		254–68
Claudius Gothicus		268–70

Aurelian	270–5
Tacitus	275–6
Probus	276–82
Carus, Carinus, Numerian	282–5
Diocletian	284–305
Maximian	286–305
Constantius	305–6
Galerius	305–11
Constantine	307–37

ABBREVIATIONS

AJA	*American Journal of Archaeology*
BAR	*British Archaeological Reports* (International Series)
BCH	*Bulletin de Correspondance Hellénique*
BSA	*British School at Athens*
CAH	*Cambridge Ancient History*, edns. 1 and 2
CIL	*Corpus Inscriptionum Latinarum*
CQ	*Classical Quarterly*
CRAI	*Comptes Rendus de l'Académie des Inscriptions et Belles-Lettres*
ILS	*Inscriptiones Latinae Selectae*
JHS	*Journal of Hellenic Studies*
JRS	*Journal of Roman Studies*
LCM	*Liverpool Classical Monthly*
MEFR	*Mélanges de l'Ecole Française de Rome*
OCD²	*Oxford Classical Dictionary*, ed. 2
PBSR	*Papers of the British School at Rome*
PW	A. Pauly, G. Wissowa, W. Kroll, *Real-Encyclopädie der classischen Altertumswissenschaft*

SUGGESTIONS FOR FURTHER READING

These modest suggestions are intended for the high school or student reader who wishes to know where to turn first for more information on a particular area or topic. Quite deliberately, therefore, most references are to modern publications in English; they are arranged in order of appearance.

In addition to material cited under the specific headings, the following general works are of notable value:

CAH
T. Frank (ed.), *An Economic Survey of Ancient Rome*, Baltimore, 1933–40.
M. Cary, *The Geographic Background of Greek and Roman History*, Oxford, 1949.
OCD²
R. Stillwell and others (eds), *The Princeton Encyclopedia of Classical Sites*, Princeton, 1976.

For very full detail, *PW* and E. de Ruggiero and others (eds), *Dizionario Epigrafico di Antichità Romane*, Rome, 1895-(in progress), may be consulted.

The Aegean in the Bronze Age
Minoan Crete
Mycenaean Greece

J.D.S. Pendlebury, *The Archaeology of Crete*, London, 1939.
C. Renfrew, *The Emergence of Civilization: The Cyclades and the Aegean in the Third Millenium B.C.*, London, 1972.
P. M. Warren, *The Aegean Civilizations*, London, 1975.
R. Hope Simpson, *Mycenaean Greece*, New Jersey, 1981.
V. Karageorghis, *Cyprus from the Stone Age to the Romans*, London, 1982.

Troy

H. H. Schliemann, *Ilios: The City and Country of the Trojans*, London, 1880.
W. Döpfeld, *Troja und Ilion: Ergebnisse der Ausgrabungen in den vorhistorischen und historischen Schichten von Ilion, 1870–1894*, Athens, 1902.
C.W. Blegen *et al.*, *Troy: Excavations Conducted by the University of Cincinnati, 1932–1938*, Princeton, 1950–8, together with *Supplementary Monographs* I-III.
C. W. Blegen, *Troy and the Trojans*, London, 1963.

Knossos

A. J. Evans, *The Palace of Minos*, London, 1921–35.
S. Hood, *The Minoans: Crete in the Bronze Age*, London, 1971.
S. Hood and W. Taylor, *The Bronze Age Palace at Knossos: Plan and Sections*, BSA Suppl. vol. 13, London, 1981.
S. Hood and D. Smyth, *Archaeological Survey of the Knossos Area*, BSA Suppl. vol. 14, London, 1981.

Mycenae

A. J. B. Wace, *Mycenae, An Archaeological History and Guide*, Princeton, 1949.
W. D. Taylour, *The Mycenaeans*, London, 1964.
G. E. Mylonas, *Mycenae and the Mycenaean Age*, Princeton, 1966.
S. E. Iakovidis, *Mycenae-Epidaurus*, Athens, 1981.

Mainland Greece in the Homeric Poems
The Homeric World

W. Leaf, *Troy: A Study in Homeric Geography*, London, 1912.
A. J. B. Wace and F. H. Stubbings, *A Companion to Homer*, London, 1962, chapters 8, 9, 13.
R. Hope Simpson and J. F. Lazenby, *The Catalogue of the Ships in Homer's Iliad*, Oxford, 1970.

Dark Age Greece
Late Geometric Greece

A. M. Snodgrass, *The Dark Age of Greece*, Edinburgh, 1971.

V. R. d'A. Desborough, *The Greek Dark Ages*, London, 1972.

J. N. Coldstream, *Geometric Greece*, London, 1977.

Greek Colonisation (Eighth to Sixth Centuries BC)

J. Boardman, *The Greeks Overseas: Their Early Colonies and Trade*, edn. 2, London, 1980.

CAH² III.3. chapters 37–39a.

Archaic Greece

L. H. Jeffery, *Archaic Greece: The City-States c. 700– 500 B.C.*, London and Tonbridge, 1976.

CAH² III.3.

The Persian Empire *c.* 550–330 BC

A. T. Olmstead, *History of the Persian Empire*, Chicago, 1948.

J. M. Cook, *The Persian Empire*, London, 1983.

Persepolis

R. N. Frye, *The Heritage of Persia*, London, 1962.

S. A. Matheson, *Persia: An Archaeological Guide*, London, 1972, esp. pp. 223–33.

Marathon, 490 BC

W. K. Pritchett, 'Marathon', *University of California Publications in Classical Archaeology*, 4, 1960, pp. 137–90.

——, *Studies in Ancient Greek Topography I*, Berkeley, 1965, chapter 6; *II*, 1969, chapter 1.

C. Hignett, *Xerxes' Invasion of Greece*, Oxford, 1963, pp. 55–74.

E. Vanderpool, 'The deme of Marathon and the Herakleion', *AJA*, 70, 1966, pp. 319–23.

——, 'A monument of the battle of Marathon', *Hesperia*, 35, 1966, pp. 93–106.

A. R. Burn, *Persia and the Greeks*, edn. 2, London, 1970, chapter 12.

N. G. L. Hammond, *Studies in Greek History*, Oxford, 1973, chapter 7.

V. Massaro, 'Herodotus' account of the battle of Marathon and the picture in the Stoa Poecile',

Ant. Class., 47, 1978, pp. 458–75.

G. S. Shrimpton, 'The Persian cavalry at Marathon', *Phoenix*, 34, 1980, pp. 20–37.

J. A. G. van der Veer, 'The battle of Marathon: a topographical survey', *Mnemosyne*, 35, 1982, pp. 290–321.

Thermopylae: Ephialtes' Route

G. B. Grundy, *The Great Persian War and its Preliminaries*, London, 1901, chapter 7.

J. A. R. Munro, 'Some observations on the Persian wars, 2', *JHS*, 22, 1902, pp. 294–332.

A. R. Burn, 'Thermopylai and Callidromus', in *Studies Presented to David Moore Robinson I*, St Louis, 1951, pp. 480–9.

——, 'Thermopylai revisited and some topographical notes on Marathon and Plataiai', in *Greece and the Eastern Mediterranean in Ancient History and Prehistory (Festschrift Schachermeyr)*, Berlin, 1977, pp. 89–105.

W. K. Pritchett, 'New light on Thermopylai', *AJA*, 62, 1958, pp. 203–13.

C. Hignett, *Xerxes' Invasion of Greece*, chapter 2 and Appendices 2–4.

Artemisium, 480 BC

C. Hignett, *Xerxes' Invasion of Greece*, chapter 3.

W. K. Pritchett, 'Xerxes' fleet at the "Ovens" ', *AJA*, 67, 1963, pp. 1–6.

——, *Studies in Ancient Greek Topography II*, chapter 2.

Salamis, 480 BC

W. K. Pritchett, 'Towards a restudy of the battle of Salamis', *AJA*, 63, 1959, pp. 251–62.

——, *Studies in Ancient Greek Topography I*, chapter 7.

A. R. Burn, *Persia and the Greeks*, pp. 436 ff.

N. G. L. Hammond, *Studies in Greek History*, chapter 8.

G. Roux, 'Eschyle, Hérodote, Diodore, Plutarque racontent la bataille de Salamine', *BCH*, 98, 1974, pp. 51–94.

J. Delorme, 'Deux notes sur la bataille de Salamine', *BCH*, 102, 1978, pp. 87–96.

Plataea, 479 BC

W. K. Pritchett, 'New Light on Plataia', *AJA*, 61, 1957, pp. 9–28.
——, *Studies in Ancient Greek Topography I*, chapter 8.
C. Hignett, *Xerxes' Invasion of Greece*, chapter 7 and Appendices 10–12.
A. R. Burn, *Persia and the Greeks*, pp. 503 ff.

Delphi

F. Poulsen, *Delphi*, London, 1920.
H. W. Parke and D. E. W. Wormell, *The Delphic Oracle*, edn. 2, Oxford, 1956.
CAH² III.3, chapter 41, section V.

Sparta

Annual of the British School at Athens, 12–16 and 26–30, 1906–10 and 1924–30.
W. G. Forrest, *A History of Sparta 950-192 B.C.,*, edn. 2, London, 1980.
P. Cartledge, *Sparta and Lakonia: A Regional History, 1300–362 B.C.*, London, 1979.

Attica

C. W. J. Eliot, *Coastal Demes of Attica*, Phoenix Suppl. vol. V, 1962.
J. S. Traill, *The Political Organization of Attica*, Hesperia Suppl. XIV, 1975.

Classical Athens
Roman Athens

R. J. Hopper, *The Acropolis*, London, 1971.
J. Travlos, *Pictorial Dictionary of Ancient Athens*, London, 1971.
H. A. Thompson and R. E. Wycherley, *The Athenian Agora, XIV. The Agora of Athens*, Princeton, 1972.
The Athenian Agora: A Guide to the Excavation and Museum, edn. 3, Athens, 1976.
R. E. Wycherley, *The Stones of Athens*, Princeton, 1978.

Halicarnassus

G. E. Bean and J. M. Cook, 'The Halicarnassus peninsula', *BSA*, 50, 1955, pp. 85–171.
G. E. Bean, *Turkey Beyond the Maeander: An Archaeological Guide*, London, 1971, chapter 9.
S. Hornblower, *Mausolus*, Oxford, 1982.

Miletus

G. E. Bean, *Aegean Turkey: An Archaeological Guide*, London, 1966, chapter 10.
G. Kleiner, *Alt-Milet*, Wiesbaden, 1966.
——, *Die Ruinen von Milet*, Berlin, 1968.

Priene

T. Wiegand and H. Schrader, *Priene*, Berlin, 1904.
M. Schede, *Die Ruinen von Priene*, edn. 2, by G. Kleiner and W. Kleiss, Berlin, 1964.

Greek Sicily

M. I. Finley, *Ancient Sicily to the Arab Conquest*, edn. 2, London, 1979.
E. Gabba and G. Vallet (eds), *La Sicilia Antica I–II, I*, Naples, 1980.
E. Manni, *Geografia Fisica e Politica della Sicilia Antica*, Kokalos Suppl. 4, 1981.

Syracuse

A. W. Gomme, A. Andrewes and K. J. Dover, *A Historical Commentary on Thucydides* vol. 4 (Books V.25–VII), Oxford, 1970.
P. Green, *Armada from Athens*, London, 1970.
H.-P. Drögemüller, *PW* Suppl. 13, s.v. Syrakusai, cols. 815–36.

Akragas

P. Griffo, *Nuovissima Guida per il Visitatore dei Monumenti di Agrigento*, Agrigento, 1961.
J. A. de Waele, *Acragas Graeca I*, 's-Gravenhage, 1971.

Cyrene

R. G. Goodchild, *Kyrene und Apollonia*, Zurich, 1971.
S. Applebaum, *Jews and Greeks in Ancient Cyrene*, Leiden, 1979.

Olympia

E. Curtius and F. Adler, *Olympia: die Ergebnisse der Ausgrabung*, Berlin, 1896–7.
Berichte über die Ausgrabungen in Olympia, Berlin, 1937– (in progress).
A. Mallwitz, *Olympia und seine Bauten*, Munich, 1972.

Greek Dialects *c.* 450 BC

C. D. Buck, *The Greek Dialects*, edn. 2, Chicago, 1973.
J. Chadwick, *The Decipherment of Linear B*, edn. 2, Cambridge, 1967.
R. J. Buck, 'The Aeolic dialect in Boeotia', *Class. Phil.*, 63, 1968, pp. 268–80.
CAH² II.2, chapter XXXIX (a).

The Athenian Empire

R. Meiggs, *The Athenian Empire*, Oxford, 1972.

Pylos/Sphacteria

W. K. Pritchett, *Studies in Ancient Greek Topography I*, chapter 1.
R. A. Bauslaugh, 'The text of Thucydides IV 8.6 and the south channel at Pylos', *JHS*, 99, 1979, pp. 1–6.
J. B. Wilson, *Pylos 425 B.C.*, Warminster, 1979, with review by C. J. Tuplin, *LCM*, 6, 1981, pp. 29–34.

The Bosporan Realm and its Neighbours

CAH VIII, chapter 18.
D. E. W. Wormell, 'Studies in Greek tyranny II. Leucon of Bosporus', *Hermathena*, 68, 1946, pp. 49–71.

C. M. Danoff, *PW* Suppl. 9, cols. 866–1175, s.v. Pontos Euxeinos.
H. Berve, *Die Tyrannis bei den Griechen*, Munich, 1967, part 3 chapter 3.3.

Trade in the Classical Greek World

M. M. Austin and P. Vidal-Naquet, *Economic and Social History of Ancient Greece: An Introduction*, London, 1977.
J. F. Healy, *Mining and Metallurgy in the Greek and Roman World*, London, 1978.
R. J. Hopper, *Trade and Industry in Classical Greece*, London, 1979.
A. W. Johnston, *Trademarks on Greek Vases*, Warminster, 1979, chapter 11.
P. Garnsey *et al.*, (eds), *Trade in the Ancient Economy*, London, 1983.

The Ancient Explorers

J Needham, *Science and Civilization in China*, vol. 1, Cambridge, 1954, chapter 7 sections (*e*)–(*g*).
R. E. M. Wheeler, *Rome Beyond the Imperial Frontiers*, Harmondsworth, 1955.
M. Cary and E. H. Warmington, *The Ancient Explorers*, edn. 2, Harmondsworth, 1963.
C. F. C. Hawkes, *Pytheas: Europe and the Greek Explorers*, Oxford, 1975.

Archaeological Sites of Greece

Archaeological Reports (for work in progress)
M. I. Finley, *Atlas of Classical Archaeology*, London, 1977.
P. MacKendrick, *The Greek Stones Speak*, edn. 2, London, 1981.
S. Rossiter, *Benn's Blue Guide to Greece*, edn. 4, London, 1981.

The Anabasis

C. F. Lehmann-Haupt, 'Zum Ruckzug der Zehntausend', in J. Kromayer (ed.), *Antike Schlachtfelder* IV, Berlin, 1931, pp. 243–60.
R. D. Barnett, 'Xenophon and the wall of Media', *JHS*, 83, 1963, pp. 1–26.

Leuctra, 371 BC

W. K. Pritchett, *Studies in Ancient Greek Topography I*, chapter 3.
J. K. Anderson, *Military Theory and Practice in the Age of Xenophon*, Berkeley, 1970, chapter 10.
G. L. Cawkwell, 'Epaminondas and Thebes', *CQ*, 22, 1972, pp. 254–78.
J. Buckler, 'Plutarch on Leuctra', *Symb. Osl.*, 55, 1980, pp. 75–94.

The Second Athenian League

F. H. Marshall, *The Second Athenian Confederacy*, Cambridge, 1905.
J. L. Cargill, *The Second Athenian League: Empire or Free Alliance?*, Berkeley, 1981.

Chaeronea, 338 BC

W. K. Pritchett, 'Observations on Chaironeia', *AJA*, 62, 1958, pp. 307–11.
N. G. L. Hammond, *Studies in Greek History*, chapter 16.
——, and G. T. Griffith, *A History of Macedonia II*, Oxford, 1979, pp. 596–603.
P. A. Rahe, 'The annihilation of the Sacred Band at Chaeronea', *AJA*, 85, 1981, pp. 84–7.

The Growth of Macedonian Power, 359–36 BC

J. R. Ellis, *Philip II and Macedonian Imperialism*, London, 1976.
N. G. L. Hammond and G. T. Griffith, *A History of Macedonia II*, part 2.

River Granicus, 334 BC

E. Badian, 'The battle of the Granicus: a new look', in *Archaia Makedonia II*, Thessaloniki, 1977, pp. 271–93.
C. Foss, ibid., pp. 495–502.
N. G. L. Hammond, 'The battle of the Granicus river', *JHS*, 100, 1980, pp. 73–88.
A. B. Bosworth, *A Historical Commentary on Arrian's History of Alexander I*, Oxford, 1980, pp. 114 ff.

Issus, 333 BC

A. B. Bosworth, *A Historical Commentary on Arrian's History of Alexander I*, pp. 198 ff.
A. Devine, 'The location of the battlefield of Issus', *LCM*, 5, 1980, pp. 3–10.
N. G. L. Hammond, *Alexander the Great: King, Commander and Statesman*, London, 1981, chapter V(B).

Gaugamela, 331 BC

G. T. Griffith, 'Alexander's generalship at Gaugamela', *JHS*, 67, 1947, pp. 77–89.
A. R. Burn, 'Notes on Alexander's campaigns, 332–330', *JHS*, 72, 1952, pp. 81–91.
E. W. Marsden, *The Campaign of Gaugamela*, Liverpool, 1964.
P. A. Brunt, *Arrian I*, Loeb series, 1976, Appendix 9.
A. B. Bosworth, *A Historical Commentary on Arrian's History of Alexander I*, pp. 297 ff.
N. G. L. Hammond, *Alexander the Great: King, Commander and Statesman*, chapter VI(C).

River Hydaspes, 326 BC

B. Breloer, *Alexanders Kampf gegen Poros*, Stuttgart, 1933.
A. Stein, *Archaeological Reconnaissances in North-Western India and South-Eastern Iran*, London, 1937, chapter 1.
J. R. Hamilton, 'The cavalry battle at the Hydaspes', *JHS*, 76, 1956, pp. 26–31.
J. F. C. Fuller, *The Generalship of Alexander the Great*, London, 1958, pp. 180–99.
R. L. Fox, *Alexander the Great*, London, 1973, chapter 25.
N. G. L. Hammond, *Alexander the Great: King, Commander and Statesman*, pp. 204–12.

Ai Khanum

Reports in *CRAI* 1965 onwards.
P. Bernard, 'Ai Khanum on the Oxus: a Hellenistic city in central Asia', *Proc. Brit. Acad.*, 53, 1967, pp. 71–95.

——, 'An ancient Greek city in central Asia', *Scientific American*, 246, 1982, pp. 126–35.

The Hellenistic Kingdoms

W. W. Tarn and G. T. Griffith, *Hellenistic Civilization*, edn. 3, London, 1952.

M. M. Austin, *The Hellenistic World from Alexander to the Roman Conquest*, Cambridge, 1981.

F. W. Walbank, *The Hellenistic World*, London, 1981.

Pergamum

E. V. Hansen, *The Attalids of Pergamon*, edn. 2, Cornell, 1971.

Delos

P. Bruneau and J. Ducat, *Guide de Délos*, Paris, 1965.

Major Cult Centres of the Classical World

W. K. C. Guthrie, *The Greeks and their Gods*, London, 1950.

R. F. Willetts, *Cretan Cults and Festivals*, London, 1962.

H. W. Parke, *Greek Oracles*, London, 1967.

——, *Festivals of the Athenians*, London, 1977.

R. M. Ogilvie, *The Romans and their Gods in the Age of Augustus*, London, 1969.

G. Dumézil, *Archaic Roman Religion*, Chicago, 1970.

J. Ferguson, *The Religions of the Roman Empire*, London, 1970.

M. Grant, *Roman Myths*, London, 1971.

R. MacMullen, *Paganism in the Roman Empire*, Yale, 1981.

Alexandria

P. M. Fraser, *Ptolemaic Alexandria*, Oxford, 1972.

Etruria and Etruscan Expansion in Northern Italy

M. Pallottino, *The Etruscans*, London, 1974.

M. Cristofani, *The Etruscans: A New Investigation*, London, 1979.

Early Italy

J. Reich, *Italy Before Rome*, Oxford, 1979.

A. C. Brown, *Ancient Italy Before the Romans*, Oxford, 1980.

Early Latium
The Environs of Imperial Rome

T. Ashby, *The Roman Campagna in Classical Times*, London, 1927.

L. Quilici, *Roma Primitiva e le Origini della Civiltà Laziale*, Rome, 1977.

The Languages of Italy Prior to the Spread of Latin

L. R. Palmer, *The Latin Language*, London, 1954.

E. Pulgram, *Italic, Latin, Italian 600 B.C. to A.D. 1260: Texts and Commentaries*, Heidelberg, 1978.

Veii

J. B. Ward-Perkins, *Veii: The History and Topography of the Ancient City*, PBSR, 29, 1961.

A. Kahane, L. Murray Threipland and J. B. Ward-Perkins, *The Ager Veientanus, North and East of Rome*, PBSR, 36, 1968.

Cosa

E. T. Salmon, *Roman Colonization Under the Republic*, London, 1969, esp. Appendix to chapter 1.

F. E. Brown, *Cosa: The Making of a Roman Town*, Ann Arbor, 1980.

Luna

A. Frova, *Scavi di Luni I and II*, Rome, 1973 and 1977.

B. Ward-Perkins, 'Luni: the decline and abandonment of the Roman town', in H.McK. Blake *et al.* (eds),*Papers in Italian Archaeology I, BAR*, 41, 1978, pp. 313–21.

Republican Rome
The Centre of Rome in the Age of Caracalla
Rome in the Age of the Severi

S. B. Platner and T. Ashby, *A Topographical Dictionary of Ancient Rome*, Oxford, 1929.
D. R. Dudley, *Urbs Roma*, London, 1967.
E. Nash, *Pictorial Dictionary of Ancient Rome*, edn. 2, London, 1968.
F. Coarelli, *Roma*, Bari, 1980.

Roman Expansion in Italy to 268 BC

E. T. Salmon, *Samnium and the Samnites*, Cambridge, 1967.
——, *The Making of Roman Italy*, London, 1982.

Roman Colonisation

E. T. Salmon, *Roman Colonization Under the Republic*.
A. N. Sherwin-White, *The Roman Citizenship*, edn. 2, Oxford, 1973.

The Punic Wars

J. F. Lazenby, *Hannibal's War*, Warminster, 1978.
B. Caven, *The Punic Wars*, London, 1980.

Cannae, 216 BC

J. F. Lazenby, *Hannibal's War*, pp. 77–85.

Zama, 202 BC

H. H. Scullard, *Scipio Africanus: Soldier and Politician*, London, 1970, chapter 6.

Carthage

B. H. Warmington, *Carthage*, edn. 2, London, 1969.
H. Hurst and L. E. Stager, 'A metropolitan landscape: the late Punic port of Carthage', *World Archaeology*, 9, 1977/8, pp. 334–46.

Cynoscephalae, 197 BC

F. W. Walbank, *A Historical Commentary on Polybius II*, Oxford, 1967, pp. 576–84.
W. K. Pritchett, *Studies in Ancient Greek Topography II*, chapter 11.

Thermopylae, 191 BC

W. K. Pritchett, *Studies in Ancient Greek Topography I*, chapter 5.

The Roman Empire in 60 BC

D. Braund, *Rome and the Friendly King: The Character of the Client Kingship*, London, 1984.

Roman Campaigns of 49–30 BC

J. F. C. Fuller, *Julius Caesar, Man, Soldier and Tyrant*, London, 1965.
J. M. Carter, *The Battle of Actium: The Rise and Triumph of Augustus Caesar*, London, 1970.

Pharsalus, 48 BC

Y. Béquignon, *PW* Suppl. 12, cols. 1071–84, s.v. Pharsalos.
C. B. R. Pelling, 'Pharsalus', *Historia*, 22, 1973, pp. 249–59.
Y. Béquignon, 'Etudes Thessaliennes XII', *BCH*, 98, 1974, pp. 119–23.
P. Greenhalgh, *Pompey: The Republican Prince*, London, 1981, pp. 243–55.

Augusta Praetoria

I. A. Richmond, 'Aosta', in P. Salway (ed.), *Roman Archaeology and Art*, London, 1969, pp. 249–59.
F. Castagnoli, *Orthogonal Town Planning in Antiquity*, Cambridge, Mass., 1971, pp. 112–13.
J. B. Ward-Perkins, *Cities of Ancient Greece and Italy: Planning in Classical Antiquity*, New York, 1974, esp. figs. 52–3.

Archaeological Sites of Italy

J. B. Ward-Perkins, *Cities of Ancient Greece and Italy: Planning in Classical Antiquity*.

F. Coarelli *et al.* (eds), *Etruscan Cities*, London, 1975.

H. McK. Blake *et al.* (eds), *Papers in Italian Archaeology I, BAR*, 41, 1978.

D. and F. Ridgway (eds), *Italy Before the Romans: the Iron Age, Orientalizing and Etruscan Periods*, London, 1979.

T. W. Potter, *The Changing Landscape of South Etruria*, London, 1979.

M. Aylwin Cotton, *The Late Republican Villa at Posto, Francolise*, London, 1979.

K. Painter (ed.), *Roman Villas in Italy: Recent Excavations and Research*, British Museum, London, 1980.

G. Barker and R. Hodges (eds), *Archaeology and Italian Society: Prehistoric, Roman and Medieval Studies, BAR*, 102, 1981.

Ostia

A. Boëthius and J. B. Ward-Perkins, *Etruscan and Roman Architecture*, Harmondsworth, 1970, pp. 279–89.

R. Meiggs, *Roman Ostia*, edn. 2, Oxford, 1973.

F. B. Sear, *Roman Architecture*, London, 1982, pp. 118–33.

Second Battle of Cremona, AD 69

K. Wellesley, *Cornelius Tacitus, The Histories, Book III*, Sydney, 1972, pp. 85–126.

——, *The Long Year A.D. 69*, London, 1975, pp. 141–50.

Campania

K. J. Beloch, *Campanien. Geschichte und Topographie des antiken Neapel und seiner Umgebung*, Breslau, 1890.

J. Heurgon, *Recherches sur l'Histoire, la Religion et la Civilization de Capoue Preromaine, des Origines à la Deuxième Guerre Punique*, Paris, 1942.

J. H. d'Arms, *Romans on the Bay of Naples*, Harvard, 1970.

M. W. Frederiksen, *Campania*, British School at Rome, London, 1984.

Pompeii
Herculaneum

A. Maiuri, *Ercolano: I Nuovi Scavi 1927–1958*, Rome, 1958.

H. Eschebach, *Die städtebauliche Entwicklung des antiken Pompeji, Römische Mitteilungen* Suppl. 17, 1970.

M. Grant, *Cities of Vesuvius: Pompeii and Herculaneum*, London, 1971.

J. B. Ward-Perkins and A. Claridge, *Pompeii A.D. 79*, London, 1976.

A. and M. De Vos, *Pompei, Ercolano, Stabia*, Bari, 1982.

Italian Towns with Alimentary Schemes

R. Duncan-Jones, *The Economy of the Roman Empire: Quantitative Studies*, edn. 2, Cambridge, 1982, chapter 7 and Appendix 5.

Trade in the Roman World

J. B. Ward-Perkins, 'Quarrying in antiquity: technology, tradition and social change', *Proc. Brit. Acad.*, 57, 1971, pp. 137–58.

J. F. Healy, *Mining and Metallurgy in the Greek and Roman World*.

J. du Plat Taylor and H. Cleere (eds), *Roman Shipping and Trade: Britain and the Rhine Provinces*, London, 1978.

G. Rickman, *The Corn Supply of Ancient Rome*, Oxford, 1980.

K. Muckelroy (ed.), *Archaeology Under Water: An Atlas of the World's Submerged Sites*, New York, 1980, chapter 2.

J. H. d'Arms, *Commerce and Social Standing in Ancient Rome*, Harvard, 1981.

P. Garnsey and C. R. Whittaker (eds), *Trade and Famine in Classical Antiquity*, Cambridge, 1983.

P. Garnsey *et al.* (eds), *Trade in the Ancient Economy*, chapters 7–13.

The Roman Empire in AD 60 and 211

F. Millar *et al.*, *The Roman Empire and Its Neighbours*, edn. 2, London, 1981.
Note the summary account of legions and their bases in *OCD²* pp. 591–3 s.v. Legion.

Roman Britain

Ordnance Survey, *Map of Roman Britain*, edn. 4, Chessington, 1978.
S. S. Frere, *Britannia: A History of Roman Britain*, edn. 2, London, 1978.
A. L. F. Rivet and C. Smith, *The Place-Names of Roman Britain*, London, 1979.
R. J. A. Wilson, *A Guide to the Roman Remains in Britain*, edn. 2, London, 1980.
P. Salway, *Roman Britain*, Oxford, 1981.
M. Todd, *Roman Britain 55 B.C. – A.D. 400*, London, 1981.

Hadrian's Wall
Antonine Wall

Ordnance Survey, *Map of Hadrian's Wall*, edn. 2, Chessington, 1972.
Ordnance Survey, *Map of the Antonine Wall*, edn. 2, Chessington, 1975.
D. J. Breeze and B. Dobson, *Hadrian's Wall*, edn. 2, Harmondsworth, 1978.
W. S. Hanson and G.S. Maxwell, *Rome's North West Frontier: The Antonine Wall*, Edinburgh, 1983.

Silchester

G. C. Boon, *Silchester: The Roman Town of Calleva*, Newton Abbot, 1974.
M. Fulford, *Guide to the Silchester Excavations 1979–81*, Reading, 1982.

Lutetia Parisiorum

P.-M. Duval, *Paris Antique, des Origines au Troisième Siècle*, Paris, 1961.
P.-A. Février *et al.*, *Histoire de la France Urbaine, I: La Ville Antique*, Paris, 1980.

Roman Gaul and the Alpine Region

O. Brogan, *Roman Gaul*, London, 1953.
E. M. Wightman, *Roman Trier and the Treveri*, London, 1970.
C. E. Stevens, 'Roman Gaul', in J. M. Wallace-Hadrill and J. McManners (eds), *France: Government and Society: A Historical Survey*, edn. 2, London, 1970, pp. 19–35.
P. MacKendrick, *Roman France*, London, 1971.
D. van Berchem, *Les Routes et l'Histoire: Etudes sur les Helvètes et leurs Voisins dans l'Empire Romain*, Geneva, 1982, chapter 14.
J. F. Drinkwater, *Roman Gaul: The Three Provinces 58 B.C.-A.D. 260*, London, 1983.
L. Pauli, *The Alps: Archaeology and Early History*, London, 1984.

Germanies-Raetia-Noricum

C. B. Rüger, *Germania Inferior*, Cologne and Graz, 1968.
J. J. Hatt, *Celts and Gallo-Romans*, London, 1970.
H.-J. Kellner, *Die Römer in Bayern*, Munich, 1971.
G. Alföldy, *Noricum*, London 1974.
A. Mócsy, *Pannonia and Upper Moesia*, London, 1974.

The Rhine-Danube Limes from *c.* AD 40 to AD 259–60

W. Schleiermacher, *Der römische Limes in Deutschland*, Berlin, 1961 and later editions.
H. Schönberger, 'The Roman frontier in Germany: an archaeological survey', *JRS*, 59, 1969, pp. 144–97.

The Danubian Provinces/Balkan Area *c.* AD 200

J. J. Wilkes, *Dalmatia*, London, 1969.
A. H. M. Jones, *The Cities of the Eastern Roman Provinces*, edn. 2, Oxford, 1971, chapter 1.
E. Condurachi and C. Daicoviciu, *The Ancient Civilization of Romania*, London, 1971.
A. Mócsy, *Pannonia and Upper Moesia*.
P. MacKendrick, *The Dacian Stones Speak*, Chapel Hill, 1975.

R. F. Hoddinott, *Bulgaria in Antiquity: An Archaeological Introduction*, London, 1975.

A. G. Poulter (ed.), *Ancient Bulgaria: Papers Presented to the International Symposium on the Ancient History and Archaeology of Bulgaria*, Nottingham, 1983.

Iberian Peninsula

C. H. V. Sutherland, *The Romans in Spain 217 B.C.–A.D. 117*, London, 1939.

F. J. Wiseman, *Roman Spain*, London, 1956.

A. Tovar and J. M. Blázquez, *Historia de la Hispania Romana*, Madrid, 1975.

J. M. Blázquez, *Economia de la Hispania Romana*, Bilbao, 1978.

J. Arce, *El Último Siglo de la España Romana: 284–409*, Madrid, 1982.

Corsica and Sardinia

E. Pais, *Storia della Sardegna e della Corsica Durante il Dominio Romano*, Rome, 1923.

M. C. Ascari, *La Corsica nell'Antichità*, Rome, 1942.

J. and L. Jehasse, 'La Corse romaine', in P. Arrighi (ed.), *Histoire de la Corse*, Toulouse, 1971, pp. 97–128.

P. Meloni, *La Sardegna Romana*, Sassari, 1975.

R. J. Rowland, Jr., *I Ritrovamenti Romani in Sardegna*, Rome, 1981.

Roman Sicily

M. I. Finley, *Ancient Sicily*, chapters 10–13.

E. Gabba and G. Vallet (eds), *La Sicilia Antica, II.2*.

E. Manni, *Geografia Fisica e Politica della Sicilia Antica*.

North African Provinces
Africa Proconsularis

T. R. S. Broughton, *The Romanization of Africa Proconsularis*, Baltimore, 1929.

B. H. Warmington, *The North African Provinces from Diocletian to the Vandal Conquest*, Cambridge, 1954.

P. D. A. Garnsey, 'Rome's African empire under the Principate', in P. D. A. Garnsey and C. R. Whittaker (eds), *Imperialism in the Ancient World*, Cambridge, 1978, pp. 223–54.

P. MacKendrick, *The North African Stones Speak*, London, 1980.

C. M. Wells (ed.), *L'Afrique Romaine: Les Conférences Vanier 1980*, Ottawa, 1982.

Imperial Estates in the R. Bagradas Valley

J. Carcopino, 'L'inscription d'Aïn-el-Djemala: contribution à l'histoire des *saltus* Africains et du colonat partiaire, IV. La région des "saltus" ', *MEFR*, 26, 1906, pp. 365–481 at pp. 423–40.

J. Kolendo, *Le Colonat en Afrique sous le Haut-Empire*, Besançon, 1976.

D. J. Crawford, 'Imperial estates', in M. I. Finley (ed.), *Studies in Roman Property*, Cambridge, 1976, pp. 35–70.

Timgad

C. Courtois, *Timgad; Antique Thamvgadi*, Algiers, 1951.

J. Lassus, *Visite à Timgad*, Paris, 1969.

Lepcis Magna

M. F. Squarciapino, *Lepcis Magna*, Basel, 1964.

R. Bianchi Bandinelli *et al.*, *The Buried City: Excavations at Leptis Magna*, London, 1966.

African Limes

M. Bénabou, *La Résistance Africaine à la Romanisation*, Paris, 1976.

E. W. B. Fentress, *Numidia and the Roman Army: Social, Military and Economic Aspects of the Frontier Zone, BAR*, 53, 1979.

Greek and Roman Crete

CAH² III.3, chapter 39b and c.

I. F. Sanders, *Roman Crete: An Archaeological Survey and Gazetteer of Late Hellenistic, Roman and Early Byzantine Crete*, Warminster, 1982.

Roman Cyprus

G. F. Hill, *A History of Cyprus I*, Cambridge, 1940, chapter 11.
V. Karageorghis, *Cyprus from the Stone Age to the Romans*, chapter 10.

Bithynia and Asia *c.* AD 100
Roman Asia Minor

A. H. M. Jones, *The Greek City from Alexander to Justinian*, Oxford, 1940.
D. Magie, *Roman Rule in Asia Minor*, Princeton, 1951.
J. Deininger, *Die Provinziallandtage der römischen Kaiserzeit, Vestigia*, 6, Munich, 1965.
D. Nörr, *Imperium und Polis in der hohen Prinzipatszeit*, edn. 2, Munich, 1969.
A. H. M. Jones, *The Cities of the Eastern Roman Provinces*, chapters 2–8.
C. Habicht, 'New evidence on the province of Asia', *JRS*, 65, 1975, pp. 64–91.
G. P. Burton, 'Proconsuls, assizes and the administration of justice under the empire', *JRS*, 65, 1975, pp. 92–106.
M. Stahl, *Imperiale Herrschaft und provinziale Stadt, Hypomnemata*, 52, Göttingen, 1978.
R. J. A. Talbert, 'Pliny the Younger as governor of Bithynia-Pontus', in C. Deroux (ed.), *Studies in Latin Literature and Roman History II, Collection Latomus*, 168, Brussels, 1980, pp. 412–35.
J. Reynolds, *Aphrodisias and Rome*, London, 1982.

Roman Syria, Western Parthia and Armenia

A. H. M. Jones, *The Cities of the Eastern Roman Provinces*, chapters 9 and 10.
D. Oates, *Studies in the Ancient History of Northern Iraq*, Oxford, 1968, chapters 1 and 4.
J. I. Miller, *The Spice Trade of the Roman Empire 29 B.C. to A.D. 641*, Oxford, 1969.
G. W. Bowersock, *Roman Arabia*, Harvard, 1983.

Masada

Y. Yadin, *Bar-Kokhba: The Rediscovery of the Legendary Hero of the Last Jewish Revolt Against Imperial Rome*, London, 1971.

G. Vermes, *The Dead Sea Scrolls in English*, edn. 2, London, 1975.
Y. Yadin, *Bar-Kokhba: The Rediscovery of the Legendary Hero of the Last Jewish Revolt Against Imperial Rome*, London, 1971.

Jerusalem

K. M. Kenyon, *Jerusalem: Excavating 3000 Years of History*, London, 1967.
Y. Yadin (ed.), *Jerusalem Revealed: Archaeology in the Holy City, 1968–1974*, Jerusalem, 1975.

Palestine

M. Grant, *The Jews in the Roman World*, London, 1973.
E. M. Smallwood, *The Jews Under Roman Rule from Pompey to Diocletian: A Study in Political Relations*, edn. 2, Leiden, 1981.

Roman Egypt

A. H. M. Jones, *The Cities of the Eastern Roman Provinces*, chapter 11.
N. Lewis, *Life in Egypt Under Roman Rule*, Oxford, 1983.

Christianity by the Early Fourth Century

A. H. M. Jones, *Constantine and the Conversion of Europe*, edn. 2, London, 1962.
K. Baus, *From the Apostolic Community to Constantine*, London, 1965.
H. Chadwick, *The Early Church*, London, 1968.
R. A. Markus, *Christianity in the Roman World*, London, 1974.
C. Thomas, *Christianity in Roman Britain to A.D. 500*, London, 1981.

The Dioceses and Provinces of the Roman Empire in AD 314

A. H. M. Jones, *The Decline of the Ancient World*, London, 1966.
T. D. Barnes, *The New Empire of Diocletian and Constantine*, Harvard, 1982, chapters 11–13.

GAZETTEER

Entries refer first to the page where the name appears; the letter and number which follow refer to figures on the map at the top/bottom and sides respectively. Thus Aballava, for example, is to be found on p. 133 within the rectangle formed by letter A (at top left) and number 2 (at bottom right).

Normally every appearance of a name is listed. This is not necessarily the case, however, with very well known names (Athens or Italy, for instance), especially in the Aegean area.

In addition most monuments and features on battle or site plans are *not* listed; the main exceptions are pp. 90, 121 and 123, where all the names appearing on these maps of Rome *are* listed under 'Roma'.

Variant endings in os/us and on/um have generally been ignored in the gazetteer. Names which cannot be found under 'Ae', 'J' and 'K' should be checked under 'Ai', 'I' and 'C' respectively.

Aalen 140 C3
Abacaenum 38 E2; 148 E2
Abae 72 C3
Aballava 133 A2
Abantes 7 D2, 3
Abarnahara 18 C3
Abassium 73 H3
Abdera [Baetica] 96 B4; 144 C4
Abdera [Thracia] 15 G1; 23 C1; 32 F1; 44 B1; 143 D4
Abella 84 C4; 92 E3; 94 D3; 119 C4
Abellinum 94 D3; 109 E4; 119 C4
Aberffraw 131 B5
Abila 166 C4
Abila/Seleuceia 74 B5; 166 D2
Abona 131 C7
Abona, R. 131 C7
Abonuteichus 161 E1
Abrettene 158 B2
Abus, R. 131 D5
Abusina 140 E3
Abydos [Hellespont] 9 D1; 27 B2; 31 F2; 33 A1; 44 C1; 160 A2
Abydus [Aegyptus] 167 C4
Acadama 162 B4
Acamas, M. 156 A5
Acamas, Pr. 156 A5
Acampsis, R. 162 C1
Acanthus 15 F1; 23 C1; 30 D1; 32 E2; 44 A1
Acarnania 30 B3
Acci 144 C4
Ace/Ptolemais 74 B4; 166 B1; 173 F5
Acelum 108 C1; 119 B1
Acerrae 92 D3; 115 B2
Acesines, R. [India] 65 H3
Acesines, R. [Sicilia] 38 E2
Achaea [Peloponnesus] 16 B2; 30 B4
Achaea, Achaia (Roman Province) 105 E3; 129 D4; 171 D4, E4; 177 D4
Achaea Phthiotis 30 C3; 62 B3
Achaeon Acte 156 D4
Acharnae 34 B3; 46 C3
Achates, R. 148 D4
Acheloos, R. 6 B2; 7 B2; 30 B3; 32 B3; 62 B3
Acheron, R. 7 A2; 32 B3

Achilleum 27 A2
Acholla 97 F5
Aciris, R. 109 F4
Acium 148 E3
Acmonia 160 C3
Acoris 76 B3
Acquarossa 82 C5
Acra Leuce 96 C3
Acrabeta 166 B3
Acrae 14 B2; 38 D4; 148 D4
Acraea, Cautes 38 E3
Acritas, Pr. 29 C1
Acrothooi 44 B1
Acruvium 143 B4
Acte [Attica] 34 B4
Acte [Chalcidice] 30 D1
Action, Actium 32 B4; 105 D3
Acuricum 143 A3
Ad Ansam 131 E7
Ad Duas Lauros 122 C2
Ad Fl. Tigrim 162 D3
Ad Fluvium Lanaricum 148 B3
Ad Gallinas Albas 122 B1
Ad Herculem 146 B3
Ad Lunam 140 C4
Ad Maiores 154 B1
Ad Medias 146 B4
Ad Olivam 148 B2
Ad Pontem [Britannia] 131 D6
Ad Pontem [Mesopotamia] 162 D3
Ad Spem Vetus 122 B1
Ad Turres 154 C1
Adana/Antioch 74 B3; 161 F4
Adara 162 C4
Addua, R. 108 B2
Adiabene 162 D2
Adora 166 B5
Adraha 162 B4
Adramytteion, Adramyttium 23 D2; 31 F2; 33 B1; 73 E2; 158 A2; 160 A3
Adramyttenus Sinus 33 A1
Adranum, Hadranum 38 D3; 148 D3
Adria, Atria 82 C1; 108 C2
Adrianopolis *see* Hadrianopolis
Adriaticum Mare 107; 109 E3, F3
Adys 97 F4
Ae- *see also* Ai-

Aeane 32 C2
Aecae 97 G2
Aeclanum 92 E2; 109 E4
Aedui 136 C3
Aegae [Macedonia] 32 C2; 56 B1; 62 B2
Aegae [Peloponnesus] 29 C1
Aegaeum Mare 31 E4
Aegaleos, M. 34 B3
Aegates Is. 38 A2; 97 F4; 148 A2
Aegilia 34 C5
Aegina 16 C2; 29 D2; 30 D4
Aeginion 32 B3
Aegion, Aigion 6 B3; 29 C1; 72 C3
Aegira, Aigeira 6 C3; 29 C1
Aegithallus 38 A2
Aegitium 46 C3
Aegospotami 47 E1
Aegospotami, R. 27 B1
Aegosthena 29 D1; 56 B2
Aegusa, Aethusa [Aegates Is.] 38 A2; 148 A2
Aegyptus (Egypt) 76; 167
Aegyptus (Roman Province) 129 E6; 171 E6
Aegyptus Herculia 177 E5, F5
Aegyptus Iovia 177 E5
Aelana 76 D2; 167 D2
Aelanites, Sinus 167 D2
Aelia Capitolina *see* Jerusalem
Aemilia 108 C2; 176 C3
Aemilia, Via 108 C2
Aemilia Scauri, Via 108 B3
Aeminium 144 A2
Aenaria 109 E4; 115 B3
Aene(i)a 32 D2; 44 A1
Aenis 23 B2; 62 B3
Aenona 143 A4
Aenos, M. [Cephallenia] 29 A1; 30 A4
Aenus, Ainos 9 C1; 15 G1; 31 E1; 44 B1; 143 E4
Aeoliae Is. 148 D1
Aeolis 16 E2; 18 B2; 31 F3
Aequi 84 B3, C3
Aequum 143 B4
Aequum Tuticum 84 C3
Aerae 47 E3
Aesernia 94 D2; 109 E4

Aesica 133 B1
Aesis 108 D3
Aesis, R. 108 D3
Aesium 95 C2
Aeso 144 D1
Aethiopia, Ethiopia 18 B5; 167 C6
Aethusa, Aegusa [Aegates Is.] 38 A2; 148 A2
Aethusa Is. [inter Siciliam et Africam] 148 A4
Aetna 38 D3; 148 E3
Aetna, M. 38 E2; 97 G4; 148 E2
Aetolia 16 B2; 30 B3
Aexone 34 B4
Aezani 160 C3
Africa (Continent) 54
Africa (Diocese) 176 B5
Africa (Roman Province) 102 B3, C3; 128 C5; 150-1; 154; 170 C5
Africa Proconsularis 150; 176 C4
Agatha 14 B3
Agathyrnum 38 D2; 148 D2
Agedincum 138 A3
Agia Eirene 2 C3; 10 C3; 12 C3; 56 C3
Agia Marina 6 C2
Agia Pelagia 4 C2
Agia Triadha 4 C3; 56 C4
Agidus 86 C2
Agios Andreas 2 C3
Agios Ilias 6 B2
Agios Kosmas 2 C3; 6 D3
Agios Stephanos 6 C4
Agnone 92 D2
Agora 27 C1
Agri Decumates 128 C3; 136 D2, 3; 138 B4, C3
Agrianians 62 B1
Agrigentum see Akragas
Agrinion 29 B1; 32 B4
Agryle 34 B3
Agylla see Caere
Agyrium 38 D3; 148 D3
Ahdem, R. 58 A3
Ai- see also Ae-
Ai Khanum 69 (Plan); 71 H2
Aiacium 146 B2
Aigythallus, Pr. 148 A2
Ain-el-Jemala 151 B2
Ain Wassel 151 A2
Aisepos, R. 9 D1
Aislingen 140 D4
Akragas/Agrigentum 14 A2; 38 C3; 40 (Plan); 97 G4, 5; 148 C3
Akroterion 6 A3
Akrotiri 2 C4; 56 C3
Aigeira see Aegira
A1 Mina 15 G4; 53 G4
Ala Miliaria 154 A1
Alabanda/Antioch 33 C4; 73 F4; 158 B4; 160 B4
Alabon, R. 38 E3
Alabum 131 B7
Alaina 162 C3
Alalia 14 C3

Alarodioi 18 D2
Alauna [1, Britannia] 130 C3
Alauna [2, Britannia] 130 C4
Alauna [3, Britannia] 130 D4
Alauna [4, Britannia] 131 C5
Alauna [5, Britannia] 131 C6
Alauna, R. 130 C4
Alauni 138 D4
Alba Fucens 94 C2; 97 G2; 109 D3; 111 E3; 119 C3
Alba Longa 86 C2; 122 C2
Alba Pompeia 108 A3
Alban Hills 86 C2
Albanum (Domitiani) 122 C2; 170 C3
Albanus, L. 108 D4
Albanus, M. 81
Albingaunum 108 B3
Albintimilium, Albium Intemelium (Ventimiglia) 108 A3; 110 A3
Albis, R. 128 C2; 138 D2; 170 D2
Alcantara Bridge 144 B2
Alcester 131 C6
Alchester 131 D7
Alcmona, R. 140 F3
Aleria 84 A3; 97 F2; 146 C2; 176 C3
Alesia 136 C3
Aletrium 92 C3
Alexandria [Aegyptus] 76 B1; 81 (Plan); 129 E5; 167 B1; 171 E5; 173 E5; 177 E5
Alexandria (Bactra, Zariaspa) 65 G2
Alexandria [Bactria] 71 H3
Alexandria (Buchephala) 65 H3
Alexandria (Carmania) 65 F4
Alexandria (Iomoussa) 65 H3
Alexandria (Nicaea) 65 H3
Alexandria (Oreitae) 65 G4
Alexandria (Paropamisadae), 65 G2
Alexandria (Prophthasia) 65 F3; 71 G4
Alexandria on the Caucasus 71 H3
Alexandria [Ad Indum] 65 H3
Alexandria (By Issus) 64 B3; 74 B3; 161 F5; 162 B3
Alexandria ad Latmum 64 A2
Alexandria ad Oxum 65 G2
Alexandria/Antioch 64 D4; 71 E4
Alexandria/Herat (Areia) 65 F3; 71 G3
Alexandria/Kandahar (Arachosia) 65 G3; 71 G3
Alexandria/Merv (Margiane) 65 F2; 71 G2
Alexandria Eschate 65 G2; 71 H2
Alexandr(e)ia Troas 64 A2; 73 E2; 158 A2; 160 A2
Alexandrion 166 C3
Alfaterna see Nuceria
Alfoldean 131 D8
Alista 146 C2
Alkofen 140 E3
Allava 148 B3
Allia 84 B3
Allifae 84 C3; 92 D3; 94 D3; 97 G2; 109 E4; 119 C3

Allobroges 97 E1; 136 C4
Allumiere 82 C5
Alope 46 C3
Alopece 34 B3
Alopeconnesus 27 B1; 143 E4
Aloros 32 C2
Alpes 128 C3; 136 D4; 170 C3; 176 C3
Alpheios, R. 16 B3; 29 C2; 30 B4
Alsium 94 B2; 108 D4; 122 B1
Altava, 150 B1; 154 A1
Altenstadt 140 B1
Altilia see Saepinum
Altinum 108 C1
Aluca 146 B1
Alutus, R. 143 D3
Alveria 143 A4
Alvona 143 A3
Alyzia 32 B4
Amantia 143 C4
Amanum Portus 144 C1
Amanus, M. 161 F4, 5; 162 B3
Amarus, L. 167 C2
Amaseia 74 B1; 161 F2; 177 F3
Amastris 74 A1; 129 F4; 158 D1; 160 D1; 171 F4; 173 E3
Amathus [Cyprus] 156 B6
Amathus [Palaestina] 166 C3
Amber Is. 54 B1
Ambiani 138 A2
Ambisontes 138 D4
Amblada 160 D4
Ambra, R. 140 E4
Ambracia 16 A2; 23 A2; 30 B3; 32 B3; 62 B3
Ambracicus Sinus 32 B4
Ambre 140 E4
Amenanus, R. 38 E3
Ameria 92 B3; 108 D3; 119 B3
Ameselum 38 D3
Amestratus 148 D2
Amiata, M. 82 C4
Amida 162 C2; 177 F4
Amisus 15 G3; 50 C4; 161 F1
Amiternum 92 C2; 109 D3
Ammaedara 150 B4; 154 C1
Ammonium 64 A4
Amnias, R. 161 E1
Amnisos 4 C2; 9 C4; 80 C4
Amorgos 16 D3; 31 E5; 33 A5; 44 B3
Amorium 160 D3
Ampelum 143 D2
Amphiaraus, Sanctuary of (Attica) 34 C1
Amphilochia 30 B2, 3
Amphipolis 30 D1; 32 E1; 44 A1; 143 D4
Amphipolis/Thapsacus 58 D2; 64 C3; 74 C3
Amphissa 12 B2; 29 C1; 30 C3; 32 C4; 62 B3
Amsanctus 92 E2
Amyclae, Amyklai 7 C5; 10 B3; 12 B3; 29 C3
Amyzon 73 F4

Anactorion, Anactorium 16 A2; 23 A2; 30 B3; 32 B4
Anaea 47 F4
Anagnia 84 B3; 86 D2; 92 C3; 119 B3; 122 D2
Anagyrus 34 C4
Analipsis 6 C4
Anaphe 31 E5; 33 A5; 60 D4
Anaphlystus 34 D5
Anapus, R. 38 E4; 148 E4
Anas, R. 96 A3; 144 A3
Anasartha 162 B3
Anaunium 108 B1
Anava, R. 130 C4
Anazarbus 161 F4
Ancaster 131 D6
Anchialus 143 E3; 173 E3
Ancona 84 C2; 92 B1; 108 D2; 110 D2
Ancyra [Galatia] 74 A2; 129 F4; 158 D2; 160 D2; 171 F4; 173 F4; 177 F4
Ancyra (Julia) [Asia] 158 B3; 160 B3
Ancyro(no)polis 76 B2; 167 B2
Andania 72 B4
Andautonia 143 B2
Andemantunnum 136 C3
Anderitum 131 E8
Androna 162 B3
Andros 16 C2; 31 E4; 44 B3
Anemurium 160 D5
Angli 138 C1
Angrivarii 138 C2
Anio, R. 86 C1
Anisa 161 F3
Annia, Via 109 F4, G5
Ansium 143 A4
Antaeopolis 167 B3
Antandros 9 D2; 23 D2; 31 F2; 44 C2
Antaradus 74 B4
Antemnae 86 B1
Anthedon [Boeotia] 6 D2; 7 D3; 29 D1
Anthedon [Palaestina] 166 A5
Anthela 16 B2
Anthemus 62 C2
Anticaria 144 B4
Anticythera 29 D4
Antigoneia 72 A1
Antilibanus, M. 162 B4
Antinoe/Antinoopolis 167 B3
Antioch [Asia] 73 G3
Antioch [Cilicia] 74 A3; 160 D5
Antioch(ia) (Caesareia) [Pisidia] 74 A2; 158 C3; 160 D3; 177 E4
Antioch(ia) [Syria] 74 B3; 129 F4; 161 F5; 162 B3; 171 F4; 173 F4; 177 F4
Antioch/Adana 74 B3; 161 F4
Antioch/Alexandria 71 E4
Antioch/Charax 71 E4
Antioch/Hippus 74 B4
Antioch/Mallus 74 A3; 161 F5
Antioch/Nisibis 74 D3; 162 C3
Antiochia/Perrhe 162 B2
Antioch in Persis 71 E4
Antioch see Alabanda
Antioch see Edessa

Antioch see Tarsus
Antipatre(i)a 72 A1; 143 C4
Antipatris 166 B3
Antiphrae 167 A1
Antipolis 14 B3
Antipyrgus 151 H2
Antirrhion Pr. 29 B1
Antissa 33 A2; 44 B2
Antitaurus, M [Armenia] 162 C2
Antitaurus, M. [Cappadocia] 161 F3, 4
Antium 81; 84 B3; 92 C3; 94 B2; 108 D4; 122 C3
Antivestaeum, Pr. 131 A8
Antonini Murus 130 B3, C3; 134 (Plan)
Antoninopolis 162 C3
Antron 7 C2
Antunnacum 140 A1
Aoi Stena 30 A1; 32 A2
Aoos, R. 30 A1; 32 A2
Aornus 65 H2
Aosta see Augusta Praetoria
Aous, M. 156 A5
Apaisos 9 D1
Apamea [Ad Euphratem] 162 B3
Apamea [Ad Orontem] 70 C3; 74 C3; 162 B3
Apame (i)a Celaenae, Kelainai 58 B2; 70 B3; 73 H3; 158 C3; 160 C4; 173 E4
Apamea/Myrle(i)a 73 F1; 158 B2; 160 B2
Ap(p)enninus, M. 108 C2-109 E4
Aperopia 29 D2
Aphaia 56 B3
Aphetae 23 B2
Aphidna 34 C2
Aphrodisias 80 E2; 125 E4; 158 B4; 160 B4; 177 E4
Aphrodisium 156 C4
Aphroditopolis [1, Aegyptus] 76 B2; 167 B2
Aphroditopolis [2, Aegyptus] 76 B3; 167 B3
Aphytis 32 D2; 44 A1
Apodhoulou 4 C2
Apollonia [Chalcidice] 32 D2
Apollonia [Cyrene] 151 G2
Apollonia [Illyricum] 14 D3; 72 A1; 97 H3; 105 D3; 143 C4
Apollonia [Ad Maeandrum] 73 G3
Apollonia [Mesopotamia] 70 D3
Apollonia [Mysia] 73 F2
Apollonia [Palaestina] 74 B5; 166 A3
Apollonia [Phrygia] 73 H3; 158 C3; 160 C4
Apollonia [Pontus Euxinus] 15 F3; 143 E3
Apollonia [Sicilia] 38 D2
Apollonia [Thracia] 32 E1
Apollonia Mygdonia 72 C1
Apollinopolis (Magna) 76 C4; 167 C4
Apollonopolis Heptacomias 167 B3
Apollonopolis Parva 167 C4

Appia, Via 90 C4; 109 D4, F4; 115 A2, C1; 122 C2; 123 D1
Aprus 143 E4
Apsorus 143 A3
Aptera 156 A1
Apthungi 150 C4
Apuani 84 A2
Apuli 84 C3
Apulia 109 F4; 176 D3
Apulum 143 D2; 171 E3
Apurytai 19 H3
Aquae 140 B3
Aquae Arnemetiae 131 C6
Aquae Flaviae 144 A2
Aquae Hypsitanae/Forum Traiani 146 B4
Aquae Larodes/Thermae Selinuntinae 148 B3
Aquae Lesitanae 146 C4
Aquae Mattiacorum 140 B2
Aquae Neapolitanae 146 B5
Aquae S. 143 B3
Aquae Segestanae 148 B2
Aquae Sextiae 136 C5; 176 C3
Aquae Statiellae 108 B2
Aquae Sulis 131 C7
Aquae Vescinae 115 A2
Aquileia [Italia] 95 C1; 108 D1; 110 D1; 124 C3; 176 C3
Aquileia [Raetia] 140 C4
Aquilonia 92 D2
Aquincum 138 F4; 143 B2; 170 D3
Aquinum (Aquino) 92 D3; 94 C2; 109 E4; 111 E4
Aquitani 104 B2
Aquitania 128 B3; 136 B4; 138 A4; 170 B3
Aquitanica 176 B2, 3
Arabia 18 C4; 162 B5; 171 F5; 177 F5
Arabia Nova 177 F5
Arabia Petraea 167 D2
Arabiates 138 E4
Arabicus, Sinus 167 D3
Arabissus 161 G3
Aracha 162 B4
Arachosia 19 G3; 65 G3; 71 H4
Aradus 74 B4; 162 B4
Arae Flaviae 138 C4; 140 B4
Arae Philaenorum 151 G2
Araithyrea 7 C4
Araks, R. see Araxes, R.
Aral Sea 19 F1; 71 F1
Arausio 136 C4
Aravorum Civitas 144 A2
Araxes, Araks, R. 58 D3; 162 D2
Araxos 6 B3
Arba 143 A3
Arbeia 133 D1
Arbela [Assyria] 64 D3; 162 D3
Arbela [Palaestina] 166 C2
Arcesine 73 E4
Archelais [Cappadocia] 161 E3
Archelais [Palaestina] 166 C4
Arconnesos 33 B5

192

193

Aveia 92 C2
Aventicum 136 D3; 138 B4
Avernus, L. 111 G1
Avon, R. 134 D2
Axia 82 C5
Axima 136 D4
Axios, R. 2 B1; 9 B1; 30 C1; 32 C1,
 D1; 62 C2; 143 D4
Azali 138 E4
Azotus 74 B5; 166 A4
Azov, Sea of 50 C1

Babba 150 A1
Babylon [Aegyptus] 167 B2
Babylon [Mesopotamia] 18 D3; 58 A4,
 E4; 64 D3; 162 D4
Babylonia 18 D3; 64 D4
Bacchias 167 B2
Bacoli (Bauli) 111 G1; 115 B2
Bactra 19 G2; 65 G2; 71 G2
Bactria 19 G2; 65 G2; 71 H3
Bad Cannstatt 140 C3
Bad Nauheim 140 B1
Badias 154 B1
Baecula 96 B3
Baelo 144 B4
Baeterrae 136 C5
Baetica 124 A4; 128 A4; 144 B3; 170
 A4; 176 A4
Baetis, R. 96 B3; 144 B3
Baetocaece 74 B4; 162 B4
Baetulo 144 E2
Baeturia 144 B3
Bagacum 138 A3
Baginton 131 D6
Bagradas, R. 97 E4; 104 C3; 150 C3;
 151 B1
Bahr Yusuf, R. 167 B3
Baiae (Baia) 111 G1; 115 B2
Balad 162 D3
Balaneae 162 B3
Balari 146 B4, C3
Balatoni 146 B2
Balbura 73 G4
Baldock 131 D7
Baleares (Gymnesiae) Is. 96 D3; 144
 E2
Balearicum Mare 144 D2
Balmuildy 134 B2
Balsa 144 A4
Bambyce see Hierapolis
Banasa 150 A1
Banna 133 B1
Bannatia 130 C3
Bannaventa 131 D6
Bannovalium 131 D6
Bantia 92 E2; 109 F4
Baquates 150 A2, B2
Bar Hill 134 B1
Barbarium, Pr. 144 A3
Barca 14 D5; 151 G2
Barcino 144 E2

Bargylia 73 F4; 158 A4; 160 B4
Bargylus, M. 162 B3
Baria 144 C4
Barium 84 D4; 109 F3
Barochan 134 A2
Barra 94 E4
Barygaza 54 E3
Basileus, R. 156 B5
Basilica Therma 161 F3
Bassae 56 B3; 80 B3
Bassiana 143 C3
Bastuli 144 B4
Batavi 138 B2
Batiae 62 B3
Batitas 162 C3
Batnae 162 B3
Bauli (Bacoli) 111 G1; 115 B2
Bautica, R. 108 A2
Bauzanum (Pons Drusi) 108 C1
Bearsden 134 A2
Beberaci. L. 162 C3
Bedriacum 108 B2
Beersheba 166 A5
Begastrum 144 C3
Begorritis, L. 30 B1; 32 C1
Belbina 29 E2
Belerium 54 A1
Belerium, Pr. 131 A8
Belgae 131 C7
Belgica 128 C2; 136 C2; 138 A3, B3;
 140 A2; 170 C2; 176 B2, C2
Belginum 140 A2
Bellunum 108 C1
Benacus, L. 108 B1
Bendorf 140 A1
Beneventum/Malventum (Benevento)
 84 C4; 92 E2; 94 D3; 97 G3; 109 E4;
 111 F4; 115 C1
Benningen 140 C3
Berbati 6 C3
Berenice [Aegyptus] 70 B5; 167 D5
Berenice [Cyrene] 151 G2; 173 D5
Berenice/Pella [Palaestina] 74 B5; 166
 C2
Berezan Is. 15 F2; 50 A1
Bergen 140 B2
Bergidum 144 B1
Bergomum 108 B2
Beroe 62 D1
Beroea [Macedonia] 32 C2; 72 C1
Beroea [Syria] 74 C3; 161 G5; 162 B3
Berones 144 C1
Bertha 130 C3
Berytus/Laodicea 74 B4; 162 A4
Bessi 105 E2
Beth Gabra/Eleutheropolis 166 B4
Beth Horon 166 B4
Bethar 166 B4
Betharamatha/Livias-Julias 166 C4
Bethlehem 166 B4
Bethletephe 166 B4
Bethsaida/Julias 166 C1
Bettolle 82 D4
Beulah 131 C6

Bezabde 162 D3
Bezereos 154 C2
Bibra 133 A2
Bilbilis 144 C2
Bilechas, R. 162 C3
Billaeus, R. 160 D1
Bingium 140 A2
Biora 146 C5
Biricianis 140 D3
Bisanthe 73 F1
Bishopton 134 A2
Bistonis, L. 31 E1
Bistue Nova 143 B3
Bistue Vetus 143 B3
Bithia, Bitia 97 E3; 146 C5
Bithynia 18 B2; 129 E4; 158 C1; 160
 C2, D1; 171 F4; 177 E4
Bithynium/Claudiopolis 74 A1; 158
 D2; 160 D2
Bituriges 136 B3, B4; 176 B2
Bizye 143 E4
Black Sea 50 B2
Blakehope 130 C4
Blanda Iulia 109 F4
Blandianus Saltus 151 A2
Blatobulgium 133 A1
Blaudus 73 F2
Blera 82 C5
Blestium 131 C7
Bocarus, R. 156 A5
Bochastle 130 B3
Bodotria Aestuarium 134 D1
Bodotria, R. 130 B3, C3
Boeae 29 D4
Boebe, Boibe, L. 7 C1; 30 C2; 32 D3
Böhming 140 E3
Boeotia 30 C3
Boii [Italia] 84 B2; 97 F1
Boii [Pannonia] 138 E4
Bola 94 B2
Bolbe, L. 30 C1; 32 D1
Bolbitine Mouth (Nile) 167 B1
Boliscus 47 E3
Bolsena see Volsinii
Bonna 128 C2; 136 C2; 138 B2; 170 C2
Bononia/Felsina 82 B2; 84 B2; 95 B1;
 97 F1; 108 C2
Borbetomagus 138 C3; 140 B2
Bormiscus 46 C1
Borysthenes, R. 15 F2; 50 B1
Bosa 146 B4
Bospori Regnum 50; 105 F2; 129 F3;
 171 F3
Bosporus [Thracian] 15 H1
Bosporus, Cimmerian 50 C2, D2
Bostra 74 C5; 162 B5; 171 F5; 173 F5;
 177 F5
Bothwellhaugh 134 C2
Botrys 162 B4
Bouprasion 7 B3
Bourton-on-the-Water 131 C7
Bovianum 92 D2; 94 D2; 109 E4
Bovianum Vetus 92 D2; 94 D2
Bovillae 122 C2

Bovium 131 C7
Bracara Augusta 144 A2; 176 A3
Bracciano, L. 86 B1
Bradanus, R. 109 F4
Braintree 131 E7
Brampton 131 E6
Branodunum 131 E6
Branogenium 131 C6
Bratananium 140 E4
Braughing 131 D7
Brauron 6 D3; 12 C3; 29 E2; 34 D4
Bravoniacum 130 C4
Brea 44 A1
Brecon Gaer 131 C7
Bremenium 130 C4
Bremetenacum, 131 C5
Bremia 131 B6
Brescia *see* Brixia
Bricindarioi 44 C4
Bricinniae 38 D3
Briga 131 D7
Brigantes 131 C5, D5
Brigantium [Hispania] 144 A1
Brigantium [Raetia] 138 C4
Brigetio 138 E4; 170 D3
Brindisi *see* Brundisium
Britannia 128 B2; 130-131; 176 B1
Britannia Inferior 171 B2
Britannia Superior 171 B2
Britanniae (Diocese) 176 B1
Britannicus Oceanus 131 D8
Brithdir 131 B6
Brixellum 95 B1; 108 B2
Brixia (Brescia) 95 B1; 108 B2; 110 B1;
    119 A1
Brocavum 130 C4
Brocolitia 133 C1
Brocomagus 140 A3
Brompton 131 C6
Broomholm 133 A1
Broxtowe 131 D6
Bructeri 138 B2
Brundisium (Brindisi) 84 D4; 94 B3;
    97 H3; 109 G4; 111 G3
Bruttii 84 D5
Bruttium 109 G5
Bryn-y-Gefailiau 131 B6
Bu Njem 154 D2
Bubastis 76 C1; 167 C1
Bubon 73 G4; 158 B4
Buch 140 D3
Buchephala 65 H3
Buchetium 62 B3
Bucra, Pr. 148 D4
Burdigala 128 B3; 136 B4; 170 B3; 176
    B3
Bulla Regia 97 E4; 150 C3
Burgh-by-Sands 133 A2
Burghwallis 131 D5
Burgundiones 138 E2
Burnum 128 D3; 143 A4
Burrium 131 C7
Burunitanus, Saltus 151 A1
Busiris 76 B1; 167 B1

Butadae 34 B3
Buthroton 32 A3
Buto 76 B1; 167 B1
Butua 143 B4
Butzbach 140 B1
Buxentum, 94 E4; 109 F4
Byblus 74 B4; 162 A4
Byllis 143 C4
Byzacena 176 C4
Byzantium 15 H1; 44 D1; 143 F2; 158
    B1; 160 B1

Cabeira 74 C1
Caburrum 108 A3
Cabyle 62 D1; 143 E3
Cacyparis, R. 38 E4
Cacyrum 38 C3
Cadder 134 B2
Cadi 73 G2; 160 C3
Cadousioi 19 E3
Caecina, R. 108 C3
Caedrus, R. 146 C4
Caelia 109 F4
Caelio Monte 140 C4
Caelis, R. 130 C2
Caenepolis 29 C4
Caenys, Pr. 109 G6
Caer Gai 131 C6
Caere (Agylla) (Cerveteri) 82 C5; 84
    B3; 86 B1; 92 B3; 110 D4; 122 B1
Caermote 133 A2
Caerphilly 131 C7
Caersws 131 C6
Caesaraugusta 144 D2
Caesarea Germanica 158 B2
Caesarea Paneas or Philippi (Panion)
    162 A4; 166 C1
Caesarea/Strato's Tower 129 F5; 166
    B2; 171 F5; 173 F5; 177 F5
Caesarea (Iol) *see* Iol
Caesarea (Mazaca) *see* Mazaca
Caesareia [Pisidia] *see* Antioch(ia)
Caesariensis, Mauretania 128 A5, B5;
    150 C1; 170 B5; 176 B4
Caesarobriga 144 B2
Caesaromagus 131 E7
Caesena 82 C2
Caiatia 92 D3; 115 B1; 119 C4
Caicos, R. 16 E1; 31 F3; 33 B2
Caister-by-Yarmouth 131 E6
Caistor 131 D5
Calabria 109 F4, G4; 176 D3
Calacte, Caleacte 38 D2; 148 D2
Calacum 131 C5
Calagurris 144 C1
Calama 150 B4
Calatia 92 D3; 94 D3; 115 B1
Calauria 12 B3; 16 C3; 29 D2
Calcaria 131 D5
Calchedon *see* Chalcedon
Caleacte, Calacte 38 D2; 148 D2
Caledonii 130 B2
Cales (Calvi Vecchia) [Campania] 109

E4; 111 E4; 115 B1; 119 C4
Cales [Umbria] 84 C4; 94 D3; 108 D3
Callatis 15 F3; 143 E3
Calleva Atrebatum (Silchester) 131
    D7; 135 (Plan)
Callinusa, Pr. 156 A5
Callipolis 27 C1; 143 E4
Calloniana 148 C3
Calor, R. 115 B1
Calpe, M. 144 B4
Calvi Vecchia *see* Cales
Calvisiana 148 D4
Calycadnus, R. 74 B3; 161 E5
Calydnioi 44 C3
Calydon 6 B3; 7 B3; 10 B2; 29 B1
Calymnos 31 F5; 33 B4
Calynda 44 D3; 73 G4; 160 B5
Camacha 161 H2
Camarina 14 A2; 38 D4; 97 G4; 148 D4
Cambodunum [Britannia] 131 D5
Cambodunum [Raetia] 138 C4
Camboglanna 133 B1
Camboritum 131 E6
Camelon 134 C1
Camerinum 92 B2; 108 D3
Camerton 131 C7
Camicus 38 C3
Camirus, Kameiros 9 D4; 12 E3; 16
    E3; 33 C5; 44 C4; 73 F5
Campana, Via 90 A2; 115 B2
Campani [Italia] 84 C4
Campani [Sardinia] 146 C4, C5
Campania 109 E4; 115; 176 C3
Campanus, Ager 115 B2
Campi Magni 97 E4, F4
Campovalano 84 C3
Camulodunum [1, Britannia] 131 C5
Camulodunum [2, Britannia] 131 E7
Cana 166 B2
Canastraion, Pr. 32 E3
Canatha 162 B4
Candidum, Pr. 97 F4
Canelata 146 C1
Cannae (Canne della Battaglia), 97
    G3; 99 (Battle); 109 F3; 111 F3
Canonium 131 E7
Canopic Mouth (Nile) 167 B1
Canopus 76 B1; 167 B1
Canovium 131 B5
Cantabri 144 B1
Cantiaci 131 E7
Cantium 54 B2
Cantium, Pr. 131 E7
Canusium 84 C3; 92 E2; 97 G3; 109 F4;
    119 D4
Capena 86 B1; 92 B3; 119 B3; 122 B1
Capera 144 B2
Capernaum 166 C1
Capestrano 84 C3
Caphareus, Pr. 29 E1
Caphyae 29 C2; 72 C3
Capitoniana 148 C3
Capitulum 92 C3

Cappadocia 18 C2; 129 F4; 161 F3; 162 B2; 171 F4; 177 F4
Cappadox, R. 161 F3
Cappuck 130 C4
Capraria [Baleares] 144 E3
Capraria [Italia] 108 C3
Capreae (Capri) 109 E4; 111 H2; 115 C3
Capsa 150 B5
Capua 84 C4; 92 D3; 94 D3; 97 G3; 109 E4; 115 B2; 119 C4
Caput Ferentinae 86 C2
Caput Tyrsi 146 C4
Carales, Caralis 52 C4; 97 F3; 128 C4; 146 C5; 170 C4; 176 C4
Carana 105 G2; 162 C2
Caranis 76 B2; 167 B2
Carbantoritum 130 C3
Carbia 146 B4
Carcine 50 B1
Cardamyle [Chios] 33 A3
Cardamyle [Messenia] 7 C5; 29 C3
Cardean 130 C2
Cardia 27 C1; 31 F1
Cardiff 131 C7
Cardouchoi 18 D2; 58 D2
Cargill 130 C3
Caria 16 E3; 18 B2; 31 G4
Caria (Roman Province) 177 E4
Carians 9 D3
Carkin Moor 130 D4
Carmana 71 F4
Carmania 19 F4; 65 F4; 71 F4
Carmo 144 B3
Carni 84 C1
Carno 131 B6
Carnuntum 128 D3; 138 E4; 143 B1; 170 D3
Carnutes 136 B3
Carpasia 156 D4
Carpathium Mare 31 F6, G6; 33 B6
Carpathos 31 F6
Carpetana, Iuga 144 B2, C2
Carpetani 96 B2, 3; 144 B2
Carpow 130 C3
Carrara 124 C3
Carreum Potentia 108 A2
Carrhae 74 C3; 161 H4; 162 C3
Carriceni 84 C3
Carriden (Veluniate) 134 D1
Carron, R. 134 C1
Carseoli, Carsioli (Carsoli) 94 C2; 109 D4; 110 D3
Carsulae 92 B3; 110 D3
Carteia 96 A4; 144 B4
Cartenna(e) 96 C4; 150 C1
Carthaea 60 C3
Carthage, Carthago 97 F4; 100 (Plan); 128 C4; 150 C3; 151 E1; 154 C1; 170 C4; 172 C4; 176 C4
Carthaginiensis 176 A3, B4
Carthago Nova 96 C3; 144 D3; 176 B4
Carvetii 130 C4
Caryae 46 C4

Caryanda 33 B4
Carystos 29 E1; 31 D4; 44 B3; 124 E4
Carzield 130 C4
Cascantum 144 C1
Casilinum 92 D3; 94 D3; 97 G3; 109 E4; 115 B2
Casinum 92 D3; 94 C2; 109 E4
Casium 167 C1
Casius, M. 162 B3
Casmenae 14 B2; 38 D4
Caspia 19 F2
Caspian Gates 65 E3
Caspians 18 D2
Caspium Mare (Caspian Sea) 19 E2; 54 D2; 64 D1
Cassandreia 70 A2; 72 C2
Cassia, Via 108 D3; 122 B1
Cassiope 32 A3
Cassope 32 B3; 62 B3; 72 B2
Castabala/Hierapolis 74 B3; 161 F4
Castel Collen 131 C6
Castel di Decima 82 D6; 86 B2
Castellammare di Stabia (Stabiae) 111 H1; 115 C2
Castellina Chianti 82 B3
Castelluccio di Pienza 82 C4
Castellum Dimmidi 154 B1
Castellum Mattiacorum 140 B2
Castellum Tibubuci 154 C2
Castlecary 134 C1
Castledykes 130 C3
Castlehill 134 A2
Castleshaw 131 C5
Castra Exploratorum 133 A1
Castra Hannibalis 94 A4
Castra Regina 138 D3; 140 E3; 170 C3
Castrum Inui 86 B2
Castrum Novum [Etruria] 94 A2; 108 D4
Castrum Novum [Picenum] 94 C1
Castrum Truentinum 92 C2; 109 D3
Castulo 96 B3; 144 C3
Castulonesis, Saltus 144 B3, C3
Casuentus, R. 109 F4
Catada, R. 97 F4
Catana, Catane, Catina 14 B2; 38 E3; 148 E3
Cataonia 18 C2
Cataractonium 130 D4
Cataracts (R. Nile) 76 C5; 167 C5
Catina see Catana
Catuvellauni 131 D7
Cauca 144 B2
Caucana 148 D4
Caucasus, M. 162 D1
Caudine Forks 92 E3; 115 C1
Caudini 84 C4
Caudium 84 C4; 92 E3
Caulonia 14 B2; 97 H3
Caunus 44 D3; 47 G4; 73 G4; 160 B5
Caurium 144 B2
Causennae 131 D6
Cautes Acraea 38 E3
Cavares 97 E1

Cayster, R. 9 D2; 16 E2; 31 G3; 33 B3, C3; 158 A3
Cebren 44 C2
Cecryphalea 29 D2
Celaenae see Apame(i)a
Celeia 138 E4
Celenderis 161 E5
Celenza val Fortore 94 D2
Celetron 32 B2
Celeusum 140 E3
Celsa 144 D2
Celtiberi 96 C2; 144 C1
Celtici 144 A3
Cemenelum 136 D4
Cena 148 B3
Cenabum 138 A3
Cenchreae 29 D2
Cenestum 146 C2
Cenis, Mont 97 E1
Cenomani 84 A1; 97 F1
Centrites, R. 58 D2; 162 D2
Centumcellae 122 A1
Centurinum 146 C1
Centuripae 38 D3; 148 D3
Ceos 29 E2; 31 D4; 44 B3; 60 C3
Cephale 34 D5
Cephallenia 29 A1; 30 A3
Cephaloedium 38 C2; 148 C2
Cephisia 34 C3
Cephisos, R. 29 E1; 30 D4
Cepi 50 D2
Cerameis 34 B3
Ceramicus Sinus 33 C4, 5
Ceramos 33 C4; 44 C3
Ceras(o)us/Pharnaceia 15 G3; 50 D4; 58 D1; 74 C1; 161 G1; 162 B1
Cercina 97 F5; 150 C5
Cercinitis 15 G2; 50 B2
Cercinitis, L. 30 D1; 32 E1
Ceresius, L. 108 B2
Ceretani 144 D1
Ceretapa/Diocaesareia 160 C4
Cerinthos 7 D2; 9 B2; 32 D4
Cerveteri see Caere
Cervini 146 B1
Cerynia 156 B4
Chaboras, R. 162 C3
Chaeronea 29 C1; 30 C3; 32 D4; 61 (Battle)
Chala 148 D4
Chalandriani 2 C3
Chalastra 32 D2
Chalce 33 B5; 47 F5
Chalcedon, Calchedon 15 H1; 44 D1; 158 B1; 160 B1
Chalcidice 30 C1
Chalcis, Chalkis [Aetolia] 7 B3; 29 B1; 30 B3
Chalcis [Euboea] 16 C2; 29 D1; 30 D3
Chalcis [1, Syria] 74 C3; 162 B3
Chalcis [2, Syria] 74 B4
Chalos, R. 58 C2
Chalybes, 58 D1
Chamavi 138 B2

Chaonia [Epirus] 30 A2
Chaonia [Syria] 74 C3
Chaonians 62 A2
Characmoba 162 A5
Charax [Pontus Euxinus] 50 C2
Charax/Antioch 71 E4
Charterhouse 131 C7
Chatti 138 C2
Chauci 138 C1
Cheimerion, Pr. 32 A3
Chelif, R. 150 C1; 154 A1
Chelonatas, Pr. 29 B1
Chemtou 124 C4
Cherronesitae 44 C1
Cherronesus 44 C3
Chersonesos [Creta] 156 C2
Chersonesus [Hellespontus] 27 B1; 31
    F1
Chersonesus [Pontus Euxinus] 15 G3;
    50 B2
Chersonesos, Pr. [Euboea] 29 E1; 32
    E4
Chersonesus, Pr. [Sardinia] 146 B6
Cherusci 138 C2
Chesterfield 131 D6
Chesterton [1, Britannia] 131 C6
Chesterton [2, Britannia] 131 D6
Chianciano 82 C4
Chieti 111 E3
Chios 16 D2; 31 E3; 33 A3; 44 B2; 158
    A3; 160 A3
Chiusi see Clusium
Chorasmia 19 F1
Chorienes, Rock of 65 G2
Chrysas, R. 38 D3; 148 D3
Chrysopolis 47 G1; 58 A1
Chullu 97 E4; 150 D1
Chytri 156 C5
Cibalae 143 B3
Cibyra 73 G4; 158 B4; 160 C4
Ciciliano 119 B3
Cicucium 131 C7
Cierion 32 C3
Cierus/Prusias-on-Hypius 73 H1; 158
    C2; 160 D2
Cilbiani 158 B3
Cilices 9 D2
Cilicia 18 B2; 102 E3; 158 D4; 161 E4,
    F4; 162 A3; 171 F4; 177 F4
Cilicius, Aulon 156 B4
Cilium 150 C4
Cilurnum 133 C1
Cimmerian Bosporus 50 C2, D2
Cimmericum 50 C2
Ciminius, L. 82 C5
Cimolos 31 D4; 62 D4
Cindye 44 C3
Cingulum 108 D3
Cinna 161 E3
Circeii 94 B3; 109 D4
Circesium 162 C3
Circidius, R. 146 B2

Cirrha 16 B2; 29 C1; 30 C3
Cirta/Constantina 97 E4; 150 D1; 172
    C4; 176 B4
Cirtensis, Numidia 176 B4
Cisalpina, Gallia 102 C2
Cissa 143 A4
Cissia 19 E4
Cissos, M. 30 C1; 32 D2
Cithaeron, M. 29 D1; 30 C4
Citium, Kition 2 E4; 53 G5; 74 B4; 156
    C5
Cius/Prusias 73 G1; 158 B2
Civitas Camunnorum 108 B1
Clampetia 109 F5
Clanis, R. 82 C4
Clanius, R. 115 B2
Clapier, Col du 97 E1
Clarenna 140 C4
Claros 56 D2; 80 D2
Clastidium 97 F1; 108 B2
Claudianus, M. 125 F6; 167 C3
Claudiopolis 161 E5
Claudiopolis/Bithynium 74 A1; 158
    D2; 160 D2
Clausentum 131 D8
Clazomenae 16 D2; 31 F3; 33 B3; 44
    C2; 73 E3
Cleddans 134 A2
Cleides Is. 156 D4
Cleitor 29 C2
Cleonae [Chalcidice] 44 B1
Cleonae [Peloponnesus] 7 C3; 29 C2
Cleopatris/Arsinoe 76 C2
Clodia, Via 108 C3, D3; 122 B1
Clota, R. 130 B3; 134 B2
Clunia 144 C2
Clunium 146 C1
Clupea 97 F4; 150 D3
Clusium (Chiusi) 82 C4; 84 B3; 92 B3;
    95 B2; 108 D3; 110 D3
Cluviae 92 D2
Clyro 131 C7
Clysma 167 C2
Cnidos (Nova) 31 G5; 33 B5; 44 C3;
    158 A4; 160 A5
Cnidos (Vetus) 16 E3; 31 G5; 33 B5
Cnossus see Knossos
Coccium 131 C5
Cocinthus, Pr. 109 G5
Coclearia 146 C3
Cocusus 161 F4
Coela 143 E4
Coelbren 131 B7
Coele (Syria) 70 C3; 162 B3; 171 F5;
    177 F4
Cömlekci, 10 E3
Colania 134 C1
Colchians 18 D1
Collatia 86 C1
Colline Metallifere 82 B4
Colline Pass 97 F2
Collippo 144 A2
Colonae 27 C1
Colonia Agrippina, Colonia Claudia

Ara Agrippinensium 136 C2; 138
    B2; 176 C2
Colonia Ulpia Traiana 138 B2
Colonus 34 B3
Colophon 16 E2; 31 F4; 33 B3; 44 C3;
    160 A4
Colossae, Kolossai 58 A2; 158 B4; 160
    C4; 173 E4
Columbarium, Pr. 146 C3
Columnata 154 A1
Comama 158 C4; 160 C4
Comana [Cappadocia] 74 B2; 161 F3
Comana [Pontus] 74 C1; 161 F2
Combretovium 131 E7
Comiciana 148 C3
Commagene 129 F4; 161 E4, G4; 162
    B2
Complutum 144 C2
Compsa 92 E2; 97 G3; 119 C4
Comum 108 B2; 119 A1
Concangis 133 D2
Concavata 133 A2
Concordia 95 C1; 108 C1
Condate 131 C5
Condercum 133 D1
Confluentes 140 A1
Conimbriga 144 A2
Consabura 144 C3
Consentia, Cosentia 84 D5; 94 A4; 97
    G3; 109 F5
Constantina see Cirta
Contestani 144 D3
Contrebia 144 C2
Copais 6 C2; 29 D1; 30 C3
Cophen, R. 65 G3
Copia 94 A3
Coptus 76 C4; 167 C4
Cora 94 B2; 122 C2
Coracesium 160 D5
Corconiana 148 C3
Corcyra 30 A2; 32 A3
Corda 130 C3
Corduba 96 B3; 128 A4; 144 B3; 170
    A4; 172 A4; 176 A4
Coresia, Coressus 44 B3; 60 C3
Corfinium 84 C3; 92 C3; 109 E3
Corinium 143 A4
Corinium (Dobunnorum) 131 C7; 176
    B2
Corinthiacus Sinus 29 C1
Corinthos 29 D2; 30 C4; 129 D4; 171
    D4; 173 D4; 177 E4
Coriosopitum 133 C1
Coritani 131 D6
Cornovii 131 C6
Cornus 146 B4
Corone(i)a 7 C3; 29 D1; 30 C3
Corsi 146 B3, C3
Corsica 146; 170 C4; 176 C3
Cortona 82 C4; 92 A2; 97 F2; 108 C3
Corupedium 73 F3
Corycus 74 B3
Corycus, M. 33 A3
Corydallus, M. 34 A3, B3

Dionysopolis 143 E3
Dioscurias 15 H3
Dioscurias, Pr. 109 G5
Diospolis/Lydda 166 B4
Diospolis Magna/Thebae, Thebes 76 C4; 167 C4
Diospolis Parva 167 C4
Diospontus 177 F3
Dium [Macedonia] 30 C2; 32 C2; 72 C1; 143 D4
Dium see also Dion
Divodurum 138 B3
Dobrudja 171 E3
Dobunni 131 C7
Docimium 125 E4; 160 C3
Doclea 143 C4; 177 D3
Dodecaschoenus 167 C5
Dodona 7 A1; 30 B2; 32 B3
Dolaucothi 131 B7
Doliche [Syria] 161 G4; 162 B3
Doliche [Thessalia] 32 C2
Dolopes 7 B2, C2
Dolopia 23 B2; 30 B3; 62 B3
Domavia 143 C3
Domitiana, Via 115 B2
Domitianopolis/Sala 158 B3
Domitianus, Saltus 151 A2
Dora 74 B5; 166 B2
Dorchester-on-Thames 131 D7
Dorion 6 B4; 7 B4
Doris 30 C3; 62 B3
Doriscos 23 D1; 31 E1
Dorn 131 D7
Dorylaeum 73 H2; 160 C2
Doschi 50 D1
Doulichion 7 A2; 9 A2
Doune 130 C3
Dramesi 6 D3
Drangiana, Drangiane 65 F3, G3; 71 G3
Dravus, R. 143 B2
Drepana, Drepanum 38 A2; 97 F4; 148 A2
Drepanum, Pr. [Aegyptus] 167 C3
Drepanum, Pr. [Cyprus] 156 A5
Dreros 12 D4; 16 D4; 73 E5; 156 C2
Drobeta 143 D3
Druentia, R. 97 E1
Drumquhassle 134 A1
Drymusa 33 A3
Dubris 131 E7
Dumnonii, 131 B8
Dumnonium, Pr. 131 A8
Dunblane 130 C3
Duntocher 134 A1
Dunum 131 C8
Dura Europus 70 C3; 74 D4; 162 C4
Duria, R. 108 A2
Durius, R. 96 A2; 144 B2
Durnovaria 131 C8
Durobrivae [1, Britannia] 131 D6
Durobrivae [2, Britannia] 131 E7
Durocobrivis 131 D7
Durocornovium 131 C7

Durocortorum 128 C2; 136 C2; 138 A3; 170 C2
Duroliponte 131 E6
Durolitum 131 E7
Durostorum 143 E3; 171 E3
Durotriges 131 C8
Durovernum Cantiacorum 131 E7
Durovigutum 131 D6
Dyme 29 B1; 72 B3
Dyrrachium, Dyrrhachium 72 A1; 97 H2; 105 D2; 143 C4; 177 D3; see also Epidamnus
Dystos 29 E1; 56 C2

Easter Happrew 130 C3
Ebora 144 A3
Eburacum 131 D5; 170 B2; 176 B1
Eburodunum 136 D4; 176 C3
Ebusus 52 B4; 96 C3; 144 D3
Ecbatana/Epiphaneia 19 E3; 64 D3; 71 E3
Echetla 38 D3; 148 D3
Echinades Is. 29 B1
Echinai 7 A3
Echinos 32 D4
Echzell 140 B1
Ecnomus, M. 38 C3; 97 G4
Edessa [Macedonia] 30 C1; 32 C1; 72 C1
Edessa/Antioch [Osrhoene] 74 C3; 161 H3; 162 C3; 173 F4; 177 F4
Edetani 96 C2
Eetionea 34 B3
Egnatia, Via 105 E2; 143 D4
Egnazia (Gnathia) 84 D4; 111 G3
Egypt (Aegyptus) 76; 167
Eileithyia 4 C2
Eileithyiapolis 167 C4
Eion 23 C1; 32 E1; 44 A1
Elaea 33 B2; 73 F3
Elaea, Pr. 156 C4
Elaeus 15 G1; 27 A2; 143 E4
Elaeussa/Sebaste 161 E5
Elaiticus Sinus 33 A2, B2
Elam 19 E3
Elaphonisi 6 C5
Elate(i)a 2 B2; 30 C3; 32 D4; 62 C3
Elatos, M. 29 A2; 30 B4
Elatria 62 B3
Elea see Velia
Elefantaria 146 C3
Eleon 6 D3
Elegeia 162 C1
Elephantine 76 C5; 167 C5
Eleusis 29 D1; 30 D4; 34 A3
Eleutherna 72 D5; 156 B2
Eleutheropolis/Beth Gabra 166 B4
Eleutherus, R. [Sicilia] 148 B2
Eleutherus, R. [Syria] 162 B4
Elginhaugh 130 C3
Elimiotis 62 B2
Elis 16 B2; 29 B2; 30 B4
Ellingen 140 D3

Elslack 131 C5
Elusa 176 B3
Elymais 71 E4
Elymi 38 A2
Elyros 156 A2
Emathia 9 B1
Emborio 2 D2; 12 D2; 56 C2
Emerita Augusta 128 A4; 144 B3; 170 A4; 176 A3
Emerkingen 140 C4
Emesa 74 C4; 162 B4; 173 F4; 177 F4
Emmaus/Nicopolis 166 B4
Emona 143 A2
Emporia [Africa] 97 F5
Emporiae, Emporium 14 B3; 96 D2; 144 E1
Ems 140 A1
Engedi 166 C5
Engyum 38 D2; 148 D2
Enienes 7 A1, B1
Enkomi 2 E4
Enna, Henna 38 D3; 81; 97 G4, H5; 148 D3
Ennetach 140 C4
Enope 7 C5
Entella 38 B2; 148 B2
Eordaea 62 B2
Epeians 7 A3, B3
Ephesos/Arsinoe 16 E2; 31 F4; 33 B3; 44 C3; 73 F3; 129 E4; 158 A3; 160 A4; 171 E4; 173 E4; 177 E4
Ephyra 7 A2; 80 A2
Epiacum 133 B2
Epidamnus 14 D3; 46 A1; 72 A1; see also Dyrrachium
Epidauros 16 B3; 29 D2; 30 C4
Epidauros Limera 6 C5; 29 D3; 30 C5
Epidaurum 143 B4
Epidium, Pr. 130 B4
Epiphan(e)ia [Syria] 74 C4; 162 B3
Epiphaneia/Ecbatana, see Ecbatana
Epirus 16 A1; 30 A2; 105 D3
Epirus (Roman Province) 171 D4
Epirus Nova 177 D4
Epirus Vetus 177 D4
Eporedia 95 A1; 108 A2
Eravisci 138 F4
Ercavica 144 C2
Erchia 34 C3
Ercolano see Herculaneum
Eresos, Eressus 33 A2; 44 B2
Eretria 16 C2; 29 E1; 30 D3
Eretum 86 C1; 92 C3
Ericus(s)a 38 D1; 148 D1
Erineos 46 B3
Eriza 73 G4
Ermoucha, R. 151 B2
Erucium 146 B3
Erymanthos, M. 7 B3; 30 B4
Erythrae [Boeotia] 29 D1; 30 C3
Erythrae [Ionia] 16 D2; 31 F3; 33 A3; 44 C2
Erythraeum, Mare 54 D3, E3; 167 D3
Eryx 38 A2; 97 F4; 81; 148 A2

Erzerum 58 D1
Esdraelon, Plain of 166 B2
Eteocretans 9 D4
Ethiopia, Aethiopia 18 B5; 167 C6
Ethiopians (Asiatic) 19 G4
Etruria 82; 108 C3; 122 B1
Etrusci 84 B3
Euboea [Graecia] 29 E1; 30 D3; 32 E4
Euboea [Sicilia] 38 D3
Euboean Hollows 23 C2, 3
Eucarpia 160 C3
Euchaita 161 F2
Euhemeria 167 B2
Euhesperides 14 D5
Eulbach 140 C2
Eumeneia 73 G3; 160 C3; 173 E4
Euonymum 34 B4
Euonymus 38 E1; 148 E1
Eupalium 46 B3
Eupatoria 74 C1
Euphrates, R. 18 D3; 65 C3; 70 D3;
    161 H2, 5; 162 D4; 177 G5
Eurydiceia see Smyrna
Euripos 30 C3; 32 D4
Euromos 33 B4
Europa (Roman Province) 177 E3
Europos, R. 30 C2; 32 C3
Europus [Syria] 74 C3; 162 B3
Europus/Rhagae 65 E3; 71 E3
Eurotas, R. 29 C3; 30 C5
Eurymedon, R. 160 D4
Eurymenae 32 B3
Eusebeia see Mazaca
Eusebeia see Tyana
Eutaea 29 C2
Eutresis 2 B2; 6 C3; 7 D3
Euxinus, Pontus 50 C3; 162 B1
Ewell 131 D7
Ezion-Geber 53 G5

Fabrateria Nova 94 C2
Fabrateria Vetus 92 C3
Faesulae (Fiesole) 82 B3; 92 A2; 95
    B2; 97 F2; 108 C3; 110 C2
Fagifulae 92 D2
Faimingen 140 D4
Falacrium, Pr. 148 E1
Falerii Novi (S. Maria di Falleri) 81; 82
    C5; 84 B3; 92 B3; 108 D3; 110 D3;
    119 B3
Falerio 95 C2; 109 D3
Falernus, Ager 115 A2, B2
Falisci 84 B3
Falkirk 134 D1
Fanum Carisi 146 C4
Fanum Cocidi 133 B1
Fanum Fortunae (Fano) 84 B2; 95 C2;
    97 G2; 108 D2; 110 D2
Faustinopolis 161 E4
Faventia 82 C2; 108 C2
Fayum 76 B2; 167 B2
Febiana 140 C4
Felsina see Bononia

Feltria 108 C1
Fendoch 130 C3
Ferentinum (Ferentino) 86 D2; 92 C3;
    111 E4; 119 B3
Ferentum 108 D3
Ferraria 146 C5
Ficana 86 B2
Ficaria 146 B3
Ficulea 119 B3
Fidenae 82 D5; 86 B1; 94 B2; 108 D4;
    122 B1
Fiesole see Faesulae
Finglandrigg 133 A2
Firmum Picenum 95 C2; 109 D3
Flanona 143 A3
Flaminia 176 C3
Flaminia, Via 90 D1; 108 D3; 122 B1;
    123 B4
Flavia Caesariensis 176 B1
Flavia Solva 138 E4
Flaviobriga 144 C1
Flaviocaesarea/Daldis 158 B3; 160 B3
Flaviopolis [Cilicia] 161 F4
Flaviopolis [Thracia] 143 E4
Flaviopolis/Crate(i)a 158 D2; 160 D2
Flaviopolis/Lora 158 B3
Flaviopolis/Temenothyrae 158 B3;
    160 C3
Fleet Marston 131 D7
Florentia 95 B2; 108 C3; 119 B2
Flosis, R. 108 D3
Forden Gaer 131 C6
Forentum 92 E2
Formia, Formiae 92 D3; 109 E4; 111
    E4; 119 C4
Forum Appii 109 D4
Forum Claudii 115 A2
Forum Clodii [N. Etruria] 108 C3
Forum Clodii [S. Etruria] 108 D4; 119
    B3; 122 B1
Forum Cornelii 108 C2
Forum Fulvii Valentinum 108 B2
Forum Gallorum 104 C2
Forum Germanorum 108 A3
Forum Hadriani 138 B2
Forum Iulii [Narbonensis] 136 D5
Forum Iulii [Venetia] 108 D1
Forum Iulium 108 B2
Forum Novum 108 B2
Forum Popilii [Aemilia] 108 C2
Forum Popilii [Campania] 115 A2
Forum Sempronii 108 D2
Forum Traiani/Aquae Hypsitanae 146
    B4
Forum Vibii 108 A3
Fossae Phoeniciae 97 E5, F5
Franchthi Cave 2 B3
Francolise Villas 111 E4
Frankfurt a. M. 140 B2
Frauenberg 140 E3
Fregellae 92 D3; 94 C2; 109 E4
Fregenae 94 B2
Frentani 84 C3
Friedberg 140 B1

Friniates 84 A2
Frisii 138 B1
Frusino 92 C3
Fucinus, L. 109 D4
Fulfinium 143 A3
Fulginiae 92 B2
Fundi 92 D3; 109 E4; 119 C3

Gaba 166 B2
Gabae 71 E4
Gabala 162 B3
Gabii (Osteria dell' Osa) 86 C2; 110
    D4; 119 C1
Gabrosentum 130 C4
Gabula 162 B3
Gadara [Gaulanitis] 74 B5; 166 C2
Gadara, Gadora [Peraea] 166 C4
Gades, 52 A4; 54 A2; 96 A4; 144 B4
Galatia 70 B3; 129 F4; 158 D3; 160
    C4-161 F2; 171 F4; 177 F4
Galava 130 C4
Galepsos 32 E1; 44 A1; 46 D1
Galeria 38 D3
Galilee 166 B1, C1
Galilee, Sea of 166 C2
Gallaeci 144 A1
Gallaecia 176 A3
Gallia 136; 138
Gallia Cisalpina 102 C2
Gallia Transalpina 102 B2
Galliae (Diocese) 176 B2
Gallicum Fretum 131 E8
Gamala 166 C2
Gandara 19 H2
Ganganorum, Pr. 131 B6
Ganges, R. 54 E3
Gangra/Germanicopolis, 74 B1; 161
    E2; 173 F3; 177 F3
Ganos 62 E2
Garamantes 151 E2, F2
Garganus, Pr. 109 F3
Gariannum 131 E6
Gariannus, R. 131 E6
Gaudos 97 G4
Gaugamela 64 C3; 68 (Battle)
Gaul 136, 138
Gaulanitis 166 D1, 2
Gaulus 148 A4
Gauraina 161 G3
Gaurion 31 D4
Gavdhos 4 B3; 156 A2
Gaza 64 B3; 74 B5; 166 A5; 173 F5
Gazara 166 B4
Gedrosia 19 G4; 54 D3; 65 G4; 71 G4
Geislingen am Rhein 140 B4
Gela 14 A2; 38 D3
Gela, Gelas , R. 38 D3, 4; 148 D3
Gelligaer 131 C7
Gemellae [Africa] 154 B1
Gemellae [Sardinia] 146 C3
Gemelli Colles 148 C3
Genava 136 C4
Genèvre, Mont 97 E1

Genoni 97 F3
Genua 97 F1; 108 B3
Georgikon 6 B1
Geraestos 29 E1
Geraistos, C. 9 C3
Gerania 30 C4
Gerasa 74 B5; 166 D3; 167 D2
Gerizim, M. 133
Germa 158 D2; 160 D2
Germania 176 C2
Germania Inferior 128 B2; 136 C2; 138
  B2; 170 C2
Germania Magna 136 D1; 138 C2
Germania Superior 128 C3; 136 D3;
  138 B4; 140 B4; 170 C3
Germanic(e)ia 161 G4; 162 B2
Germanicopolis 160 D5
Germanicopolis see also Gangra
Germanicum 140 E3
Germanicum Mare 138 A1
Germanicus Oceanus 130 D3, 4
Gernsheim 140 B2
Geronthrai 29 C3
Gerunda 144 E1
Gerunium 97 G2
Gesoriacum 136 B2; 138 A2
Getae 62 E1
Ghadames 154 C2
Gheria-el-Garbia 154 C2
Gigia 144 B1
Gigthis 150 C6
Gindarus 74 C3; 162 B3
Girba 150 C5
Gischala 166 C1
Gitane 32 A3
Gla 6 C2; 56 B2
Glannoventa 130 C4
Glanum 136 C4
Glasgow Bridge 134 B2
Glaucus, R. 162 C1
Glemona 108 C1
Glenlochar 130 B4
Glevum 131 C7
Glycys Limen 32 A3
Gnathia (Egnazia) 84 D4; 111 G3
Gnotzheim 140 D3
Gobannium 131 C7
Golgi 156 C5
Gomadingen 140 C4
Gomphoi 30 B2; 32 C3; 72 B2
Gonnos 12 B1; 30 C2; 32 C3
Gophna 166 B4
Gorbeus 160 D2
Gorditanum, Pr. 146 B3
Gordium 64 B2; 74 A2; 160 D2
Gordyene 162 D2
Gorgippia 50 D2
Gorneae 162 D1
Gortyn(a) 9 C4; 16 C4; 56 C4; 73 D6;
  129 E5; 156 B2; 171 E5; 173 E4;
  177 E4
Gournia 4 D2
Grabaei 62 A1
Graccurris 96 C2; 144 C1

Graiae et Poeninae, Alpes 136 D3,
  4; 176 C3
Granianum, Pr. 146 C2
Granicos, R. 27 C2; 31 F1; 64 A2; 67
  (Battle); 160 A2
Gravisca(e) 52 D3; 82 C5; 84 B3; 94
  A1; 110 D3
Great Casterton 131 D6
Great Chesterford 131 E7
Great Dunmow 131 E7
Great St. Bernard 97 E1
Greta Bridge 130 D4
Grimenothyrae/Traianopolis 158 B3
Grinario 140 C4
Gr.-Gerau 140 B2
Gr.-Krotzenburg 140 B2
Grotta 2 C3; 10 C3
Grumentum 94 E4; 97 G3; 109 F4
Gryneion 33 B2
Gubbio see Iguvium
Gulf Is. 19 F5
Guntia 140 D4
Gunugu 150 C1
Gunzenhausen 140 D3
Gurulis Nova 146 B4
Gurulis Vetus 146 B4
Gyaros 31 D4
Gygaian, L. 9 D2
Gymnesiae (Baleares) Is. 96 D3; 144
  E2
Gymnias 58 D1
Gyrton(e) 7 C1; 46 C2
Gytheion 29 C3; 30 C5; 72 B4

Habitancum 133 C1
Hadranum see Adranum
Hadria 94 D1; 109 E3
Hadriana, Via 167 C3
Hadrianeia 160 B3
Hadriani Murus 130 C4, D4; 133
  (Plan)
Hadrianopolis [Lycaonia] 160 D2
Hadrianopolis [Thracia] 143 E4; 177
  E3
Hadrianutherae 160 B2
Hadrumetum 97 F4; 150 C4; 151 E1;
  176 C4
Haemimontus 177 E3
Haemus, M. 62 D1; 143 E3
Haerae 44 C3
Hafa 146 B4
Hagnus 34 C4
Hainstadt 140 B2
Halae 32 D4
Halae Aexonides 34 C4
Halae Araphenides 34 D3
Halaesa 38 D2; 148 D2
Halheim 140 D3
Haliacmon, R. 2 B1; 30 B2, C1; 32 C2;
  62 B2
Haliartos 6 C3; 7 C3; 29 D1
Halicarnassos 16 E3; 31 G5; 33 B4; 36
  (Plan); 44 C3; 73 F4; 158 A4; 160
  B4

Halicyae 148 B2
Halieis 29 D2; 46 C4
Halimus 34 B4
Halonnesos 31 E2; 62 D2
Halos 32 D4
Haltwhistle Burn 133 B1
Haluntium 148 D2
Halus 23 B2; 62 C3
Halycus, R. 38 B3; 148 C3
Halys, R. 18 C2; 58 C1; 74 B2; 161 E2,
  F2
Hamaxitus 47 E2
Hamworthy 131 C8
Hanau-Kesselstadt 140 B2
Hardham 131 D8
Harpagium 47 F1
Harpasos, R. 58 D1
Hassocks 131 D8
Hasta 108 A2
Hatra 162 D3
Hayton 131 D5
Heba 82 B5; 94 A1; 108 C3
Hebron 166 B5
Hebros, R. 31 F1; 62 D1; 143 E4
Hecale 34 C2
Hecatompylus 65 E3; 71 F3
Hecatonnesi 33 A2
Heddesdorf 140 A1
Heftrich 140 B1
Heidekringen 140 B2
Heidelberg 140 B3
Heilbronn-Böckingen 140 C3
Heircte, M. 38 B2; 97 G5
Heldenbergen 140 B1
Helice 29 C1
Heliopolis [Aegyptus] 76 B1; 167 B2
Heliopolis [Syria] 162 B4
Hellas 7 C2
Hellespont(os) 27; 31 F2; 33 A1
Hellespontus (Roman Province) 177
  E4
Helorus 14 B2; 38 E4; 97 H6; 148 E4
Helorus, R. 38 E4; 148 E4
Helos 7 C5; 29 C3
Helvetii 136 D3; 138 B4
Hemeroscopeum 96 C3
Henchir Mettich 151 B2
Heniochi 162 C1, D1
Henna see Enna
Hephaestia 31 E2; 44 B1
Heptanomia 167 B2
Heracleia [Caria] 56 D3; 160 B4
Heracleia, Heraclea (Policoro)
  [Lucania] 97 H3; 109 F4; 111 G4
Heracle(i)a [Lyncestis] 30 B1; 32 B1;
  62 B2; 143 C4
Heracleia [Thracia] 143 D4
Heraclea Minoa 38 B3; 97 G4, 5; 148
  B3
Heraclea (Pontica) 15 F3; 50 A4; 74
  A1; 158 D1; 160 D1
Heraclea (Trachinia) 32 C4; 46 C3; 72
  C3
Heraclea/Pleistarcheia 73 F4

Heracleia *see* Perinthus
Heracleion 30 C2
Heracleopolis (Magna) 76 B2; 167 B2
Heraea 72 B4
Heraei, M. 38 D4; 148 D4
Heraeum (Argos) 12 B3
Heraeum, Heraion [Samos] 2 D3; 10 D3
Heraeum (Cymbe) 148 D4
Heraion Teichos 62 E1
Herat/Alexandria (Areia) 65 F3; 71 G3
Herbessus [1, Sicilia] 38 B3; 97 G5
Herbessus [2, Sicilia] 38 D4
Herbita 38 D2
Herculaneum (Ercolano) 111 H1; 115 C2; 118 (Plan)
Hercules Musinus (Shrine) 86 B1
Herculeum, Pr. 109 G6
Herculis, Pr. 131 B7
Herdonia(e) (Ordona) 92 E2; 97 G2; 109 F4; 111 F3
Hermaeum, Pr. [Africa] 97 F4
Hermaeum, Pr. [Sardinia] 146 B4
Herminius, M. 144 A2
Hermione 7 D4; 23 B3; 29 D2
Hermonassa 50 D2
Hermonthis 76 C4; 167 C4
Hermopolis 76 C1
Hermopolis (Magna) 76 B3; 167 B3; 173 F5
Hermopolis (Parva) 76 B1; 167 B1
Hermos, R. 9 D2; 16 E2; 31 G3; 33 C2; 158 A3; 160 A3
Hernici 84 B3
Herodion 166 B4
Heroopolis 76 C1; 167 C1
Heroopoliticus, Sinus 167 C2
Heshbon 166 D4
Hesselbach 140 C2
Hestiaea *see* Histiaea
Hexalophos 6 B1
Hibernia 130 A4
Hibernicus Oceanus 131 A5
Hibis 167 B4
Hiera 38 A2
Hiera Hephaesti Insula/Vulcani(a) 38 D1; 148 E1
Hieracopolis 167 C4
Hierapolis [Asia] 160 B4; 173 E4
Hierapolis/Bambyce 74 C3; 161 G5; 162 B3; 177 F4
Hierapolis/Castabala 74 B3; 161 F4
Hierapytna 73 E6; 156 C2
Hierasus, R. 143 E2
Hierasycaminus 167 C5
Hieron Oros 62 E2
Hieropolis 73 G3
Hierosolyma *see* Jerusalem
Himera 14 A2; 38 C2
Himera, R. [N. Sicily] 38 C2; 148 C2
Himera, R. [S. Sicily] 38 C3; 97 G5; 148 C3
Hippana 38 B2; 148 B2

Hipparis, R. 38 D4; 148 D4
Hippo Diarrhytus (Acra) 97 F4; 150 C3
Hippo Regius 97 E4; 150 B3, D1
Hipponium/Vibo Valentia 14 B1; 84 D5; 94 A4; 109 G5; 111 G5; 119 D5
Hippus/Antioch 74 B4
Hirminus, R. 148 D4
Hirpini 84 C4
Hispalis 104 A3; 144 B3
Hispania Citerior 96 B3, C3; 102 A2, B2
Hispania Ulterior 96 B3; 102 A3
Hispaniae (Diocese) 176 A3
Hispellum (Spello) 95 C2; 108 D3; 110 D3
Histiaea, Hestiaea/Oreus 9 B2; 30 C3; 32 D4; 44 A2; 72 C3
Histonium 109 E3
Histri 84 C1
Histria 108 D1; 138 D4; 176 C3
Histria/Istrus 15 F3; 143 E2
Hod Hill 131 C8
Hofheim a. Ts. 140 B2
Holzhausen 140 B1
Horncastle 131 D6
Horreum Margi 143 C3
Hostilia 108 C2
Hunzel 140 A1
Hyampolis 7 C2
Hybla 148 D4
Hybla Geleatis 38 D3
Hyccara 38 B2; 148 B2
Hydaspes, R. 65 H3; 69 (Battle)
Hyde 9 D2
Hydissus 44 C3
Hydraotes, R. 65 H3
Hydrea 29 D2
Hyllos, R. 9 D2
Hymettus, M. 34 C3
Hypanis, R. 15 F2; 50 B1
Hypata 32 C4
Hyperesia 7 C3
Hyphasis, R. 65 H3
Hypsa(s), R. 38 B2; 148 B3
Hypselis 167 B3
Hyrcania [ad Caspium Mare] 19 E3, F3; 65 E2; 71 E3
Hyrcania [Palaestina] 166 C4
Hyrcanis 73 F3
Hyrgales 158 B3, C3
Hyrie 7 D3
Hyrtakina 156 A2
Hysiai 16 B3
Hyssus, R. 162 C1
Hytenneis 18 B2

Iaca 144 D1
Iader 97 G2; 143 A4
Iaitas, Ietas 38 B2; 148 B2
Ialysos 2 E3; 9 E3; 10 E3; 12 E3; 16 E3; 33 C5; 44 C4
Iamo 144 E2

Iapudes 104 D2
Iapyges 84 D4
Iapygium, Pr. 109 G4
Iasos 2 E2; 33 B4; 44 C3; 47 F4; 73 F4
Iazyges 138 E4, F4; 171 D3
Iberi 162 D1
Ibericum Mare 144 C4, D4
Iberus, R. 96 C2; 144 D2
Icaria, Icaros 31 F4; 33 A4; 60 D3
Icarium 34 C2
Icarus [Persian Gulf] 71 E4
Iceni 131 E6
Ichnae 74 C3; 162 C3
Ichthyophagi 167 D4
Ichthys, Pr. 29 B2
Iconium, Ikonion 58 B2; 74 A2; 158 D4; 160 D4; 173 F4
Icos 32 E3; 60 C2
Icosium 96 D4; 150 C1
Ida, M. [Creta] 4 C2; 80 C4; 156 B2
Ida, M. [Troas] 9 D2; 31 F2; 33 A1
Idaean Cave 4 C2; 12 C4; 156 B2
Idalium 156 B5
Idomene 46 B2
Idubeda, M. 144 C2
Idumaea 166 B5
Idyma 44 D3; 160 B4
Iesso 144 D2
Ietas *see* Iaitas
Igaeditani 144 A2
Igilium 82 B5; 108 C4
Iguvium (Gubbio) 84 B2; 92 B2; 108 D3; 110 D3
Ikonion *see* Iconium
Ilerda 104 B2; 144 D2
Ilergavones 144 D2
Ilergetes 96 C2; 144 D1
Iliberis 96 D2
Iliberris 144 C4; 172 A4
Ilici 96 C3; 144 D3
Ilienses 146 C4
Ilion, Ilium 27 A2; 31 F2; 33 A1; 158 A2; 160 A2; *see also* Troy
Ilipa 96 A3; 144 B3
Iliturgi [Hispania Citerior] 96 C3
Iliturgi [Hispania Ulterior] 96 B3
Illyricum 102 C2; 105 D2
Ilorci 96 C3
Iluro 144 E2
Ilva 82 A4; 108 C4
Ilyratum 50 C2
Imachara 148 D3
Imbros 27 A2; 31 E2; 33 A1; 44 B1
Inatos 4 D3; 156 C2
India 19 H4; 54 E3; 65 H3
Indus, R. [India] 19 H3, 4; 54 E2; 65 H4
Indus, R. [Lycia] 158 B4; 160 B4
Industria 108 A2; 119 A2
Ineravon 134 D1
Inessa 38 D3
Infer(n)um/Tyrrhenum Mare 107; 108 B4, C4
Ingauni 84 A2

160 B4; 173 E4; 177 E4
Laodice(i)a Catacecaumene
  (Combusta) 74 A2; 160 D4
Laodicea *see also* Berytus
Lapethus 156 B4
Lappa 156 B2
Laranda 161 E4; 173 F4
Larinum 84 C3; 92 D2; 109 E3
Larisa [Troas] 9 C2
Larissa [Ionia] 56 D2
Larissa [Mesopotamia] 58 E2
Larissa [Syria] 74 C4; 162 B3
Larissa [Thessalia] 23 B2; 30 C2; 32
  C3; 62 B2; 177 D4
Larissa Cremaste 32 D4
Larius, L. 108 B1
Las *see* La(a)s
Lata, Via 90 C2; 121 B1; 123 C3
Latina, Via 90 C4; 115 A1; 122 C2
Latini 84 B3
Latium 86; 109 D4; 122 B2, C2
Latmos, M. 31 G4; 33 B4
Latmus 44 C3
Lato 56 C4; 156 C2
Latopolis 76 C4; 167 C4
Laurentium, Vicus Augustanus 122 B2
Lauriacum 138 D4; 170 D3
Laurium 34 D5
Lauro 144 D2
Laus 14 B1
Laus Pompeia 108 B2
Lautlingen 140 B4
Lautulae 92 D3
Lavatris 130 C4
Lavinium 86 B2; 92 C3; 110 D4; 122 B2
Lease Rigg 131 D5
Lebade(i)a 29 C1; 62 C3; 80 B2
Lebedos/Ptolemais 33 B3; 44 C3; 73 F3
Lebena 2 C4; 4 C3; 80 C4
Lecce *see* Lupiae
Lechaeon 29 D2
Lecton, Pr. 33 A1
Lefkandi 2 C2; 6 D3; 10 C2; 56 B2
Legio VII Gemina 144 B1; 170 A3
Lelantine Plain 16 C2
Lemesus (Nemesus, Neapolis) 156 B6
Lemnos 31 E2; 44 B1
Leon 38 E4
Leontini 14 B2; 38 E3; 97 H5; 148 E3
Leontion 29 C1
Leontopolis [1, Aegyptus] 76 B1; 167
  B1
Leontopolis [2, Aegyptus] 76 B1; 167
  B2; 177 F5
Lepcis Magna 97 G6; 124 C5; 151 F2;
  153 (Plan); 154 D2; 176 C5
Lepcis Minor 97 F4
Lepreon, Lepreum 23 B3; 29 B2; 46
  B3
Leptis 104 C3
Lerna 2 B3; 29 C2; 30 C4; 56 B3
Leros 33 B4; 60 D3
Lesbos 16 D1; 31 F2; 33 A2; 160 A3
Letocetum 131 C6

Letopolis 76 B1; 167 B2
Leucarum 131 B7
Leucas, Leukas 2 A2; 23 A2; 30 A3; 32
  A4, B4
Leucate, Pr. 29 A1; 32 A4
Leuce 27 C1
Leuce Is. 50 A2
Leuci 138 B3
Leucimme 46 A2
Leucimme, Pr. 32 A3
Leucolla 156 C5
Leucomagus 131 D7
Leuconium 47 E3
Leuconoe 34 B3
Leucos Limen 167 D4
Leucosia 156 B5
Leucovia 130 B4
Leuctra 29 D1; 30 C4; 59 (Battle)
Libanus, M. 162 B4
Libarna 108 B2
Libisosa 144 C3
Liburnia 143 A3, B3
Libya 18 A3
Libya Inferior 177 E5
Libya Superior 177 D5
Libycum Mare 38 B3; 148 B4
Licca, R. 140 D4
Ligures 84 A2
Ligures Baebiani 119 C3
Liguria 108 A3; 176 C3
Ligusticum Mare 107
Ligusticus Sinus 108 B3
Lilaea 32 C4; 72 C3
Lilybaeum 38 A2; 97 F4, G5; 148 A2
Limenia 156 A5
Limes (Africa) 154
Limes (Rhine/Danube) 140
Limnae 15 G1; 27 A1
Limonum 136 B3
Lindinis 131 C7
Lindos 9 D4; 10 E4; 12 E4; 16 E4; 33
  C6; 44 C4
Lindum 128 B2; 131 D6; 176 B1
Lingones [Gallia] 136 C3; 138 B4
Lingones [Italia] 84 B2
Lipadusa 148 A4
Lipara 14 B2; 38 D1; 97 G3; 148 D1
Liparaeae Is. 38 D1; 97 G3
Lipsydrium 34 B2
Liris, R. 109 D4, E4; 115 A1
Lissos [Creta] 156 A2
Lissus [Dalmatia] 97 H2; 105 D2; 143
  C4
Liternum (Literno) 94 C3; 111 G1; 115
  B2
Little St. Bernard 97 E1
Livias-Julias/Betharamatha 166 C4
Lixus 52 A4; 96 A4; 150 A1
Llandovery 131 B7
Llanfor 131 C6
Locra, R. 146 B2
Locri (Epizephyrii) 14 B2; 84 D5; 97
  G4; 109 G5; 111 G5; 119 D5
Locris 23 B2; 30 C3

Locris, East 16 B2; 62 C3
Locris, West 16 B2; 62 B3
Londinium (Augusta) 124 B2; 128 B2;
  137 D7; 170 B2; 176 B2
Long Melford 131 E7
Long Preston 131 C5
Long Walls (Athens) 34 B3
Longanus, R. 38 E2
Longaricum 148 B2
Longovicium 133 D2
Longthorpe 131 D6
Lopodunum 138 C3; 140 B2
Lopsica 143 A3
Lora/Flaviopolis 158 B3
Lorch 140 C3
Lorium 122 B1
Loryma 47 F4
Losodica 140 D3
Loudoun Hill 130 B3
Lousoi 12 B3
Lousonna 138 B4
Low Borrow Bridge 130 C4
Loxa, R. 130 C2
Luca 95 B2; 108 C3
Lucani 84 C4
Lucania 109 F4; 176 D4
Lucentum 144 D3
Luceria 84 C3; 94 E2; 97 G2; 109 E4
Lucus Augusti 144 A1
Lucus Deae Diae 122 B2
Lucus Feroniae 82 D5; 86 C1; 94 B2;
  108 D4; 119 B3; 122 C1
Luentinum 131 B7
Lützelbach, 140 C2
Lugdunensis 128 B3; 136 B3; 138 A3,
  4; 170 B3; 176 B2, C2
Lugdunum 128 C3; 136 C4; 138 A4;
  170 C3; 172 C3; 176 C3
Lugudunum 131 D7
Luguido 146 C3
Luguvalium 133 A2
Luna (Luni) 89 (Plan); 95 B2; 108 B3;
  110 B3
Lupia, R. 138 C2
Lupiae (Lecce) 84 D4; 109 G4;
  111 H4
Lurinum 146 C1
Lusitani 104 A2
Lusitania 128 A4; 144 A2, B2; 170 A4;
  176 A3
Lutetia Parisiorum (Paris) 135 (Plan);
  136 B3; 138 A3
Lycaeum, M. 80 B3
Lycaonia 18 B2; 161 E4
Lychnidos 72 B1; 143 C4
Lychnitis, L. [Armenia] 162 D1
Lychnitis, L. [Macedonia] 30 A1; 32
  A1, B1; 62 B2
Lycia 18 B2; 129 E4; 158 B4; 160 C5;
  171 E4; 177 E4, F4
Lycians, Lycioi 9 E3; 44 D4
Lycopolis 76 B3; 167 B3
Lycos, R. [Aeolis] 31 G3; 33 B2
Lycosura 29 C2; 56 B3

162 C3
Mesopotamia (Roman Province) 177 G4
Mesopotamium 148 D4
Mespila 58 E2
Messana/Zancle 14 B2; 38 E2; 97 G4; 148 E2
Messapii 84 D4
Messene 29 B3; 30 B5; 62 B4
Messenia 16 B3; 30 B5
Messeniacus Sinus 29 C3
Metagonium, Pr. 96 B4
Metalla 146 B5
Metallifere, Colline 82 B4
Metapontum 14 B1; 84 D4; 97 H3; 109 F4; 111 G4
Metaris Aestuarium 131 E6
Metaurus 14 B2
Metaurus, R. 97 F2; 108 D2
Metchley 131 C6
Metellinum 144 B3
Methana 29 D2; 46 C4; 72 C4
Methone [Macedonia] 15 F1; 30 C1; 32 C2; 44 A1
Methone [Messenia] 29 B3; 30 B5
Methone [Thessalia] 32 D3
Methydrium 46 C4
Methymna 16 D1; 31 F2; 33 A2; 44 C2
Metulum 104 D2; 143 A3
Mevania 92 B2
Midea 6 C3
Milatos, Miletos [Creta] 156 C2
Miletos [Ionia] 16 E3; 31 F4; 33 B4; 37 (Plan); 44 C3; 158 A4; 160 A4
Milev 150 D1; 172 B4
Militana, Numidia 176 B4, C4
Miltenberg-Altstadt 140 C2
Miltenberg-Ost 140 C2
Milton 130 C4
Milyai 18 B2
Mimas, M. 9 D2; 33 A3
Mincius, R. 108 C2
Minervium 94 A4
Minturnae 92 D3; 94 C3; 109 E4; 111 E4; 115 A2
Mirobriga [Baetica] 144 B3
Mirobriga [Lusitania] 144 B2
Misenum 109 E4; 115 B3
Mistea 160 D4
Moab 166 C5
Mochlos 2 D4; 4 E2
Modiana 167 D3
Modiin 166 B4
Modrene 160 D2
Moenus, R. 138 C3
Moeris, L. 167 B2
Moesia (Diocese) 177 D4
Moesia (Roman Province) 129 D4
Moesia Inferior 143 E3; 171 E3, 4; 177 E3
Moesia Superior 143 C3; 171 D3
Moesia Superior Margensis 177 D3
Mogentiana 143 B2
Mogontiacum, Moguntiacum 128 C2;

136 D2; 138 C3; 140 B2; 170 C2; 176 C2
Molaria 146 B4
Mollins 134 B2
Molossian Kingdom 62 B2
Molossis 30 A2; 60 A2
Mona 131 B5
Monastiraki 4 C2
Monoeci Portus 108 A3
Monte Cavo 86 C2
Monte Giove 95 C2
Monteriggioni 82 B3
Monti Sirai 97 E3
Mopsuestia 74 B3; 161 F4
Morae, R. 146 B2
Morbium 130 D4
Morgantina 38 D3; 97 H5; 148 D3
Moricambe Aestuarium 131 C5
Moridunum 131 B7
Morini 138 A2
Mosa, R. 138 B2
Moschi 18 D2; 162 C1
Mosella, R. 138 B3; 140 A2
Mossynoeci 18 C2; 58 D1
Motya 38 A2
Motyum 38 C3
Moxeani 158 C3
Müskebi 2 D3
Mulucha, R. 150 B2
Mumrills 134 D1
Munda 104 A3; 144 B3
Munichia 34 B4
Municipium Augustum Veiens see Veii
Municipium Iasorum 143 B2
Munigua 144 B3
Murgi 144 C4
Murlo 82 C4; 84 B3
Murrhardt 140 C3
Mursa 143 B2
Mursella 143 B2
Muş 58 D2
Muthul, R. 150 B4
Mutina 95 B1; 108 C2
Mutyca 148 D4
Mycale, Mykale, M. 9 D3; 23 D3; 31 F4; 33 B4
Mycalessus 46 C3
Mycenae 5 (Plan); 6 C3; 29 C2
Myconos 31 E4; 44 B3
Mygdonia 23 B1; 46 C1
Mygdonis, R. 162 C2, 3
Mylae 14 B2; 38 E2; 97 G4; 148 E2
Mylasa 33 B4; 44 C3; 73 F4; 158 A4; 160 B4
Myndos 33 B4
Myonnesos 33 B3; 73 E3
Myra 129 E5; 160 C5; 171 E5; 177 E4
Myrcinus 46 D1
Myriandros 58 C2
Myrina [Aeolis] 44 C2; 73 F3
Myrina [Lemnos] 31 E2; 44 B1
Myrle(i)a/Apamea 73 F1; 158 B2; 160 B2

Myrmecium 50 C2
Myrrhinus 34 D4
Myrsinochori 6 B4
Myrtilis 144 A3
Myrtos 2 D4; 4 D3
Myrtoum Mare 29 D3; 30 C5, D5
Mysia 16 E1; 18 B2; 31 G2; 160 A2, B2
Mysians 9 D1
Mytilene 16 D2; 31 F3; 33 A2; 44 C2; 158 A2; 160 A3
Myus 33 B4; 44 C3
Myus Hormus 76 D2; 167 C3
Myxorrouma 4 B2

Nabataea 129 F5
Nabataei 162 B4, 5; 167 D2
Nacoleia 160 C3
Nacrasa 73 F2
Naissus 143 C3
Nanstallon 131 B8
Naples see Neapolis
Napoca 143 D2
Naraggara 97 E4
Narbo (Martius) 128 B3; 136 C5; 170 B3
Narbonensis 128 B3, C3; 136 C4; 170 B3, C3; 176 B3, C3
Narce 82 D5
Narnia 94 B1; 108 D3
Narona 143 B3
Narthacion 32 C4
Nasamones 151 G2
Natiso, R. 108 D1
Naucratis 15 F5; 53 G5; 76 B1; 167 B1
Naulochus 104 D3
Naupactus 16 B2; 29 B1; 30 B3
Nauplion 29 D2
Naustathmus, Pr. 148 E4
Nautaca 65 G2
Navio 131 D5
Naxos [Cyclades] 16 D3; 31 E5; 44 B3
Naxos [Sicilia] 14 B2; 38 E2; 148 E2
Nazareth 166 B2
Nazianzus 161 E3
Nea Makri 2 C2
Nea Nikomedia 2 B1
Neapolis (Naples) 14 A1; 92 D3; 97 G3; 109 E4; 111 H1; 115 B2; 119 C4
Neapolis (Nemesus, Lemesus) 156 B6
Neapolis [Africa] 97 F4; 150 D3
Neapolis [Mesopotamia] 70 D3
Neapolis [Palaestina] 166 B3
Neapolis [Propontis] 44 C1
Neapolis [Sardinia] 146 B5
Neapolis [Thracia] 15 F1; 31 D1; 32 E1
Neatham 131 D7
Nebrodes, M. 38 D2
Nechesia 167 D4
Neckarburken 140 C3
Nedinum 143 A4
Nemausus 136 C4; 176 B3
Nemea 12 B3; 29 C2; 30 C4
Nemesus (Lemesus, Neapolis) 156 B6

Nemetostatio 131 B8
Nemus Dianae 86 C2; 122 C2
Neocaesarea 162 B1; 173 F3; 177 F3
Nepet(e) 82 C5; 94 B1; 119 B3
Nepheris 97 F4
Nepta 154 B2
Neptunia 94 A3
Neptunius, M. 148 E2
Neronianus, Saltus 151 B1
Nertobriga 144 C2
Nervii 138 A2
Nesactium 108 D1
Nestos, R. 31 D1; 32 F1; 62 C1; 143 D4
Ne(e)tum 38 E4; 148 E4
Nether Denton 133 B2
Neuburg 140 D4
Neuenheim 140 B3
Neviodunum 143 A2
Newbrough 133 C1
Newton-on-Trent 131 D6
Nicaea [Bithynia] 73 G1; 158 C2; 160 C2; 173 E4
Nicaea [Gallia] 14 B3
Nicaea [India] 65 H3
Nicaea [Locris] 32 C4; 62 C3
Nicephorium 74 C3; 162 C3
Nicer, R. 138 C3; 140 C3
Nichoria 6 B4; 10 B3
Nicomed(e)ia 73 G1; 129 E4; 158 C1; 160 C2; 171 E4; 173 E3; 177 E3
Niconium 50 A1
Nicopolis [Aegyptus] 129 E5; 171 E5
Nicopolis [Armenia Minor] 105 F2; 161 G2; 162 B1
Nicopolis [Epirus] 56 A2; 171 D4; 177 D4
Nicopolis [Syria] 161 G4; 162 B3
Nicopolis ad Istrum 143 D3
Nicopolis ad Nestum 143 D4
Nicopolis/Emmaus 166 B4
Nida 140 B2
Nidri 2 A2
Nidum 131 B7
Niederberg 140 A1
Niederbieber 140 A1
Niedernberg 140 C2
Niger, R. 54 B3
Nilopolis 173 F5
Nilus, R. 76 C5; 167 C5
Niniveh (Ninus) 162 D3
Niphates, M. 162 C2, D2
Nirou Khani 4 D2
Nisaea 29 D1
Nisibis/Antioch 74 D3; 162 C3
Nisyros 9 D3; 33 B5; 44 C4
Nola 92 E3; 94 D3; 97 G3; 109 E4; 115 C2
Nomentana, Via 122 C1; 123 A3
Nomentum 92 C3; 119 B3; 122 C1
Nora 97 F3; 146 C5
Norba [Latium] 94 B2
Norba [Lusitania] 144 B3
Norchia 82 C5
Norici 138 D4

Noricum 128 C3, D3; 138 D4; 170 C3, D3
Noricum Mediterraneum 176 C3
Noricum Ripense 176 D2
Norium, Pr. 144 A1
Notion 33 B3; 47 F3
Nova Traiana, Via 162 A5
Novae 129 E3; 143 B4; 171 E3
Novaesium 128 C2; 138 B2
Novantae 130 B4
Novantarum, Pr. 130 B4
Novaria 108 A2
Novem Populi 176 B3
Novilara 84 B2
Noviodunum Equestrium 136 C3
Noviomagus [Batavorum] 138 B2
Noviomagus [Cantiacorum] 131 E7
Noviomagus [ad Mosellam] 140 A2
Noviomagus [ad Rhenum] 138 C3; 140 B3
Noviomagus Reginorum 131 D8
Novius, R. 130 B4
Nuceria (Alfaterna) 92 E3; 94 D3; 97 G3; 109 E4; 115 C2
Numana 84 C2
Numantia 96 C2; 144 C2
Numerus Syrorum 154 A1
Numidia 97 E4; 128 B5; 150 D1; 170 B5, C5
Numidia Cirtensis 176 B4
Numidia Militana 176 B4, C4
Nuntia 146 C1
Nure 146 B3
Nursia 92 B2
Nymphaei Portus 146 B4
Nymphaeum 50 C2
Nymphaeum, Pr. 32 E2
Nysa 73 F3
Nyssa 161 E3

Oa 34 C3
Oanis, R. 38 D4
Oasis Magna 167 A4, B4
Oasis Minor 167 A1
Oberflorstad 140 B1
Obernburg 140 C2
Oberscheidental 140 C2
Oberstimm 140 E4
Obulco 144 B3
Occaraba 162 B4
Ocelum, Pr. 131 E5
Ocelumduri 144 B2
Ochrid, L. 62 B2
Ocriculum 92 B3; 108 D3
Ocrinum, Pr. 131 A8
Octapitarum, Pr. 131 B7
Octodurum 176 C3
Odenwald 140 C2, 3
Odessus 15 F3; 143 E3
Odysseum, Pr. 148 E4
Oe 34 B3
Oea [Africa] 97 F5; 151 E2
Oea [Thera] 31 E5

Oeasso 144 C1
Öhringen 140 C3
Oeneon 46 B3
Oeniadae 29 B1; 46 B3; 56 A2
Oenoanda 73 G4; 160 C5
Oenoe [N.E. Attica] 34 D2
Oenoe [N.W. Attica] 34 A2
Oenoe [Corinthia] 29 D1
Oenoe, Oine [Icaros] 33 A4; 44 B3; 60 D3
Oenophyta 29 D1
Oenotri 84 C4
Oenussae Is. 29 B3
Oescus 129 E3; 143 D3
Oesyme 32 E1; 46 D1
Oetylos 7 C5; 29 C3
Offenburg 140 A4
Oglasa 108 C4
Oine see Oenoe
Oisyme 15 F1
Oitylos see Oetylos
Okarben 140 B1
Okehampton 131 B8
Olba 74 B3; 161 C5
Olbasa 158 C4; 160 C4
Olbia [Gallia] 14 B3
Olbia [Pontus Euxinus] 15 F2; 50 B1
Olbia [Sardinia] 97 F3; 146 C3
Olcades 144 C2, 3
Olcinium 143 C4
Old Carlisle 133 A2
Old Church 133 B2
Old Kilpatrick 134 A1
Olenacum 131 C5
Olenos 29 B1
Olgassys, M. 161 E1
Oliaros 31 E5
Olizon 7 D2; 32 D3
Ollius, R. 108 B2
Oloosson 7 B1; 23 B1; 32 C3
Olophyxus 44 A1
Olous 12 D4; 156 C2
Olpae 32 B4; 46 B3
Olympene 158 B2
Olympia 16 B3; 29 B2; 30 B4; 41 (Plan)
Olympus [Lycia] 160 C5
Olympus, M. [Bithynia] 160 C2
Olympus, M. [1, Cyprus] 156 B5
Olympus, M. [2, Cyprus] 156 D4
Olympos, M. [Ionia] 31 F3; 33 B3
Olympos, M. [Macedonia] 30 C2; 32 C3
Olynthos 23 B1; 30 C1; 32 D2; 44 A1
Ombi 167 C4
Ombi, Ombos 76 C4; 167 C5
Omphace 38 C3
Onchestos 7 C3
Onnum 133 C1
Onoba 144 A4
Onugnathos, Pr. 29 D4
Ophis, R. 162 C1
Ophiussa 144 D3
Opie 140 D3

Opini 146 C2
Opinum 146 C2
Opis 58 B4, E3; 64 D3
Opitergium 108 C1
Oplontis (Torre Annunziata) 111 H1
Opoeis 7 C2
Opous, Opus 16 B2; 23 B2; 29 D1; 32 D4
Oppidum Novum 154 A1
Opus, Pr. 29 C1
Orbetello 82 B5
Orca 54 B2
Orchoi/Uruk 70 D4
Orchomenos [Boeotia] 2 B2; 29 D1; 30 C3; 32 D4
Orchomenos [Peloponnesus] 7 C4; 16 B2; 29 C2; 30 C4
Orcistus 160 D3
Ordessus 50 A1
Ordona see Herdonia(e)
Ordovices 131 B6
Oreitae 65 G4
Orestis 62 B2
Oretana, Iuga 144 B3
Oretani 96 B3; 144 B3
Oretum 144 C3
Oreus see Histiaea
Orgus, R. 108 A2
Oricum, Oricus 72 A1; 97 H3; 105 D3
Oriens (Diocese) 177 F5
Orisa 162 B4
Orneae, Orneai 7 C4; 46 C4
Orolaunum 138 B3
Orongis 96 B3
Orontes, R. 74 B4; 161 F5; 162 B3
Oropia 34 B1
Oropos 29 E1; 30 D3; 34 C1
Orospeda, M. 144 C3
Orthosia 162 B4
Ortoplina 143 A3
Orvieto 82 C4; 110 D3
Osca 96 C2; 144 D1
Oscela 108 A2
Osci 84 C4
Ospringe 131 E7
Osrhoene 162 B3, C3; 177 G4
Ossa, M. 7 C1; 30 C2; 32 D3
Ossonoba 144 A4
Osteodes 38 B1
Osterburken 140 C3
Osteria dell' Osa see Gabii
Ostia 86 B2; 94 B2; 108 D4; 110 D4; 113 (Plan); 119 B3; 122 B2
Ostiensis, Via 90 A4; 123 E1
Ostracine 167 C1
Othoca 146 B4
Othona 131 E7
Othrys, M. 30 C3
Otrus 173 E4
Otzaki 2 B1
Ourania 156 D4
Outioi 19 F4
Ouxioi 19 E4
Ovetum 144 B1

Ovilava 138 D4; 176 C2
Owmby 131 D5
Oxus, R. 19 G2; 54 E2; 65 F5; 71 G2
Oxyrhynchus 76 B2; 167 B2

Pachynum, Pachynus, Pr. 38 E4; 97 G4; 148 E4
Pactolos, R. 31 G3; 33 C3
Pactye 27 C1
Padus, R. 97 E1, F1; 108 C2
Paeania 34 C3
Paeligni 84 B3, C3
Paeonians 9 B1; 62 B1
Paeonidae 34 B2
Paestum (Poseidonia) 14 B1; 81 ; 84 C4; 92 E3; 94 D4; 109 F4; 111 F4
Paesus 27 C1
Pagae 29 D1
Pagasae 30 C2; 32 D3
Pagasaeus Sinus 32 D3
Palaea 156 C5
Palaepercote 27 C2
Palaestina (Roman Province) 177 F5
Palaestina, Syria 171 F5
Palaikastro [Creta] 4 E2
Palaiokastro [Peloponnesus] 6 B4
Palaipaphos 2 E4; 156 A6
Palantia 146 B1
Pale 23 A3; 60 A3
Palestine 166
Palestrina see Praeneste
Palice 38 D3
Palinurus, Pr. 109 F5
Pallae 146 C3
Pallantia 144 B1
Pallantion 29 C2
Pallene [Attica] 34 C3
Pallene [Chalcidice] 23 B1, C1; 30 C2
Pallia, R. 108 D3
Pallicum Fretum 146 B3
Palma 144 E2
Palmae (Tamaricii) 148 E2
Palmyra 162 B4
Paltus 162 B3
Pamisos, R. 29 C2, 3; 30 B4, 5
Pamphylia 18 B2; 129 E4; 158 C4; 160 D4, 5; 171 E4; 177 E4, F4
Pandateria 109 E4
Pandosia 32 A3; 62 B3
Paneas 166 C1
Pangaeus, M. 30 D1
Panhormus see Panormus
Panion see Caesarea Philippi
Panionion 16 E2
Pannonia 128 D3
Pannonia Inferior 138 E4, F4; 143 B3, C3; 170 D3; 176 D3
Pannonia Superior 138 E4; 143 B2; 170 D3; 176 D2
Pannoniae (Diocese) 176 D3
Panopeos 6 C2; 7 C3
Panopolis 76 C3; 167 C3
Panormus [Achaea] 46 B3

Panormus, Panhormus [Sicilia] 38 B2; 97 G4; 148 B2
Pantagias, Pantagyas, R. 38 E3; 148 E3
Panticapaeum 15 G2; 50 C2
Pantimathoi 19 F2
Panzano 82 B3
Paphlagonia 18 B2; 58 B1
Paphlagonia (Roman Province) 177 F3
Paphus 129 F5; 156 A6; 171 F5; 177 F4
Pappa/Tiberiopolis 160 D4
Paraetacene 65 E3
Paraetonium 76 A1; 167 A1
Parapamisos 19 H3; 65 G2
Parauaea 62 B2
Parentium 95 C1; 108 D1
Parga 6 A1
Parikanioi 19 E3
Parikaroi 19 G4, H4
Parion, Parium 27 C1; 31 F1; 44 C1; 158 A2; 160 A2
Paris see Lutetia Parisiorum
Parisata 6 A3
Parisi 131 D5
Parisii 138 A3
Parium see Parion
Parlais 158 C3; 160 C4
Parma 95 B1; 108 B2
Parnassus 161 E3
Parnassos, M. 7 C3; 29 C1; 30 C3; 32 C4
Parnes, M. 30 D4; 34 B2
Parnon, M. 30 C5
Paroikia 2 C3
Paropamisadae 65 G2
Paropus 38 C2; 148 C2
Paros 16 C3; 31 E5; 44 B3
Parrhasia 7 B4
Parrodunum 140 D4
Parthenicum 148 B2
Parthenios, R. 58 B1
Parthia 19 F3; 65 E3, F3; 71 F3; 105 G3; 129 G5; 162 D4; 171 G4
Parthini 105 D2
Pasargadai 19 E4; 65 E4
Passaron 32 B3
Pat(t)ala 65 H4; 71 H4
Patara/Arsinoe 73 G5; 158 B5; 160 C5
Patavium 108 C1
Patelles 2 D3
Pathyris/Crocodilopolis 167 C4
Patmos 31 F4; 33 A4
Patrae, Patras 6 B3; 29 B1; 30 B4
Patraea 50 D2
Patulcenses 146 C4, 5
Pauca 146 B2
Paucae, R. 146 B2
Pausikani 19 F2
Pautalia 143 D3
Pax Julia 144 A3
Paxos 32 A3
Pedalium, Pr. 156 C5
Pedasa 44 C3
Pedasos 9 D2

Pediaeus, R. 156 B5, C5
Pedum 92 C3
Pegae 46 C3
Pelagonia 62 B1
Pelinna 32 C3
Pelion 30 B1; 32 B2
Pelion, M. 7 C1
Pella 30 C1; 32 C1; 62 B2; 143 D4
Pella/Berenice 74 B5; 166 C2
Pellanes 6 B4
Pellene 7 C3; 46 C3; 72 C3
Peloponnesus 29
Pelorus, Pr. 38 F1; 97 H5; 148 E2
Pelos 2 C3
Peltai 58 B2
Peltuinum 92 C2; 119 C3
Pelusiac Mouth (Nile) 167 C1
Pelusium 76 C1; 167 C1; 177 F5
Pelva 143 B4
Pen Llwyn 131 B6
Pen Llystyn 131 B6
Pen-y-Darren 131 C7
Peneios, R. [Elis] 29 B2; 30 B4
Peneios, R. [Thessalia] 2 A1; 30 C2; 32
    C3; 62 B2
Penna Sant' Andrea 84 C3
Pennal 131 B6
Pennocrucium 131 C6
Pentelicon, M. 34 C3
Pentri 84 C3
Peparethos 32 E4; 44 A2
Perachora 2 B2; 12 B2; 56 B2
Peraea 166 C3, 4
Peraiboi 7 A1, B1
Perakastro 2 D3
Perati 6 D3; 10 C3; 56 C3
Percote 27 B1
Perdikaria 6 C3
Pergamon, Pergamum 31 F2; 33 B2; 73
    F2; 77 (Plan); 129 E4; 158 A2; 160
    A3; 171 E4; 173 E4
Perga, Perge 74 A3; 160 C4
Pergus, L. 38 D3; 148 D3
Perinthus (Heracleia) 15 H1; 44 C1; 73
    F1; 129 E4; 143 E4; 160 B1; 171 E4;
    177 E3
Peristeria 6 B4
Perrhaebia 23 B1, 2; 30 B2; 62 B2
Perrhe/Antiochia 162 B2
Persepolis 19 E4; 21 (Plan); 65 E4
Persian Gates 65 E4
Persian Gulf 71 E5
Persis 19 E4; 65 E4; 71 E4
Perusia 82 C4; 92 B2; 95 B2; 97 F2; 108
    D3
Pessinus 70 B3; 74 A2; 158 D3; 160 D3
Petelia 97 H3
Petiliana 148 C3
Petra [Arabia] 70 C4; 74 B5; 162 A5;
    167 D1
Petra [Hellespontus] 27 B3
Petra [Thessalia] 6 C1
Petrina 148 B3
Petsofa 4 E2

Petuaria 131 D5
Peucelaotis 65 H2
Peucetii 84 D4
Phaestus, Phaistos 2 C4; 4 C3; 9 C4; 72
    D6; 156 B2
Phalarium 38 C4
Phalasarna 156 A1
Phaleron 29 D2; 30 D4; 34 B4
Phanagoria 15 G2; 50 D2
Pharae, Pharai [Achaea] 29 B1; 72 B3;
    80 A2
Pharae [Leucas] 32 A4
Pharae [Messenia] 29 C3
Pharbaethus 167 C1
Pharcadon 32 C3
Pharmacussa 33 B4
Pharnaceia see Ceras(o)us
Pharos 97 G2
Pharsalos 16 B1; 30 C2; 32 C3; 62 B3;
    72 C2; 105 E3, G1 (Battle)
Phasaelis 166 C3
Phaselis 44 E4; 160 C5
Phasis 15 H3; 53 H3; 74 D1
Phasis, R. 58 E1, 2; 162 C1, D1
Phatnitic Mouth (Nile) 167 C1
Pheia 6 B3; 46 B3
Pheneos 6 C3; 7 C3; 29 C2
Pherai [Messenia] 7 B5
Pherae, Pherai [Thessalia] 6 C1; 7 C1;
    12 B2; 30 C2; 32 D3
Phigaleia 29 B2; 72 B4
Philadelphia [Aegyptus] 76 B2; 167 B2
Philadelphia [Asia] 73 G3; 158 B3; 160
    B3; 173 E4
Philadelphia [Cilicia] 74 B3
Philadelphia [Palaestina] 74 B5; 166
    D4
Philae Is. 76 C5; 167 C5
Philaidae 34 D4
Philetaereia 73 E2
Philia 12 B2
Philippi 30 D1; 32 E1; 62 C2; 105 E2;
    143 D4; 173 E4
Philippopolis [Syria] 162 B4
Philippopolis [Thracia] 62 D1; 143 D4;
    177 E3
Philippoupolis 62 C2
Philomelium 74 A2; 158 C3; 160 D3;
    173 E4
Philosophiana 148 D3
Philotera 76 C2; 167 D3
Philoteria 74 B5
Phintias 38 C4; 148 C4
Phlegraei, Campi 115 B2
Phlius 23 B3; 29 C2; 30 C4
Phlya 34 C3
Phocaea 16 D2; 31 F3; 33 A2; 44 C2
Phocis 16 B2; 23 B2; 30 C3
Phoenice 32 A2; 72 A2; 97 H3
Phoenice (Syria) 162 A4, B4; 171 F5;
    177 F4
Phoenicia 18 C3
Phoenicum 167 C4
Phoenicum Mare 162 A4

Phoenicus 167 A1
Phoenicus(s)a 38 D1; 148 D1
Phoinix 156 A2
Phokaia see Phocaea
Pholegandros 31 E5
Phorbantia 38 A2; 148 A2
Phraaspa 105 G3
Phrearrhii 34 C5
Phrygia 16 F1; 18 B2; 160 C4, D3
Phrygia (Roman Provinces) 177 E4
Phrygians 9 E1
Phthia 7 C2
Phthiotis (Achaea) 23 B2; 30 C3; 62 B3
Phylakopi 2 C3; 56 C3
Phyle 34 B2
Physkos, R. 58 B3
Picentes 84 C3
Picentia 115 D2
Picenum 109 D3; 176 C3
Pictones 136 B3
Piercebridge 130 D4
Pieria [Macedonia] 9 B1
Pieria [Syria] 74 B3; 162 B3
Pietrabbondante 84 C3
Pighadia 2 D4
Pindos, M. 2 A1, 2; 30 B2
Pinna 92 C2
Pinnata Castra 130 C3
Piquentum 108 D1
Piraeon 29 D1
Piraeus 29 D2; 30 D4; 34 B3
Pirama 148 B2
Pisa 29 B2
Pisae 95 B2; 97 F2; 108 C3
Pisatis 16 A2, B2
Pisaurum 95 C2; 108 D2; 119 B2
Pisaurus, R. 108 D2
Pisidia 18 B2; 160 C4, D4
Pisidia (Roman Province) 177 F4
Pistoria 97 F2; 108 C3
Pitane 16 D2
Pithecusa(e) 14 A1; 84 C4; 111 G1; 115
    B3
Pitiniana 148 C3
Pitinum (Mergens) 108 D2; 119 B2
Pitya 27 D1
Pityeia 9 D1
Pityussa 29 D2
Pityussae Is. 96 D3; 144 D3
Placentia 95 A1; 97 F1; 108 B2
Planasia 108 C4
Plataea 23 B3; 25 (Battle); 29 D1; 30
    C4
Platamodes, Pr. 29 B3
Platanos 4 C3
Platyvola 4 B2
Plavis, R. 108 C1
Pleistarcheia/Heraclea 73 F4
Plemmyrium, Pr. 38 E4; 148 E4
Plestia 92 B2
Pleuron 7 B3; 29 B1; 46 B3
Plotinopolis 143 E4
Pnigeus 167 A1
Podandus 161 E4

Poeessa 60 C3
Poeninae, Alpes Atrectianae et 170 C3
Poeninae, Alpes Graiae et 136 D3, 4; 176 C3
Poetovio 128 D3; 138 E4; 143 A2
Poggio Buco 82 C5
Pola 95 C1; 108 D2
Policoro see Heraclea
Poliochni 2 C1; 56 C1
Polis [Ithaca] 6 A2
Polla 94 E4
Pollentia [Baleares] 144 E2
Pollentia [Italia] 108 A3
Polyrrhenia 72 D5; 156 A1
Pompaelo 144 C1
Pompeii 94 D3; 109 E4; 111 H1; 115 C2; 116 (Plan)
Pompeiopolis 161 E1
Pompeiopolis/Soli 64 B3; 74 B3; 161 E5
Pomptine Marshes 86 C3
Pondicherry (Arikamedu) 54 E3
Pons Aelius 133 D1
Pons Aeni 138 D4
Pons Drusi (Bauzanum) 108 C1
Pons Saravi 140 A3
Pontecagnano 84 C4
Pontes 131 D7
Pontia, Pontiae Is. 94 B3; 109 D4
Pontica (Diocese) 177 F4
Pontus Euxinus 50 C3; 162 B1
Pontus 129 E4, 5; 158 D1; 161 E1; 171 F4
Pontus Galaticus 161 G2, H2
Pontus Polemonaicus 177 F3
Popilia, Via 115 D2
Popillia, Via 108 C2
Populonia 82 B4; 84 B3; 92 A3; 108 C3; 110 C3
Porolissum 143 D1
Porphyrites, M. 167 C3
Portchester 131 D8
Porthmium 50 C2
Porticenses 146 C4
Portuensis, Via 123 E3
Portus Ardaoni 131 D8
Portus Argous 108 C3
Portus Cale 144 A2
Portus Favoni 146 C2
Portus Lemanis 131 E8
Portus Luguidonis 146 C3
Portus Namnetum 136 A3
Portus Romae 122 B2
Portus Syracusanus 146 C3
Pos(e)ideion, Pr. [Achaea Phthiotis] 30 C3; 32 D4
Poseideion, Pr. [Caria] 33 B4
Pose(i)donia see Paestum
Posideion, Pr. [Chalcidice] 32 D2
Posideium [Syria] 74 B3
Posidium [Aegyptus] 167 C2
Posidium, Pr. [Campania] 109 F4
Postumia, Via 108 C1
Potaissa 143 D2; 171 E3

Potentia [Lucania] 109 F4
Potentia [Picenum] 95 C2; 108 D3
Potidaea 15 F1; 30 C2; 32 D2; 44 A1
Pozzuoli see Puteoli
Praeneste·(Palestrina) 81; 82 D6; 84 B3; 86 C2; 92 C3; 94 B2; 109 D4; 110 D4; 122 C2
Praenestina, Via 90 D4; 122 C2; 123 B1
Praesidium 146 C2
Praetavi 162 D3
Praetuttii 84 C3
Praevalitana 177 D3
Praisos 4 E2;16 D4; 156 D2
Prasiae 29 D3; 46 C4
Prestatyn 131 C5
Priansos 156 C2
Priapus 27 D1; 47 F1
Priene 16 E3; 31 F4; 33 B4; 37 (Plan); 44 C3; 160 A4
Prilius, L. 108 C3
Prinias 12 C4; 156 B2
Privernum 92 C3; 94 C2
Probalinthus 34 D3
Prochyta 115 B3
Proconnesos 31 G1; 44 C1; 125 E4; 160 B2
Prodromos 2 B2
Promona 104 D2
Pronni 60 A3
Prophthasia 65 F3
Prostovitsa 6 B3
Prosymna 6 C3;.12 B3
Prote 29 B3
Prusa 73 G2; 158 B2; 160 B2
Prusias/Cius 73 G1; 158 B2
Prusias-on-Hypius/Cierus 73 H1; 158 C2; 160 D2
Prymnessus 160 C3
Psaros, R. 58 C2
Pseira 4 E2
Pselchis 167 C5
Psessi 50 E1
Psophis 29 B2
Psychro 4 D2
Psyr(i)a 9 C2; 31 E3
Pteleon [Achaea Phthiotis] 6 C2; 7 C2; 32 D4
Pteleum [Hellespontus] 27 C1
Ptoeum 80 B2
Ptolemais [Aegyptus] 76 C3; 167 C4
Ptolemais [Cyrene] 151 G2
Ptolemais [Lycia] 74 A3
Ptolemais/Ace 74 B4; 166 B1; 173 F5
Ptolemais, see Lebedos
Ptolemais Hormou 167 B2
Pulchrum, Pr. 97 F4
Pura 19 G4; 71 G4
Puteoli (Pozzuoli) 94 C3; 97 G3; 109 E4; 111 H1; 115 B2
Pydna 30 C1; 32 C2; 62 C3; 72 C1
Pygela 44 C3; 47 F3
Pylae Amanicae 161 F4
Pylae Ciliciae (Cilician Gates) 161 F4

Pylae Syriae (Syrian Gates) 161 F5
Pylai 58 E3
Pylos 6 B4; 7 B5; 29 B3; 30 B5; 49 (Plan)
Pyramos, R. 58 C2; 161 F5
Pyrasos 7 C2
Pyrenaei, M. 96 C2; 144 D1
Pyrgi (Santa Severa) 82 C5; 86 A1; 94 A2; 108 D4; 110 D4
Pyrgos 2 C4
Pyrgos Kieriou 6 B1
Pyrrha 33 A2; 44 C2; 47 E2; 60 D2
Pytho 7 C3

Quadi 138 E3; 170 D3
Quintana 138 D3
Quinto 82 B3
Qumran 166 C4

Rabbathmoba 162 B5
Raeburnfoot 130 C4
Raeti 84 B1
Raetia 128 C3; 136 D3; 138 C4; 140 D4; 170 C3; 176 C3
Raphaneae 129 F5; 162 B3; 171 F5
Raphia 70 B4; 74 B5; 166 A5
Raphina 2 C2
Rapidum 150 C1; 154 B1
Ratae Coritanorum 131 D6
Ratiaria 143 D3; 177 D3
Ravenna 108 C2; 110 C2
Reate 84 B3; 92 C3; 97 G2; 108 D3
Red House 133 C1
Red Sea 70 C5
Refugium Apollinis 148 E4
Regina 144 B3
Regini 131 D8
Regium Lepidum 108 C2
Regulbium 131 E7
Remi 136 C2; 138 A3; 176 C2
Renus, R. 82 B2; 108 C2
Resafa 162 B3
Resaina 162 C3; 171 G4
Rhagae/Europus 65 E3; 71 E3
Rhaikelos 16 B1
Rhamn(o)us 29 E1; 34 D1
Rhegium 14 B2; 84 D5; 97 G4; 109 G6
Rheingönheim 140 B3
Rhenea 31 E4
Rhenus, R. 138 C3; 140 A4; 176 C2
Rhenus, R. [Aemilia] see Renus
Rhinocolura 76 D1; 167 C1
Rhion, Pr. 29 B1
Rhizenia 156 B2
Rhizon 97 H2
Rhizus 162 C1
Rhode 96 D2; 144 E1
Rhodes, Rhodos 16 E3; 31 G5; 33 C5; 73 F5; 158 B4; 160 B5; 177 E4
Rhodope 177 E3
Rhoeteum, Rhoetium 27 B2; 47 E2
Rhoetium, Pr. 146 B2
Rhosus 74 B3; 162 B3

211

Savus, R. 104 D2; 143 B2
Saxa Rubra 122 B1
Saxones 138 C1
Scaldis, R. 138 A2
Scallabis 144 A3
Scamander, R. 9 D2; 31 F2; 33 A1, B1
Scarbantia 138 E4; 143 B1
Scardonia 143 A4
Scenitae 162 C4, D4
Scepsis 27 C3; 33 A1; 44 C1; 73 E2
Schedia 167 B1
Schierenhof 140 C3
Schlossau 140 C2
Sciathos 30 C3; 32 D3
Scillus 29 B2
Scione 15 F1; 30 D2; 32 D2; 44 A1
Sciritis 30 B4, C4
Scodra 97 H2; 105 D2; 143 C4
Scolacium, Scylacium 94 A4; 109 G5
Scole 131 E6
Scotussa 32 C3
Scupi 143 C4; 177 D3
Scyllaion, Pr. 29 D2
Scyros 31 D3; 32 E4; 44 B2
Scythi 50 C1
Scythia 54 C2
Scythia (Roman Province) 177 E3
Scythopolis 74 B5; 166 C2
Seabegs 134 C1
Sebaste [Asia] 158 C3; 160 C3
Sebaste/Elaeussa 161 E5
Sebaste/Samaria 74 B5; 166 B3
Sebaste, Via 160 C4, D4
Sebasteia 161 G2; 177 F4
Sebastopolis 161 F2
Sebennytic Mouth (Nile) 167 B1
Sebennytus 76 B1; 167 B1
Sebethus, R. 115 C2
Sebinus, L. 108 B1
Sebou, R. 150 B1
Seckmauern 140 C2
Segedunum 133 D1
Segelocum 131 D5
Segesta 38 B2; 97 G4; 148 B2
Segisama 144 C1
Segobriga 144 C2
Segontia 96 C2; 144 C2
Segontium 131 B6
Segovia 144 B2
Segusio 136 D4; 176 C3
Seleuceia [Cilicia] 74 B3; 161 E5; 177 F4
Seleucia [Osrhoene] 162 B3
Seleuceia [Pamphylia] 74 A3
Seleuceia [Persis] 71 E4
Seleuceia ad Belum 74 B3
Seleuceia (in) Pieria 74 B3; 161 F5; 162 B3
Seleuceia (on the Tigris) 70 D3; 162 D4
Seleuceia Sidera 73 H3; 160 C4
Seleuceia/Abila 74 B5; 166 D2
Seleuceia see Susa
Seleuceia see Tralles

Seleuceia see Zeugma
Seleucis 70 C3
Selge 74 A3; 160 D4
Selgovae 130 C4
Seligenstadt 140 B2
Selinus [Cilicia] 160 D5
Selinus [Sicilia] 14 A2; 38 B3; 97 G4
Sellasia 29 C3; 72 C4
Selymbria 15 H1; 44 C1
Semnones 138 D2
Sena Gallica 95 C2; 97 G2; 108 D2
Sena Iulia 95 B2; 108 C3
Senia 104 D2; 143 A4
Senones [Gallia] 138 A3
Senones [Italia] 84 B2
Sentinum 92 B2
Sepias, Pr. 30 C3; 32 D3
Sepphoris/Diocaesarea 166 B2
Septimanca 144 B2
Sequana, R. 138 A3
Sequani 136 C3; 138 B4
Sequania 176 C2
Seraglio 2 D3; 10 D3
Serapeum 76 B2
Serdica, Sardica 143 D3; 173 D3
Seriane 162 B3
Seriphos 29 E3; 31 D4; 44 B3; 60 C3
Sermigium 146 B2
Sermyle, Sermylia 32 D2; 44 A1; 46 C2
Servia 2 B1
Sesites, R. 108 A2
Sesklo 2 B2
Sessa Aurunca see Suessa Aurunca
Sestinum 119 B2
Sestos 15 G1; 27 B2; 31 F1; 33 A1; 143 E4
Seteia, R. 131 C5
Setia 94 B2
Sette Finestre Villa 110 C3
Severiana, Via 122 B2, C2
Sexi 96 B4; 144 C4
Shapwick 131 C8
Sibari see Sybaris
Sicani 38 C3
Sicca 97 E4
Sicignano 94 E4
Sicilia (Sicily) 38; 148
Sicinos 31 E5; 60 C4
Sicoris, R. 104 B2
Siculi 38 D2, 3
Siculum Fretum 38 F1, 2; 148 E2, F1
Siculum Mare 38 E3
Sicyon 16 B2; 29 C1; 30 C4
Side 74 A3; 158 C4; 160 D5
Sidicini 84 C4
Sidon 74 B4; 162 A4
Sidrona 143 A4
Siga 96 C4
Sigeion, Sigeum 15 G1; 16 D1; 27 A2
Signia 94 B2
Sigrium, Pr. 33 A2
Silarus, R. 109 F4
Silchester (Calleva Atrebatum) 131 D7; 135 (Plan)

Siliana, R. 151 B2
Silures 131 B7, C7
Simbri 146 B2
Simoeis, R. 9 D1
Simyra 162 B4
Sinda 2 E4
Sindi 50 D2
Sindimana 65 G4
Singara 74 D3; 162 C3; 171 G4
Singidunum 143 C3; 170 D3
Singiticus Sinus 32 E2
Singos 32 E2; 44 A1; 46 D2
Sinope 15 G3; 50 C4; 161 F1
Sinuessa 94 C3; 115 A2
Sinzig 140 A1
Siphae 46 C3
Siphnos 12 C3; 16 C3; 31 D4; 44 B3
Sipontum 84 C3; 94 E2; 109 F3; 119 C3
Sippar 58 A4
Sipylos, M. 9 D2; 31 F3; 33 B2
Siris 14 B1
Siris, R. 109 F4
Sirmio 108 B2
Sirmium 143 C3; 176 D3
Sisapo 144 B3
Siscia 104 D2; 143 B3; 176 D3
Sitagroi 2 C1
Siteia 156 D2
Sithonia 30 D2
Sitifensis, Mauretania 176 B4
Sitifis 150 D1; 176 B4
Sittacene 18 D3
Sittake 58 B4, E3
Siwa(h) 64 A4; 151 H2
Sklavokambos 4 C2
Skoteino 4 D2
Skudra 18 A1
Smaragdus, M. 167 D4
Smyrna/Eurydiceia 16 E2; 31 F3; 33 B3; 73 F3; 158 A3; 160 A3; 177 E4
Smyrna, Old 10 D2; 12 D2
Smyrnaeus Sinus 33 B3
Soandus 161 E3
Socnopaei Nesus 76 B2; 167 B2
Sogdian Rock 65 G2
Sogdiana 19 G2; 65 F2, G2; 71 G2, H2
Soli [Cyprus] 74 A4; 156 B5
Soli/Pompeiopolis [Cilicia] 64 B3; 74 B3; 161 E5
Sollion 30 B3; 32 B4
Solorius, M. 144 C4
Soluntum, Solus 38 C2; 97 G4; 148 C2
Solygeia 46 C3
Solyma, M. 9 F3
Sophanene 162 C2
Sophene 162 C2
Sopianae 138 E4; 176 D3
Sora 94 C2; 109 E4
Sorabile 146 C4
Soracte, M. 86 B1
Sorviodunum 131 C7
Sorviodurum 140 F4
Sossios, R. 148 B3
Sotira 2 E4

Souphli 2 B1
Sovana 82 C4
Sparta 23 B3; 27 (Plan); 29 C3; 30 C5; 80 A3
Spartolos 32 D2; 44 A1
Spata 6 D3
Spello see Hispellum
Spercheios, R. 6 C2; 7 B2, C2
Sperlonga 111 E4
Sphacteria 29 B3; 30 B5; 49 (Plan)
Sphettos 29 E2; 34 C4
Spina 14 C3; 52 D3; 82 C2; 84 B2; 110 C2
Spinis 131 D7
Spoletium (Spoleto) 94 B1; 97 G2; 108 D3; 110 D3
Stabiae (Castellammare di Stabia) 111 H1; 115 C2
Stagirus 15 F1; 23 C1; 32 E2; 44 A1
Stagna Palicorum 148 D3
Staniwells 131 D5
Stobi 143 D4
Stockstadt 140 C2
Stolos 44 A1; 46 C1
Stracathro, R. 130 C2
Strageath 130 C3
Stratonicea [Athos] 32 E2
Stratonicaea, Stratonice(i)a [Caria] 73 F4; 158 B4; 160 B4
Stratonicaea [Mysia] 73 F2
Strato's Tower see Caesarea
Stratos 32 B4; 46 B3; 72 B3
Stratton Grandison 131 C7
Strepsa 44 A1
Strongyle 38 E1; 148 E1
Strymon, R. 30 C1; 32 D1; 62 C1; 143 D4
Stuttgart 140 C3
Styberra 143 C4
Stylos 4 B2
Stymphalus, L. 29 C2
Stymphalus, Stymphelos 7 C3; 29 C2
Styra 9 C3; 23 C3; 29 E1; 44 A3
Styx, R. 7 B3
Subasani 146 C2
Sublaqueum 122 D1
Sucro, R. 96 C3
Suebjcum Mare 138 D1
Suel 144 B4
Suessa Aurunca (Sessa Aurunca) 84 C4; 92 D3; 94 C3; 111 E4; 115 A2
Suessula 84 C4; 92 D3; 94 D3; 109 E4; 115 C2; 119 C4
Sufes 150 C4
Sufetula 150 C4
Suia 156 A2
Sûk-el-Khmis, 151 A1
Sulcis [E. Sardinia] 146 C4
Sulci(s) [W. Sardinia] 97 E3; 146 B5
Sulcis, R. 146 B5
Sulloniacis 131 D7
Sulmo 84 C3; 109 E3
Sulz 140 B4
Sumelocenna 140 B4

Summerston 134 B2
Summontorium 140 D4
Sunion, Pr. 29 E2; 30 D4; 34 D5
Super(n)um (Adriaticum) Mare 107; 109 E3, F3
Sura 162 B3
Surrentum 109 E4; 115 C2
Susa/Seleuceia 19 E3; 64 D3; 71 E4
Susiana, Susiane 64 D4; 71 E4
Sutrium 82 C5; 94 B1
Syangela 44 C3
Sybaris (Sibari) 14 B1; 111 G4
Sybota 32 A3; 46 A2
Sybrita 156 B2
Syene 76 C5; 167 C5
Symaethius 148 E3
Symaethus, R. 38 D2, 3; 148 D3
Syme, 9 D3; 31 G5; 33 C5
Synnada 73 H3; 125 E4; 158 C3; 160 C3; 173 E4; 177 E4
Syracus(a)e 14 B2; 38 E4; 39 (Plan); 97 G4, H5; 128 D4; 148 E4; 170 D4; 172 D4; 176 D4
Syria 74
Syria (Roman Province) 129 F5; 162 B4; 171 F4, 5; 177 F4
Syros 31 E4
Syrtis Minor 97 F5

Tabae 160 B4
Tabernae 138 C3; 140 B3
Tabor, M. 166 C2
Tacapae 150 C5
Tader, R. 96 C3
Tadinum 92 B2
Taenaron, Pr. 29 C4
Taenarum 29 C4
Taexali 130 C2
Taexalorum, Pr. 130 D2
Tagus, R. 96 A2; 144 B2
Talcinum 146 B2
Talmis 76 C5
Tamalleni 154 C2
Taman Peninsula 50 D2
Tamaricii (Palmae) 148 E2
Tamarus, R. 131 B8
Tamassus 156 B5
Tameia 130 C2
Tamesis, R. 131 D7
Tamium 131 C7
Tamynae 29 E1; 32 E4
Tamyrace 50 B1
Tanagra 29 D1; 30 D3; 34 B1
Tanais 50 E1
Tanais, R. 50 E1
Tanarus, R. 108 A3
Tanatus 131 E7
Tanis 76 C1; 167 C1
Tanitic Mouth (Nile) 167 C1
Tannetum 97 H3; 108 B2
Taochi 58 D1
Taposiris 167 A1
Tapurioi 19 E3

Taras, Tarentum (Taranto) 14 B1; 84 D4; 94 A3; 109 G4; 111 G4
Tarentinus Sinus 109 G4
Tarichaeae 166 C2
Tarne 9 D2
Tarquinia, Tarquinii 82 C5; 84 B3; 92 B3; 108 D4; 110 D4
Tarrabeni 146 B2
Tarracina (Terracina) 84 C4; 92 D3; 94 C3; 97 G3; 111 E4; 119 B4
Tarraco 96 D2; 128 B4; 144 D2; 170 B4; 176 B3
Tarraconensis 128 B3; 144 C2; 170 B4; 176 B3
Tarsatica 143 A3
Tarsus/Antioch 58 C2; 70 C3; 74 B3; 161 F4; 162 A3; 171 F4; 173 F4; 177 F4
Tartarus, R. 108 C2
Tarvisium 108 C1
Tatta, L. 161 E3
Tauchira 14 D5
Taulantii 62 A1
Taurasia 97 E1
Tauri 50 C2
Taurianum, Pr. 109 F5
Taurini 97 E1
Tauroentum 14 B3
Tauromenium 38 E2; 97 G4; 148 E2
Taurus, M. 161 E4-G4; 162 B3
Taurus, Pr. 148 E3
Tava, R. 130 C2
Tavium 74 B2; 161 E2
Taxila 65 H3; 71 H3
Taygetos, M. 7 C5; 30 C5
Teanum (Apulum) 84 C3; 92 D2; 109 E3
Teanum Sidicinum (Teano) 84 C4; 92 D3; 94 C3; 97 G3; 109 E4; 111 E4; 115 A1
Teate 92 C2
Tebtunis 76 B2; 167 B2
Tectosages 136 B5
Tegea 16 B3; 29 C2; 30 C4
Tegula 146 B5
Tegyra 29 D1; 32 D4
Teichiussa 47 F4
Teichos Dymaion 6 B3; 56 A2
Tekoa 166 B4
Telamon 82 B5; 92 A3
Telandria 44 D3
Telesia 92 D3; 94 D3
Tell Sukas 15 G4
Telmessus 44 D3; 73 G4; 160 B5
Telos 33 B5; 60 E4
Tembris, R. 158 C2, 3; 160 C2, 3
Temenothyrae/Flaviopolis 158 B3; 160 C3
Tempe 23 B2; 30 C2
Templeborough 131 D5
Tempsa 94 A4; 109 G5
Temus, R. 146 B4
Tenedos 27 A3; 31 E2; 33 A1; 44 B2
Tenos 31 E4; 44 B3

Tentyra 76 C4; 167 C4
Teos, Teus 16 D2; 33 B3; 44 C3; 160 A3
Terenuthis 167 B1
Tergeste 95 C1; 108 D1
Terias, R. 38 E3; 148 E3
Terina 14 B1; 109 G5
Termantia 144 C2
Termera 44 C3
Termessus 73 H4; 158 C4; 160 C4
Terracina *see* Tarracina
Tetius, R. 156 B5
Tetrapolis 34 D2
Teurnia 138 D4
Teutlussa 47 F5
Thabraca 97 E4; 150 C3
Thabudeos 154 B1
Thaenae 150 C5
Thagaste 150 B4
Thalamae 80 B3
Thamalluma 154 B1
Thamgnaioi 19 F4
Thamna 166 B4
Thamugadi (Timgad) 150 D1; 153 (Plan); 154 B1
Thapsacus/Amphipolis 58 D2; 64 C3; 74 C3
Thapsus [Africa] 97 F5; 104 C3; 150 C4
Thapsus [Sicilia] 38 E3
Tharros 97 E3; 146 B4
Thasos 15 F1; 16 C1; 31 D1; 32 F1; 44 B1
Thateis 50 E1
Thaumacoi 32 C4
Theadelphia 76 B2; 167 B2
Theangela 73 F4
Thebae [Achaea Phthiotis] 32 D3
Thebae [Boeotia] 29 D1; 30 C4
Thebae, Thebes/Diospolis Magna, 76 C4; 167 C4
Thebais 167 B4, C4
Thebais (Roman Province) 177 E5, F5
Thebe 9 D2
Thebeta 162 C3
Theilenhofen 140 D3
Thelepte 150 B4
Thelpusa 29 B2
Themisonium 73 G4
Theodosia 15 G2; 50 C2
Thera 16 D3; 31 E5
Therapnae 80 B3
Thermae [Icaros] 60 D3
Thermae (Himeraeae), [Sicilia] 38 C2; 97 G4; 148 C2
Thermae Selinuntinae/Aquae Larodes 148 B3
Thermaicus Sinus 30 C2; 32 D2
Therme [Macedonia] 23 B1; 30 C1; 32 D2
Thermessa 38 D1
Thermi [Lesbos] 2 D2
Thermodon, R. 58 C1
Thermon, Thermos 6 B2; 10 B2; 12 B2; 29 B1; 32 C4

Thermopylae 23 B2; 24 (Battle, 480 BC; 30 C3; 32 C4; 101 (Battle, 191 BC)
Thermos, R. 148 C2
Thespeia, Thespiae 7 D3; 23 B3; 29 D1; 46 C3; 72 C3
Thesprotia(ns) 7 A1, 2; 9 A2; 30 A2, 3; 62 A2, B3
Thessalia, Thessaly 30 C2; 62 B3; 105 E3
Thessalia (Roman Province) 177 D4, E4
Thessalonica 56 B1; 70 A2; 72 C1; 129 D4; 143 D4; 171 D4; 177 E4
Theveste 97 E5; 128 C4; 150 B4, D1; 154 C1
Thibar, R. 151 A2
Thibilis 150 D1
Thinis 167 C4
Thisbe 6 C3; 7 C3; 29 D1
Thmuis 167 C1; 173 F5
Thoricos, Thorikos 6 D3; 10 C3; 12 C3; 29 E2; 34 D5
Thospitis (Van), L. 58 E2; 162 D2
Thouria 6 B4
Thracia 31 E1
Thracia (Diocese) 177 E3
Thracia (Roman Province) 129 E4; 143 E4; 171 E4; 177 E3
Thracium Mare 31 D1, E1
Thria 34 A3
Throni 156 C5
Thronion, Thronium 7 C2; 32 D4; 46 C3
Thryoessa 7 B4
Thryon 7 B4
Thubunae 154 B1
Thuburbo Maius 150 C4
Thuburbo Minus 150 C3
Thubursicu Numidarum 150 B4, D1
Thugga 150 C3; 151 A2
Thule 54 B1
Thuria 29 C3
Thurii 84 D4; 94 A3; 97 G3
Thyateira 73 F3; 158 B3; 160 B3
Thymbrion 58 B2
Thyrea 16 B3; 29 C2; 46 C4
Thyrides, Pr. 29 C3
Thyrreum 72 B3
Thyrsus, R. 146 C4
Thysdrus 150 C4
Thyssus 44 A1; 46 D1
Tibareni 18 C2
Tiber(is), R. 86 B2; 108 D3; 122
Tiberias 166 C2
Tiberina, Via 122 B1
Tiberiopolis 158 B3
Tiberiopolis/Pappa 160 D4
Tibiscum 143 C2
Tibula 146 C3
Tibur (Tivoli) 84 B3; 86 C1; 92 C3; 108 D4; 110 D4; 122 C1
Tibureni 58 D1
Tiburtina, Via 90 E4; 122 C1; 123 A1

Ticinum 108 B2
Ticinus, R. 97 F1; 108 B2
Tie(i)um *see* Tios
Tifata, M. 81; 97 G3; 115 B1
Tifernum (Tiberinum) 108 D3
Tifernum Mataurense 119 B2
Tigisi(s) 150 D1; 172 C4
Tigranocerta 70 D3; 74 D2; 162 C2
Tigris, R. 18 D3; 64 C2; 70 D3; 162 D4
Tigullia 108 B3
Tiliaventum, R. 108 C1
Tillibari 154 C2
Tilox, Pr. 146 B1
Timbuktu 54 B3
Timetos, R. 148 E2
Timgad (Thamugadi) 150 D1; 153 (Plan); 154 B1
Tinea, R. 130 D4; 133 C2
Tingi(s) 96 A4; 128 A4; 150 A1; 170 A4; 176 A4
Tingitana, Mauretania 128 A5; 150 B1; 170 A4; 176 A4
Tinna, R. 108 D3
Tios, Tie(i)um 15 F3; 74 A1; 158 D1; 160 D1
Tipasa 96 D4; 150 C1
Tiryns 2 B3; 7 C4; 29 D2
Tissa 148 E2
Tivoli *see* Tibur
Tmolitae 158 B3
Tmolos, M. 9 D2; 31 G3; 33 C3; 160 B3
Toletum 144 B2
Tolfa 82 C5
Tolosa 136 B5
Tomen-y-Mur 131 B6
Tomi(s) 15 F3; 143 E3; 177 E3
Tomisa 161 H3; 162 B2
Topirus 143 D4
Topsham 131 C8
Toretae 50 D2
Toronaicus Sinus 30 D2; 32 D2, E2
Torone 15 F1; 32 E2; 44 A1
Torre Annunziata (Oplontis) 111 H1
Trachis 30 C3
Traducta 144 B4
Tragana 6 B4
Tragia 33 B4
Traianopolis 143 E4; 177 E3
Traianopolis/Grymenothyrae 158 B3
Traiectum 138 B2
Traiectus 148 E2
Tralles/Seleuceia 33 B3; 73 F3; 158 B3; 160 B4; 173 E4
Transalpina, Gallia 102 B2
Transpadana 108 B1; 138 C4
Trapez(o)us 15 H3; 50 E4; 58 D1; 161 H1; 162 C1
Traversette, Col de la 97 E1
Trasimenus, L. 82 C4; 97 F2; 108 D3
Trawscoed 131 B6
Treba 92 C3
Trebia, R. 97 F1; 108 B2
Trebula Mutuesca 92 C3
Trebula Suffenas 92 C3

Trechis 7 C2
Trennfurt 140 C2
Trent Vale 131 C6
Trerus, R. 109 E4
Tres Tabernae 140 A3
Treveri 136 C2, D2; 138 B3
Treveri *see* Augusta Treverorum
Trianda 2 E3
Tricca 32 C3
Trichonis, L. 29 B1; 32 B4
Tricorii 97 E1
Tricorynthus 34 D2
Tridentum 108 C1
Trifanum 92 D3
Trikke 7 B1
Trimethus 156 C5
Trimontium 130 C3
Trinovantes 131 E7
Triocala 148 B3
Triopion 33 B5; 47 F4
Triphylia 30 B4
Tripolis [Asia] 160 B4
Tripolis [Syria] 74 B4; 162 B4
Tripolitana 176 C5
Tripontium 131 D6
Trisantona, R. [1, Britannia] 131 D6
Trisantona, R. [2, Britannia] 131 D8
Tritaea 29 B1
Trivicum 119 C4
Troad, Troas 16 D1; 31 F2; *see also*
    Alexandria Troas
Trocnades 158 C2
Troesmis 143 E2
Troezen, Troizen 7 D4; 23 B3; 29 D2;
    30 C4
Trogilium, Pr. 33 B4
Trogodos, M. 156 B5
Trogodytae 167 D5
Troia [Latium] 86 B2
Tropaeum Traiani 143 E3
Trotilum 38 E3
Troutbeck 130 C4
Troy 2 D1; 3 (Plan); 9 D1; *see also*
Ilion
Truenius, R. 109 D3
Tsangli 2 B2
Tsikalario 12 C3
Tubusuctu 150 D1
Tucci 144 C3
Tude 144 A1
Tuder 84 B3; 92 B3; 94 B1; 108 D3
Tuesis, R. 130 C2
Tullum 138 B3
Tungri 138 B2
Tunis 97 F4
Tuola, R. 146 B1, C1
Turdetani 96 A3; 144 B4
Turiaso 144 C1
Turin *see* Augusta Taurinorum
Turris Libisonis 146 B3
Turublum Minus 146 C3
Tuscania 82 C5
Tuscia 176 C3
Tusculum 86 C2; 92 C3; 108 D4; 110

D4; 122 C2
Tuvius, R. 131 B6
Tuzritanus, Saltus 151 B2
Tyana/Eusebeia 58 C2; 74 B2; 161 E4
Tylissos 4 C2
Tymphaea 62 B2
Tyndaris 38 E2; 97 G4; 148 E2
Tyras 15 F2; 50 A1; 143 F2
Tyras, R. 15 F2; 50 A1; 143 E1, F2
Tyre, Tyrus 64 B3; 68 (Plan); 74 B4;
    162 A4; 166 A1; 171 F5; 173 F5; 177 F4
Tyriaion 58 B2
Tyritace 50 C2
Tyrrhenum/Infer(n)um Mare 107; 108
    B4, C4

Ubii 136 C2
Ucubi 144 B3
Udensis, Saltus 151 A2
Ulatha 166 C1
Ulia 144 B3
Ulixis Portus 148 E4
Ulpia Traiana Sarmizeget(h)usa 143
    D2; 171 D3
Ulpianum 143 C4
Ulubrae 94 B2
Umbri 84 B2
Umbria 108 C3; 176 C3
Umbro, R. 82 B4; 108 C3
Unterböbingen, 140 C3
Urbana 94 C3
Urbinum 108 D2
Urbs Salvia 92 B2
Urci 144 C4
Urcinium 146 B2
Uria 109 G4
Urmia/Matianus, L. 58 E2; 162 D2
Ursi, Pr. 146 C3
Urso 96 B3; 144 B4
Uruk/Orchoi 70 D4
Urvinum Mataurense 119 B2
Uselis 146 B4
Usha 166 B2
Ustica 38 B1; 148 B1
Utica 97 F4; 150 C3
Uxacona 131 C6
Uxama Barca 144 C2
Uxelodunum 133 A2
Uxii 64 D4
Uzentum 84 D4; 109 G4

Vaccaei 96 B2; 144 B1, 2
Vacomagi 130 B2, C2
Vada-Cecina 82 B4
Vada Sabatia 108 B3
Vada Volaterrana 108 C3
Vadimon, L. 92 B3
Vaga 150 C3; 151 A1
Vagniacis 131 E7
Vagum, Pr. 146 C1
Valentia [Italia] 108 B2
Valentia [Sardinia] 146 C4

Valentia [Tarraconensis] 144 D3
Valeria (Roman Province) 176 D3
Valeria [Tarraconensis] 144 C2
Valeria, Via 122 C1
Valle Latina 86 C2, D2
Van/Thospitis, L. 58 E2; 162 D2
Vandali 138 E2
Vaphio 6 C4; 56 B3
Varduli 144 C1
Vareia 144 C1
Varis 131 C5
Varvaria 143 A4
Vasada 160 D4
Vascones 144 C1, D1
Vasiliki 2 D4; 4 D2
Vasio 136 C4
Vathypatro 4 C2
Vaxus *see* Axos
Vectis 131 D8
Vegium 143 A4
Veii/Municipium Augustum Veiens
    (Veio) 82 C5; 84 B3; 86 B1; 88 (Plan);
    108 D4; 110 D4; 122 B1
Veldidena 138 D4
Veleia (Velleia) 95 A1; 108 B2; 110
    B2; 119 A2
Velia (Elea) 14 B1; 84 C4; 92 E3; 97
    G3; 109 F4; 111 F4
Veliocasses 138 A3
Velitrae 81; 82 D6; 92 C3; 94 B2; 122
    C2
Veluniate (Carriden) 134 D1
Venafrum 92 D3; 94 C2; 109 E4
Venasa 161 E3
Veneria Sicca 150 B4
Veneti 84 B1
Venetia 108 C1; 138 C4; 176 C3
Venicium 146 B2
Venicones 130 C3
Venonis 131 D6
Venta Belgarum 131 D7
Venta Icenorum 131 E6
Venta Silurum 131 C7
Ventimiglia *see* Albintimilium
Venusia 92 E2; 94 E3; 97 G3; 109 F4
Verbanus, L. 108 A2
Verbeia 131 D5
Vercellae 108 A2
Vercovicium 133 C1
Vergina 10 B1; 12 B1
Verlucio 131 C7
Vernemetum 131 D6
Verona 108 C2; 110 C1
Verteris 130 C4
Vertis 131 C6
Verulae 92 C3
Verulamium 131 D7
Vescera 154 B1
Vesontio 136 C3; 138 B4; 176 C2
Vestini 84 C3
Vesuvius, M. 111 H1; 115 C2
Vetera 128 C2; 136 C2; 138 B2; 170 C2
Vetonianis 140 E3
Vetralla 82 C5

Vettones 144 B2
Vetulonia 82 B4; 84 B3; 92 A3; 108 C3
Vibo Valentia *see* Hipponium
Vicat 162 D3
Vicetia 108 C1
Victoria 130 C3
Vicus Alexandri 122 B2
Vicus Altiaiensium 140 B2
Vicus Augustanus Laurentium 122 B2
Vicus Scuttarensium 140 D3
Vicus V.V. 140 B2
Vielbrunn 140 C2
Vienna 136 C4; 172 C3
Viennensis (Diocese) 176 B3, C3
Villa Faustini 131 E6
Villa Hadriani (Tibur) 122 C1
Villa Iovis (Capri) 111 H2
Villa Magna [Latium] 122 D2
Villanova 82 B2
Viminacium 129 D3; 143 C3; 171 D3; 177 D3
Vindelici 138 C4
Vindius, M. 144 B1
Vindobala 133 D1
Vindobona 138 E4; 170 D3
Vindocladia 131 C8
Vindolanda 133 C1
Vindomora 133 C2
Vindonissa 128 C2; 138 C4
Vindonium 131 D7
Viniola [1, Sardinia] 146 B3
Viniola [2, Sardinia] 146 C4
Vinovia 130 D4
Vipasca 144 A3
Viriballum, Pr. 146 B1
Virconium (Cornoviorum) 128 B2; 131 C6
Viromandui 138 A3
Virosidum 131 C5
Virunum 128 D3; 138 D4; 176 D3
Visentium 82 C5
Vitellia 94 B2
Vivara 115 B3
Vivisci 136 B4
Vix 52 C2
Vocontii 136 C4
Voghiera 82 C2
Volaterrae (Volterra) 82 B3; 92 A3; 108 C3; 110 C3
Volcae 96 D2; 136 B5
Volcae Arecomici 136 C4, 5
Volci 108 D4
Volga, R. 54 D1
Volsci 84 B3
Volsiniensis, L. 82 C5; 108 D3
Volsinii (Bolsena) 82 C4; 84 B3; 92 B3; 97 F2; 108 D3; 110 D3
Volterra *see* Volaterrae
Volturnum (S. Maria di Capua Vetere) 94 C3; 109 E4; 111 H1; 115 B2
Volturnus, R. 109 E4; 115 B1, 2
Volubilis 150 A2
Voreda 133 B2
Votadini 130 C3

Vounous 2 E4
Vrokastro 4 D2; 10 D4; 12 D4; 156 C2
Vrysinas 4 B2
Vulcani(a)/Hiera Hephaesti Insula 38 D1; 148 E1
Vulci 82 C5; 84 B3; 92 B3; 110 D3

Waddon Hill 131 C8
Walheim 140 C3
Waldmössingen 140 B4
Wall Town 131 C6
Walldürn 140 C2
Walton 131 C6
Walton Castle 131 E7
Ward Law 130 C5
Watling Lodge 134 C1
Wearmouth 133 D2
Weltenburg 140 E3
Welwyn 131 D7
Welzheim 140 C3
Welzheim-Ost 140 C3
Wensley 131 C5
Westerwood 134 C1
Whickham 133 D2
White Mountains 4 A2, B2; 156 A2
White Walls 131 C7
Whitley Castle 133 B2
Wiesental 140 B3
Wigan 131 C5
Wilderness Plantation 134 B2
Wilderspool 131 C5
Wimborne 131 C8
Wimpfen 140 C3
Wimpole Lodge 131 D7
Wiveliscombe 131 C7
Wörth 140 C2
Worcester 131 C6
Wreay 133 B2
Würzburg 140 C2

Xanthos, R. 9 E3
Xanthus 73 G4; 80 E3; 158 B4; 160 C5
Xiphonia 38 E3
Xiphoniae, Pr. 148 E3
Xois 167 B1
Xuthia 38 E3
Xynias, L. 30 B3, C3; 32 C4
Xypete 34 B3

Zab (Greater), R. 58 E2
Zab (Lesser), R. 58 E3
Zabi 154 B1
Zacynthos 29 A2; 30 A4; 60 A3
Zadracarta 54 D2; 65 E3; 71 F3
Zaghouan 150 C4
Zagora 12 C3
Zagurae 162 D3
Zaitha 162 C3
Zakro 4 E2; 56 C4
Zama (Battle) 99
Zama Regia 97 F4; 150 C4

Zancle *see* Messana
Zapatas, R. 58 E2
Zarai 150 D1
Zarax 29 D3
Zariaspa 65 G2
Zegrenses 150 A2
Zela 74 B1; 105 F2; 161 F2
Zele(i)a 9 D1; 73 F2
Zenobia 162 C3
Zephyrium 167 A1
Zephyrium, Pr. 156 A6
Zeugma/Seleuceia 70 C3; 74 C3; 162 B3
Zilis 150 A1
Zliten 151 F2
Zoelae Civitas 144 B2
Zoster, Pr. 29 E2
Zou 4 E2
Zugmantel 140 B1
Zygouries 2 B3; 6 C3

217